Speaking Truth In Love

By
Bobby Thompson

© **Guardian of Truth Foundation 2008.** All rights reserved. No part of this book may be reproduced in any form without written permission from the publisher. Printed in the United States of America.

ISBN 13: 978-158427-222-9

ISBN 10: 1-58427-222-8

Guardian of Truth Foundation
P.O. Box 9670
Bowling Green, Kentucky 42102
1-800-428-0121
www.truthbooks.net

Table of Contents

Preface	ix
A Communication Gap	11
A Heart the Lord Opened	13
A Matter of Whose Choice?	16
A Unique Command	18
A Walk Pleasing To God	21
Accepted With God	23
An Ideal Assembly	25
An Ideal Couple	28
And Hast Been Assured Of	31
And When He Came To Himself	33
Are There Any Bereans Today?	35
Are We Still Restoring the Church?	38
Are You Following the Doctor's Orders?	40
Assumption, Assumption, and More Assumption	43
Astonishment	45
Balaam Still Lives	48
Being Spiritually Minded	50
Betrayal	52
Bridling the Tongue (1)	55
Bridling the Tongue (2)	57
Brother Going To Law With Brother	59
But He Prays	62
But Make Me Thereof a Little Cake First	64
But They Are Really Friendly	66
But Thomas Was Not With Them	69
But We All Sin	71
Church Autonomy	74
Concerning Blushing	77
Concerning Doubt	79
Concerning the Word "Easter" in Acts 12:4	81

Concerning Tithing 83
Conflicting Voices 86
Consistency Thou Art a Jewel 88
Covering Sins 90
Cutting A Little Slack 93
Daily Religion 95
Dare I Fellowship Corinth? 97
Dare To Be Involved 100
Darkness 102
Demoniacs 104
Did the Catholics Give Us the Bible? 107
Did You Ask Him To Worship With You? 109
Do You Not Yet Understand? 111
Do You Really Love God? 113
Does Every Man Do It? 116
Does Everyone Have A Right To His Own Belief? 118
Does the End Justify the Means? 120
Does The Lord Ask Too Much? 123
Encouragement—Something All Of Us Can Use 125
Enthusiasm 127
Except A Man Be Born Again 130
Excuse Making 132
Faith That One Has 134
Father, Forgive Them, For They Know Not What They Do ... 137
Give Us An Understanding Heart 139
Giving God Our Best 141
Have I Become Your Enemy? 143
Having the Preeminence 146
He Preaches Like He Means It 148
He Received Orders From His God 150
He Stirreth Up the People 152
Holding Traditions 154
How Can A Man Obey God? 157
How Close A Friend Are We To Jesus? 159
How Noble Are We? 161
I Am Not Ashamed 164
I Don't Care 166

I Don't Feel Good	168
If You Can't Convert, Join Them	171
I'm Sorry	173
Inconsistency Can Be Over Emphasized	175
Is It A Sin To Change In Religion?	178
Job's Wife	180
Jonah, The Man Who Tried the Impossible	182
Just A Christian	185
Lord, Increase Our Faith (1)	187
Lord, Increase Our Faith (2)	189
Lot's Wife	191
May As Well Say Or Do It As To Think It	194
Mind Your Own Business	196
Misrepresentation	198
More Than a Bumper Sticker	201
More Than Teaching	203
Narrow Mindedness (1)	205
Narrow Mindedness (2)	207
Necessary Inference and Authority	209
Nor Charged God Foolishly	212
Not Far From the Kingdom of God	214
Not Good If Detached	216
Offended In Christ	217
Our Calling	219
Our Double Life	222
Our Likes and Our Dislikes	224
Paul's Secret of Success	226
Personalities	229
Persuading Men	231
Placing the Proper Emphasis	233
Playing Fair (1)	235
Playing Fair (2)	238
Pollution—A Grave Concern	240
Providing Things Honest	242
Refreshing Christians	244
Regarding Love	247
Rejoice in the Lord Always (1)	249

Rejoice in the Lord Always (2) 251
Reverence For God 254
Right and Wrong 256
Salvation to the Uttermost (1) 258
Salvation to the Uttermost (2) 260
Scornful Laughter 263
See That Ye Refuse Not Him That Speaketh 265
Self-Pity 268
Set For the Defence of the Gospel 270
Set Thine House In Order: For Thou Shalt Die and Not Live 272
Some Works Revealed in the New Testament 275
Staying in the Boundary 277
Strong in the Lord 279
Stubbornness Is As Iniquity and Idolatry 282
Take Ye Away the Stone 284
Teachers of God's Word 286
Tekel 288
Tell Us Plainly 291
That's Not My Thing 293
That's The Way It Was 295
The Balance of Life 298
The Christian and Pressure 300
The Church's Responsibility 302
The Confession of An Extremist 305
The Culprit 307
The Fears of Paul 309
The Curse of Meroz 312
The Day Which the Lord Hath Made 314
The Faith Which Was Once Delivered 316
The Few in Sardis 319
The Fine Art of Forgetting 322
The Grace of God That Brings Salvation 324
The "It" of God 326
The Judgment To Come 330
The Land of Beginning Again 332
The Marks of the Owner 335
The Only Question That Really Matters 337

The Power of Love	339
The Royal Family of God	341
The Saga of Three Beer Cans	344
The Spiritual Boomerang or God's Law of Retribution	346
The Study of God's Word May Be Abused	349
The Untrodden Path	351
The Valleys of Life	353
The Value of Positive Living	356
The Verb "Continue"	358
They Have Already Been Removed	360
There Were Three Crosses	363
Therefore	365
Things That Accompany Salvation	368
Things That Are To Follow Teaching	370
Thinking Too Highly of Ourselves	372
This World of Superlatives	375
Thou Hypocrite	377
Thoughts Concerning the Greek Word *Psallo*	379
Three Valuable Words	382
Touching Jesus	384
Translations or Interpretations?	387
Troubled Hearts	389
Truth and Consequences	391
Twisting the Picture Won't Help the Scene	394
"Unto the Jews I Became As a Jew"	396
Victory Over Circumstances	398
Victory Over the World	400
Waiting For the Rapture?	403
Was Apollos A False Teacher?	406
We Have An Enemy	408
What About Doubt?	410
What About the Heathen?	413
What Baptism Does Not Do	415
What Can The Righteous Do?	417
What Does It Mean To Become a Christian?	419
What Doth The Lord Require Of Thee?	422
What Is Jesus To You?	424

What Motivates You? 427
What Offends You? 429
What Was I, That I Could Withstand God? 432
Where Is It Condemned? 434
When Is One Guilty of Being Factious? 436
When It Comes To Push and Shove 439
When Right Becomes Wrong 441
Wherefore Rebuke Them Sharply 444
Who Wears the Shoes? 446
Whom Shall We Please? 449
Why Are Not All Prayers Answered? 451
Why Didn't Paul Heal Epaphroditus? 454
Why Gaddest Thou About So Much? 456
Wisdom To Know The Difference 458
Why The Bible? (1) 461
Why The Bible? (2) 463
Why The Bible? (3) 466
Why the Early Church Gave Liberally 469
Wind Conscious More Than Christ Conscious 471
With Regard To Bitterness, Don't Confuse It! 473
Work Out Your Own Salvation 476
Ye Shall Be Free Indeed (1) 478
Ye Shall Be Free Indeed (2) 481
Ye Shall Be Free Indeed (3) 483
Yes, It Certainly Does! 485
You Never Mentioned Him To Me 488

Preface

Bobby K. Thompson was born in Henry County, Tennessee on July 25, 1925 and then reared in Paris, Tennessee. He served in the U.S. Navy from July 24, 1943 to February 19, 1946. He began preaching for churches in Henry County, Tennessee in 1947, where he preached for several years. He attended Freed-Hardeman College in Henderson, Tennessee and Bethel College in McKenzie, Tennessee, where he graduated in 1953. He preached for the Plaza church of Christ in Charlotte, North Carolina during the years of 1953-58. While at Charlotte, he married his beloved companion, Vera, on December 19, 1955 and they celebrated their 50th anniversary in 2005. They have three children, David Benson of Henry, Tennessee; Linda Wade, of Tampa, Florida; and Karen Dargan of The Woodlands, Texas. He has also preached for the North Miami Avenue church of Christ in Miami, Florida, 1958-78; the Pruett and Lobit church of Christ in Baytown, Texas, 1978-1992; and with the Manatee County church of Christ in Bradenton, Florida from 1992 to the present. He has conducted gospel meetings from coast to coast and is still active in meeting work. He has written and published the two-volume *Christian Attitudes* lesson books which have been widely used by brethren for many years, seven volumes of sermons for the flannel board, and nine volumes of fifty-two sermon outlines for making transparences.

I became acquainted with Bobby and Vera Thompson in the late 1950s and they are some of the very dearest and most revered people in my life. Much of what I learned, and came to stand for, in the early years of the institutional division came from Bobby's teaching and encouragement. Bobby and I have held numerous gospel meetings where each other have preached over the past fifty years. He is greatly loved and appreciated by brethren who have had the opportunity to sit at his feet over the past sixty years of his preaching the gospel of Christ. Several years ago, I began sending out Bobby's bulletin articles to my email list of over three hundred people, and these articles have been used all over this country in church bulletins. I encouraged him to have them printed in book form so that they can profit many more people for generations to come. Our sincere appreciation is expressed to Mike Willis and The Guardian of Truth Foundation for assisting us with this publication. May God richly bless this effort to his glory.

Dennis L. Reed
February, 2008

A Communication Gap

Communication is a very vital principle and lifeline in practically all avenues of endeavor. Organizations, firms, and homes that seem to properly function are those where communication has not become a lost virtue, but something that is respected and revered by the participants. By communication, we are referring to the imparting of information and the discussion of matters that affect the individuals who compose the work or unit. Thoughts and views of others need to be appreciated and realized. Such thoughts and views are made known where harmonious communication between individuals is practiced. Doubtlessly, many problems and misunderstandings could be eliminated if people could and would communicate.

In recent years, the phrase, "generation gap" has been coined. This has reference to differences that exist between older folks and the youth of our day. Usually it points to the parent and children relationship and so often children lament that their problems are due to a generation gap. Perhaps the gap exists, but oftentimes it is a lack of communication between parents and children that presents a problem. Many ills can be diverted or solutions reached when parents and children will discuss the problems that exist. A parent mentioned to me that he had hope for his child to do what is right. His basis of hope had been renewed in the fact that they were able to sit down and discuss what was really in the mind of the youth. Sure enough, the parent was right! The child responded to the invitation and evidently made his life right with the Lord. Individuals need to express themselves and discuss what bothers them rather than permit such to linger in their hearts. A wise mother once said that she did not always agree with her children, but she tried faithfully to listen to them express themselves and to keep the lines of communication open with them. This is the failure of some parents and the cause for the gloom that hangs over too many homes! Communication is dead!

It seems that most of us are prone to think things that are not so and to build pyramids of imagination that do harm to ourselves and to others. Proper communication could eliminate much of this! After fair and frank discussions, many times the persons involved have later expressed feeling better and having a different perspective toward others who were involved. The communication gap has been responsible for much ill in the church of the Lord. Members have retained certain unrighteous feelings and views about other members and the work in general that a better communication might have possibly eliminated. We are not inferring that in every case communication would do so, but it is certainly a step in the right direction. When one shuts himself up with his own feelings and harbors thoughts regarding others, he is refusing the value that communication could bring to him.

We do not profess to know all the reasons why individuals seem to be hesitant in communicating, but *pride* represents a great factor. On occasions, we had rather have people wondering what is wrong with us and rejoice in the notoriety of such than to express ourselves with the hope of finding a proper solution. Solomon wrote, "Pride goeth before destruction, and a haughty spirit before a fall" (Prov. 16:18). To the Philippians, Paul wrote this beautiful truth: "Let nothing be done through strife or vainglory; but in lowliness of mind let each esteem other better than themselves. Look not every man on his own things, but every man also on the things of others. Let this mind be in you, which was also in Christ Jesus" (Phil. 2:3-5). Pride has a tendency to keep the communication gap "gapping." Looking on the things of others presents an avenue of promoting communication. Brethren have been known to create something in their minds and condemn others without giving them an opportunity to discuss the matter. They depart without any consideration for

Matthew 18:15-17 or other passages that would focus on communication. Perhaps they were looking for some excuse to leave a congregation and knew proper communication would eliminate their excuse. They had rather degrade someone than to give him an opportunity to explain.

Without communication, many things can never be realized. Take for instance the admonition that is found in James 5:16: "Confess your faults one to another, and pray one for another, that ye may be healed. The effectual fervent prayer of a righteous man availeth much." Without proper communication, this could never be accomplished. Brotherly love and the respect for membership in the body of Christ should help keep the communication gap very small and even tend to eliminate it altogether. As those who endeavor to respect the doctrine of Christ, let's do our part in endeavoring to eliminate it altogether in every field of activity.

A Heart the Lord Opened
(Acts 16:11-15)

The first part of the sixteenth chapter of Acts contains the account of the "Macedonian Call." The journeys of Paul and Silas had brought them to Philippi. On the Sabbath day they went by a river side, where they found a place of prayer. The group which had gathered there was made up of women. Taking their seats, Paul and company spoke unto them. Among the women was Lydia, and since it was her heart the Lord opened, it is well that we note some facts regarding this woman.

Some Facts Concerning Lydia. She was a merchant woman and had come from Thyatira, a city of Asia. Her business in Philippi was that of a dealer in purple. Purple dye was very costly and was used only in expensive fabrics. When one became quite prosperous, it was designated in those days by the saying, "he had reached the purple." Being a dealer in this material, head of a household, and having a large home large enough to accommodate Paul and his companions indicates, while not above the necessity of working, she nevertheless was in comparatively easy circumstance. "One that worshipped God" are words descriptive of Lydia. She had carried her religion with her into a heathen city where doubtlessly the Sabbath of the Old Testament Scriptures was unknown to its inhabitants. Other merchants may have been busy on that day, but not Lydia. Temptations and competitions of trade could not seduce her from the faithful observance of worship. Since there was no synagogue to worship in, Lydia took to the river bank. Since there were no men to conduct worship, she and her associates had a prayer service on the bank of the river. Such fidelity to God is not often seen in our own more favored time. There are some professed Christians who will let business, pleasure, company, and almost anything else keep them from worship. If it is convenient for them to worship, they will; but to overcome inconveniences is something that never enters their minds.

Why Did Her Heart Need Opening? The question naturally suggests itself. The fact that the Lord opened it implies in some way it was closed. It was certainly not due to inherited depravity (if such is true and it's not), nor yet to the hardness of a sinful life. Her character is against this idea in no uncertain terms. I would conclude that her heart was closed in the same sense in which the hearts of other pious Jews were closed—misconceptions regarding Christ. Perhaps she was thinking Christ was coming to establish a earthly kingdom and her heart was closed against him as a crucified Redeemer. This condition had to be corrected or she would reject the gospel of Christ. The effect of the opening was precisely that which was intended. It led her "to give heed unto the things which were spoken by Paul."

What Is the Heart That Was Opened? Certainly the "heart" referred to is not the lobe of flesh or physical organ known as the heart! It is the heart that the Scriptures describe as being able to *think* (Prov. 23:7), *desire* (Rom. 10:1), *purpose* (2 Cor. 9:7), *believe* (Rom. 10:10), and *love* (Matt. 23:37). It is that which may be pricked by the gospel (Acts 2:37). This heart involves man's intellect, emotions, and will. We have used the expression, "his heart was opened" in reference to a stingy person becoming charitable. His contracted and narrow heart had been filled with a grander, nobler sentiment than usual.

How Did the Lord Open Lydia's Heart? Notice the order of the text. She "heard us." She listened to that which was spoken to her. Following this hearing, it is stated: "Whose heart the Lord opened." After her heart (or understanding) was opened, "she attended unto the things which were spoken by Paul." What is the order? Hearing, opening, and attending! Through the preaching of God's word, the heart of Lydia was opened that she might attend to the things which were spoken by Paul. Here is the reason why the Lord opened her heart, so that she might do the things which were appointed for her to do. "And when she was baptized." That which Lydia did in response to Paul's teaching was in complete harmony with the Great Commission, "Go ye into all the world, and preach the gospel to every creature. He that believeth and is baptized shall be saved; but he that believeth not shall be damned" (Mark 16:15-16).

The context plainly shows that the Lord followed a deliberate plan in bringing Lydia and Paul together (Acts 16:1-10). Barring any miraculous element that may have been in the case of the "Macedonian Call," it is altogether probable that the Lord, in his providential oversight, is doing the same for people today, especially those whose lives and attitudes are like Lydia. How is your heart? Does it need opening? Give heed to God's word and permit your heart and understanding to be opened that you might attend to obeying the truth.

A Matter of Whose Choice?

The Scriptures reveal that Jesus Christ is to have pre-eminence in all matters pertaining to man's soul salvation. God gave Christ this pre-eminence. "And hath put all things under his feet, and gave him to be head over all things to the church, which is his body, the fulness of him that filleth all in all" (Eph. 1:22-23). It is man's privilege to recognize that Christ has the pre-eminence and ascribe unto Christ the first place in all matters of a religious nature. He is the head of his church. It is not by a stroke of chance or by some remote accident that God placed him there.

The word of Christ is to be given first place in our lives, but so many today will not regard it so. A faithful pursuit of personal desire, emphasized regard for their own preferences, is the usual order of religion today. Men have made religion a matter of their own choice. How often have you heard it said, "Go to the church of your choice," or "Accept the faith of your choice"? How many times do you hear individuals talk about God's choice in regard to churches and faith? Why isn't the choice of Jesus Christ ever considered? By the actions of most people, one would never know that God intended for him to have the pre-eminence.

But does Christ have any choice in the matter of churches? He surely does and his choice is more pronounced than that of any individual that you know. Listen: "Every plant, which my heavenly Father hath not planted, shall be rooted up" (Matt. 15:14). Again, "Husbands, love your wives, even as Christ also loved the church, and gave himself for it" (Eph. 5:25). This plainly shows that Christ was very decided about the matter. He had as much choice about the church as he expects a man to have toward his wife. Paul wrote: "There is one body, and one Spirit, even as ye are called in one hope of your calling; one Lord, one faith, one baptism, one God and Father of all, who is above all, and through all, and in you all" (Eph. 4:4-6). The one body is the one church (Eph. 1:22-23; Col. 1:18). A person has no more a choice regarding church or faith than he does regarding the Lord to serve or God to worship. I have as much a scriptural justification to talk about the Lord or God of one's choice as any man has to talk about the church or faith of man's choice.

A man does not have a right to the church of his own choice when he expects the Lord to save him. When Jesus was in the world, he did not consider his own choice or pleasure. We read: "Christ pleased not himself," but he said, "He that sent me is with me; he hath not left me alone; for I do always the things that are pleasing to him" (John 8:29).

Men have the divine order exactly reversed. They have made churches of their own choice, not of God's order or will. They have put names on those churches entirely foreign to any expressed choice of God. They heap unto themselves teachers after their own lusts, or choice, and practice anything they desire and label it as pleasing God. So today, religion has become largely a matter of choice with humans and the divine choice is disregarded. And their choices invariably differ so that we have an unearthly multitude of churches, names, creeds, doctrines, and methods. It brings home a pertinent question that each accountable being should ponder: my religion, the church to which I belong, the life I live, the name I wear, the way I worship and the doctrine I believe—are all of these a matter of my own choice, or is it the expressed choice of God and specified in his word? Can you say with Jesus: "I do always the things that are pleasing to him," or must you say that it is a matter of your own choice?

God has granted man the choice of obeying him or disobeying him. We have the choice of accepting his truth or rejecting it. Before God, we do not have the choice of determining what constitutes truth. This God has determined through Jesus Christ and it is tragic that so many will not permit themselves to see this. If I had written or arranged the truth, there would have been doubtlessly a number of things that I would have changed. But I didn't write or compose it and I have no right to tamper with it. I have the God-given right to obey God's will and preach it to others. In this we should all rejoice and stop trying to make religion a matter of man's choice. Pleasing God is determined as one obeys God. Men are not obeying God by making the religion of Jesus Christ into a matter of one's own personal choice. We should be thankful and rejoice in the fact that God has made us creatures of choice. However, choice can be abused and we must be careful that such is not taking place in our lives. Jesus said: "Not every one that saith unto me, Lord, Lord, shall enter into the kingdom of heaven; but he that doeth the will of my Father which is in heaven" (Matt. 7:21). Let's always strive to do his will and have the hope of heaven in our lives.

A Unique Command

"And Moses gave commandment, and they caused it to be proclaimed throughout the camp, saying, Let neither man nor woman make any more work for the offering of the sanctuary. So the people were restrained from bringing" (Exod. 36:6). This portion of Scripture refers to the matter of building the tabernacle. Construction of the tabernacle was being financed by the Lord's people and they were bringing such an abundance that the wise men "that wrought all the work of the sanctuary" came to Moses telling him that they "bring much more than enough for the service of the work." In view of this, Moses gave the command that neither man nor woman was to make any more work for the offering of the sanctuary. "So the people were restrained from bringing."

Unique means "being without a like or equal; single in kind of excellence; unequaled; matchless." This is a unique command for, with a slight exception in 2 Corinthians 8:3-5, there is nothing like it in the Scriptures. It is unique in that people are restrained in their bringing to the Lord or his work. Most of the commands are to encourage bringing rather than to restrain it. It is particularly excellent in that people had to be restrained from bringing. The common and less desirable trait is that they be constrained to bring. Another unique factor is that they would have superabundance at the end. So often abundance might exist in the beginning and then the zeal burns out, toward the end there is a lack.

What did the command restrain them from bringing? It was not what was left over and undesirable. Such would have not been unique (Mal. 1:7-9; 3:8). These people were not bringing the scraps to God. Exodus 35:5-9 reveals what they were bringing: An offering unto the Lord of a willing heart.

What prompted them to bring so superabundantly that they were restrained from bringing? It was a noble effort. The offering was to be used in a grand endeavor—that of constructing the tabernacle of God. The people recognized that this was to be used for the glory of God and their religious endeavors. There was no question concerning right or wrong. This was an endeavor approved of God and in keeping with his will. There was clear, concise teaching in preparation for these offerings to be brought. Moses spoke unto all the congregation of the children of Israel, "This is the thing which the Lord commanded." The project was not undertaken in secret. All of the people were given an opportunity and an incentive to bring. Their heart was in the work. They wanted the tabernacle to be built. When people's hearts are in something, the cause will prosper. Nehemiah and his workmen had a mind to work and the walls of Jerusalem were built in fifty-two days. The offering was possible. They possessed what was needed and they made such available. When one does not have it, he can't give it. You certainly can't get blood out of a turnip! It's just not there! "For if there be first a willing mind, it is accepted according to that a man hath, and not according to that he hath not" (2 Cor. 8:12). So many cry hard times when such usually doesn't exist. It is hard for some to give up anything!

Lessons To Be Derived From This Unique Command

Example. If these wanderers in the desert could be so generous to give more than was needed, can't we give enough to reach what is required or expected of us? There has never been a nobler effort than that of supporting the preaching of the gospel, the foremost work of the Lord's church.

A Surplus is Not Desirable. Enough to complete the project was the objective. Too much was constituting a hindrance. Congregations that boast of how much they have in the treasury are not commendable. There is work to be done in spreading the gospel that could take care of such "fat treasuries." Large sums in the treasury have a tendency to create complacency and that feeling of "at ease in Zion" which is a detriment to the Lord's cause.

The Lord's People Can Accomplish the Lord's Work. It was a free will offering from the people of God. There was no solicitation from outsiders. There was no high-powered schemes of great pressure placed on the people. They had been taught and they responded to the teaching.

Scriptural Work Creates an Incentive For People to Give. It was scriptural. No one can scripturally contribute to something that is not scriptural. An active congregation keeps a program constantly before the members that gives them an added incentive in giving.

Let us bring God the best and find our lives enriched by his blessings (2 cor. 9:6-7).

A Walk Pleasing To God

"Furthermore then we beseech you, brethren, and exhort you by the Lord Jesus, that as ye have received of us how ye ought to walk and to please God, so ye would abound more and more" (1 Thess. 4:1). It is important to please God (Gal. 1:10) Without faith it is impossible (Heb. 11:6). We should be concerned with a walk pleasing in the sight of God. The service of a Christian is represented in the Scriptures by a number of different figures. Building, vineyard, temple, race, and walk are but a few of these figures. The life and conduct of the Christian is often referred to in the figure of a walk. Paul was admonishing the brethren at Thessalonica to walk in a manner pleasing to the Lord. This should be our desire and such must be our desire if we hope to live with the Lord in eternity. If our walk is to be pleasing to the Lord, we must:

Walk With God. Two individuals in the Scriptures are said to have walked with God. We have reference to Enoch (Gen. 5:24) and Noah (Gen. 6:8-9). Both are referred to in Hebrews 11 as being men of faith and their deeds being motivated by faith in God. Walking with God also indicates communion and agreement. Amos asked the question, "Can two walk together, except they be agreed?" (3:3). The man who treasures his wisdom above the wisdom of God and challenges the will of God will never walk with God. Those of us who profess to be walking with him need to carefully watch our actions and manner of life. It is highly possible for us to get ahead of God and be guilty of presumption. Moses was guilty of presumption when he struck the rock in the desert of Zin rather than speaking to it (Num. 20). We may even find ourselves following afar off as Peter did and later warming ourselves at the devil's fireside (Mark 14:54, 67). The meaning of the preposition "with" should be appropriated in our every day walk, if it be pleasing to God.

Walk Before God. The emphasis now is upon the word "before." We need to be constantly aware of the fact that we are in the presence of God. Our lives are to stand the inspecting eye of the Lord. The Hebrew writer stated: "Neither is there any creature that is not manifest in his sight. But all things are naked and opened unto the eyes of him with whom we have to do" (Heb. 4:13). Abram was directed of the Lord to walk before him. "I am the Almighty God; walk before me, and be thou perfect" (Gen. 17:1). Hezekiah reminded the Lord, "how I have walked before thee in truth and with perfect heart, and have done that which is good in thy sight" (Isa. 30:3). Rather than to walk before God, as men should, we often try to walk before God as we do before men. We have been guilty of viewing God in the manner mentioned by the Psalmist: "Thou thoughtest that I was altogether such a one as thyself" (Ps. 50:21). Man hides from man and he tries to hide from God, but in vain (Gen. 3:8). Men deceive one another and they attempt to deceive God, but God is not mocked (Gal. 6:7). How often men are slack in their promises and in turn they get to thinking that God is the same. Peter states that the Lord "is not slack concerning his promise" (2 Pet. 3:9). He is not in any respect slack concerning the fulfillment of his promises. Sinful man bribes his fellowman and the success that he encounters motivates him to thinking he can do the same to God. Humans view sin as not being so terrible and they stifle their consciences to the point of feeling that God feels the same way. All such thinking is vanity! We need to walk before God with the reverent understanding that his thoughts and his ways are high above ours as are the heavens above the earth (Isa. 55:8-9). What are you doing now? The Lord knows. He knows even the thoughts of our hearts!

Walk After God. The admonition to the children of Israel: "Ye shall walk after the Lord your God, and fear him, and keep his commandments, and obey his voice, and ye shall serve him, and cleave unto him" (Deut. 13:4). It is fatal to follow the wrong influence and teaching. The Scriptures abound in examples of those who did and the consequences that they had to pay. In this age, walking after God means walking by faith in Christ (2 Cor. 5:7), in the commandments of the Lord (1 John 5:3; Luke 1:6), in newness of life (Rom. 6:3-4), after the spirit (Rom. 8:1), and in the narrow way (Matt. 7:13-14).

Have you checked your walk lately? It may be needing a tune-up! A walk pleasing to God involves with, before, and after. Think on this!

Accepted With God
(Acts 10:34-35)

"Then Peter opened his mouth, and said, Of a truth I perceive that God is no respecter of persons: But in every nation he that feareth him, and worketh righteousness, is accepted with him." This passage, along with several others in the Scriptures, refers to individuals being accepted with God. Accepted is defined as "to receive (a thing offered) with a consenting mind; to receive with favor; to approve." A number of principles are brought to our minds in this phrase "accepted with God." Observe a few of these:

- God does not accept all—not all are accepted with him.
- There are conditions of acceptability with God. These conditions are stated in the passage.
- Where there is acceptability, rejection also exists. Acceptance implies rejection of others.
- The conditions for acceptability are the same for all. God is no respecter of persons. All may be accepted with him who are willing to comply with the conditions of acceptability.

Whom Does God Accept?
Negatively: No man's person. "Of a truth I perceive that God is no respecter of persons." From the original language, the phrase "respecter of persons" literally means "reception of faces." It signifies to regard the external circumstances of a man—his rank, wealth, etc. as opposed to his real intrinsic character. God respects character—not what men might be reputed to be (Rom. 2:11).

Not nations. The passage speaks of those in every nation. The individuals in every nation are accepted with him—not the nations themselves. The acceptability rests with the individual who will conform to the will of God. The Bible does not speak of "Christian nations." There are Christians in the nations. There were Christians in Caesar's household (Phil. 4:22).

Positively. "He that feareth him, and worketh righteousness." It is quite obvious that two conditions are stated that an individual must meet in order for that one to be accepted with God. (1) "He that feareth him, and (2) worketh righteousness." To develop one and omit the other is to forfeit our acceptability with God. We should not be amazed at these conditions. They are not new. Solomon stated the same principles in Ecclesiastes 12:13, "Let us hear the conclusion of the whole matter: Fear God, and keep his commandments: for this is the whole duty of man." The conclusion of the whole matter involved being accepted of God. To fear him and work righteousness is to fear him and keep his commandments.

What is it to fear God? One definition of fear is "awe, profound reverence, especially for the Supreme Being." Fear in this respect is akin to reverence. When one fears God, he reverences him. Fear also involves honor. When one truly fears God, he respects and honors God. Man is a foolish creature in that he so often fears the wrong thing or person. Jesus dealt with this thought when he said: "And fear not them which kill the body but are not able to kill the soul: but rather fear him which is able to destroy both soul and body in hell" (Matt. 10:28). In all that we do in being acceptable to God, we must do so in a manner of reverence for God. There is no time to make light of God. "Wherefore we receiving a kingdom which cannot be moved, let us have grace whereby we may serve God acceptably with reverence and godly fear: for our God is a consuming fire" (Heb. 12:28-29).

What is it to work righteousness? Not only are we to fear God, we are also to work righteousness. If there were no other passage in the word of God that teaches that man is to do something to be accepted with him, this passage certainly does! Man is to work God's righteousness in order to be accepted with him. How can any one say that he believes the Bible and deny such a simple observation? Have they never read Acts 10:34-35? Mind you, Cornelius "feared God with all his house" (Acts 10:2), but he was not accepted with God. Why wasn't he accepted in the new covenant that is in Christ Jesus? Simply because the gospel, which was for both Jew and Gentile, was not made known to him at this time and he was not aware of what was involved in working the righteousness of God. To work the righteousness of God is to obey the commandments of God. The Psalmist wrote: "for all thy commandments are righteousness" (Ps. 119:172). Peter preached the gospel to Cornelius and his household and "commanded them to be baptized in the name of the Lord" (Acts 10:48). When penitent believers, on a confession of faith, are baptized into Christ, they are working God's righteousness to be accepted with him. This is what God authorizes for men to do that they might be accepted with him. This is not righteousness that men have established, but that which has come from God. Having done this to be accepted with him, we must continue as his children to fear God and do the things that involve being faithful unto death (Rev. 2:10).

An Ideal Assembly

"Immediately therefore I sent to thee; and thou hast well done that thou art come. Now therefore are we all here present before God, to hear all things that are commanded thee of God" (Acts 10:33). These are the words spoken by Cornelius in explanation of his sending to Joppa for Peter. An angel of the Lord had appeared to Cornelius a few days before and told him to send for Peter, "he shall tell thee what thou oughtest to do" (Acts 10: 6). Without delay, this good man, Cornelius, set in motion the directions that were given to him. "And when the angel which spake unto Cornelius was departed, he called two of his household servants, and a devout soldier of them that waited on him continually; And when he had declared all these things unto them, he sent them to Joppa" (Acts 10:7-8). Peter, accompanied by six brethren, had returned with them to Caesarea. He had come to preach the gospel to this Gentile household and the meeting was ideal from various viewpoints. I would like to suggest some of these in hope that all of us might think on them and work to make every assembly ideal.

Unity Of Purpose: "Now therefore are we all here." We do not know the attendance count, but we are told that when Peter came to Caesarea for this meeting he "found many that were come together" (Acts 10:27). There was a reason for them being there. While Cornelius was waiting for the preacher to come, he had been busy. Note verse 24, "And Cornelius waited for them, and had called together his kinsmen and near friends." He doubtlessly wanted others to hear what he would hear. He was not ashamed of what would be taught him. If there were things that he ought to hear, he wanted his relatives and friends to be benefited by hearing the same. What a wonderful attitude! How wonderful it would be if we had such an attitude toward our assemblies! At times, we think enough of our relatives and friends to invite them to other endeavors. We want them to participate in them with us. But what about hearing the gospel? Don't we think enough of them to invite them to attend where the gospel is preached? Cornelius did and there were those who accepted the invitation. There is no better advertisement in the world than the personal invitation of a member of the church to someone who needs to hear the gospel.

Consider again the phrase, "Now therefore are we all here." Just think what a thrill it would be if all the members of this congregation were present for every assembly. In the years that I have preached, I do not recall any service where all the members of the congregation were present. There are those who are sick, and they are not expected to be present in such a condition. That is certainly understandable! But what about those who are not ready to sacrifice a little time and effort to be a part of the assembly? What about those who prefer something else rather than worshiping the Lord, when their presence could mean so much to encouraging the preaching of the gospel? Cornelius was where he was supposed to be, and we could make our assemblies ideal if we were where we are supposed to be. Satan can give us many excuses for not attending. Whose side are we on, Satan's or the Lord's?

Reverential Aspect: "Present before God." When Cornelius and his guests came together to hear the message from Peter, they knew that they were "present before God." No doubt they met worshipfully and were attentive to the things preached. "Wherefore we receiving a kingdom which cannot be moved, let us have grace, whereby we may serve God acceptably with reverence and godly fear" (Heb. 12:28). God will be present at our assemblies, too, and we need to conduct ourselves reverently during that occasion. We should arrive on time, participate heartily in the singing, and listen carefully to the things preached by the preacher with the intent of obeying the commands of God.

Noble Purpose: "To hear." They had not come together to be entertained or amused. There were other assemblies that could be attended for that purpose. They were there to hear the gospel of Christ. Some people say the service does nothing for them. Usually those who make such a statement do not understand the purpose of the assembly. They are not there to be taught the word of God. They do not have the noble purpose of Cornelius and his guests. "For whosoever shall call upon the name of the Lord shall be saved. How then shall they call on him in whom they have not believed? And how shall they believe in him of whom they have not heard? And how shall they hear without a preacher?" (Rom. 10:13-14).

Determination: "To hear all things commanded thee of God." In essence, they were saying to Peter, "Lay it on us." Whatever God has for us to know, let us hear it. Don't hold back and keep it from us. They were interested in all things commanded of God. So many people want a part of the truth, but there are other things of truth of which they want no part. Such an attitude can take the very heart out of an assembly where the gospel is preached. Peter came to preach the gospel, and those who gathered wanted to hear all the things commanded by God. Neither the preacher nor the hearers were interested in speculative theories, philosophy, psychiatry, or other rhetoric. The traditions and teachings of men cannot save; the gospel is God's power unto salvation (Rom. 1:16). We should expect the gospel to be preached in every assembly. We hope you desire to hear the word of the Lord without addition or subtraction. When Peter came to preach at Caesarea, it was an ideal assembly.

Think on these things and let every one of us work diligently to make every assembly ideal in the sight of the Lord. This is something that challenges every member of this congregation.

An Ideal Couple

The Scriptures reveal an ideal couple, and we have in mind Aquila and Priscilla. We are familiar with them to some extent; however, we fail at times to appreciate the entirety of what the Scriptures relate concerning them. This type of couple is what the church needs. Just think of what people like Aquila and Priscilla mean to congregations! Such people are the hope of some congregations surviving and prospering in the sight of the Lord. There are six passages in the New Testament books which mention Aquila and Priscilla. As we observe these passages, we can understand their lives and in turn gain profitable lessons as we apply their situations to our own lives.

The first mention of them is in Corinth (Acts 18:1-3). Aquila was a Jew born in Pontus, a northern portion of Asia Minor. They had lived in Rome from which they had been banished with all Jews by Claudius. There is no evidence that the banishment and tribulations involved had caused them to be bitter toward God. Comparable things have caused many to be extremely bitter toward life. There is no evidence of such in the life of this couple. They had come to Corinth as tentmakers and were found by Paul who was of the same craft. Here was the beginning of one of the dearest friendships in the Scriptures. Were they Christians at this time? Probably, and if not, we conclude that they were before leaving Corinth.

The next mention of them is in Ephesus (Acts 18:19). Paul departed from Corinth and went to Ephesus. Aquila and Priscilla accompanied him and remained there while Paul went on to Jerusalem. In Ephesus, they heard an eloquent preacher named Apollos, who in spite of his attainments and ability, knew only the baptism of John (Acts 18:24-28). After hearing Apollos, they took him unto them "and expounded unto him the way of God more perfectly" (Acts 18:26). From this account, we are able to conclude: (a) They knew the truth about John's baptism that Apollos at this time did not know. (b) They were courageous enough to endeavor to teach Apollos concerning his false teaching regarding the baptism of John. (c) They were not worshipers of eloquence. They could distinguish eloquence from truth. (d) They loved the souls of men to the extent that they took the time and effort to teach Apollos the truth that his error in teaching might be corrected. What would you have done if you had stood where Aquila and Priscilla stood? What are we doing today when confronted with the exponents of false teaching? So many of us adopt the course of least resistance by saying it wouldn't have done any good, and then go on our merry way, singing how we love Jesus and his truth!

The next mention of this faithful couple is in 1 Corinthians 16:19. Salutations were sent by Paul from this couple to the church at Corinth. Aquila and Priscilla knew members in Corinth and no doubt were eager to see the church at Corinth be more spiritually minded. There was a church in their house at this time. Such implies: (a) their home was open to Christians. The facilities of their house could be used as the meeting place of the church. (b) Priscilla was not so concerned with her house but that she could experience inconveniences by permitting the church to meet there. It is difficult now to find members who will open their homes for a Bible study to be conducted. How unlike the spirit manifested by Aquila and Priscilla! They could endure what some call an inconvenience—what about us?

The fourth mention of them is in Romans 16:3-5. Greetings are sent to them in Rome. They had doubtlessly moved from Ephesus to Rome. They had not forsaken the truth or Paul, the truth's servant. "Greet Priscilla and Aquila, my helpers in Christ Jesus:

who have for my life laid down their own necks: unto whom not only I give thanks, but also all the churches of the gentiles." Notice these statements concerning them: (a) my helpers in Christ Jesus. (b) for my life laid down their own necks. (c) Paul was thankful for them and so were all the churches of the Gentiles. We notice also verse 5: "Likewise greet the church that is in their house." As in Ephesus, there was also in Rome, a church meeting in their house. Everything said about them was highly commendable. They loved the truth and were faithful to it.

The last time they are mentioned is in 2 Timothy 4:19. In this brief statement, Paul saluted Priscilla and Aquila in Ephesus. They had returned to Ephesus from Rome. This probably was the apostle's last letter; yet, among the important items, he had space to remember Priscilla and Aquila.

Conclusion

Let us profit from this couple. They were industrious. They had friendship for a humble servant of the Lord. The church could meet in their house. They took their religion with them wherever they went. They knew the truth and were courageous enough to contend for it. Is the spirit of Priscilla and Aquila in us? Why not? Don't we desire to go to heaven? As we said before, so say we again: What congregations need today are members of the Lord's church who have the attitude of this faithful couple rather than hearts being filled with pride and vanity of this world!

And Hast Been Assured Of

"But continue thou in the things which thou hast learned and hast been assured of, knowing of whom thou hast learned them; And that from a child thou hast known the holy scriptures, which are able to make thee wise unto salvation through faith which is in Christ Jesus" (2 Tim. 3:14-15). Paul addressed this beautiful admonition to Timothy. Every phrase of it is filled with meaning and Christians today need to appreciate the value of these meaningful words. There were things that Timothy had been taught as a child from the Holy Scriptures. As a child, this teaching had doubtlessly come from his grandmother and mother. 2 Timothy 1:5 brings this to our minds: "When I call to remembrance the unfeigned faith that is in thee, which dwelt first in thy grandmother Lois, and thy mother Eunice; and I am persuaded that in thee also." No greater heritage can be given to a child than that of knowing the Holy Scriptures. The Holy Scriptures are the only source of making one wise unto salvation. We are to know the truth and continue following the things that we have learned and been assured of.

The assurance concerning salvation comes through the Holy Scriptures. In the Scriptures, we are taught of our need for salvation and what it takes to be saved. All the sources and references from men cannot make this available. As the Psalmist wrote: "Thy word is a lamp unto my feet, and a light unto my path" (Ps. 119:105). Again, "All scripture is given by inspiration of God, and is profitable for doctrine, for reproof, for correction, for instruction in righteousness: That the man of God may be perfect, thoroughly furnished unto all good works" (2 Tim. 3:16-17). Along with learning and obeying the Scriptures, we are to recognize the assurance that they offer. We may have doubt in certain categories that bring us to search the Scriptures to know the truth. However, God does not intend for us to live in doubt. The peace that passeth all understanding does not come through doubt of the Scriptures.

We seem to live in a time when many of the bulwarks of the

faith are being viewed in a doubtful manner. When one speaks of the steps of salvation, there are those who are prone to ridicule such a thought. We are speaking of those who from a child have been taught the Holy Scriptures. The importance of the church is no longer important to them. They were taught and given the privilege of learning, but somewhere along the line they have lost their assurance. It is such a sorrowful picture to view those who have learned the Holy Scriptures from a child, but now have no assurance of their being true.

This is occurring with all ages of people. It involves the older people as well as the young. There are preachers who have been taught the Holy Scriptures from childhood that now question the Scriptures as we have revered them though the years. When it comes to the canon of the New Testament, they utter remarks that question the authenticity of a book being included. If we do not have the truth revealed in the Scriptures, then where can it be found? A great deal of the problem lies in "our intellectuals" taking the works of philosophers and being moved by their concepts rather than the Holy Scriptures. Reference may be made to such information, but it should never be classified as truth found in the Holy Scriptures.

Years ago, I recall the sorrowful account of some preachers departing from the faith. A faithful brother commented that the first symptom of such occurring was when they would cast words of doubt regarding Jonah living in the belly of the fish and Balaam's donkey speaking to him. They were developing reservations as to the truth of these things as stated in the Holy Scriptures. The door was being opened and from there other things were doubted about the truth revealed in the Scriptures. Today, some question that an actual serpent spoke to Eve in the book of Genesis. They suggest that such was the product of ancient mythology and not some factual truth as mentioned in the Scriptures. In the years that I have endeavored to teach the Holy Scriptures, I have never viewed the serpent as other than a serpent that was told "upon thy belly shalt thou go, and dust shalt thou eat all the days of thy life" (Gen. 3:14). Those who would deny what the Scriptures say regarding the serpent have lost their assurance of the truthfulness of the Scriptures.

I have been known to "miss my mouth" and say that Jonah swallowed the whale. In correcting the matter, I have said that, if the Scriptures had said he did, I would certainly believe it with as much conviction as what it does say. Brethren, we are to continue in those things that we have learned from the Holy Scriptures. We may have as a child learned them, but they are not childish! As a faithful brother said: "If these preachers are not sure of what they are preaching, let them shut up and let people hear from those who do assuredly know and believe!" Amen!

And When He Came To Himself

This is said of the younger son who had departed from his father's house, wasted his inheritance in riotous living and experienced the shame for a Jewish boy of feeding unclean swine. He had tasted the bitter dregs of hunger and sin. In such a condition, he did what many in similar circumstances need to do today. He came to himself! Sin is an infatuation and a craze. When the blinded eyes of the soul are opened, no man is content to abide in sin, that is, in destruction. Having come to himself, he could see clearly his shameful, pitiful state and the way to do something about it. He returned to his father's house in remorse and humility, saying, "I have sinned against heaven, and before thee, and am no more worthy to be called thy son: make me as one of thy hired servants" (Luke 15:17-19). His condition was a form of spiritual insanity. It was an improper evaluation of his blessings and stewardship. But the beautiful thing in this scenario is that he came to himself and returned before it was too late.

There are those today in the church of the Lord who need to come to themselves. They are not properly evaluating their blessings and stewardship before God! They need to see themselves in the swine fields of failure before God and return to him in spiritual zeal before it is too late. We think of some who truly need to come to themselves and return to the better life of faithfulness in God that they once knew. We have in mind:

Those who shun responsibility. We are accountable to God for our talents and abilities. These are God given! Our eternal home depends upon how we respond to our responsibilities (Matt. 25:30). Some have become slothful in doing their part. They need to awaken and see just how far they are drifting from God. Yes, the work goes on, but what about our souls? Our actions may be condoned by ourselves in the haze of deception and other members may attempt to justify us, but not so of God. "For every man shall bear his own burden" (Gal. 6:5). We need to come to ourselves and cease thinking that God will accept us in our slothfulness and failure to do our part. What about you? Are you truly on the team? Are you doing your part? What if everyone were like you? We need to start thinking soberly. We need to come to ourselves and not continue in shunning our responsibilities.

The lukewarm and indifferent. Surely, you weren't always this way! Can't you see how you have drifted from faithfulness in God? Such evidently have become blinded to the true perspective of the life of faithfulness in Christ. Lukewarmness can sap the strength of any work. Diligence and zeal are commended in the Scriptures. Lukewarmness and indifference are condemned. Christ said that the lukewarm would be spewed out of his mouth. "I know thy works, that thou art neither cold nor hot: I would thou wert cold or hot. So then because thou art lukewarm, and neither cold nor hot, I will spue thee out of my mouth" (Rev. 3:15-16). To the Laodiceans, Christ said that in their lukewarmness they were blind to their true spiritual condition. "Because thou sayest, I am rich, and increased with goods, and have need of nothing; and knowest not that thou art wretched, and miserable, and poor, and blind, and naked" (Rev. 3:17). Here were members of the Lord's church who definitely needed to come to themselves and see themselves as Christ truly saw them. In their lukewarmness and indifference toward God, they were voting to defeat the greatest work on earth. Consider the following regarding voting: (author unknown)

> Last Lord's Day, I voted. Not intentionally, not maliciously, but carelessly, and thoughtlessly, lazily and indifferently, I voted! Yes, I voted for the church to cease assembling for worship. I voted to stop the class study. I voted to close the open Bible which has been

given to me by many years of struggling and by the blood of martyrs who have died that we might have it to read, obey and be saved. I voted for the preacher to cease preaching the glorious truth of God's word. I voted for the children no longer being taught God's word in the Bible classes. I voted for the church to cease singing hymns of praise, glory and thanksgiving to the Father. I voted to cease the work of the congregation. I voted for the darkness of superstition and the degrading influence of sin, the curse of the selfish greed to once again settle their damning load on the shoulders of an already overburdened world. I voted for souls, even my own, to be damned to a devil's hell for eternity. Carelessly, lazily, indifferently, I voted! For, you see, I could have gone, but I did not. I stayed away from worship. I stayed away from Bible study. Yes, I VOTED!

The prodigal came to himself and returned to his father's house. Some in the church today need to come to themselves and return to faithfulness in the Lord. Think on these things!

Are There Any Bereans Today?

Concerning the people in the Macedonian city of Berea, Luke relates a very refreshing evaluation: "These were more noble than those in Thessalonica, in that they received the word with all readiness of mind, and searched the scriptures daily, whether those things were so. Therefore many of them believed; also of honorable women which were Greeks, and of men, not a few" (Acts 17:11-12). When the word of the Lord was preached to these people, they manifested outstanding characteristics that all individuals would do well to practice. There are various and sundry reactions to the preaching of God's word. The Bereans demonstrated the proper attitude that hearers should have. Consider the outstanding qualities that they evidenced by their actions and then ask yourself if there are any Bereans today. They were:

Free of Prejudice. "They received the word with all readiness of mind, and searched the scriptures daily, whether those things were so." Hearers filled with prejudice would not have done this. How different the Bereans were as compared to some of the Lord's own countrymen: "For this people's heart is waxed gross, and their ears are dull of hearing, and their ears they have closed; lest at any time they should see with their eyes, and hear with their ears, and should understand with their heart, and should be converted, and I should heal them" (Matt. 13:15). Jesus quoted from the prophecy of Isaiah 6:9-10 which applied to the reaction of these people to his teaching. Prejudice involves folly and shame! The wise man wrote: "He that answereth a matter before he heareth it, it is folly and shame unto him" (Prov. 18:13). Prejudice is the lock on the door of the closed mind, the ignorance we usually mistake for reason, the first enemy of information and progress, intellectual stigmatism, and a perfect combination of conceit and ignorance. Prejudice never saved a soul, nor settled any question in the light of truth and justice. It is the defense of the devil, the shell of a petrified mind, and the ceiling on understanding. There is a principle which is a bar against all information and proof against argument. It cannot fail to keep a man in everlasting ignorance. That principle is condemnation before investigation. This the Bereans did not practice! Are there any Bereans today? How about ourselves? Do we have a readiness of mind to investigate or are we motivated by prejudice?

Not Gullible. This was another quality of the Bereans that was outstanding. Gullible is defined as "easily cheated or tricked; credulous." While some people are not prejudiced, they are gullible to the extent of accepting almost anything that is taught them. We should be of a mind to investigate and then make the proper investigation as the Bereans did; they "and searched the scriptures daily, whether those things were so." So many today are content to accept most anything and in so doing they are not like the Bereans. We are admonished to "prove all things; hold fast that which is good" (1 Thess. 5:21). Again, "Beloved, believe not every spirit, but try the spirits whether they are of God: because many false prophets are gone out into the world" (1 John 4:1). Anyone who is sincere does not object to his teaching being examined by the Scriptures as to whether those things are so. It is an element of insincerity when preachers object to what they teach being "tried" by the word of God.

Energetic. These people evidence an energetic spirit by searching the Scriptures daily. The Scriptures that were available to them doubtlessly involved the Old Testament Scriptures that were available in the synagogues. These Scriptures were written on material that required considerable effort to search. Yet, they did this daily! The lazy, indolent type would have been weighed in the balances and found wanting when confronted with this rather tedious work. Are there any Bereans today? In a day when the Scriptures are so conveniently arranged in books, chapters, and verses and when Bibles are available that abound in concordances and other types of helps to locate various passages, surely Bereans should exist on every hand! But the pathetic thing is that there is a lack of them. Even members of the church do not qualify at times. They are so lazy in studying the word of God that they neglect preparing the Bible lessons themselves or taking the time to help their children do the same. If they had the spirit of the Bereans, somewhere along the line, they lost it. We need to heed Paul's admonition: "not slothful in business; fervent in spirit; serving the Lord" (Rom. 12:11).

The Bereans were not willingly ignorant (2 Pet. 3:3-7). They were receptive to the will of God. They were more than hearers. Whatever may be our attitude in hearing God's word, we must be obedient to the truth. "Therefore many of them believed." May the Lord help all of us today to have the spirit of the Bereans.

Are We Still Restoring the Church?

This is a question that a brother asked me a few weeks ago. It is a question that requires some proper thought regarding its answer. Most all members of the church of Christ are familiar with what is called the Restoration Movement. In the later part of the eighteenth century and beginning of the nineteenth, there was an awakening of religious people in an effort to follow the Scriptures. The plea was back to the Bible and to speak where the Bible speaks and be silent where it is silent. Men like James O'Kelly, Dr. Abner Jones, Barton W. Stone, along with Thomas and Alexander Campbell, pled for a return to the New Testament order of things. It would appear that these preachers and others were preaching the same plea without knowledge of what the others were doing. Though respecting the work of Martin Luther, Ulrich Zwingli, and John Calvin in the reformation, they felt their efforts did not produce a return to the purity of the New Testament pattern. Many were impressed with the plea of the restoration and came out of denominations to be members of the church that Jesus built which is revealed in the Scriptures. To an extent, their work should be appreciated today. They made mistakes, but in a sense, they "shelled the corn" for generations that would follow and made understanding of many passages far more plausible. We should honor their work, but still recognize that they were fallible men subject to error as all are. Due to the ability and energetic efforts of Alexander Campbell, numbers agreed with his view of the Scriptures. Others who were determined to support denominational doctrines called them as "Campbellites."

Today, in some parts of the country, the name is ignorantly used to identify those who are endeavoring to follow the simple pattern of truth and be members of the Lord's church. I have said to those who have called me a "Campbellite" that I am following Christ and no fallible man (1 Cor. 1:10-13). Furthermore, I have had problems in understanding all that Campbell wrote and believing some things that he endorsed. His work and the work of others who might be classed as part of the restoration movement are to be viewed in the light of the Scriptures. Respect their efforts, but prove all things by a "thus saith the Lord" (1 Thess. 5:21).

Does one need to know of the Restoration Movement to be saved and be a faithful member of the Lord's church? I would say NO! The word of God is before us and the Scriptures reveal what God would have us to know in being acceptable before him. There may be profit in knowing the work of these scholarly servants of God. There may be help in reading their explanation of certain Scriptures, but we can do God's will without ever knowing of them. There might be some preachers today who quote more of the words of the restoration preachers than they do of the word of God. Such constitutes a definite abuse of their work and intentions.

We need to think about the question that is the title of this article. Are we still restoring the church of Christ? It might be said when it comes to proper zeal and enthusiasm for the truth that elements of restoration are needed. When the Jerusalem church was scattered abroad, brethren went everywhere preaching the word (Acts 8:4). Such zeal and determination may often be lacking! However, when it comes to doctrine and practice of truth, I believe the church has been restored. In what is known as the Restoration Movement, there were numerous doctrines and practices that were not being followed. Scriptural teaching regarding baptism for the remission of sins, worship in spirit and truth, the value of the name Christian, and many other things needed to be practiced or restored. Through the years, we have seen the truth regarding these matters. This was truth that needed restoring during the time called the Restoration Movement. What truth or practices need to be restored now if we are still restoring the church?

Furthermore, doesn't it imply that the church is not complete if we continue to say that we are still restoring it? What truth is yet to be restored? Please understand that the word of God can always be appreciated more, and we can see the beautiful truth more clearly through study. It has been said that the word of God is like a piece of gold. The more it is polished the brighter it shines. This is appreciation rather than restoration!

When individuals contend that the church still needs to be restored, there may be motives that they have which need to be watched. What they have in mind is advocating false practices under the guise of saying we still do not know all the truth and are still restoring the church. Some desire women to have a public place in the worship and work of the church. When the truth is related to them (1 Tim. 2:11-15), they are quick to say that we are still restoring the church and do not recognize all the truth. The house church advocates and those who deny the scriptural work of elders have been known to hide behind the thought that we are still restoring the church. More can be said, but think about what we are trying to say!

Are You Following the Doctor's Orders?

Medicines and drugs can be of great benefit. This has been demonstrated time and again. On the other hand, they can be of untold damage if not properly handled. The honesty, care, and scruples of any pharmacist are important factors in the blessing or the curse that medicines provide. The knowledge of the physician and the druggist are likewise vital factors in dealing with powerful combinations of disease fighting medicines. In religion, as in medicine, there must be no tampering with human destiny by unskillful hands and minds. Additions or subtractions to the doctor's prescription are improper. If any changes are to be made, let the doctor do the changing.

This conveys the proper position relative to the truth of God's divine directions. There are three things that must not occur if his word is to be properly followed: (1) No addition must be made to his word. (2) Any subtraction must likewise be avoided. (3) No substitution for any specification in his word must occur. There is one thing that we absolutely must have and must continue to follow and that is the word of God, as it is, in all of its truth and purity. We are to have unbounded confidence in Christ as the good physician who has properly diagnosed our case, having the proper remedy for us.

When one hears a preacher, dispensing spiritual medicine, quote Acts 8:23 in this manner: "For I perceive that thou are *yet* in the gall of bitterness, and in the bond of iniquity," one should know that he is hearing a preacher add to the divine directions. He adds the word "yet" to indicate Simon the sorcerer had not become a Christian, and had not therefore fallen from grace. The word of God did not state that Simon was "yet" lost. It does say that he had believed and been baptized (Acts 8:13), and Jesus said in Mark 16:16 that all who do that were to be saved. Then Simon sinned, and Peter told him that he and his money were on the road to perdition. But preachers, who are sometimes unscrupulous and dishonest, will insert the word "yet" to preserve their unfounded and false doctrine that a child of God cannot sin and be lost. They are guilty of tampering with the doctor's orders and sinning themselves.

We frequently find some religious "quacks" slipping a little narcotic into their preaching prescription of John 3:16. In this verse, Jesus said, ". . .whosoever believeth in him should not perish, but have everlasting life." The Bible teaches that faith is essential to salvation, but it does not teach that faith only will save. The narcotic in this case is the idea of "only." These teadhers affirm that to only believe, and that alone, is sufficient for salvation without anything else being necessary. This is not what the Bible says, but it is the view that many denominational preachers place on the passage. It is a narcotic, this "only" idea, because it lulls the believer into a sleep of false security, causing him to think that salvation is attained without any other acts of obedience to God.

What about love? Is a man saved without loving God? No, for "he that loveth not knoweth not God, for God is love" (I John 4:8). Then, a man is not saved by faith only. Faith is one thing and love is another. "Now abideth faith, hope and love, these three; and the greatest of these is love" (1 Cor. 13:13). What about repentance? It is certainly essential to one's salvation! "And the times of this ignorance God winked at; but now commandeth all men every where to repent" (Acts 17:30). Repentance being recognized as necessary for salvation, then man cannot be saved by only believing. What about praying? Those who speak so often of only believing are very adamant in stressing the necessity of prayer. Then, once again, it is evident a man cannot be saved by only believing in Christ and those who teach such really do not believe it themselves. What about baptism? Regardless of what men might say, Jesus said that it is essential. "Except a man be born of water and the Spirit, he cannot enter into the kingdom of God" (John 3:5). Laying aside the figure of birth, Jesus stated in Mark 16:16: "He that believeth and is baptized shall be saved, but he that believeth not shall be damned." Any preacher who preaches that a man can be saved by faith only is definitely tampering. with the doctor's orders by adding a narcotic that is not in the prescription.

Men are usually very practical in matters of a temporal and physical nature. They would abhor the thought of any man changing the prescription given by the doctor without the doctor's knowledge or permission, but not so in matters that affect our souls. Myriads listen to most anything and never stop to consider if it is the divine truth. They seldom read for themselves and the idea of investigation is nauseating to them. Such an attitude is very impractical and quite tragic. We should be more concerned with seeing that we are following the purity of God's words and his directions than anything else on this earth. How closely is God's word being obeyed in your life (1 Thess. 5:21)?

Assumption, Assumption, and More Assumption

We recently received a bulletin, which contained an article entitled "Sponsoring Church Arrangement." The writer defines the arrangement: "A sponsoring church arrangement is when a congregation takes on a particular work in evangelism or benevolence and other congregations or individuals assist in that work." He contends, "We have New Testament precedent for this arrangement in evangelism and benevolence." This arrangement that he refers to is one of the innovations that has led to division in the Lord's church. Those believing such have brought upon themselves the designation of "liberal." They have taken liberties with the Scriptures that they have no right to do. Such an arrangement is not found in the Scriptures! Congregations are not equal in size, but they are equal in their obligation and responsibility in practicing evangelism and benevolence to the extent of their ability.

The sponsoring church arrangement violates the pattern of truth and creates centralization that finds one church or churches becoming superior to others in receiving funds from other churches to finance their projects. Though evidently innocent in the minds of some over zealous brethren, they have nevertheless promoted their programs to the dividing asunder of the Lord's people. What this preacher says is a New Testament precedent for the arrangement constitutes nothing but assumption. Webster defines "assumption" as "**a:** the supposition that something is true; **b:** a fact or statement (as a proposition, axiom, postulate, or notion) taken for granted." The preacher's article on the sponsoring church arrangement is filled with assumption rather than evidence from the Scriptures. He refers to an example of benevolence in Acts 11:27-30. The passage speaks of disciples sending relief unto the brethren which dwelt in Judea. "Which also they did, and sent it to the elders by the hands of Barnabas and Saul." He assumes the elders were the elders in the church at Jerusalem and that they received the relief, and that they then in turn distributed it to the other churches in Judea and in so doing became a sponsoring church. Can't one see that this is entirely assumption? The Scriptures speak of *churches* in Judea (Gal. 1:22; 1 Thess. 2:14). When the passage speaks of the relief being sent to the elders, how can one assume that the elders of the churches in Judea were not the ones to whom it was sent? By sending to each local church, the autonomy of the local church is respected and one group of elders is not above another. Elders are to feed the flock which is among them and take the oversight over that flock alone (1 Pet. 5:1-3). He further states: "Luke tells us that these two returned to Antioch from Jerusalem" (Acts 12:25). There is nothing in the inspired record that tells us that Paul and Barnabas went personally to all the churches of Judea." The fact that they returned from Jerusalem and that the Scriptures do not mention them personally visiting the churches of Judea is proof to him that the Jerusalem church was involved in a sponsoring church arrangement. His argument is just more assumption that denies the pattern of truth that God has given to the church to follow and the meaning of church autonomy.

The article further states: "Since evangelism and benevolence go hand in hand, that which can be done in benevolence, can be done in evangelism. In other words, if one church can send money to another church to do a work of benevolence, then, the same can be done in evangelism." This again is something that he assumes without authority from the Scriptures. He is under the assumption that one assumption makes another one right. There is no authority for one church receiving funds from churches and distributing those funds to other churches whether it is in benevolence or evangelism. Furthermore, it is assumption to say that, if it can be done in benevolence, it can also be done in evangelism. We do note that other churches could help a church with needy saints (Rom. 15:25-27; 1 Cor. 16:1-2; 2 Cor. 8, 9), and other passages relate to help being sent to the poor saints in Jerusalem. The contribution in Romans 15:25-27 and 1 Corinthians 16:1-2 and 2 Corinthians 8-9 was a later contribution than that mentioned in Acts 11 and is not to be confused with it. However, on both occasions there is no evidence of any church receiving funds to sponsor any other work whether it is in benevolence or evangelism.

The writer labors to find a sponsoring church in Philippians 4 where he argues that Philippi channeled other congregation's funds to Paul. This was not so! Philippians 4:15-16 speaks of Philippi alone sending to Paul at Thessalonica, while Paul says he received support from other churches at Corinth (2 Cor. 11:8-9). Furthermore, Paul credits only Philippi for the funds he received in Macedonia. If Philippi were a sponsoring church, why aren't those other churches mentioned? The argument on Philippians 4:15-16 is more assumption rather than truth.

To the credit of the writer, he disowns the Herald of Truth, which he now calls another organization. But he fails to see that the Herald of Truth was begun in a sponsoring church arrangement which was an unscriptural arrangement in the beginning. Brethren want their pet projects and they keep on assuming justification for them that is not found in the Scriptures. Beware and don't be deceived by assumption!

Astonishment

The reaction to the teaching of Christ brought varied results and conclusions in the hearts of those who heard him. On a number of occasions, the gospel writers mention that "the people were astonished at his doctrine." This was the reaction of the people when Jesus preached the Sermon on the Mount. "And it came to pass, when Jesus had ended these sayings, the people were astonished at his doctrine" (Matt. 7:28). He caused astonishment in his own country. "And when he was come into his own country, he taught them in their synagogue, insomuch that they were astonished, and said, Whence hath this man this wisdom, and these mighty works?" (Matt. 13:54). Mark states on one occasion that even his disciples "were beyond measure astonished" (Mark 7:37). On another occasion, "And they were astonished with a great astonishment" (Mark 5:42). The meaning of the word "astonish" from the original language is "to be greatly struck." Webster supplies this definition: "to strike with sudden fear or wonder; astound; amaze."

When the word of the Lord is preached today, we shouldn't be astonished to find people "astonished at his doctrine." Human nature and reaction have not changed through the years! I would suppose the astonishing thing in a great way would be to find the mass of people not being astonished at his doctrine. We have noted that some seem to use their astonishment to offset the weight and power of the truth. But such will not work! I may say in astonishment that "I never heard of such a thing!" or "How ridiculous can one become!" But if the message is the truth and it remains the truth, regardless of my astonishment or any other reaction.

What is it about the doctrine of Christ that caused the people to be astonished? What causes individuals to be astonished today when they come in contact with the simple truth?

"For he taught them as one having authority and not as the scribes" (Matt. 7:29). This is the answer of explanation for the people being astonished in verse 28. Christ spoke the words of the Sermon on the Mount with definiteness. The Scribes, whom the people were accustomed to hearing, quoted Moses, but Christ said, "I say unto you." They weren't used to this! In our time, there are those reared in the haze of denominationalism and so accustomed to indefiniteness, that they are "beyond measure astonished" to hear a gospel sermon preached by one truly respecting the authority of the Lord. There is to be no vagueness in our teaching and preaching and this invariably astonishes those who are not accustomed to such.

Christ had the answer for false teachers and their error. The manner in which he answered the Sadducees regarding their question about the resurrection demonstrates the certainty of his answers. The Sadduceeds posed a question about a woman who married seven brothers. They asked whose wife the woman would be in the resurrection (Matt. 22:23-33). Jesus told them that "in the resurrection they neither marry, nor are given in marriage, but are as the angels of God in heaven." He called to their minds that God was "not the God of the dead, but of the living." His wisdom in answering these Sadducees astonished the multitude which heard. Religious questions demand and deserve an answer from the word of God, the wisdom of God. When ready answers are given from the Scriptures, there are those today who stand astonished. Inspired men in the New Testament did not have to hesitate when asked by sinners what to do to be saved. We can answer in their words today (Act 2:37-38; 16:30-33; 22:16). It astonishes some to hear the answer spoken with such plainness, confidence, and boldness. But why shouldn't it be so? People were astonished at the doctrine of Christ then and we shouldn't be astonished when they are still being astonished.

Regardless of what reaction may come, we need to continue to follow and preach the truth with all the fiber of our being. Astonishment does not nullify truth! We may expect people to cry astonishment when they hear the truth of the one church that Jesus built (Matt. 16:18; Eph. 4:4), baptism for the remission of sins (Acts 2:38), Christ before all (Matt. 10:37-38), the sin of mechanical music in worship (Eph. 5:19), and many other things that involve the doctrine of Christ. But the truth is still the truth whether it astonishes *you* or *me* or anyone else. Christ astonished people with his teaching, and we shouldn't be afraid to do so today. There is no time for compromise and the middle of the road concept when truth is involved. In many areas, it appears that members of the Lord's church, who should know and love the truth, cry astonishment when the word of God is preached with forcefulness and conviction. The old denominational attitude of softness has reached the hearts of those who should be ashamed to cry astonishment at the simple truth. Remember, astonishment is not going to change the truth and it takes the truth to save (1 Pet. 1:22).

Balaam Still Lives

Jude makes mention of the error of Balaam. He speaks of those who "ran greedily after the error of Balaam for reward" (Jude 11). Peter refers to those "which have forsaken the right way, and are gone astray, following the way of Balaam the son of Beor, who loved the wages of unrighteousness; but was rebuked for his iniquity: the dumb ass speaking with man's voice forbade the madness of the prophet" (2 Pet. 2:15-16). The more complete record concerning Balaam is to be found in Numbers 22-24. As a prophet, he was given great opportunity to do good, but unfortunately, he chose to do contrary to God's will.

The will of the Lord was plain and definite regarding the reply that Balaam was to make to Balak's request. Balak, king of Moab, had sent men to Balaam with rewards of divination in their hands requesting that Balaam, as a prophet, might curse the children of Israel who were coming into his land. "Behold, there is a people come out of Egypt, which covereth the face of the earth: come now, curse me them; peradventure I shall be able to overcome them, and drive them out. And God said unto Balaam, Thou shalt not go with them; thou shalt not curse the people: for they are blessed" (Num. 22:11-12). How could words be any plainer? How could Balaam keep from understanding the Lord's will regarding his decision in this matter? His understanding is evident in the reply given the princes of Moab, "Get you into your land: for the Lord refuseth to give me leave to go with you" (Num. 22:13). This didn't suffice with Balak. He was persistent and he sent other princes more honorable than the first with greater words of enticement "for I will promote thee unto very great honor and I will do whatsoever thou sayest unto me: come therefore, I pray thee, curse me this people" (Num. 22:17). Balak was saying that Balaam could name his own price. The Lord had spoken to Balaam. He knew the will of the Lord in this matter, but rather than sending these princes on their way, he said, "Tarry ye also here this night, that I may know what the Lord will say unto me more" (Num. 22:19).

Even after God had revealed his will in the matter, Balaam wanted to see what God would speak to him "more" (Num. 22:19). The word "more" seems to be the key to the index of Balaam's heart. Though his words feigned devotion, by seeking more from the Lord, he was demonstrating the true sentiment of his heart. People have the same attitude today when they seek to justify by the word of God what they already believe, or what they want to believe. No doubt, any doctrine can be supported by taking the Scripture from its proper context and its intended meaning. By such procedure those who want God to say "more" can have him say just what they want to hear. Balaam had been told what God wanted. His will was plain and Balaam didn't misunderstand it. His ears heard one thing, but his heart desired another. He wanted those rewards of divination that Balak offered. His heart's sentiment sought to seek what the Lord would say "more."

We are aware of a couple who had no scriptural right to marry. They went from gospel preacher to gospel preacher and after relating their circumstances, asked if they had a right to marry. In every case, the answer was "NO." Finally, they came to some one who said "YES." This was all they wanted to hear. The other negative answers meant nothing! They now heard what they wanted to hear. A thousand preachers in the light of truth could have said, "NO" and it would not have satisfied. They wanted "more" than God's will. They wanted to hear the one word "YES." And as you might conclude, they married. In all probability, they were determined to do it anyway! The amazing thing is that they did ask others concerning God's will in the matter.

Balaam still lives! There are many people who still profess his spirit of a fixed heart. They hear the word of God. They know the word and what it means, but it means little to them for their hearts are fixed to the contrary. They crave the popularity of the world and the rewards of divination. The mission of the Lord's church is not to provide social functions and entertainment for its members.

Such activities fall upon the responsibility of the individual and the home life. The mission of the church in preaching the gospel, edifying its members in the truth and caring for indigent members is outlined in the word of God. Yet, there are those who want "more." They want to make a social function of the blood-bought body of Christ. When the word of God is brought to their attention, they are not content to accept its authority. They want "more" because their hearts are fixed. Hence they seek congregations to provide such for them. And there are congregations ready to provide the "more"—congregations that are foreign to the pattern of God's truth. All the Balaams are not dead by any means! May God help us always to be content with "a thus saith the Lord."

Being Spiritually Minded

In Romans chapter 8, Paul speaks of the two great realms that affect man's thinking and his behavior—the flesh and the Spirit. He speaks of those who are governed by these realms as being so minded. "Minded" refers to what a man thinks of; aims at; cares for; one's purpose, aspiration and goal. "For they that are after the flesh do mind the things of the flesh; but they that are after the Spirit, the things of the Spirit" (Rom. 8:5).

Observe These Outstanding Facts

A Christian can become carnally minded. To make the saints in Rome aware of such was Paul's purpose in writing as he did in this chapter. Be it understood that a spiritual mind is required as one becomes a Christian, but later one can serve the flesh and certainly cease to be spiritually minded. "There is therefore now no condemnation to them which are in Christ Jesus, who walk not after the flesh, but after the Spirit" (Rom. 8:1). Remaining free of condemnation is conditional upon walking "not after the flesh, but after the Spirit."

These two minds are diametrically opposed to one another. The great conflict that engages the Christian is that of overcoming and subduing the flesh. "And they that are Christ's have crucified the flesh with the affections and lusts" (Gal. 5:4). The apostle was aware of this ever present conflict: "but I keep under my body, and bring it into subjection: lest that by any means, when I have preached to others, I myself should be a castaway" (1 Cor. 9:27). These two minds are opposed in purpose and aim. The spiritual mind delights in serving God—the carnal mind delights in rebellion toward God's law. In results or end, they continue to be opposed one to another. The carnal mind results in death, to be spiritually minded is life and peace (Rom. 8:6-7).

Just Who Is Spiritually Minded?

One in whom the Spirit is supreme. Barnabas and Stephen are good examples of those being spiritually minded (Acts 7:55; 11:24). The spirit of man has asserted its rightful position in bringing the lower passions under control—thus, obeying the will of God and following the directions of the Spirit of God. One in whom the Spirit is supreme does not practice the works of the flesh (Gal. 5:19-21), but produces in his life the fruit of the Spirit (Gal. 5:22-23).

One who discerns the excellence of spiritual objects. He recognizes the Scriptures as being God's divine word (1 Cor. 2:14; Ps. 19:7-10). He thinks of God with veneration and affections. He respects the blessing of salvation and of the life to come. Men may witness the same scene or deed, yet how different are their emotions. The one gloats over the sin, the other loathes the wickedness. Their training and preparation of mind cause them to discern to the point of gloating or loathing! An artist has trained himself to discern the beauty of a modernistic painting, while to me, it may represent nothing more or less than paint splattered on a canvas. It does nothing for me! However, the artist has developed a sensitive appreciation for such and is able to discern the value. In like manner, the spiritually minded are following the direction of the Spirit and have developed the love and appreciation to discern the excellence of spiritual objects.

He loves spiritual exercise. To the spiritually minded these exercises are not deemed as a round of duties but enjoyments. To the activities and services of the church, he flies as a refuge from cares and anxieties confronted in life. To the fleshly minded, these are burdens and at times elements of sheer boredom. The fleshly minded are deaf to the charms of the spiritual melody and blind to the glory of the spiritual sunrise. The spiritual are rejoicing in the truth being preached and drink it into their souls, while the fleshly minded are bored and wondering when it will be over. He is intent upon how little he can do in spiritual exercise and at the same time salve his conscience in thinking he is faithful rather than doing more and wanting to do more for the cause of Christ. What are you minding—the Spirit or the flesh?

How Does One Become Spiritually Minded?

By being led by the Spirit of God. "For as many as are led by the Spirit of God, they are the sons of God" (Rom. 8:14). Not by some special decree or mysterious operation from God does one become spiritually minded. Nor is spiritual wickedness accomplished by hereditary and environmental means. Some with the best backgrounds seem to be at times less spiritually minded. But becoming spiritually mind comes by the word of God as the Spirit directs (Rev. 1:11; 2:11), we must continually obey God's word and appreciate its value. The proper diet of spiritual food in study of God's word and exercise in practicing such are essential to the development and retainment of a spiritual mind. *We can train our minds to appreciate spiritual things and become spiritually minded that we might have the hope of eternal life.*

Betrayal

As a rule, we turn to Christ and the apostles or other great men of God for our precepts and examples. This lesson is somewhat different in its approach because, on this occasion, we find ourselves sitting at the feet of a great traitor that we might appreciate some important lessons. There are a number of valuable lessons that can be learned from the life of Judas Iscariot. As one considers the life of this man who placed the hypocritical kiss on Jesus in the garden of Gethsemane, the question almost immediately arises as to what prompted Judas to do what he did? Was it a matter of compulsion on the part of Judas in order to fulfill a prophecy? Old Testament prophecies such as Psalms 41:9 and Zechariah 11:10-13 most assuredly point to the fact that one would betray the Lord, but Judas by name is not mentioned. If he were compelled to betray Jesus, God must have compelled him; hence, Judas was not to be blamed for what he did. It would be the deed of God himself! It is folly to conclude that Judas was the victim of prophecy or that he had to do what he did! Furthermore, the Scriptures express that his betrayal was a voluntary transaction. From Matthew 26:14-16, we know that Judas voluntarily went to the chief priests. Before them, he voluntarily asked what would they give him to deliver Jesus unto them, "And they covenanted with him for thirty pieces of silver" which Judas voluntarily agreed to accept. After the betrayal, Judas confessed his own guilt in the betrayal saying, "I have sinned in that I have betrayed the innocent blood" (Matt. 27:3-5). The expression that the devil put it into the heart of Judas further disqualifies the thought of compulsion (John 13:25-30). Judas was probably chosen because he was fitting himself to do just such work (John 6:70-71).

Lessons To Be Learned From This Traitor

Sin Is Worse Than Men Think It Is. Probably, Judas was surprised when Jesus was condemned. Witnessing the miracles and power which Jesus demonstrated, Judas might well have thought that, when the Lord was delivered to the chief priests and elders, nothing would come of it. Here was an opportunity for Judas to pick up a little extra cash and no one would be the worse off for it. Many sinners in our time have begun as simple opportunists! History reveals that sin has always been worse than men had thought. Think of Adam (Rom. 5:12), Cain (Gen. 4:13), and David (Ps. 51:3). Who can foresee the end of even the least sin? Who can see the end of an idle word or a foolish deed? We must never underestimate the consequence of a single sin! Jokes are made about sin, but sin is not a joking matter!

Sin and Its Consequence Cannot Be Escaped. "And he cast down the pieces of silver in the temple, and departed, and went and hanged himself" (Matt. 27:5). Who had accused him? Why was

Judas smitten with remorse? Why was he driven to suicide? The answer must be sin and its consequence! It has been said that there are four courts which have a possible bearing upon our lives: (1) Court of the land, civil law; (2) Court of public opinion, social law or what the public thinks; (3) Court of the conscience, moral law; (4) Court of God, divine law. Men may escape one or more of these courts but it is certain that he cannot escape them all. Doubtlessly the court of conscience was the strong element affecting Judas at this time! But who can escape the court of God, divine law? "And as it is appointed unto men once to die, but after this the judgment" (Heb. 9:27).

In Sin We May Have Encouragement, But In Consequences We Must Bear Our Own Burden. "Then Judas, which had betrayed him, when he saw that he was condemned, repented himself, and brought again the thirty pieces of silver to the chief priests and elders, saying, I have sinned in that I have betrayed the innocent blood. And he cast down the pieces of silver in the temple, and departed, and went and hanged himself."

What is that to us? Judas had done what they wanted him to do. He had served the purpose in their plot. Now, they wanted nothing to do with him. In like manner, when the prodigal's inheritance was depleted, the narrative implies that he was in want of his worldly companion (Luke 15). A lustful boy speaks all manner of "love" to a young girl. They engage in fornication and the girl becomes pregnant. Who bears the consequences? For the time being the burden is usually evaded by the boy, but not for always!

Sin Cannot Be Undone. Evidence points to the fact that Judas tried to undo his crime. It was impossible for him to have done so! No ugly word can be unspoken. No sinful deed can be undone. God does not require the impossible—that of undoing. But he does require that sinners conform to his will to be forgiven—that aliens believe, repent, confess Christ, and be baptized. Erring children are to prayerfully repent and confess the sin committed (Prov. 28:13).

Bridling the Tongue (1)

James wrote: "If any man thinketh himself to be religious while he bridleth not his tongue but deceiveth his heart, this man's religion is vain" (Jas. 1:26). And again, "For in many things we offend all. If any man offend not in word, the same is a perfect man, and able also to bridle the whole body" (Jas. 3:2). "And the tongue is a fire, a world of iniquity: so is the tongue among our members, that it defileth the whole body, and setteth on fire the course of nature; and it is set on fire of hell" (Jas. 3:6). Sins of the tongue are probably the most prevalent sins among men today. The religion of many is made vain because of improper use of the little member, the tongue. But what are some of these sins of the tongue that cause a man's religion to be vain? We suggest some of the more common ones:

Murmuring and Complaining. This was one of the besetting sins of the children of Israel (Num. 11:1; 16:41; 17:5, 10). Many of them were destroyed because of their murmurings. Paul wrote, "These things were our examples" and gave this warning, "Neither murmur ye, as some of them murmured, and were destroyed of the destroyer" (1 Cor. 10:10). True followers of Christ do not complain and "growl" about the weather, their financial status, or circumstances about them. They simply seek God first having full assurance that he will take care of them (Matt. 6:33). They have learned with Paul to be content in whatsoever state they are to be found. Let us, therefore, learn to "do all things without murmurings and disputings" (Phil. 2:14). Forasmuch as all such grumbling and complaining are sinful and destructive. How can anyone hope to influence someone else to be a Christian with the same lips that utter murmurings and complainings of the circumstances of life? We are only deceiving ourselves.

Profanity and Filthy Talk. God's name is holy and should not be spoken except with reverence and awe. "Holy and reverend is His name" (Ps. 111:9). When men and women use God's name in vain, either as a byword or as a curse word, they are guilty of sin. Sometimes professed members of the body of Christ will praise God's name on Sunday and with the same tongue curse their fellow man on Monday. James said, "Out of the same mouth proceedeth blessing and cursing. My brethren, these things ought not so to be" (Jas. 3:10). Filthy, obscene, lewd talk is likewise sinful. Smutty jokes and vulgar language ought never to fall from the lips of the saints. "Let no corrupt communication proceed out of your mouth, but that which is good to the use of edifying, that it may minister grace unto the hearers" (Eph. 4:29). This is an admonition that all should heed.

Angry Words. We sing the hymn, "Angry words are lightly spoken, bitterest thoughts are rashly stirred, brightest links of life are broken by a single angry word." How true! How true! Solomon declared: "A soft answer turneth away wrath; But grievous words stirreth up anger" (Prov. 15:1). Paul charged, "Be ye angry, and sin not: let not the sun go down upon your wrath" (Eph. 4:26). Christians should guard their tongues at all times but especially when they are angry, because "a fool uttereth all his anger" (Prov. 29:11).

Harsh and Unkind Words. Some people possess a razor sharp, caustic tongue. Some even boast of such. With it they can cut friend and foe alike. Such persons seemingly delight in taking little digs at others. There is very little kindness in their speech. Homes at times are covered with a fog of unhappiness because of harsh and unkind remarks from one member to another. "Let all bitterness, and wrath, and anger, and clamour, and evil speaking, be put away from you, with all malice: And be ye kind one to another, tenderhearted, forgiving one another, even as God for Christ's sake hath forgiven you" (Eph. 4:31-32). "A word fitly spoken is like apples of gold in pictures of silver" (Prov. 25:11). Some people seem to ignore that these statements are in the word of God!

Gossiping. The gossiper is an idle tattler, whisperer, and busybody. All that he hears he tells, and oftentimes he tells more than he hears. "A talebearer revealeth secrets" (Prov. 26:20). He "separateth chief friends" (Prov. 16:28). Like a fly the whisperer picks up all of the filth that he can and scatters it wherever he goes. The gossiper is a snake in the grass. "Thou shalt not go up and down as a talebearer among thy people" was a commandment given unto the Israelites (Lev. 19:16). Paul condemned certain women for being tattlers and busybodies (1 Tim. 5:13). The Lord despises this odious sin of the tongue. Children of God should always be careful how they repeat what they hear lest they be found guilty of gossiping. We need to bridle our tongues that we might not be guilty of sinning with it.

Bridling the Tongue (2)

All of us are confronted with many and varied dangers every day of our lives. Some are easily detected and recognized and are much more apparent than others. Others are more subtle. The more concealed a danger is the more dangerous it becomes. The tongue certainly fits into the latter group. The improper use of one's tongue can bring more sorrow to more people than most any one thing. It not only brings great sorrow to those involved here on earth but will also make their religion vain. Remember the statement from James: "If any man among you seem to be religious, and bridleth not his tongue, but deceiveth his own heart, this man's religion is vain" (Jas. 1:26). Every individual should give the greatest care to the use of the tongue.

In the previous article, we mentioned some of the sins of the tongue. This list included murmuring and complaining, profanity and filthy talk, angry words, harsh and unkind remarks, and, lastly, gossiping. This is quite a list, but the list by no means has exhausted the sins of this little member that is capable of "setting on fire the course of nature." To this gruesome list, we add the following:

Foolish Talking. There are people who seem to talk constantly and say nothing. The wise man cautioned: "Be not rash with thy mouth and let not thy heart be hasty to utter anything before God: for God is in heaven, and thou upon earth: therefore let thy words be few" (Eccl. 5:2). Christians should "study to be quiet" (1 Thess.

4:11). We need to train ourselves in the art of being sober minded rather than being frivolous and silly (Tit. 2:1-6). Foolish talking is plainly forbidden by the apostle Paul: "But fornication, and all uncleanness, or covetousness, let it not even be named among you, as becometh saints; nor filthiness nor foolish taking, or jesting which are not convenient, but rather giving of thanks" (Eph. 5:3-4). Jesus said: "And I say unto you, that every idle word that men shall speak, they shall give account thereof in the day of judgment. For by thy words thou shalt be justified, and by thy words thou shalt be condemned" (Matt. 12:36-37). I recall hearing an individual describe a person who talked a great deal by saying that the person had a mouth large enough for two sets of teeth. Perhaps it was somewhat of an extreme statement, but it should make all of us stop and think about verbal habits!

Lying. There are no big lies and little lies, black lies and white lies in the Lord's sight. "All liars shall have their part in the lake that burneth with fire and brimstone" (Rev. 21:8). God hates "a lying tongue" (Prov. 6:17). "Lying lips are an abomination to Jehovah; but they that deal truly are his delight" (Prov. 12:22). Satan is the father of lies (John 8:44). As God's children, we must "lie not one to another." But "putting away lying, speak every man truth with his neighbour: for we are members one of another" (Eph. 4:25). We must strive to let our "yea be yea, and our nay, nay" (Jas. 5:12). Let us therefore weigh our words carefully lest we speak that which is untrue and lose our soul. The first sin in the church of the Lord was that of lying. Consider the sins of Ananias and Sapphira in Acts 5:3-4! Are we saying that members of the church can lie? There is nothing wrong with your hearing. You heard it right, brother!

False Teaching. "Many false prophets are gone out into the world" (1 John 4:1). Quite often they come in sheep's clothing and devour the flock (Matt. 7:15; Acts 20:29-30; 2 Pet. 2:1). False teachers are deceitful workers, pretending to be ministers of righteousness (2 Cor. 11:13-15) "and by good words and fair speeches deceive the hearts of the simple" (Rom. 16:18). Paul places an anathema upon all of those who pervert God's word (Gal. 1:6-9). Any person who uses his tongue to preach false doctrine will probably lead more souls to hell than all of the talebearers, slanderers, and filthy talkers put together. There is no sin more pronounced in the word of God than the sin of false teaching. An immoral person may teach the truth to others and lead some to Christ, but a false teacher can never save himself or help anyone else to be saved. False teaching condemns both the teacher and the disciple. The true disciple is to take heed to himself and to the doctrine (1 Tim. 4:16). By so doing, he can save himself and others!

Failure To Speak. Solomon said that there is "a time to keep silence, and a time to speak" (Eccl. 3:7). The trouble with many is that we get the times all confused. Not only are we to hold our tongue from evil, but we must use it to speak that which is good. When one fails to speak the truth as he has opportunity or does not strive to refute false teaching when he hears it, is he not sinning by the silence of his tongue? Every Christian is charged with the responsibility of "speaking the truth in love" (Eph. 4:15). **Let Us Think!**

Brother Going To Law With Brother

As one reads the sixth chapter of 1 Corinthians, he must be impressed with the fact that a brother going to law with another brother is severely condemned. This evidently was one of the sins committed by the Corinthian brethren and deserved condemnation.

> I speak to your shame. Is it so, that there is not a wise man among you? No, not one that shall be able to judge between his brethren? But brother goeth to law with brother, and that before the unbelievers. Now therefore there is utterly a fault among you, because ye go to law one with another. Why do ye not rather take wrong? Why do ye not rather suffer yourselves to be defrauded? Nay, ye do wrong, and defraud, and that your brethren (1 Cor. 6:5-8).

It is generally understood that brethren going to law with brethren would involve lawsuits among brethren or a brother suing another brother. Such things come about when brethren refuse to respect and follow the teaching of Matthew 18:15-17: "Moreover if thy brother shall trespass against thee, go and tell him his fault between thee and him alone: if he shall hear thee, thou hast gained thy brother. But if he will not hear thee, then take with thee one or two more, that in the mouth of two or three witnesses every word may be established. And if he shall neglect to hear them. Tell it unto the church; but if he neglect to hear the church, let him be unto thee as an heathen man and a publican."

This is the procedure for settling disputes among brethren! Christ's method of dealing with personal offences involves brethren handling their affairs without engaging in lawsuits or suing one another before unbelievers. But does 1 Corinthians 6 prohibit a brother seeking protection from a brother when that one becomes violent? Though one hates to think of such happening, there are occasions when brethren conduct themselves as criminals and jeopardize the lives of other brethren.

Recently, we have come in contact with such cases and brethren thought it was needful to call the law for a restraining order to protect their families. Be it understood that such should be done with caution and careful consideration. However, is a brother going to law with a brother when protection of the police or some other law enforcement agency is called upon? It appears that some brethren feel that it does, and they strongly condemn the ones who have followed such a course. The cases of which I am aware involved brethren who have been faithful to the Lord for many years and evidence lives of spirituality. Yet, they are condemned for seeking help from the law in protection of their families. Evidently, others reason to seek the law's protection against some mentally disturbed brother is the same as going to law against a brother. Would they feel the same if such a person was seeking to rape a member of their family? Would this be their conclusion if the life of one of their family was being threatened with murder? Think!

Though a Christian should seek no pleasure in doing so, I think it proper for a Christian at times to appeal to civil law for protection. We have an example of this when Paul appealed to Caesar to protect him from the Jews who were using the law and the offices of the law to punish him. "And as they bound him with thongs, Paul said unto the centurion that stood by, Is it lawful for you to scourge a man that is a Roman, and uncondemned? When the centurion heard that, he went and told the chief captain, saying, Take heed what thou doest: for this man is a Roman" (Acts 22:25-26). Paul appealed to his rights as a Roman citizen on this occasion to save himself from punishment. At Philippi, the keeper of the prison came to Paul and said the magistrates told them to go in peace. "But Paul said unto them, They have beaten us openly uncondemned, being Romans, and have cast us into prison; and now do they thrust us out privily? Nay, verily; but let them come themselves and fetch us out" (Acts 16:37). These passages show that the Christian has a right to appeal to the law for protection. It seems to make no difference if the protection is needed from a brother or from one who does not profess to be a member of the body of Christ. Paul made the authorities come and release them, but there is no evidence that he sought to prosecute them. To prosecute goes beyond the thought of protection from injury and involves vengeance for wrong done. It is more than protection!

I definitely believe there is a difference between what is condemned in 1 Corinthians 6 of a brother going to law with a brother and a brother seeking protection of the law from a brother. Generally, lawsuits come about with individuals desiring gain or other objectives rather than the thought of physical protection from harm. They can be eliminated when brethren will follow what God teaches and reason, as they should on the basis of God's word. On the other hand, when brethren display violence and threaten bodily harm to other brethren, there is at times reason for looking to the law of the land for protection. One should never desire for such things to happen, but sometimes they do and Christians have a right to be protected regardless of whom it is that seeks to harm them.

But He Prays

Prayer is a wonderful thing and we should never lose sight of how valuable it is. However, like most every other Bible subject, it is often abused and practiced contrary to the truth of the word of God. We must never overlook what the Scriptures relate regarding prayers being acceptable in the sight of God. Prayers are the privilege of righteous people. James wrote: "The effectual fervent prayer of a righteous man availeth much" (Jas. 5:16). Peter speaks of whom the Lord hears: "For the eyes of the Lord are over the righteous, and his ears are open unto their prayers: but the face of the Lord is against them that do evil" (1 Pet. 3:12). The righteous are those who keep the commandments of the Lord. "...for all thy commandments are righteousness" (Ps. 119:172). Righteous people are those who obey the gospel of Christ and observe the commandments of the Lord. "For therein (in the gospel) is the righteousness of God revealed from faith to faith" (Rom. 1:17). People may pray, but are they righteous people and do they have God's promise that he will hear their prayers? Prayer can be so abused that individuals use such to exempt them from obeying other commandments of the Lord. Every commandment of the Lord has its definite purpose in the lives of those who obey. One commandment obeyed does not atone for those that are disobeyed or neglected. However, it appears that even some members of the church are not in agreement with this conclusion. They are inclined to praise people and view them to be righteous due to the fact that they pray.

Why does one pray? What purpose does one have in mind when he prays? The Lord spoke of the prayers of hypocrites. He told his disciples: "And when thou prayest thou shalt not be as the hypocrites are: for they love to pray standing in the synagogues and in the corners of the streets, that they may be seen of men. Verily I say unto you, They have their reward" (Matt. 6:5). The Lord knew the hearts of men and he knew there were those praying to be seen of men or to have their praise. Prayer was nothing more than a figurehead for them. Their purpose was not right and pleasing to the Lord. We may not be able to scrutinize the hearts of men as Jesus did, but we can safely conclude that there are those who pray today to be seen of men. It is a token of esteem for others to say of them "but he prays." Hear again the words of Christ: "Woe unto you, scribes and Pharisees, hypocrites! For ye devour widows' houses, and for a pretence make long prayers: therefore ye shall receive the greater damnation" (Matt. 23:14). These hypocrites were taking advantage of widows, and to cover their ungodliness, they were making long prayers. Did their prayers make their ungodly deeds right before God? Certainly not! It is possible for the same to exist today. Still today men commit ungodly deeds and endeavor to hide their guilt by making long prayers. What good is any prayer to God when the hands of men are covered with blood? Isaiah wrote: "And when ye spread forth your hands, I will hide mine eyes from you: yea, when ye make many prayers, I will not hear: your hands are full of blood" (Isa. 1:15). God calls upon men to obey his will and as penitent children to fervently pray to him.

Quite often, we observe those over television and other news media stating that they hoped and prayed for people suffering in disasters or tragedies of life. Their sentiment sounds good and it is far better than their saying that they cursed them or wished them additional harm, but do they really mean what they are saying? Do they really practice prayer and believe in it? Or is it just an appropriate phrase that amounts to nothing more than some figurehead? I may not be able to answer these questions, but what good is prayer that does not come from the heart of the Christian or righteous soul? Yet, people who should know better have been known to say that others are righteous and their prayers acceptable simply on the basis that they advocate praying.

There have been politicians who have impressed voters on the basis that the candidate spoke of prayer. Whatever might have been said for or against him, their approval was on the basis of "but he prays." Years ago, as a young man in Tennessee, I recall a political race for governor of the state. One of the candidates was reputed to be a Bible reader and believer in prayer. His opponent spoke of him carrying a Bible in one hand and a deck of cards with liquor in the other. People are prone to ignore this and dwell on the fact "but he prays."

We are to live lives consistent with our prayers. What we pray for is what we should be working to accomplish. "And why call ye me, Lord, Lord, and do not the things which I say?" (Luke 6:46). When we consider praising any official or anyone on the basis of his praying, we need to think about what he is doing in keeping with his prayers. Individuals can be like the hypocrites who devour widows' houses and for a pretence make long prayers.

But Make Me Thereof a Little Cake First

(1 Kings 17:13)

These words were spoken by the prophet Elijah to a widow in Zarephath. In the time of famine, the Lord directed Elijah: "Arise, get thee to Zarephath, which belongeth to Zidon, and dwell there: behold, I have commanded a widow woman there to sustain thee." As Elijah came to the gate of the city, he saw the woman gathering sticks. He requested of her a drink of water. As she went her way to fetch the water, Elijah's second request was "bring me a morsel of bread in thy hand." Her reply was, "I have not a cake—only a handful of meal and a little oil in a cruse—I am preparing it now for me and my son, that we may eat it, and die." Then the words from Elijah were, "Make me thereof a little cake first. . . ."

Consider her position! It had not rained for months. She had only enough food for her son and herself for one meal. From a physical standpoint, this was "it." She seemed to have reconciled herself to the fate of starvation. Her words were: "that we may eat it, and die."

Consider now the appearance of Elijah's command! It appeared exceedingly unreasonable. If he could multiply food, why ask her for bread? Furthermore, it assumed the appearance of being selfish and harsh. The prophet asked to be served before the widow and her son.

The Action of the Woman Reveals:
A. The genuineness of her faith.
  1. She went and did according to the saying of Elijah.
  2. She could have set up a strong defense. She might have thought this man is a stranger, perhaps he is a deceiver! Or, she might have acted upon the principle "charity begins at home"—my child comes first.
  3. Her ray of hope rested upon verse 14: "For thus saith the Lord God of Israel, The barrel of meal shall not waste, neither shall the cruse of oil fail, until the day that the Lord sendeth rain upon the earth."
B. Faith is often times found in unlikely places.
  1. Who would expect to find faith in the land of Jezebel?
  2. A Gentile woman sustained Elijah when his own people rejected him. Jesus referred to this in Luke 4:24-26 as he illustrated the fact that "no prophet is accepted in his own country."
C. That obedient faith is rewarded.
  1. She did as she was told and never lacked.
  2. The barrel of meal wasted not, neither did the cruse of oil fail. Furthermore, Elijah raised her son to life while staying in this home. Surely, her obedient faith was rewarded. What does it take for us to realize this great lesson?

Lessons For Us
A child of God is to recognize the priority of God's claim.
We are to make God's cake first. God is not a beggar asking for alms or the crumbs that fall from our tables. We are stewards of his manifold grace. Actually, what we have we hold in trust for him. We cannot honestly use trust funds to gratify our desires, while we

only give the leftovers to assist his work. Plain living, high thinking, and large giving should characterize the disciples of Christ. We are to make God's cake not only before pleasures and luxuries, but also before those things that might be termed as necessities. Remember that Jesus said, "But seek ye first the kingdom of God, and his righteousness; and all these things shall be added unto you" (Matt. 6:33).

There is a bright side to adversity. Adversity makes men look to the source of their comforts. In seasons of plenty, men are disposed to place their trust in the full barn. Think of the rich farmer in Luke 12:16-19! God called him a fool because, in his prosperity, he had left God out of his plans. Adversity reveals the boundless supply of the Almighty. He blessed Elijah and the widow and her son apart from nature. Nature is not exhausted by blessing man.

Prosperity comes not by saving, but by sharing. Had the widow withheld from the prophet of God, she would have doubtlessly perished. She was saved by her generosity. She was enriched by her sharing. We need to understand that giving is an investment. It is laying up treasures in heaven. "Lay not up for yourselves treasures upon earth, where moth and rust doth corrupt, and where thieves break through and steal: But lay up for yourselves treasures in heaven, where neither moth nor rust doth not corrupt, and where thieves do not break through nor steal" (Matt. 6:19-20). It is sowing for a harvest (2 Cor. 9:6). When we make God's cake first, he is able to bless us with more. "Here lies a man, men thought him mad; the more he gave, the more he had." Make God's cake first and see your life enriched, as God wants it to be. Regardless of what might come, we need to always obey God and keep him first in our lives.

But They Are Really Friendly

Friendliness is an outstanding quality and should certainly characterize the Lord's people. Visitors to the services should be impressed with friendliness shown to them. It is a good thing for a congregation to have the reputation of being friendly regarding visitors. More emphasis should be given by members in making people feel welcomed at the services. There have been occasions when visitors are virtually ignored when a warm handshake and a few words could mean so much. Such could easily determine whether they would return and be in the assembly again to hear the gospel of Christ. The unfortunate thing is that some members never seem to feel the importance of being friendly.

Years ago, we were coming home from a meeting in one of the western states. We needed a place to worship on Sunday and found the location of a church that was said to be conservative. We even made a trip from the motel Saturday evening to locate the building where we would attend on Sunday. We were there early for Bible Study and remained through the worship that followed. We stayed around after service and didn't run out at the moment the "amen" was said. In all of this, there was not one soul who made any effort to speak to us or make us feel welcome. Mind you, it didn't keep us from worshiping the Lord and doing what was expected in praising him, but how much more joyful it would have been for a little friendliness to be shown those visiting. This reminds me of the account of a man attending a service when the preacher was discussing would there be recognition in heaven. After the cold reception the man received, he commented that the preacher ought to preach about would there be recognition on earth for it seemed to be lacking in that congregation regarding visitors.

The wise man wrote, "A man that hath friends must shew himself friendly: and there is a friend that sticketh closer than a brother" (Prov. 18:24). Some individuals do not give others an opportunity to be friendly. They come in late and leave early, commenting later about how unfriendly the people were toward them. It is difficult to be friendly with those who do not desire such. There are times when some are looking for something that will give them fuel to speak derogatorily about a congregation. Perhaps no one could please such individuals, but we should do our best to show ourselves friendly as servants of the Lord.

We now come to the real heart of this article. We have known members of the church who would attend services where the truth on various issues is not being taught. Some of these have been forewarned about such situations. Nevertheless, they attend and when it is discussed with them, their justification was, "But they were really friendly." In essence, they were saying the friendliness shown them made the wrong that was being practiced all right. Friendliness is admirable, but it can never make right what is being practiced that is wrong. Yes, God's people are to be friendly. We have related how true this is, but friendliness does not determine what is truth. Think about where this could lead. On occasions one might be impressed with the friendliness of Methodists, Baptists, Catholics, Mormons, Jehovah Witnesses, Lutherans, Quakers, etc. Are we saying that the showing of themselves friendly to visitors will make what they teach the truth? If brethren can justify their visiting with congregations not standing for the truth by saying "but they are really friendly," why couldn't the same apply to denominations? Why wouldn't their friendliness make their corrupt doctrines right in the sight of God? I suppose one could say the Devil is friendly. Paul wrote, "...for Satan himself is transformed into an angel of light" (2 Cor. 11:14). Without doubt, Satan wants to be on the friendly side of all of us, but is that making him any less wicked? No, these are just more of his deceitful tactics of which we must not be ignorant.

With the view that some manifest about friendliness, a number of passages should read differently. 2 John 9 should read, "Whosoever transgresseth, and abideth not in friendliness, hath not God. He that abideth in friendliness, he hath both the Father and the Son." They seem to dwell on being friendly and place such above recognition of the doctrine of Christ. Hence, friendliness is inserted to take the place of the doctrine of Christ. We notice 1 Timothy 4:16: "Take heed unto thyself, and unto friendliness; continue in them: for in doing this thou shalt both save thyself and them that hear thee." Why bother with the doctrine? Leave it out of the verse and replace it with friendliness. We could do this with all the passages that refer to the doctrine of Christ.

Friendliness has its virtue and we readily admit that such exists. But friendliness like everything else can be abused and we must guard against such. Know the doctrine of Christ and always stand for the truth. All the friendliness in the world can not take the place of truth. Don't let Satan deceive you by thinking that it can.

But Thomas Was Not With Them
(John 20:24-25)

After the resurrection, the writer John mentions three appearances of Christ—one on the resurrection day, one eight days later, the last on the shore of the Sea of Tiberias. It was at this first meeting that Thomas was not present, the one where the disciples had assembled behind shut doors for fear of the Jews. Outside of being one of the Twelve, we do not know a great deal about Thomas. The Greek name Didymus means "twin." He displayed loyalty in suggesting that the disciples accompany Jesus to Bethany. "Let us also go, that we may die with him" (John 11:16). On another occasion he asked of Jesus, "We know not whither thou goest; and how can we know the way?" (John 14:5-6). However, the fame of Thomas usually lies in this event recorded in John 20. The word "doubt" is used synonymous with Thomas—the man whose faith might be described as being in his finger tips.

Let Us Observe . . .

Why Was Thomas Absent From This Assembly? There is no definite explanation or reason given in the Scriptures. We might suggest:

A lack of knowledge of the meeting. This would appear to be less plausible than some other possible explanations. Mary Magdalene had told the disciples that Jesus had risen (v. 20; Matt. 28:5-7). To say the least, Thomas had as much information as did the other disciples who were present when Jesus appeared. If he had been with the other disciples, he would have doubtlessly been present.

He was for some reason apart from his regular place.

Not reasonable to say that it was from a lack of teaching concerning the value of assembling. Could he have forgotten so soon the words of Jesus, ". . . gathered together in my name, there am I in the midst of them" (Matt. 18:20)? He had experienced many occasions with Jesus and the disciples conducive to make him appreciate the value of assembling.

By accident not being there or being "providentially hindered." The statement of the other disciples to Thomas gives no support to this. "We have seen the Lord." Furthermore, the action and statements by Thomas suggests something was ill with Thomas, but not of a physical nature.

Discouragement or spiritual despondency seems to be more plausible. Elijah (1 Kings 19) and John the Baptist (Matt. 11) experienced such on occasions. Due to his suggestions at Bethany (John 11:16), we conclude that his character would leave him open to profound discouragement at the death of Jesus—if he dies, we may as well go and die with him. His apparent temperament would incline him to await in solitude the solution of the death of Christ. Perhaps given to moody fear, he shrank into solitude.

We can never know *why* he was absent. The fact remains that he was absent and look what he missed. When we absent ourselves from any assembly of the saints, we are impairing our spiritual life as did Thomas. Thomas probably didn't realize what he was missing or what was happening to him. The other disciples were eager to tell him, but he appeared insensible to his condition.

Had He Actually Lost Anything By Being Absent?

He lost much good and gained much evil, two effects of neglecting the assembling of ourselves together.

He lost the opportunity of seeing and hearing Jesus. He had to spend needless days in the evil disposition of doubt (v. 20).

He missed the blessings that Jesus gave to those who were present. These involved peace, promise of the Holy Ghost and ministry.

He gained the hardening and darkening of his heart through deceitfulness of sin.

The Consequence of His Absence
Separated from the fellowship of kindred spirits, he augmented his gloom. He became utterly unreasonable. Ten of his brethren witnessed that they had seen Christ (v. 25), but Thomas rejected their testimony and deep interest in him.

He became obstinate—"except... I will not believe." He was determined not to believe on evidence that it might please God to give him. He would believe according to his own prejudices, or not at all—faith at the finger's tip.

He became presumptuous and insolent. A view of the person of Christ would not suffice. He said he would not believe until he had put fingers into the nail holes and hand into the wound in his side.

Conclusion
It was through God's mere mercy that Thomas was convinced of his error (John 20:27-28). Thomas saw and believed. "Blessed are they that have not seen, and yet have believed" (v. 29). Have you obediently believed in Christ (John 20:30-31)? Thomas forfeited many blessings by not being in the assembly. Jesus will appear again! Where will he find you? Faithful in the general assembly, church of the firstborn (Heb. 12:23)?

But We All Sin

This is a phrase that is often spoken. It is certainly nothing of which to boast or be thankful. Sin is a horrible, hideous, and degrading thing. Rather than these words coming from a contrite and humble heart that is ashamed of sin, they are usually spoken in an entirely contrary light. Let someone be rebuked about his life that is lacking in the sight of God and it is not uncommon to hear him say, "But we all sin." In so doing he is endeavoring to retaliate for the rebuke and even justify his actions. The sentiment of these words is used as a form of refuge for his sinful actions. The words are not commonly uttered with the spirit of confession, but with the defiant attitude of justification. In summation, one is sayihng, "You have your sin; I have my sin; we all sin—so leave me alone!"

The word of God teaches that we do sin! A student of God's word will not deny this. In fact, if he does, he places himself in the very presumptuous category of making God a liar. Read 1 John 1:8-9: "If we say that we have no sin, we deceive ourselves, and the truth is not in us. If we confess our sins, he is faithful and just to forgive us our sins, and to cleanse us from all unrighteousness. If we say that we have not sinned, we make him a liar, and his word is not is us." The "we" and the "us" in these verses must refer to those who have established covenant relationship with God through Jesus Christ. As they prayerfully confess their sins, they are the only ones God has promised to forgive (v. 9). God will hear their prayers that their sins might be forgiven. These are "my little children" as John graciously and affectionately refer to them in the beginning of chapter 2. So we should humbly and shamefully recognize that we do sin!

Regarding the subject that we have under consideration, a few points need to be pointed out.

There is a classification of sin. This may startle some readers, as they have heard throughout their lives that sin is sin or one sin is not to be considered more heinous than another. Perhaps we could improve upon the word "classification"; nevertheless, the book of 1 John makes a distinction with sin. John writes in 1 John 3:8, "He that committeth sin is of the devil." We are told in the first chapter that we all sin and if we deny such, we make God a liar. Therefore, if no classification or distinction exists, we are all of the devil and to deny such makes God nothing more than a liar. This is obviously a false conclusion. Sin is classified by John: "If any man see his brother sin a sin which is not unto death, he shall ask, and he shall give him life for them that sin not unto death. There is a sin unto death: I do not say that he shall pray for it. All unrighteousness is sin: and there is a sin not unto death" (1 John 5:16-17). There is sin "not unto death" and there is "sin unto death" (1 John 5:17). The sin unto death is a sin that a brother will not confess that God might forgive him (1 John 1:9). I am far from admitting that "we all sin" in a rebellious and habitual manner. In 1 John 1:8-10, John is saying that we have not reached a sinless state in which we no longer need the blood of Christ to cleanse us. He is establishing the need for our continually walking in the light (v. 7) that the blood of "Jesus Christ his Son cleanseth us from all sin." A part of our walking in the light involves recognizing our imperfect state and confessing our sins unto the Lord when they are committed.

Sins are to be confessed and forsaken. When individuals say, "But we all sin," they seem to suggest that God licenses sin or that he will ignore such. I never read of any such principle in the word of God. Even in the proper evaluation of the subject, John isn't writing to encourage sin or endorse it with his statements in 1 John 1:7-10. In these words, he is calling upon Christians to appreciate that God doesn't ignore sins, but is ready to forgive them as we confess our sins, which certainly implies forsaking them. When we sin and we are aware of such, what do we do about it? Do we with an arrogant, defiant spirit say, "But we all sin" and leave it there? Or do we humbly evaluate the subject and with a penitent heart ask the forgiveness of God and then proceed to do what we have to do in making the matter right? In some respect, we may all sin, but not all are so hardened and indifferent that they will continue on in their sins. To do so is to "sin unto death" and forfeit any right for an eternal home with God. "Whosoever is born of God doth not commit sin; for his seed remaineth in him: and he cannot sin, because he is born of God" (1 John 3:9). John does not contradict himself. To commit sin here refers to a practice of sin. Even Williams, a Baptist scholar, renders it to "practice sin" in his translation of the New Testament. We need to obey the Lord and cease trying to justify our sins by saying, "But we all sin"!

Church Autonomy

The word "autonomy" is defined as meaning: "1. independence; self-government (contrasted with heteronomy); 2. a self-governing state or community" (*The World Book Dictionary*). In God's wisdom and prudence, he has designed his church as being self-governed and every local church as being independent of all others. At times this design has been illustrated with a window pane. A rock or flying object striking one huge window pane would destroy the entire glass. But what if the window were composed of various panes? One or so might be destroyed while the others are not ruined. In like manner one congregation might depart from God's truth while others are not necessarily affected. Thus, we can see the wisdom of God in granting such an arrangement to the church.

Some one may ask where is the word "autonomy" found in the Scriptures? I have never encountered a version that uses the word. However, the very principle or truth of the word is found in the Scriptures. Think about 1 Peter 5:1-2 as Peter gives directions to elders. Observe in these verses the phrase "which are among you" or "which is among you." Elders are over a local church and that is where their work begins and ends. The "among you" conveys this thought and the self-government of the local church. The same thought is brought to our minds when we read Acts 20:28: "Take heed therefore unto yourselves, and to all the flock, over the which the Holy Ghost hath made you overseers, to feed the church of God, which he hath purchased with his own blood." This was spoken to the Ephesian elders (v. 17) and defines the area of their work. "And to all the flock, over the which the Holy Ghost hath made you overseers." The feeding of the flock conveys the idea of an autonomous group over which they were the overseers. Other passages might be given to show the autonomous feature of each local congregation.

Unfortunately, church autonomy, like most every other Bible subject, has been abused. There have been elders in other churches trying to tell other churches what to do. They have had programs that involved their being over more than the local church. Such undertakings like the Herald of Truth Radio and TV programs were and are financed by funds sent from churches to another church to do a work that the contributing elders could not possibly govern or supervise. Such activities as these are just exactly what in years gone by gave birth to Catholicism with its centralization of power and authority. Every congregation is responsible before God for doing what it can do. This is true if the congregation is composed of ten members or a thousand. We need to truly appreciate the meaning of church autonomy and keep it where God placed it.

More recently there has surfaced another abuse of autonomy and that has developed along the line of every church doing what it wants to do and no one has any right to say anything about what the practice might be. Be it understood that nothing is right in a practice of a local church that is not approved by the word of God. Autonomy does not grant any church the right to do what they design as right and to ignore what the Scriptures authorize. But this seems to be a prevailing view among some today and you have no right to say anything about it. If you do say something, then you are to be branded as "church watchdogs" who violate church autonomy. They view fellowship as being entirely local and none of your business if you are not a part of that local church. Paul spoke of "my ways which be in Christ, as I teach every where in every church" (1 Cor. 4:17). What he taught in one church, he taught in all churches. Autonomy did not grant a church the right to decide what is truth. The word of God does that! It would appear that some view church autonomy as a fence around a church that protects it against warnings and rebukes of whatever their practices might be. Jesus condemned or commended each of the seven churches of Asia by the same standard. Each church was certainly an autonomous body, but each had to answer to the Lord regarding what they were teaching and practicing. To the church at Ephesus, Christ wrote: "Remember therefore from which thou art fallen, and repent, and do the first works; or else I will come unto thee quickly, and will remove thy candlestick out of his place, except thou repent" (Rev. 2:5). Was Jesus proposing to violate their autonomy? Certainly not!

The purpose of this abuse of autonomy is an attempt to deal with those who point out the truth that is not being taught in some congregations regarding marriage, divorce, and remarriage and their effort to sanction unity-in-diversity by dumping all things into Romans 14. If fellowship is only local, how could Paul speak of us all partaking and being "one bread" and "one body" in 1 Corinthians 10:16, 17? He was not there with them, yet spoke of their "communion" and of his being one body, "for we are all partakers of that one bread." How were they all partakers of that one bread, if he was not there with them when he wrote? Did "the church" controlled by Diotrephes have the "autonomy" to allow it to reject John and refuse those who accepted him (1 John 4:6; 3 John 9)? How extensive, or far reaching, is to "walk by the same rule" and "mind the same things" to be understood (Phil. 3:16-17)? The irony is this: Can these "church autonomy" enthusiasts bind their concept of church autonomy on the rest of us? If they continue to teach their concept of autonomy and expect us to abide by it, do they not violate their very rule? **Think**—are they not doing what they say in others is unscriptural? **Be Not Deceived!**

Concerning Blushing

"Were they ashamed when they had committed abomination? Nay, they were not at all ashamed, neither could they blush; therefore they shall fall: at the time that I visit them they shall be cast down, saith the Lord" (Jer. 6:15; 8:12). These were the words of the Lord describing the doom of Jerusalem and Judah. While reading the Bible through this year, I am now in the last of Jeremiah. A few weeks ago I read these verses speaking of blushing and several thoughts came to my mind. Jeremiah is speaking of the condition that would bring about the doom of Jerusalem and Judah. Judah had chosen to commit abomination in preference to the way of the Lord. In describing their attitude toward these crimes, it is stated that the people "were not at all ashamed, neither could they blush." These words indicated the depth into which they had gone in rejecting the will of God. They were *not at all ashamed*. There wasn't any symbol of shame in what they were doing. Invariably people commit sins in which they are grossly ashamed. Of these, there appears far more hope of their repentance than for those who experience no shame at all.

But notice the other phrase, "neither could they blush." Webster defines the word "blush": "1. to become red in the face from shame, embarrassment, etc. 2. To be ashamed (at or for). 3. To be or become rosy. v.t. to redden." Experiencing no shame, it is no wonder that they could not blush. To be able to blush is a very complimentary thing. Rather than it being something that one would attempt to hide or conceal, it is on many occasions a symbol of honor. Perhaps the most outstanding makeup that a young girl can wear are rosy cheeks that have become so by blushing at improperly spoken words or suggested scenes. May God help all of us abhor sin and flirtations of sin to such an extent that we can blush when confronted with immoral filth.

In many respects blushing is an index to character. People who have been taught and trained in the righteousness of God recognize the shame of sin. They are embarrassed when confronted with immodesty of dress, off-colored stories, and suggestive acts, etc. Their blushing conveys that such is abnormal with them. On the other hand, the person who rejoices in such and seeks pleasure from such circumstances might never be expected to blush. Hardness in sin eliminates grounds for blushing. We are not concluding that a blushing person will refrain from the sin or partaking in the suggestive acts, but at least it conveys that he is embarrassed at the time and he recognizes that what is occurring is not routine. In this "mod" society of our day, the blushing cheek is deemed naïve and old-fashioned. Sin is "watered down" to such a degree that it is very seldom referred to as sin any more. In fact, it is hard to find a plain, old-fashioned sinner any more! Alcoholism is deemed just another illness. Cursing is just an expression of one's society-caused feelings. Pre-marital relations are not sinful any more; rather they serve as useful media for two people to get to "know each other better" and to know if they are suited for marriage. Even some of the modern "clergymen" are advocating trial marriages. A murderer is not a sinner; he is just a sick man, and who would be so heartless as to execute a sick man who caught his disease from the "sick society" of which he is a mere part! On and on it goes! By society's view of things, it is hard for one to find anything for which to blush. This is why all who profess to be God's children must stay close to the book of books and not be caught up with worldly thinking. It will damn one to hell.

In a sense one is trained to blush. Blushing may be more pronounced in some individuals than in others. Hereditary factors may play a decided part in demonstrating this, but we cannot discount the principle of training. As parents teach their children what is wrong and point them to the word of God, they are training them in a sense to blush. They need to be schooled in abstaining from the suggested acts that should prompt blushing. Why should one want to be a part of something that has caused them to blush? Is not the point of blushing the signal that something is wrong in the mind of one educated in the way of God's righteousness? There are parents who are failing miserably in rearing their children to blush. They permit them to follow the fashions of the world in wearing clothing not in keeping with Christianity and displaying their nudity on every hand. How do any parents expect children to blush at immodesty when they are a part of the same (1 Tim. 2:9)? They encourage them to flirt with sin!

Blushing can be lost. The Lord said of Judah, "neither can they blush." Was this always their condition? We hardly think so! They had not always been unfaithful. In the innocence of the former days of faith, they knew what shame was in failing to do the will of God. But such was not the case in the days of Jeremiah. The same can definitely happen to God's children today. We need to keep our lives in tune to the will of God lest we find that **we cannot blush.**

Concerning Doubt

Webster defines "doubt" as "to be unsettled in opinion or belief; be uncertain or undecided." Doubt might be said to be opposed to assurance and peace of mind. With caution and in a limited sense, it might be said it is good at times for an individual to experience doubt. We are told to "prove all things; hold fast that which is good" (1 Thess. 5:21). Doubt on occasions has caused individuals to examine their religious positions and to find them not in keeping with the word of God. The sincere ones, having come to the knowledge of truth, were obedient to the truth and have the peace of mind that God intends for them to have. Perhaps all of us at one time or another have experienced doubt which has motivated us to change that we might remove the doubt which was robbing us of the peace of mind that God desires for his people to enjoy.

Though doubt sometimes brings good results, it is not to be denied that doubt in itself is misery. Who can say that they were happy while doubt engulfed their heart? Regardless of the situation or endeavor of life, doubt represents misery. Think of a husband or a wife who doubts the fidelity of his/her mate! Are they happy as they should be in their marriage? Use whatever example or illustration that one might desire, but the results picture doubt and misery as being hand in hand.

We come now to the heart of what we have in mind regarding the subject of doubt. On occasions we have known people who have professed to obey the will of God manifest doubt about what they have done and continually be governed by doubt. We have reference to some who have professed to be Christians for years and yet on some of the most fundamental subjects they still do not know what is truth. They profess to study and be searchers, but they are still in doubt. A novice is not who we have in mind. The firmness of some novices would even put these people to open shame! We are writing about some who might fit the description of those Paul had in mind when he wrote: "Ever learning, and never able to come to the knowledge of the truth" (2 Tim. 3:7). Perhaps, for a limited period, doubt can serve an admirable function in one's life, but we fail to accept the thought that doubt can prevail in one's life and be an asset.

The truth is available to all men and we are confident that it is not hidden to anyone who desires it and is ready to pay the price for it. The apostle wrote, "But if our gospel be hid, it is hid to them that are lost: In whom the god of this world hath blinded the minds of them which believe not, lest the light of the glorious gospel of Christ, who is the image of God, should shine unto them" (2 Cor. 3:3-4). Jesus stated in the Sermon on the Mount, "Ask, and it shall be given you; seek, and ye shall find; knock, and it shall be opened unto you: For every one that asketh receiveth; and he that seeketh findeth; and to him that knocketh it shall be opened" (Matt. 7:7-8). Does this mean that one must seek throughout his entire life in order to find what constitutes the truth he is to obey in order to be saved? Must one remain in doubt the greater part of life while seeking to find? Such reasoning would defeat the concept of assurance, confidence, and peace of mind that the Scriptures vividly portray. Those who were the converts in the book of Acts were people who obeyed the word the first time it was preached to them. It was not so complicated that they had to spend a life time studying to find the truth before they could remove the doubt of their life. Some one is ready to say, "O, but they didn't have to confront the various doctrines that we do today." Error has always existed. They had to confront Judaism that seemed to have an influence on people in a sense far greater than anything we might picture in prevailing error today. Perhaps we have hit upon one of the grounds of doubt. It appears that some feel that they have to know all the error in the world to know what truth is. Be it understood that it is good to know about false doctrines, but one can read the Bible and know the truth without knowing about every false doctrine that exists.

I firmly believe that anyone who continues in doubt about the fundamental principles of God's will toward man has a problem other than recognizing the plainness of those things that we are to believe.

Unbelieving Jews came to Jesus and said: "How long dost thou make us to doubt? If thou be the Christ, tell us plainly. Jesus answered them, I told you and ye believed not: the works that I do in my Father's name, they bear witness of me. But ye believe not, because ye are not of my sheep, as I said unto you" (John 10:24-26). These Jews accused Jesus of causing them to doubt and not being plain in his teaching. The Lord told them the reason for their lack of faith, "ye are not of my sheep." They did not possess the sheep-like qualities to condescend to the obedience required in accepting the truth. When we doubt, we need to examine ourselves. Look inward where the problem truly exists. God wants his people to have peace and peace we can truly have!

Concerning the Word "Easter" in Acts 12:4

Each spring a religious holiday comes that many in the religious world call "Easter Sunday." This day is so honored by them as being the day of Christ's resurrection from the dead. There is no biblical record of the observance of Easter, or any of its related activities such as Lent, etc. Actually, Easter originated from paganism, Judaism, and Catholicism rather than from the authority of God's word. However, when statements like these are made, someone may remark, "Doesn't Acts 12:4 speak of Easter?" Yes, it does in the King James Version, but not in numerous other versions. We must bear in mind that, though the Bible itself is inspired, the various translations, or versions, are not. The translators of the King James Version simply made an error in translating Acts 12:4 as "Easter."

The Bible, correctly translated, makes no mention of Easter. The Revised Version with Weymouth, Moffatt, Goodspeed, and Young correct the mistranslation of the King James Version and make it read "after the Passover." The King James mistranslates Acts 12:4 and makes it read "after Easter," without any scriptural authority for such a change. The language of the original says *meta to pascha*, which means "after the Passover." Even the Catholic Version reads "after the pasch." *Clarke's Commentary* says that John Wycliff, the first to translate the Bible into the English language, used the word "*paske,*" i.e., "passover." But someone remarks: "This is rather confusing to me for I am not able to determine which version is preferable above another." All right, granting that this is so and the difficulty does exist, I believe that you and I can understand from a careful study of the context of Acts 12:4 that the word should have been translated "Passover" instead of "Easter." Let's notice the passage that is under consideration! It reads:

> Now about that time Herod the king stretched forth his hands to vex certain of the church, and he killed James the brother of John with the sword. And because he saw it pleased the Jews, he proceeded further to take Peter also. (Then were the days of unleavened bread.) And when he had apprehended him, he put him in prison, and delivered him to four quaternions of soldiers to keep him; intending after Easter to bring him forth to the people. Peter therefore was kept in prison: but prayer was made without ceasing of the church unto God for him (Acts 12:1-5).

The significance of this passage is that Herod kept Peter in prison because it was the Passover season; thus giving honor to this event. Would Herod, being of Jewish blood and the ruler of the Jews, have cared whether Easter, if such it was, was thus desecrated or not? Certainly not! It is foolish to think that he would have kept Peter in prison to honor a "holy day" to Christians or especially one designed to commemorate the resurrection of Christ from the dead. On the other hand, it is plausible to conclude that he would have so honored a Jewish holy day—the Passover.

Then why did the King James translators not translate it "Passover" instead of "Easter"? There could possibly have been a number of reasons. It might possibly have been one of those human errors that will slip into any undertaking not directly controlled by God. It could have been for some ulterior motive which we do not, and may never, know. Again, they may have translated it "Easter" instead of "Passover" because of the close connection which has existed in the minds of people between the Passover and the resurrection of Christ.

We are aware of the fact that Christ did arise during the Passover season. The translators knowing this, and the fact that Easter was designed to commemorate Christ's resurrection, naturally translated it Easter. This idea is brought out in the following comments of the *Cambridge Bible*, published by the Cambridge University Press: "Intending after Easter (the Passover). The rendering 'Easter' is an attempt to give by an English word the notion of the whole feast." The term "whole feast" in the above quotation includes both the Passover of verse 4 and the days of unleavened bread of verse 3. However, Mr. Clarke in his commentary on this passage says that the King James translators were probably influenced by the Anglo-Saxon service books and versions of the Gospel records. He points out that the Anglo-Saxons consistently translated "Passover" as "Easter" and cites as examples Matthew 26:2, 19; Mark 14:12. But the King James translators were not consistent. They translated it "Easter" only in Acts 12:4. Mr. Clarke calls this an unhappy and absurd translation.

Christians are content on every Lord's day in the year, to assemble and worship God according to the New Testament pattern (Acts 2:42; 20:7; 1 Cor. 16:1-2). There is no authority for exalting one Sunday above the others and calling it Easter. It is to go beyond the doctrine of Christ and have not God (2 John 9; Gal. 4:10-11).

Concerning Tithing

A few years ago, a periodical entitled *Tithing Digest for Pastors* came in the mail to the church office. It was published by Layman Tithing Foundation and, as you might expect, the publication dealt with articles and hints that "Pastors" might use to encourage their members of various denominations to be fervent in giving a tenth of their income to their treasuries. Tithing was a law of God in the Old Covenant which was abrogated at the cross of Christ (Col. 2:14-17). The law of tithing is not taught in the New Covenant and to endeavor to bind such upon Christians is to pervert the gospel and make Christ to be of no effect (Gal. 5:4). But in an effort to show that individuals are to practice tithing in this age, we quote the following article that appeared in this digest:

> The LAW of the TITHE runs all the way through the Scriptures and is stated clearly:
>
> FIRST, in the PATRIARCHAL DISPENSATION, where the REVELATION of God was an appeal to the MIND of man. Study the following passages together: Genesis 4:3; Genesis 4:7; Leviticus 27:30; and Numbers 18:21. (The last two passages from the law of Moses and the first two from the account of the sacrifices offered by Cain and Abel do not mention the principle of tithing. A far better passage from the Patriarchal age would be Genesis 12:20 when Abram paid tithes to the priest of the most high God, Melchizedek. bkt)
>
> SECOND, in the MOSAIC DISPENSATION, where the LEGISLATION of God makes an appeal to the WILL of man. Study the following passages together: Deuteronomy 14:22; Proverbs 3:9 and 10; and Deuteronomy 8:18.
>
> THIRD, in the CHRISTIAN DISPENSATION, where the SALVATION of God comes with an appeal to the HEART of man. Study the following passages together: Matthew 23:23; 1 Corinthians 16:1 and 2; Luke 19:8 (Thomas Kane, 8).

There is no definite reason to question that the law of the tithe ran through the Patriarchal and Mosaic Dispensations, but we certainly deny that it is found in this dispensation identified as the Christian. This writer makes a very feeble effort to prove that it is God's will that Christians are to practice tithing. Doubtlessly you have already observed that he has only used three Scriptures from the New Testament. Only one of the Scriptures mention tithing and it lacks much in teaching that we are under the law of tithing in this age. We have in mind Matthew 23:23, which reads: "Woe unto you, scribes and Pharisees, hypocrites! For ye pay tithe of mint and anise and cummin, and have omitted the weightier matters of the law, judgment, mercy and faith; these ought ye to have done, and not to leave the other undone." "Not to leave the other undone" refers to their obligation to tithe. This is not to be denied! But under what dispensation were these living? This was under the Mosaic dispensation or the Old Covenant in which tithing was definitely taught as the law of God. The Old Law was not fulfilled until Jesus died on the cross and at this time he was very much alive as he spoke this woe to the scribes and Pharisees.

The passage from Luke 19:8 does not even refer to the principle of tithing and, even if it did, the setting again was under the period of the Old Covenant before the New Testament Law went into effect. This passage involves the words of Zaccheus, the publican: "And Zaccheus stood, and said unto the Lord: Behold, Lord, the half of my goods I give to the poor; and if I have taken any thing from any man by false accusation, I restore him fourfold" (Luke 19:8). How can one get paying a tenth to the Lord out these words? These words are the testimony of a man in which he was pleading his fairness and honesty in dealing with his fellowman. I fail to see how anyone could feel tithing is authorized in such a passage.

The final passage is 1 Corinthians 16:1-2 which is quite ironic that it should be cited to teach tithing. It is one of the passages that shows what God expects in giving to him in this age. A passage that clearly points to the fact that the law of tithing is not in existence now. The passage reads: "Now concerning the collection for the saints, as I have given order to the churches of Galatia, even so do ye. Upon the first day of the week let every one of you lay by him in store, as God hath prospered him, that there be no gatherings when I come." Christians are to contribute on the first day of the week "as God hath prospered" them. There is no law of tithing in the verse or any other in the New Covenant. There is no set standard of determining how we prosper. However, we live under a better covenant and have a better hope than those who were under the Old Covenant when tithing was commanded. Perhaps, we should consider blessings received as Christians and even strive to give more than a tenth of our income when we purpose giving as God has prospered us. Giving is an individual responsibility that certainly can affect our souls!

Conflicting Voices

It is an apparent fact that we live in a world of conflicting voices. Voices of the world are conflicting with the word of God in matters of obedience, concerning the church, true worship, or practically any subject that is found in the Bible. Our soul salvation depends upon accepting God's voice and being true to it. In 1 Kings 13:1-32, we read a narrative that deals with the subject of conflicting voices. The idolatrous stroke of policy by Jeroboam had just been completed when the facts of this narrative come before us. Jeroboam feared for the people to go to Jerusalem for worship. He feared that they might be drawn again to their former allegiance and serve Rehoboam. He had set up a false worship in Bethel and Dan—a substitutionary worship. His act was a bold stroke and at the scene of the text he was engaged in the very performance of this false religion. He "stood by the altar to burn incense." Let us notice the characters and things involved in this narrative.

The Prophet from Judah. He had come to Bethel and was acting by "the word of Jehovah" (v. 1). The incident before us illustrates the invincible courage of a divinely authorized messenger. His divine authority aided him in the full and faithful declaration of the message which the Lord had given to him. It rendered him fearless in the presence of an angry and unscrupulous king. It enabled him to resist the strongest of temptations to disobedience—namely, flattery and avarice. "And the man of God said unto the king, if thou wilt give me half thine house, I will not go in with thee, neither will I eat bread nor drink water in this place: for so was it charged me by the word of the Lord, saying, Eat no bread, nor drink water, nor turn again by the same way that thou camest" (vv. 8-9).

The Old Prophet in Bethel. The record does not tell us who this prophet was, or whether he was genuine. His sons were present at the destruction of the altar and reported the events to their father. After learning of the exploits of this prophet from Judah, he pursued him, lied to him, and induced him to return to his house in violation of the plain commandments of God. This brings us to consider . . .

The Conflicting Voices. When the old prophet found the man from Judah, he was sitting under an oak. Probably he was weak and hungry and meditating on the command that shut him out from the king's hospitality. Much depends on the mood we are in when a message comes to us. There is the possibility that the prophet wanted to accept the old prophet's invitation though he was restrained by the divine inhibition. The old prophet lied to him saying, "the angel spake . . . bring him back with thee into they house." He was assuring the prophet from Judah that he had a divine message countermanding the previous order. The conflict has arisen . . . which shall he believe? Reason and conscience said, "Hold on to what you know to be true." Appetite assured him to believe what he wanted to be true. To appetite he yielded. Many people view it unjust and cruel that the man of God should be condemned for a mistake imposed on him by the lie of another. That brings us to ask: Was the way of duty really obscured by the old prophet? Was it a mere mistake that the prophet from Judah accepted it? Was he the helpless victim of a falsehood? As one considers these questions, he must confront the facts in the case. The first message came directly to him and he knew that it came from God. It was confirmed by miracles. The second message came from a total stranger and it was void of divine evidence. All presumptions, therefore, were against the truthfulness of this new message. Here was a prophet living in Bethel that evidently was not recognized of God as being faithful. If he had been, why didn't God use him to denounce the acts of Jeroboam rather than having to send the prophet of Judah?

The value of the lesson to us. It is definitely a part of God's revelation which has been preserved for us (Rom. 15:4). Similar experiences can and do happen to people now. If we heed this lesson thus preserved for us, we know how to act under like circumstances. How then may we know what is right in such cases, or that we are in the right way? We need to always stay within the territory of revealed truth (Matt. 15:14; Gal. 1:6-9; 2 Thess. 2:10-12). We need to beware of the voice of sentiment. Sentiment can make a lie appear to be the truth. We should never turn a deaf ear to the voice of conscience (Acts 23:1; 24:16). We should always be cautious of the voice of opinion (Col. 2:8; 2 Kings 5:11). Voices in the world are saying that baptism isn't necessary, have the church of your choice, and worship as one pleases. What does the word of God say? Read Mark 16:16; Ephesians 1:22-23; and John 4:23-24 as well as many other passages. To whom will you listen? Will you believe a lie and be damned or obey the truth spoken from God and be saved? **Be cautious of conflicting voices!**

Consistency Thou Art a Jewel

This is a statement or quotation that we hear quite often. I do not know the source or originator of the quote. A jewel is a very valuable, enduring, and beautiful thing. Consistency is a jewel in view of the fact that it also possesses the like qualities of being valuable, enduring, and quite beautiful. Consistency is defined as "possessing firmness or coherence; living or acting conformably to one's own belief or profession."

Why Should Christians Strive to be Consistent in Life?

Christ, our example, lived such a life. He taught and lived in harmony with what he taught. Luke begins the Acts of the Apostles with this statement: "The former treatise have I made, O Theophilus, of all that Jesus began both to do and teach" (Acts 1:1). We are to always remember that Jesus is our example in the life that we are to live (1 Pet. 2:21). We must be consistent with teaching and practicing the truth.

Christ condemned inconsistencies. In Matthew 11:18-19, Jesus pointed to the inconsistent reasoning of the people regarding John and him. "For John came neither eating nor drinking, and they say, He hath a devil. The Son of man came eating and drinking, and they say, Behold a man gluttonous, and a winebibber, a friend of publicans and sinners. But wisdom is justified of her children." They were inconsistent in their standard or criteria of judgment. The twenty-third chapter of Matthew abounds in Christ's condemnation of the inconsistencies of the Scribes and Pharisees. The nine woes that are pronounced in this chapter are either directed against an inconsistency in their teaching and manner of life or such is definitely implied. Our Lord referred to them as follows: "Ye blind guides, which strain at a gnat, and swallow a camel" (Matt. 23:24). They didn't possess the jewel of consistency!

Lest we become hypocrites. An individual who dwells upon the practice of inconsistencies is hypocritical. Jesus referred to those who were inconsistent in their teaching and practice as being hypocrites (Matt. 23). In condemning inconsistent, unrighteous judgment, Jesus asked, "And why beholdest thou the mote that is in thy brother's eye, but considerest not the beam that is in thine own eye? Or how wilt thou say to thy brother, Let me pull out the mote out of thine eye; and behold a beam is in thine own eye? Thou hypocrite, first cast out the beam out of thine own eye; and then shalt thou see clearly to cast out the mote out of thy brother's eye" (Matt. 7:3-5). Hypocrisy is an eventual fruit of continued inconsistency! It is difficult to separate the two!

Lest we lose our influence. No one knows what to actually expect from an inconsistent individual. They are one way one time and another way the next time. It is quite obvious that such actions are not conducive for one having a good influence. Uniformity is very important to a good influence. Paul spoke of inconsistencies in Romans 2:21-24: "Thou therefore which teachest another, teachest thou not thyself? Thou that preachest a man should not steal, dost thou steal? Thou that sayest a man should not commit adultery, dost thou commit adultery? Thou that abhorrest idols, dost thou commit sacrilege? Thou that makest thy boast of the law, through breaking the law dishonorest thou God? For the name of God is blasphemed among the Gentiles through you, as it is written."

After depicting their manner of not practicing what they preached and calling attention to their inconsistent life, Paul states that such had led the Gentiles to blaspheme the name of God. "For the name of God is blasphemed among the Gentiles through you." Their manner of life in failing to live in accord with the truth that they preached was a hindrance to the cause of Christ. Rather than leading men to glorify God by their life, they were causing them to blaspheme the name of God. Their inconsistency condemned themselves and turned others from the truth of God's word. Such is the curse of inconsistency!

To save ourselves and others, our life must be consistent with the teaching of Christ. In writing to Timothy, Paul gave the true qualifications of a true servant of the Lord: "Take heed unto thyself and unto the doctrine; continue in them: for in doing this thou shalt both save thyself, and them that hear thee" (1 Tim. 4:16). There are two factors involved that must not be ignored. Heed is to be given to living a pure life and preaching the true doctrine of Christ. Both legs are to be equal if one is to be pleasing to the Lord. There must be a pure life and the pure doctrine of Christ must be preached. Jesus asked: "And why call ye me, Lord, Lord, and do not the things which I say?" (Luke 6:46). We need to truly appreciate how beautiful a jewel consistency is and let it always be a part of our lives.

Covering Sins

"He that covereth his sins shall not prosper: but whoso confesseth and forsaketh them shall have mercy" (Prov. 28:13). "Blessed is he whose transgression is forgiven, whose sin is covered" (Ps. 32:1). These two passages appear almost contradictory, one stating, "He that covereth his sins shall not prosper" and the other "Blessed is he whose sins are covered." The answer of course, lies in the fact that there are two ways to cover sins. There is a right and a wrong way. It is always wrong when man refuses to follow God's directions and devises his own way of dealing with his sins. The right way is when man follows the will of God in doing what God has for him to obey that he might be forgiven by the Lord. Let us observe.

Wrong Ways To Cover Sins

To deny that we have them. To the Romans, Paul wrote: "For all have sinned, and come short of the glory of God" (Rom. 3:23). All accountable beings need to obey the gospel of Christ in order that their sins might be forgiven (Rom. 1:16-17; Mark 16:16). In writing to "my little children" or those in covenant relationship with the Lord, John said, "If we say we have no sin, we deceive ourselves, and the truth is not in us. If we confess our sins, he is faithful and just to forgive us our sins, and to cleanse us from all unrighteousness. If we say that we have not sinned, we make him a liar, and his word is not in us" (1 John 1:8-10). When we sin, to endeavor to cover our sins by denying that we have them is "to deceive ourselves," "the truth is not in us," "make him a liar, and his word is not in us." This is quite tragic!

To hold others responsible—attempting to excuse ourselves. This is one of the oldest devices of man in an effort to cover his sins before God. Rather than stand on his own two feet and recognize responsibility for his deeds, he has tried to exempt himself by blaming others. Adam attempted such (Gen. 3:12); Aaron tried this approach when Moses questioned him about the calf worship (Exod. 32:21-25). Men do it today, but it will not work. "For every man shall bear his own burden" (Gal. 6:5). We must answer to God for our deeds (2 Cor. 5:10).

To commit another sin. David is an example of this. He committed adultery with Bathsheba. In an effort to cover his sin, he resorted to having Uriah, the husband of Bathsheba killed (2 Sam. 11:15-12:7). He only made bad matters worse by adding sin to sin. His covering of sin in this approach was a vain failure. How many people have at times followed such a vain approach to covering sins and virtually destroying their lives by committing another sin in an effort to hide the first! This is the futile and hard way!

Believing that doing a good act will cover for sin committed. A command obeyed does not justify a commandment disobeyed. People have been known to use James 5:19-20 to teach that converting an erring brother hides or covers the sins of the one that is instrumental in doing the converting. The multitude of sins hidden are the sins of the one converted as the erring brother does the will of God in repenting and confessing his sins. We cannot offset sins by doing other things that are right in the sight of the Lord. Be not deceived, brethren!

Finding inconsistencies in others. There are those who seem to think that the failure of some professed Christians in doing what is right, will justify them or cover their sins. We hear people say, "Why, look at _____, he is supposed to be faithful and see what he has done. Surely I am no worse than he is." God will certainly deal with the hypocrite. But the deeds of others will neither condemn nor justify me. His sins will not grant any cover to the sins that I have committed. Remember: "For every man shall bear his own burden" (Gal. 6:5).

Having ill will toward those who would mention our sins. John the Baptist preached to Herod, saying, "It is not for lawful thee to have her" (Matt. 14:4). Such cost John his head, but it didn't cover Herod's sins. The end of those who cover their sins in such a fashion is this: "He shall not prosper" (Prov. 28:13). We should be thankful that sins are pointed out that we might truly cover them in obeying the will of God. In this respect, Peter wrote, "for charity shall cover the multitude of sins" (1 Pet. 4:8).

Right Way To Cover Sins (Ps. 32:1)

The alien is to obey the gospel. As a penitent believer, he is to confess the name of Jesus Christ and be baptized for the remission of his sins (Mark 16:16; Acts 2:38; Rom. 10:10).

The erring child of God is to confess and forsake his sins. God does not require torture or asceticism. To confess is to acknowledge our sins and our own guilt. To forsake is to turn from them. This is the right way and in many cases the easier way. May God help us to cover our sins in the right way!

Cutting A Little Slack

There are phrases which we use that are at times very interesting as pertaining to their origin and history. As you might recognize, we are thinking about individuals viewing others with the attitude of "cutting them a little slack." Recently I read in western novels where the phrase was used and it appears that the words were referring to a cowboy with his lariat or rope around the neck of a horse or cow. He could put too much force on the rope and possibly do harm to the animal and himself. Hence, it was suggested that he slack up some and prevent injury from occurring. The task would be completed or accomplished with the slack being given.

From this original use, the words in a figurative sense have been adopted to apply to individuals or circumstances in life today. This involves an attitude toward others with whom we have contact. To practice this principle is certainly in keeping with what Jesus spoke in Matthew 7:12. "Therefore all things whatsoever ye would that men should do to you, do ye even so to them for this is the law and the prophets." It is quite certain that none of us would have our brethren judge us with such severity that they never cut us any slack. Paul perhaps had this principle in mind when he wrote, "Let nothing be done through strife and vainglory; but in lowliness of mind let each esteem other better than themselves. Look not every man on his own things, but every man also on the things of others. Let this mind be in you, which was also in Christ Jesus" (Phil. 2:3-5).

There Are Certain Things Involved When One Follows the Principle of "Cutting A Little Slack"

Mercy. We serve a merciful heavenly Father who expects his children to show mercy. One of the beatitudes speaks of this. "Blessed are the merciful: for they shall obtain mercy" (Matt. 5:7). James stressed the importance of mercy by writing: "For he shall have judgment without mercy, that hath shewed no mercy; and mercy rejoiceth against judgment" (Jas. 2:13). If we aren't careful, we get so involved in stressing some of the requirements of God that we lose sight of being merciful to those who need it. We have known individuals who actually expected more of some brethren in obedience than God has ever commanded. I have felt that mercy involves helping a person obey the commandments and requirements of God just as easily as possible. Are we saying that mercy grants a person the privilege of ignoring God's commandments? No indeed! But it does help the guilty party to comply with God's requirements in cutting one as much slack as possible. We should be merciful because God commands it and also in the consideration that we may be needing it in the event of weaknesses in our lives that could often develop. Those who have shown mercy can normally expect it from others if and when they need it.

Righteous Judgment. This is another factor involved in cutting one some slack. Oftentimes individuals make judgments before the facts are known. Some do not even care to know the facts. They make no effort at giving a person the benefit of the doubt. Jesus said, "Judge not according to the appearance, but judge righteous judgment" (John 7:24). There is judgment that is condemned (according to the appearance) and then there is judgment that is commanded (but judge righteous judgment). Jesus spoke of hypocritical judgment in Matthew 7:3-5. "And why beholdest thou the mote that is in thy brother's eye, but considerest not the beam that is in thine own eye? Or how wilt thou say to thy brother, Let me pull out the mote out of thine eye; and, behold, a beam is in thine own eye? Thou hypocrite, first cast out the beam out of thine own eye; and then shalt thou see clearly to cast out the mote out of thy brother's eye?" Such judgment is not helping a brother in cutting him any slack. We need to practice righteous judgment by not expecting of others what we would not do ourselves. We need to think of a possible beam in our own eye when we are beholding a mote in our brother's eye.

Consistency. This is a word that should be a very vital part of our lives. It is highly possible for one to cut a great deal of slack for the friend and withhold such from the one that is not considered a friend. We do not deny that it takes more effort and heart to cut the slack for one that is less friendly than it does for the one who shows friendship. This is where our influence can greatly be lacking in quality. Be ready to cut the slack to all those who would desire it. There have been incidents where individuals have strongly voiced criticism of other people's children. They have been known to be very vocal in condemning their behavior. They didn't take any effort to cut these parents any slack! Guess what? Now they have children and what do they desire? You guessed it! "Cut us a little slack in the problems we have of discipline and teaching them the proper manners, etc." This comes back again to the previous statements of mercy and righteous judgment that we should be careful to exert. I am reminded of the preacher who had three sermons on how to rear children. Sometime later, he had three children and no sermons. Don't you suppose he would desire someone to cut him a little slack as he faces the problems he once failed to see that others were having?

Finally brethren, the word of God is the word of God. We have no right to change any of it. Help people to obey it, but never think we can be slack in obeying the truth.

Daily Religion

The religion that Christ gave to the world is not a one day a week affair—but for everyday. "So teach us to number our days, that we may apply our hearts to wisdom" (Ps. 90:12). We need to realize the value of time. Time is a tremendously precious commodity! "Dost thou love life? Then do not squander time, for that is the stuff life is made of" (Benjamin Franklin). There is a vast difference between existing and using one's time well. Too many people appear content to exist without giving thought to using their time well. Perhaps they are striving to pattern their existence after Methuselah. "And all the days of Methuselah were nine hundred sixty and nine years: and he died" (Gen. 5:27). Thomas Edison said, "Time is the most important thing in the world." It is one of the best remedies for our heartaches and the most efficient detective to uncover error and bring truth to light. Many things can be regained; time is not one of them. The very familiar slogan, "Live today as if it will be the last—work today as if you will live forever," certainly has its merits. As one approaches each day as if it will be the last, he will be practicing in that day the principles of Jesus Christ.

What Constitutes Daily Religion?

Daily Prayer. It is difficult to think of one who professes to be a Christian letting a day pass without praying to God. David's sentiments were: "Be merciful unto me, O Lord: for I cry unto thee daily" (Ps. 86:3). We need to pray to be spared from temptation and evil. Daily we should confess our sins. Daily we need the cleansing blood of the Lamb (1 John 1:7-10). Christians are admonished to "pray without ceasing" (1 Thess. 5:17). A time element is involved in the phrase, "without ceasing." No day is complete without prayer!

Daily Bread. Jesus taught his disciples to pray, "Give us this day our *daily* bread" (Matt. 6:11). To the Israelites God gave a day's supply of manna at a time. We need to trust in the Lord! The fact that we have a part in obtaining the daily bread by honest labor doesn't deny that the Lord provides and that daily bread is even a part of daily religion (Matt. 6:33-34). Paul wrote to the Thessalonians, "For even when we were with you, this we commanded you, that if any would not work, neither should he eat" (2 Thess. 3:10). An indolent, lazy spirit is not the spirit of true daily religion.

Daily Gratitude. Our days should be spent with an attitude filled with gratitude for the blessings that have come from the Lord. Only one of the healed lepers came back to thank the Lord for the blessing received. Jesus asked, "But where are the nine?" (Luke 17:17). Nine offered no evidence of gratitude for being healed of the dreaded disease. Hearts that are grateful will express it! "Blessed be the Lord, who daily loadeth us with benefits, even the God of our salvation. Selah" (Ps. 68:19). The complaining and murmuring of some displays a lack of true faith rather than an evidence of the true religion of Jesus Christ. What about you?

Daily Vigilance. The Christian must constantly stay alert. "Be sober, be vigilant; because your adversary the devil, as a roaring lion, walketh about, seeking whom he may devour" (1 Pet. 5:8). "Take heed, brethren, lest there be in any of you an evil heart of unbelief, in departing from the living God. But exhort one another daily, while it is called Today; lest any of you be hardened through the deceitfulness of sin" (Heb. 3:12-13). Carelessness for one day invites failure. The admonition of truth is to watch and pray.

Daily Cross Bearing. Self-denial is a daily requirement of the Scriptures. Rather than remove our crosses, Jesus said to take up the cross and follow him. "Then said Jesus unto his disciples, If any man will come after me, let him deny himself, and take up his cross and follow me" (Matt.16:24). With faith in God, we can bear the cross and be victorious each day. "But God forbid that I should glory, save in the cross of our Lord Jesus Christ, by whom the world is crucified unto me, and I unto the world" (Gal. 6:14).

Daily Study. Christians talk to God through prayer. God speaks to Christians through his word. We need to keep the conversation complete by praying daily and reading God's word each day. No day is complete when the word of God has not been read. We need this food for the soul (1 Pet. 2:2). We should seek to follow the example of the noble Bereans ". . . in that they received the word with all readiness of mind, and searched the Scriptures daily, whether those things were so" (Acts 17:11).

How is your daily religion?

Dare I Fellowship Corinth?

Some time ago, I read an article with this title, "Dare I Fellowship Corinth?" The writer spoke of the prevailing sins of the church at Corinth and that Paul fellowshipped the Corinthian church. It seems the purpose of the article was to reason that, if Paul did so with Corinth, we should certainly be able to fellowship most anything that is practiced in churches today. In his estimate it would be difficult to find any congregation today with as many unscriptural practices as existed in the church at Corinth. Therefore, if Paul fellowshipped Corinth, we should not have any difficulty or difference over the question of fellowshipping churches.

This is not a new approach in condoning sinful practices in congregations. Others have made it and many others will continue to make it. Some know better in making such an argument while others possibly are not aware of the positions that they are accepting. What fellowship Paul extended to the church at Corinth in his first epistle to the Corinthians was certainly a fellowship with rebuke. As one reads the epistle, the reader is confronted with the stern denunciations uttered against this church. In the first few chapters, the sin of division and appeal to worldly wisdom are condemned. In the fifth chapter, the church at Corinth is rebuked for condoning the sin of fornication. The brethren were going to law one with another in that which was opposed to the spirit of Christ and there is the rebuke of their behavior in chapter 6 of this epistle. Among other failures, their abuse of the Lord's supper is stated in the eleventh chapter as well as their questioning the resurrection truth in chapter 15. What fellowship existed at this time was truly a fellowship with strong rebukes. "And I, brethren, could not speak unto you as unto spiritual, but as unto carnal, even as unto babes in Christ. I have fed you with milk, and not with meat: for hitherto ye were not able to bear it, neither yet now are ye able. For ye are yet carnal: for whereas there is among you envying, and strife, and divisions, are ye not carnal, and walk as men?" (1 Cor. 3:1-3).

When individuals use Paul's action and demeanor toward the Corinthians as an example for fellowshipping sin in congregations today, is this the fellowship they have in mind? I hardly think so! They don't desire or sanction the rebukes and denunciations, but rather expect sins to be ignored and peace to exist without any objections to what practices may occur in a particular congregation. Paul pointed out their sins and called upon them to repent. He manifested a confidence in them that they would repent and correct their behavior. When Paul's attitude toward the church at Corinth is used as an example for fellowshipping sinful practices in churches today, consistency demands that the rebukes and condemnations have a place in that fellowship. However, in most cases, when such things are preached against, the objectors are told to be quiet or "hit the road" with no regard for the Scriptures or God's pattern of truth.

Paul preached truth in every church. He promised the Corinthians that he would send Timothy "who shall bring you into remembrance of my ways which be in Christ, as I teach every where in every church" (1 Cor. 4:15). I find it difficult to conclude that Paul preached in every church that he fellowshipped sins that existed in some churches. If Paul were living today, it makes you wonder what congregations would have the faith to endure his teaching and say "amen" to his sermons.

Concerning Paul's fellowship of the Corinthian church, we need to realize that God in his longsuffering grants churches and individuals an opportunity to repent. "The Lord is not slack concerning his promise, as some men count slackness; but is longsuffering to us-ward, not willing that any should perish, but that all should come to repentance" (2 Pet. 3:10). In the writing of this first epistle, the Corinthians were warned of their sins and given an opportunity to repent. According to the scope of the second epistle, it appears that they did repent and correct what needed to be done. "For though I made you sorry with a letter, I do not repent, though I did repent: for I perceive that the same epistle hath made you sorry, though it were but for a season. Now I rejoice, not that ye were made sorry, but that ye sorrowed to repentance" (2 Cor. 7:8-9). They had sorrowed to repentance! But what if such had not occurred? What if they had turned a deaf ear to the need for repentance and continued in the sinful practices? We must always be careful with the "what ifs," but it would appear that this would have presented a different scenario. Whatever fellowship existed before their sins were pointed out would cease to be if they continued in defying the will of God. This is what we must not ignore when answering the question, "Dare I fellowship Corinth?" What Corinth do you have in mind—the one that was practicing sin or the one that repented as mentioned in the second epistle? "Wherefore come out from among them, and be ye separate, saith the Lord, and touch not the unclean thing; and I will receive you" (2 Cor. 6:17).

Dare To Be Involved

It has become a rather common occurrence to read of someone being molested on our public streets and viewers failing to offer any assistance or help to the victims. Various explanations may be given for the public's failure in coming to the rescue or aid of one being abused. One of the apparent explanations is that most of the people fear to become involved. No doubt the same people who would strongly desire assistance if they were in such a situation fail to help others due to their not wanting to be involved.

In the church of the Lord today, there are cases where injustice and unfairness in the spiritual realm prevail simply because there are brethren who do not want to be involved. There is work that is never undertaken because it takes involvement that members refuse. The faithful involvement that exists in a congregation accounts for its growth and spiritual strength. The pathetic thing is that so few seem to be of the spirit to be involved. They are content to let others do it without bearing their own responsibility before the Lord. Time, energy, expense, and even mental anguish are some of the costs of being involved. Is it a wonder why some do not want to be involved? How wonderful it was that the Samaritan dared to be involved in helping the man who had been left half dead by the robbers on the Jericho road! The priest and the Levite saw the man's plight, but they passed on the other side of the road. No involvement! "But a certain Samaritan, as he journeyed, came where he was: and when he saw him, he had compassion on him, and went to him, and bound up his wounds, pouring in oil and wine, and set him on his own beast, and brought him to an inn, and took care of him. And on the morrow when he departed, he took out two pence, and gave them to the host, and said unto him. Take care of him; and whatsoever thou spendest more, when I come again, I will repay thee" (Luke 10:33-35). What the Samaritan did required time, energy, and expense in involvement that the others were not ready to give. He showed mercy that the others lacked regarding one who was definitely in sore need. He became involved.

Barnabas dared to be involved in coming to Saul's rescue when brethren in Jerusalem were doubtful of his conversion. "And when Saul was come to Jerusalem, he assayed to join himself to the disciples: but they were all afraid of him, and believed not that he was a disciple. But Barnabas took him, and brought him to the apostles, and declared unto them how he had seen the Lord in the way, and that he had spoken to him, and how he had preached boldly at Damascus in the name of Jesus" (Acts 9:26-27). Barnabas knew of Saul's conversion and he was ready to stand up for his brother. He mentioned evidences that suggested that Saul was now a true disciple of the Lord and was preaching boldly now in the name of Jesus. Think what this must have meant to Saul at this critical time in his life! Doubtlessly, it helped to knit together the friendship that these two had in the years that followed in their service and journeys for the Lord.

Christians need to be involved in teaching others the truth. We hear of cases of personal work and marvel at what some are doing. These should be common cases due to the fact that more of God's people are involved in telling others of Jesus and his truth. Andrew brought his brother, Peter, to the Lord. He dared to become involved in pointing another to Christ (John 1:40-42). Aquila and Priscilla heard Apollos preaching the baptism of John that was not present truth. They became involved in declaring unto him the way of God more perfectly. It appears that he was receptive to their teaching and went to Achaia preaching that Jesus was Christ. In these cases and many others, there were those who dared to be involved. The results were wonderful!

Christians need to be involved in the work of restoring the unfaithful to the Lord. "Brethren, if a man be overtaken in a fault, ye which are spiritual, restore such an one in the spirit of meekness; considering thyself, lest thou also be tempted. Bear ye one another's burdens, and so fulfil the law of Christ" (Gal. 6:1-2). How can one restore another without being involved with the failures and problems of another? How can one bear another's burdens without being involved in knowing what constitutes these burdens? At times, individuals hide behind the excuse that they do not want to be busybodies. When we are dealing with men's souls and their sins, we are not busybodies in the sight of the Lord. Some of us today are faithful in the Lord because someone dared to be involved in helping us be converted from the error of our way (Jas. 5:19-20). Men of faith do not do an about face or live by a double standard when truth is at stake or when men of God are being abused. Decisions of haste are to be avoided, but all of us should be more and more involved in doing and contending for what is right. How about you?

Darkness

"When I was daily with you in the temple, ye stretched forth no hands against me: but this is your hour, and the power of darkness" (Luke 22:53). These words from the Lord were addressed to the chief priests, and captains of the temple, and the elders, which were come to him with the purpose of arresting him in the Garden of Gethsemane. Jesus recognized the power of darkness! Darkness certainly has its power or attraction. Such makes men bold in their evil deeds. "And this is the condemnation, that light is come into the world, and men loved darkness rather than light, because their deeds were evil. For every one that doeth evil hateth the light, neither cometh to the light, lest his deeds should be reproved. But he that doeth truth cometh to the light, that his deeds may be made manifest, that they are wrought in God" (John 3:19-21). Men do not just love darkness; they love it rather than light. It might be said that there are two great powers that influence lives today: God's power (the gospel of Christ) and Satan's power (evil conveyed in darkness). One is light while the other is darkness! Those who follow darkness here will live for eternity in darkness—the place of "outer darkness" (Matt. 25:30).

Darkness betrayed itself in the voices that cried, "Away with this man, and release unto us Barabbas" (Luke 23:18). It was the voice of darkness that cried out, "Crucify him, crucify him." The hatred and prejudice of the Jews evidenced the darkness that controlled them. They were asking that Christ be crucified—he who had tried to do so much for them (John 5:40; Matt. 23:37). Only blind men could do this! The request that he be crucified was an expression of a gross ingratitude and identified the power which controlled them. Men continue to maintain these same attitudes today. The masses still say, "Away with what He teaches. . . . Any doctrine, any church or any way" rather than what the Christ authorizes. So many say they lament the way Jesus was abused and in the very next breath, sanction practices that he never authorized as evidence of the power of darkness that now is in them.

Paul's commission was to the Gentiles "to open their eyes, and to turn them from darkness to light, and from the power of Satan unto God, that they may receive forgiveness of sins" (Acts 26:18). To turn men from darkness to light, requires labor, prayer, and an unrelenting spirit. Why? Because darkness exerts a tremendous power over men! Note Paul's labor at Athens. Why was he so unsuccessful there as compared to other places where he preached the gospel? *Darkness!* The sooner Christians learn that it is not some sort of playful game in which we are engaged, but that it is a real task, the sooner will the church grow.

Tell me not that darkness has no power, when I see men turn down the invitation of a loving Savior as if it were nothing more than garbage under their feet. There are old men and women who are almost through with this life who continually turn down an opportunity to live in peace with God in eternity. An aged man who seemingly had one foot in the grave and the other on a banana peeling told me in his rejection of the gospel that he wasn't ready to settle down yet! Tell me not that darkness has no power, when I see young boys and girls refuse obedience to Christ because they want a taste of worldly living and even boast that they never will become a Christian. And there is the drunkard who refuses to give up his drink and continues to wreck both body and soul. If darkness doesn't control them, then please tell what does? Again, when men are so prejudiced that they will not hear the truth that they might be saved, what is it but the power of darkness influencing their lives? When men will wrest the Scriptures to make them fit some false theory (2 Pet. 3:16) and when educated men, big men otherwise, will labor to protect their faith when they know it is not New Testament teaching, what accounts for such other than the power of darkness?

What should be our conduct with respect to darkness? Those who were once in darkness are told to have no fellowship with it. Paul admonished the Ephesians: "And have no fellowship with the unfruitful works of darkness, but rather reprove them. For it is a shame even to speak of those things which are done of them in secret" (Eph. 5:11-12). Christians are not to sanction, endorse, or support anyone or anything that is not compatible with the teaching of Christ. Some say, "I am too strong, or my children are too strong to be harmed or affected by this or that." Do we know more than God? Be not deceived! The religion of Christ is not a passive religion. We must fight darkness and reprove those participating in the unfruitful works of darkness. Our warfare is "against the rulers of the darkness of this world" (Eph. 6:12). Don't let darkness have control over your life—it can be fatal!

Demoniacs

A demoniac is defined as "a person supposedly possessed by a demon." This word is frequently used in the New Testament, and applied to persons suffering under the possession of a demon or evil spirit. Much is being said lately about individuals in our times being possessed of demons. The film, "The Exorcist," that received so much publicity several years ago, was built around demon possession. It is no uncommon thing to read of modern religionists who have cast demons out of individuals in our day and made them whole again. People seem to accept demon possession today as a fact and also that there are those who have the power now to cast out demons. The prevailing thought with many who accept such views is that being possessed accounts for the evil so many perform for which they are not accountable. As in the case of so many false beliefs, it is another effort to lessen man's responsibility and accountability for the crimes and evils that men commit.

Anyone who reads the New Testament must accept the fact that during the days of the Lord and his apostles there were evil spirits subject to the Devil. These evil spirits were permitted by God to exercise a direct influence over the souls and bodies of certain individuals. The New Testament Scriptures abound in evidence of people being possessed with demons. Christ had power over these demons and he in turn gave such power to his apostles and certain disciples. "And the seventy returned again with joy, saying, Lord, even the devils are subject unto us through thy name" (Luke 10:17). God doubtlessly permitted them in the days of Christ and his apostles in order to demonstrate the power that Christ had in being able to cast them out. This involved evidence of the divinity of Christ that we might believe him to be the Son of God. "And many other signs truly did Jesus in the presence of his disciples, which are not written in this book: But these are written, that ye might believe that Jesus is the Christ, the Son of God; and that believing ye might have life through his name." Included in the signs were the occasions of Christ casting out these demons from certain individuals.

In the long ago, Zechariah prophesied that "there shall be a fountain opened to the House of David and to the inhabitants of Jerusalem for sin and for uncleanness" (Zech. 13:1). This prophecy referred to the inauguration of the New Covenant and events of Pentecost in Acts 2. In the latter portion of verse 2, he stated, "I will cause the prophets and the unclean spirit to pass out of the land." With the revealing of the truth of the New Covenant in Jesus Christ, the unclean spirit or demoniacs did pass out of the land. As the perfect law of liberty was available and confirmation was in the written word, there was no more need for signs and miracles to confirm the deity of Christ or the word of truth. Hence, no men are possessed with demons in our time for the purpose of such and demonstration over them is no longer needed. Paul wrote, "For we know in part, and we prophesy in part. But when that which is perfect is come, then that which is in part shall be done away" (1 Cor. 13:9-10). That which is perfect refers to the complete revelation of God's will. It has come and is found in the New Testament Scriptures. We have the complete revelation of God's will "that the man of God may be perfect, thoroughly furnished unto all good works" (2 Tim. 3:16-17). Demon possession has passed out of the land!

Concerning the subject of demoniacs, we quote from *Smith's Bible Dictionary*:

> It has been maintained by many persons that our Lord and the evangelists, in referring to demonical possession, spoke only in accommodation to the general belief of the Jews, without any assertion as to its truth or its falsity. It is concluded that, since the symptoms of the affliction were frequently those of bodily disease (as dumbness, Matt. 9:32; blindness, Matt. 12:22; epilepsy, Mark 5:1-5), the demoniacs were merely persons suffering under unusual diseases of body and mind. But demoniacs are frequently distinguished from those afflicted with bodily sickness, see Mark 1:32; Mark 16:17-18; Luke 6:7-18; the same outward signs are sometimes referred to possession, sometimes merely to disease, comp. Matthew 4:24 with Matthew 17:15; Luke 4:41, etc. All of these things speak of a personal power of evil. Twice our Lord distinctly connects demonical possession with the power of the evil one. Luke 10:18. Lastly, the single fact recorded of the entrance of the demons at Gadara, Mark 5:10-14, into the herd of swine, and the effect which that entrance caused, is sufficient to over throw the notion that our Lord and the evangelists do not assert or imply any objective reality of possession. We are led, therefore, to the ordinary and literal interpretation of these passages that there are evil spirits, subjects of the evil one, who, in the days of the Lord himself and his apostles especially, were permitted by God to exercise a direct influence over souls and bodies of certain men.

The above is certainly worthy of study and consideration. However, in the last sentence, I would say, "there were evil spirits, etc." rather than "there are evil spirits" as if the possibility of them existing now exists.

Did the Catholics Give Us the Bible?

The claim is often made by the Roman Catholics that they gave our Bible to the world. I have even heard some unlearned members of the church make such an observation. From a magazine advertisement of some years back published by the Knights of Columbus bearing the title, "Who Gave the Bible to the People?", we copy these words:

> For the first three hundred years of Christianity, the Bible existed, but not as we have it today. During those early times parts of the Bible were scattered among the various churches, no one of which had the complete Bible as we have it now. Then in 390 A.D., at the council of Hippo, the Catholic church gathered together the various books which claimed to be the Scriptures, passed on the merits and claims of each, and this council decided which were inspired books and which were not. The Catholic church put all the inspired books and epistles together in one volume and that is the Bible as we have it today. The Catholic church therefore gave to the people and the world, the Bible as we have it today. Her students copied it in longhand for centuries before the invention of printing.

Is this claim true? Did the Catholics give the Bible as we have it today to the people and the world? Are we dependent upon the Council of Hippo in A.D. 390 for collecting the books of the Bible?

Some Facts That Prove This Claim To Be False
We are happy to read that the Catholics said the Bible existed in the first three hundred years of Christianity and also that from the above statement they imply that it is complete now, however . . .

Copies of the original manuscripts such as the Codex Sinaiticus existed before the Council of Hippo. It contains the entire Greek New Testament and half of the Greek Old Testament.

There are versions or translations available which date back to the second century, two centuries before the council of Hippo. The Peshito Syriac was written in the Armenian tongue within half a century of the original writings. It is the oldest version that has all the Old Testament. Another version, the Old Latin, dates back to about A.D. 150. This version was in existence 240 years before the Council of Hippo. How do the Catholics explain these versions being in existence (books collected in versions) before A.D. 390 if they thought the Council of Hippo gave us our Bible?

The Catholics have yet to prove that the Roman Catholic church was in existence in A.D. 390. If it were proven that we are indebted to the Council of Hippo for giving us our Bible, it remains to be proven that the council was Catholics and this was done by approval of the Catholic church. The Roman Catholic church was a "hatching" of gradual apostasies from the true church and it is difficult to determine just when it did begin. It is generally accepted by church historians to have begun in A. D. 606. The year 1054 saw the separation into Roman and Greek Catholic churches.

Furthermore, the work of the council of Hippo does not prove consistent with the catalogs of the early religious writers commonly termed "church fathers." Athanasius died in A.D. 373. In his catalog (listing of books) were the books of the Old Testament as we have them. Cyril died in A.D. 382. He mentions all the New Testament books. So even secular history disproves rather than proves the claim of the Catholics.

Some interesting questions for our Catholic friends—if they gave us the Bible, why then . . .

- Did they hate John Wycliffe for translating it into English?
- Was William Tyndale burned at the stake in 1536?
- Was there such an age as "the dark ages" when the Bible was almost a forgotten book?
- Do they refuse to recognize it as sole authority in matters of religion?

We concede that the early monks were quite diligent in preserving the early writings and that the Catholic church gave us the Apocryphal Books which gift we reject, *but never that they gave us the*

Bible! History verifies the fact that the Roman Catholic church has been the enemy rather than the friend of the Bible. To allege is one thing, but to present the proof is entirely another thing!

Did You Ask Him To Worship With You?

We might not feel we can accomplish great tasks, but there is something all of us can do. We can invite those with whom we have contact during the week to worship with us on the Lord's day. This certainly does not require a great deal of effort and the ability to invite others is within the capability of all of us. There is power in suggestion and suggesting that one worship with you may bring about wonderful results. We should never underrate the power of suggestion. Think about the suggestion that the captive maid made regarding a prophet in Samaria who could heal Naaman of his leprosy. "And she said unto her mistress, Would God my Lord were with the prophet that is in Samaria! For he would recover him of his leprosy" (2 Kings 5:3). This suggestion set the wheels in motion that eventually led to the healing of Naaman, who was a leper. I personally have known of a simple invitation to worship that was accepted and in time brought about a conversion of a precious soul to Christ. The prevalent attitude of many is that it will do no good to invite another to worship with them. With most people, the invitation will be ignored, but that should not keep us from continuing to make the effort. To feel it will do no good is to admit defeat! That is just exactly what Satan desires for all of God's children to feel.

Rather than thinking of inviting someone to worship with us, we have thoughts and actions that often conflict with our doing so. On numerous occasions, I have mentioned the account of a Christian boasting about how he with anger spoke to an individual and as he described it, "telling him off and putting the person in his place." They took delight in relating the circumstances. A Christian hearing what was said calmly made the observation: "In the scenario, did you invite the person to worship with you on Sunday?" You know the answer! That was no doubt the farthest from the mind of the person speaking in anger. The concern was for telling the person off without any thought of his spiritual welfare. The moral of this story is that we should labor to keep our behavior in such a manner that it might be consistent with us inviting others to worship with us. Think of the statement made by Paul in Galatians 2:20: "I am crucified with Christ: nevertheless I live; yet not I, but Christ liveth in me: and the life which I now live in the flesh I live by the faith of the Son of God, who loved me, and gave himself for me." Again from Philippians: "According to my earnest expectation and my hope, that in nothing I shall be ashamed, but that with all boldness, as always, so now also Christ shall be magnified in my body whether it be by life or by death" (Phil. 1:20). He speaks of magnifying Christ in his body. We should strive to live in such a way that others can see Christ in us. We should live in such a way that our behavior would be consistent with asking someone to worship with us. We may gloat in having told someone off, but something else usually happens. We have turned someone off in influencing that one to worship with us, "Let your light so shine before men, that they may see your good works, and glorify your Father which is in heaven" (Matt. 5:16).

A young Christian was stopped for a traffic violation. You may be assured that this was not a joyful incident in her day's activity. No one gets a thrill at being apprehended for a traffic violation. When the officer gave her the citation, she was humble and apologetic. She knew that she was wrong and accepted the consequences. When she received the ticket, she replied by giving the officer an invitation to attend a gospel meeting that was in progress. Who would have thought of her at such a time doing this? But she did it! Guess what followed? The officer accepted the invitation and came to the meeting. It wasn't long until he and his family were converted to Christ. This happened because a Christian thought of a person's soul and acted in such a way in a trying circumstance to adorn the gospel. What if she had angrily told the officer off and acted in an unbecoming manner? Doubtlessly, in such a mood she would never thought of inviting him to attend the meeting. Furthermore, what would he have thought of one behaving in such a manner as being spiritually minded? "Only let your conversation be as becometh the gospel of Christ: that whether I come and see you, or else be absent, I may hear of your affairs, that ye stand fast in one spirit, with one mind striving together for the faith of the gospel" (Phil. 1:27).

A couple was in close embrace dancing in the nightclub. The girl asked the boy if he were a Christian. He replied in the negative and added, "If I were a Christian, I would not be here doing this." If Christians were being arrested, would there be enough evidence in your life to find you guilty? We need to keep our lives pure that we can consistently show that Jesus dwells within us and invite others to worship with us!

Do You Not Yet Understand?

On more than one occasion Jesus asked his disciples, "Do ye not yet understand" concerning certain truth that he had presented to them (Matt. 15:17; 16:9). They had been given the opportunity to know and understand, yet they were slow to grasp the true application of what Jesus was teaching. I have often felt that, if there were any times when our Lord was perturbed with his disciples, it might possibly have been on these occasions when they were slow to comprehend simple truth and he was compelled to ask them,"Do ye not yet understand?"

Today, as in every age, God desires that men understand his word. There is no premium on ignorance! Ignorance is not bliss when it comes to our responsibility to God's will. The word of the Lord can be understood. Paul wrote in Ephesians 3:3-5, ". . . when ye read, ye may understand my knowledge in the mystery of Christ." Again, "Be not unwise, but understanding what the will of the Lord is" (Eph. 5:17). For a person with average intelligence to state that he can't understand the will of God as revealed in the Scriptures is a gross reflection upon God himself. God has given us his word and told us to follow it. We must understand it to do so, and if we can't understand our duty to the Lord, then he has greatly deceived us and withheld mercy from us. Peter stated that brother Paul wrote "some things hard to be understood" (2 Pet. 3:16). He didn't say that everything Paul wrote was hard to be understood. Furthermore, he didn't say that these things couldn't be understood. Some of the things were harder to understand than some of the other things that Paul wrote.

After much teaching has been done on various subjects, issues, problems, etc. that confront the Lord's people in our time, it is still amazing how little some people know of what is going on. Others, with no more capacity to comprehend than their brethren, have no trouble in seeing and understanding—yet, some still do not yet understand. Why is this so? Bear with me as I mention a possible explanation or so for their failure to understand. Some people . . .

Understand But They Are Hesitant To Admit It. Actually with this class, they understand too much. They know that it is far more convenient for them to say, "We do not understand." This attitude doesn't exempt anyone from his responsibility in following the truth, but at times it does encourage sympathy from others that some brethren long to have. The problem with such people in this class is not that of understanding but conviction to stand for what is right.

Do Not Desire To Understand. Jesus said of some, "For this people's heart is waxed gross, and their ears are dull of hearing, and their eyes they have closed; lest at any time they should see with their eyes, and hear with their ears, and should understand with their heart, and should be converted, and I should heal them" (Matt. 13:15). These words that Jesus uttered were first spoken in prophecy by Isaiah (6:9-10), and they are found in more than one place in the New Testament as they describe the action of individuals in hearing and not understanding the truth of God's word. It is not uncommon to witness individuals who have closed their eyes and ears to certain truth today. They do not want to be bothered. Their minds are fixed and set like concrete and that's all there is to the matter as far as their hearts are concerned. To understand would be to find themselves condemned, and that they will not tolerate.

Will Not Exert the Effort to Understand. To understand the truth on some subjects and issues, one must exert some time and effort. So many are so intellectually lazy that they will not think for themselves that their hearts might be filled with understanding. They had rather someone else do the thinking for them. Hence, they simply follow along with the crowd in the course of least resistance. Solomon wrote, "Buy the truth, and sell it not" (Prov. 23:23). Buying the truth requires understanding and understanding necessitates effort that many people will not expend.

The fact that his disciples did not yet understand did not deter Christ in continuing to teach them. We may at times be amazed at the lack of understanding that some have. Perhaps, we have been guilty of taking too much for granted! Teaching is the hope of understanding and we should never be weary in teaching what the Lord says about every subject. Take every opportunity to teach the truth, perhaps, they will yet understand!

Do You Really Love God?

"But I know you, that ye have not the love of God in you" (John 5:42). These words were spoken by Christ in evaluation of some of his Jewish contemporaries. This was a very grave and tragic condition! The first and great commandment is that of loving God with "all the heart, and with all thy soul, and with all thy mind. This is the first and great commandment" (Matt. 22:37-38). The Spirit of God moved Paul to write "without love . . . we are nothing" (1 Cor. 13:1-3). Yet, Jesus said of some professing to be followers of God that they had not the love of God in them. If it happened then, it could well be the case with us today. We could present ourselves as following God and find ourselves void of the love of God in our hearts.

Jesus knew what was in man (John 2:25). He was able to determine what was in the hearts of men. He was capable of saying with surety that these had not the love of God in them. We may find ourselves asking, "Do we really love God?" and then wondering how we might really determine our love for God. If nothing more, we at times need to prove ourselves regarding our love for God.

How May We Measure Our Love For God?

Our general attitude toward God. Those who love him accept his attributes and truly reverence his name. "He sent redemption unto his people: he hath commanded his covenant for ever: holy and reverend is his name" (Ps. 111:9). Do you feel a great dependence upon him? This is part of our love for him. "For in him we live, and move, and have our being" (Acts 17:28).

Our attitude toward sin. Sin is transgression of God's law (1 John 3:4). We cannot love sin and God at the same time. The one is the antithesis of the other. Christians are called upon to "abhor that which is evil; cleave to that which is good" (Rom. 12:9). Do we abhor sin and genuinely repent when we sin? Can we say the love of God is in us when we fail to do so? Be honest!

Our attitude toward this present world. "Love not the world, neither the things that are in the world. If any man love the world, the love of the Father is not in him. For all that is in the world, the lust of the flesh, and the lust of the eyes, and the pride of life, is not of the Father, but is of the world. And the world passeth away, and the lust thereof: but he that doeth the will of God abideth for ever" (1 John 2:15-17). Demas loved this present world. Paul said, "For Demas hath forsaken me" (2 Tim. 4:10). If we love the world that John defines as the lust of the flesh, the lust of the eyes, and the pride of life, the love of God is not in us!

Our love for the Son of God. One who rejects Christ does not love God. Herein was the great failure and inconsistency of the Jews who felt that they loved God. In their rejection of him, Christ could say that they had not the love of God in them. Paul wrote: "If any man love not the Lord Jesus Christ, let him be Anathema Maranatha" (1 Cor. 16:22). Let him be accursed at the coming of the Lord is how the words *Anathema maranatha* are rendered in other versions. Our love for Christ is determined by keeping his commandments. "If ye love me, keep my commandments" (John 14:15). Again, "For this is the love of God, that we keep his commandments: and his commandments are not grievous" (1 John 5:3). It is foolish for one who does not love Christ to speak of loving God, and it is also foolish to speak of loving Christ without obeying his commandments. And remember, Christ said commandments—not just one or so which might be obeyed without sacrifice or might come with little effort! Do you really love God?

Love for the word of God—the truth. Do we seek guidance from it? "O Lord, I know that the way of man is not in himself: it is not in man that walketh to direct his steps" (Jer. 10:23). Do we subordinate our opinions to God's word? His thoughts and ways are as high above ours as are the heavens above the earth (Isa. 55:8-9). We should cherish his word as a delayed letter from an old friend. When we defy or reject God's word, we are evidencing a lack of love for God.

Love for God's people. Listen to John truly lay it on the line: "If a man say, I love God, and hateth his brother, he is a liar: for he that loveth not his brother whom he hath seen, how can he love God whom he hath not seen?" (1 John 4:20). This love is to be characterized by "deed and in truth" (1 John 3:18). It is to be free of hypocrisy or dissimulation (Rom. 12:9-10). It is to be with earnest care (1 Thess. 4:9-10).

Knowing our hearts, would Jesus say of us that we have not the love of God in us? We need to examine ourselves!

Does Every Man Do It?

Jesus said, "Ye have heard that it was said by them of old, Thou shalt not commit adultery: but I say unto you, That whosoever looketh on a woman to lust after her hath committed adultery with her already in his heart" (Matt. 5:27-28). This passage became more conspicuous due to a statement made by one of the presidential candidates several years ago. In this publicized interview, he was quoted as saying, "I've looked on a lot of women with lust. I've committed adultery in my heart many times." In defense of his confession and the sins that have been committed by others in high positions, there are those who are quick to say, "Why, every man does this. He is no different than any other man." I beg to differ with such a statement offered in the justifying of their deeds. I challenge a person making the statement that every man does it. The political overtones do not bother me. I have no axe to grind there. The thing that always bothers me is when I hear individuals misuse and misapply God's word. I believe it is an obvious misunderstanding of Matthew 5:28 when anyone makes a blanket charge that every man commits adultery through lust.

What does the passage mean? What is it to look upon a woman to lust after her in the heart? Brother Gene Frost has some good observations on this passage and some timely comments of reputable Bible scholars. We submit the following:

> First, it needs to be noted that the "looketh on" is literally a "seeing with a view to," i.e. it is "not . . . the casual evil thought which is checked by holy watchfulness, but the gazing with a view to feed that desire. . ." (Henry Alford, *The Greek Testament*, I:42). God created the woman to be attractive to man, and it is not the attraction that is sinful. Sin results when the attraction becomes a viewing with an intent to inflaming the passions and contemplating adultery. "The intent is strongly marked in the Greek. It is not the passing glance, not even the momentary impulse of desire, but the continued gaze by which the impulse is deliberately cherished until it becomes a

passion" (Charles John Ellicott, *Ellicott's Bible Commentary*, 693). Thus "the look is supposed to be not casual but persistent, the desire not involuntary or momentary, but cherished with longing" (Alexander B. Bruce, *The Expositor's Greek Testament*).

Second, the "lust" or "desire" is an intent. The man who can do this —viz. "gaze with a view to feed unlawful desire" has already in his heart passed the barrier of criminal intent; made up his mind, stifled his conscience; in thought, committed the deed (Henry Alford, *op. cit.*, I:42). Such a man has already in his mind committed the overt act. Where "the lust is dwelt upon and approved, and the wanton desire is rolled under the tongue as a sweet morsel, it is the commission of the sin, as far as the heart can do it; there wants nothing but a convenient opportunity for the sin itself" (Matthew Henry, *Commentary*, V:61). "Whosoever cherishes unchaste desire and intentions, or, as it is expressed in the tenth precept, whosoever covets his neighbor's wife, is really guilty of adultery, though he never should find an opportunity of committing the act with her" (James MacKnight, *Harmony of the Gospels*, I:435).

Jesus thus teaches that not only is the overt act of adultery sinful, but the intent of the man who would commit it. The man who would if he could is guilty before God as though he did. And so Jesus very forcefully emphasizes the necessity of our keeping our minds pure. Evil thoughts must be put away, the mind being controlled as to what it will dwell upon. As someone has said, "We cannot prevent birds of evil from flying into the mind, but we can keep then from roosting there!"

Lust, or desire, in itself is not evil. God created man with physical appetites. And, with every desire, God has ordained legitimate means of satisfaction. For example, man experiences hunger, and this is good, else man could starve himself without realizing it. God has supplied nutritious foods to satisfy that hunger. However, it is an abuse of the appetite to engage in gluttony or to ingest harmful substances. Even so, the sexual appetite is good, but it is to be satisfied in God's lawful way. "Nevertheless, to avoid fornication, let every man have his own wife, and let every woman have her own husband" (1 Cor. 7:2). God has ordained marriage as the answer to satisfying the sexual appetites, but fornication and adultery are sinful.

To charge all men with being guilty of adultery by reason of lusting is unfounded. It assumes that every man has intended to commit adultery; those who have not have only lacked the opportunity. And that is not so! We cannot accept as fact the proposition that all husbands either have already, or will plan to be unfaithful. This is to say that no man can be godly, and that all Christians are hypocrites. Are you ready to accept such reasoning?

We should all be careful as to how we use any passage of Scripture. A perversion of Scripture is a poor defense for any man, whether he is the president of the United States or the poorest of street people. Be careful.

Does Everyone Have A Right To His Own Belief?

In 2 Thessalonians 2:10-12, the apostle speaks of some who perish, the reason being that they received not the love of the truth that they might be saved. Due to their lack of love for the truth, a strong delusion or working of error governs their life that they might believe a lie and be damned. All people believe something! Even to disbelieve is to believe that something is false or not worthwhile. Furthermore, it might be said that there are two classes of believers. There are those who believe the truth and there are believers of that which is false. This passage strongly emphasizes that people can believe the truth and be saved and with equal emphasis that individuals can believe a lie and be damned.

Does everyone have a right to his own belief? What does this question involve? Consider the terminology: The word "right" is one granted the privilege of determining what he will believe? And will what he believes be acceptable in the sight of God? Their own belief refers to whether or not individuals are expected to believe the same way religiously or can one differ from another in matters of faith and be right with God.

The question is truly a very important one. It deals with the salvation of the soul and any subject dealing with the salvation of one's soul is highly important. A person's life is affected by what he believes. As long as one feels he has a right to his own belief, he'll be satisfied to the degree that a search for truth will not be made. Furthermore, the subject certainly affects the principle of unity. How can there ever be oneness when men believe that in the sight of God everyone has a right to his own belief?

Does everyone have a right to his own belief? What shall the answer be?

Legally, Yes. Our constitution grants religious freedom to its citizens. We may worship what, when, and how we please, so long as it does not violate existing civil laws. Constitutionally, one may worship the one true God, a stone idol, a man, or even a bird or beast. He may offer a bloody animal sacrifice, burn incense, or dance as a religious rite. He may trust in Christ, Mohammed, or Buddha as his savior, or he may legally be an infidel or atheist. Constitutional freedom is a wonderful privilege! We should be thankful for the phrase, *E Pluribus Unum* and be grateful that the colonies could melt and weld their political beliefs together and frame our constitution. However, constitutional freedom does not guarantee acceptance with God. What is God's answer to the question?

Scripturally, No. Our religious belief is to be controlled by truth and truth does not offer man a preference. This is true in the fields of mathematics and chemistry. Why should it be an element of amazement for some to think of it being equally true in religion? Jesus said his Father's word was truth (John 17:17). Some people seem never to grasp the thought that there is truth in religion as in other fields of endeavor. If solutions to a mathematical problem differ, can they all be right? Certainly not! Again, if all "beliefs" in religion are true how could one believe a lie as stated in 2 Thessalonians 2:10-12? There actually could be no lie! For a lie to exist, there must be truth. Futhermore, why should the Scriptures speak of religious truth, if one has a right to his own belief? There could be no abiding value in truth (1 Pet. 1:22; 2 Tim. 4:4).

When individuals contend that everyone has a right to his own belief in the sight of God, I find myself thinking upon some rather familiar accounts in the Old Testament—thinking on these things that were written aforetime for our learning (Rom. 15:4). If everyone has a right to his own belief and is acceptable to God in this belief, Why then . . .

- Was Cain's offering rejected and Abel's accepted (Gen. 4:3-5; Heb. 11:4)?
- Wasn't Naaman right in what he believed should occur in reference to his being cured of leprosy (2 Kings 5:10-12)?
- Should God have sent fire from heaven to devour Nadab and Abihu (Lev. 10:1-3)?

On and on it goes! These people, and many more who could be mentioned, held their own beliefs and were wrong. Are we more privileged than they (Heb. 2:1-3)? If anything, our obligations to the truth in this age warrants even more respect (Heb. 10:26-29). Christ has the right to command our belief and to refuse him this prerogative is to minimize his authority. Politically, man has a right to his own belief. Scripturally, before God, man has only the right to believe that which is based on the revelation of God (Gal. 1:6-9; Eph. 4:4-6). Let's labor to know, believe, and obey the truth.

Does the End Justify the Means?

What do we mean by this question? By "end" that which is accomplished or the results of any project. By "means" that which is being performed, the acts used to reach the end. By "justify" make right, or sanction, condone. The question may be paraphrased: "Does the result or conclusion of any project (being good) make the means or acts performed right that were used to gain the results?"

There are different views regarding the subject. We need to have a better understanding of it. People who ordinarily would not say that this principle is just are known to say "Amen" to it in religious or benevolent matters. At times we may unconsciously condone this very principle that we condemn in others. So often we hear people say, "Oh, why object to what is being done, look at the results (or the end) of their work."

Our attitude toward the subject has a great effect upon our obedience to God's word. One who feels that the end justifies the means will reason that the end of all endeavors is to please God; hence, he will not be zealous in obeying since he believes that as long as he has the right end in sight, then the other doesn't make much difference. On the other hand, a person who believes the means must be correct to have the right end will be fervent in obeying the word to bring about the right results of pleasing God.

This is one of the principles which cause divisions among people professing to follow God. The denominational world advocates such a principle. "We are all worshiping God, you one way and others another; we all have the same end in mind, so why quibble over the acts employed." This sounds like Saul of old when the best of the flocks and herds were spared rather than kill them in obeying the command of God. Evidently, Saul felt that the end justified the means. He was told by Samuel, "Behold, to obey is better than sacrifice, and to hearken than the fat of rams" (1 Sam. 15:22). People true to the Lord have always contended that the means must be divine as well as the end in view. God must be worshiped, but in spirit and in truth. Let's notice a few practices that have come about on the basis of some believing that the end justifies the means.

Gambling or Lottery for Church or School Revenues. Many people argue that gambling is permissible if the revenue goes to a school or church. They are leaning on the old crutch, the end justifies the means. However, if an activity is illegal, it is just as illegal for a church or school to do it as for a gambling syndicate. Many people who would never play at a roulette wheel think nothing about buying a chance on a car, etc. to help a school. Laws to outlaw gambling have failed to pass because of its sanction in some states by certain religious groups. They profit from gambling. Bingo in some churches is quite popular! The end justifying the means doubtlessly is one of their customer attractions and they profit by deceiving people in believing such is right.

Advocates of the Missionary Society View the Movement in Light of the End Justifying the Means. They have contended: "Spread the gospel, the means is not the important thing." Isn't it important to glorify God? ". . .to the intent that now unto the principalities and powers in heavenly places might be known by the church the manifold wisdom of God" (Eph. 3:10), "unto him be glory in the church by Christ Jesus throughout all ages, world without end. Amen" (Eph. 3:21). The Lord's church never worked through the machinery of any society in the New Testament days and the Lord's church doesn't do it in the twenty-first century. The church was sufficient then; the church is sufficient now!

Advocates of Mechanical Instruments of Music in Worship Have Defended Their Positions By This Principle. They contend that music glorifies God; the end justifies the means. But who are we to determine what glorifies God? Such is one of the purposes of the Scriptures! The word of God would have us to sing and make melody in our hearts (Eph. 5:19; Col. 3:16). This is what glorifies God and we are to abide in the doctrine of Christ that authorizes singing (2 John 9-11).

Reliance Upon This View Has Closed the Minds of Some Brethren To Various Issues in the Brotherhood. Poor little orphans—see that they are cared for—who cares about the means. So prejudiced are some to this principle that they will not reason as to what the Bible says regarding what is the work of the church. On and on go the results of this principle! Keep the young people in the church even if it takes youth movements—give them what they want—the end justifies the means. Brethren, we need to obey God in his appointed way and the end will take care of itself.

Does The Lord Ask Too Much?

Jeroboam taught his subjects in the Northern Kingdom that he did.

And Jeroboam said in his heart, Now shall the kingdom return to the house of David. If this people go up to do sacrifice in the house of the Lord at Jerusalem, then shall the heart of this people turn again unto their lord, even unto Rehoboam king of Judah, and they shall kill me, and go again to Rehoboam king of Judah. Whereupon the king took counsel, and made two calves of gold, and said unto them, It is too much for you to go up to Jerusalem: behold thy gods, O Israel, which brought thee up out of the land of Egypt (1 Kings 12:26-28).

The kingdom had been divided and Jeroboam was king over ten tribes. God had assured him that as long as he kept his commandments that things would be well with him. Jeroboam did not have the faith to accept God's assurance. Though the kingdom was divided, the people were still commanded to go to Jerusalem for worship. Jerusalem was where Rehoboam, the son of Solomon, reigned over Judah. Jeroboam felt, if the people went to Jerusalem, that their hearts would be turned from him and they would become subjects of Rehoboam in the kingdom of Judah. How would he keep them from going to Jerusalem for worship? His approach was this: "It is too much for you to go to Jerusalem." He placed in their minds the thought that the Lord was asking too much of them.

Evidently this thought was one of the primary considerations that led the people to follow the false worship that Jeroboam inaugurated. It may have not been the only factor, but it certainly had a part in persuading the people to accept Jeroboam's human-originated religion. We have a craving for convenience! We desire that which is the easier! Jeroboam hit a tender concept and the people chose to follow his direction. There was not a great distance for most of the people to travel to reach Jerusalem. They had been going there through the years to the place where God had recorded his name. Perhaps, they had not really considered it being "too much" until Jeroboam instilled the thought into their minds. But instill, he did!

When the truth is taught to people today, there are some who come to realize what truth is, but they reject it on the basis that they feel the Lord is asking too much. The spirit of Jeroboam prevails in their hearts rather than the spirit of obedience to the Lord. John wrote, "For this is the love of God, that we keep his commandments: and his commandments are not grievous" (1 John 5:3). Grievous is from the Greek word *barus* which Vine's says, "denotes heavy, burdensome (causing a burden on him who fulfils them)." What God gives for us to obey involves "much," but never "too much" for our abilities to perform. Jesus said, "For my yoke is easy, and my burden is light" (Matt. 11:30).

Some Feel It Is Asking Too Much to Obey the Gospel of Christ. Having heard the gospel, this involves believing in Christ, repenting of sins, confessing the name of Christ, and being baptized for the remission of sins (Mark 16:16; Acts 2:38; 8:35-39). Many in the book of Acts responded to obeying the gospel, and they didn't consider doing so was asking too much of them. Though effort and sacrifice may be involved, these are minor as compared to the blessings that are offered in Christ (Eph. 1:3). Satan has his ministers preaching "just believe" and to obey the gospel is asking too much. Today, the spirit of Jeroboam is very much alive!

Some Feel It Is Asking Too Much to Faithfully Worship God. They do what they desire in worship and do this when they desire to do it. What pleases them is their criteria of worship! This is so contrary to what Jesus said about worship. He said, "But the hour cometh, and now is, when the true worshippers shall worship the Father in spirit and in truth: for the father seeketh such to worship him. God is a Spirit: and they that worship him must worship him in spirit and in truth" (John 4:23-24). The "spirit" involves the heart of the worshipers; while the "truth" is the word of God which authorizes the acts of worship (Acts 2:42; 20:7; Eph. 5:19). How is worship in spirit and truth asking too much? Once again, the spirit of Jeroboam continues to work in the minds of men!

Some Feel It Is Asking Too Much To Live Godly Lives. They are aware of what is expected of them (Tit. 2:10-11). They know what the Scriptures teach regarding being faithful. However, their love for this present world motivates them to cry that God is asking too much. We generally do what we want to do. Yes, there are some exceptions, but in most cases we find the energy and ability to perform what we want to do. We can be faithful and every command that God gives is for our good here and for eternal welfare. Keep on listening to the spirit of Jeroboam, which cries too much and find out how futile and horrible it will be in the Judgment Day!

Encouragement—Something All Of Us Can Use

Life is so complicated and perplexing at times that we all face certain difficulties in living as Christ like as we should. So many know what is right and have experienced doing what is right, yet at times, they feel a definite drag in executing the performance of righteousness. We all need encouragement! Frequently, individuals talk about how the young people need encouragement. This should be of grave concern to parents and older Christians. It would appear that we at times are prone to forget that we were once young and sorely needed encouragement to get our feet on the ground in doing the things that are approved of God. But the young people are not the only ones who need encouragement. There are middle-aged folks and old folks who sorely need encouragement in living like Christ. So many seem to think that the field of encouragement is limited to the young people. All ages need encouragement as much or more than they do.

There is a tendency of man to be selfish in all fields. The field of encouragement is not excluded! The next time you lament the lack of encouragement you have received, stop and think about how much you have given to the brother who is standing next to you. You just might be amazed at how selfish you have become! And there is even such a thing as self-encouragement that comes when we work toward helping someone else. It can make us realize how insignificant a matter our problems are as compared to the other person. Let's not forget the man who complained about not having new shoes until he observed an individual who had both feet missing.

It is understood that at one time or another, we do or will need some encouragement from others. Like most other subjects, there are some guidelines that Christians should consider and be inclined to follow. Let us observe:

Encouragement should be scriptural. What do we mean by such an observation? Simply, that we should not use something unscriptural in an attempt to influence anyone. Some people have the mistaken view that the end justifies the means. This principle is unscriptural! King Saul attempted to justify his disobedience through the appeal to such a principle, but he was told by Samuel "Behold, to obey is better than sacrifice, and to hearken than the fat of rams" (1 Sam. 15:22). In order to keep people interested, there are those who appeal to gimmicks and procedures that are not compatible with truth. It has been suggested by some that they do not approve of the procedures, but they are tolerant of such since it is encouraging others. But we ask, encouraging them to what? If it is encouraging them in anything, it is to be lax toward scriptural practices due to the fact that unscriptural practices encouraged them. If the word of God, properly applied, will not work, then individuals cannot be scripturally encouraged. Paul told the elders of Ephesus, "And now, brethren, I commend you to God, and to the word of his grace, which is able to build you up, and to give you an inheritance among all them which are sanctified" (Acts 20:32). When one is commended to the word of God which is able to build one up, he is not being encouraged in some unscriptural practices of man's foolishness. I'm afraid that some who cry for encouragement are really crying for innovations rather than the purity of God's word with which they have become bored.

Encouragement should not be by condoning sin. Some people seem to have the idea that participation in sinful practices with others will grant one an opportunity to lift them out of sin. The concept is this: Join them to defeat them. There have been those who have even construed Paul's statements in 1 Corinthians 9:19-23 as meaning this. Paul was speaking of practices of custom and expedient situations that did not conflict with matters of faith "that I might by all means save some." The Christian is to live a transformed life that is not conformed to the world. "And be not conformed to this world, but be ye transformed by the renewing of your mind, that ye may prove what is that good, and acceptable, and perfect, will of God" (Rom. 12:2). We do not encourage individuals to forsake sinful practices by engaging in such practices with them. Perhaps again, some people, when they cry lack of encouragement, really mean lack of condoning our sinful practices. That's the encouragement they want—encouragement to do what they want to do without any restraint. Such is never from the word of God. To say "No" to such people is in their eyes a token of discouragement. They desire to do as they please and any negative view toward them is then a breach of encouragement. Such views breed rebellion and rejection of scriptural authority. We are to do all things in the name of the Lord Jesus or by his authority (Col. 3:17).

Finally, we must be aware of the fact that a man must be willing to be encouraged if he is to be encouraged. Try me—I could use it!

Enthusiasm

Enthusiasm is defined as "ardent zeal or interest; fervor." The word itself is not found in the Scriptures but its definition abounds throughout the entire Bible as pertaining to those who are devoted to the Lord. Enthusiasm is a very beautiful thing to behold and it is a principle that the people of God should surely possess. Their cause is great! It warrants enthusiasm! Can one say he is truly dedicated to the Lord and not be enthusiastic regarding the Lord's cause?

Concerning Enthusiasm, We Note the Following

Enthusiasm is Contagious. When individuals are enthusiastic, others observe the enthusiasm. It catches on and invariably effects the actions of others. We like to be around people who are enthusiastic. It makes one feel that he truly believes what he professes that he believes. Speaking of Christ, Paul wrote, "Who gave himself for us, that he might redeem us from all iniquity, and purify unto himself a peculiar people, zealous of good works" (Tit. 2:14). As we are enthusiastic for the truth, we have the possibility of causing others to be the same. Remember, an indifferent spirit cannot lead to a spirit of enthusiasm.

Proper Enthusiasm Must Be Grounded In Faith. To be enthusiastic religiously is not enough. We must have enthusiasm that is motivated by and from the word of God. Fanatics abound in the world of religion. Who will deny that they are enthusiastic? But what profit is such if they are not following the truth? Paul wrote of his own countrymen, "Brethren, my heart's desire and prayer to God for Israel is, that they might be saved. For I bear them record that they have a zeal of God, but not according to knowledge. For they being ignorant of God's righteousness, and going about to establish their own righteousness, have not submitted themselves unto the righteousness of God" (Rom. 10:1-3). They had a zeal of God, but such was not according to knowledge. It was not grounded in the faith of God's word. Had it been grounded in God's word, they would have been Christians and contending for the truth that is in Christ rather than contending for the law of Moses. Their enthusiasm was to no avail! What about your life? Do you have enthusiasm that is grounded in faith? Are you doing those things that are authorized by the Lord? Those of Matthew 7:21-23 were no doubt enthusiastic but such was vain in that they failed to do the will of God.

Enthusiasm Must Be Fed. For most anything to continue and prosper, there is vital need that it be nourished. Enthusiasm is by no means an exception! Individuals can at one time be enthusiastic and then find that they have lost it. The less honest and sincere may blame any number of circumstances for their failure, but the most frequent reason is that they have failed in feeding their enthusiasm. We must not lose sight of the value of study of God's word and spiritual exercise. As one's faith develops, his enthusiasm develops. On the other hand, as one's faith weakens, so goes his enthusiasm for spiritual things. You admit your lack of zeal? How much effort do you exert in feeding your enthusiasm? "As newborn babes, desire the sincere milk of the word, that ye may grow thereby" (1 Pet. 2:2). "But grow in grace, and in the knowledge of our Lord and Saviour Jesus Christ. To him be glory both now and for ever. Amen" (2 Pet. 3:18).

Enthusiasm Must Be Sustained. The religion of Jesus Christ is a day by day need. Constant vigilance must be sustained against our adversary (1 Pet. 5:8). As some people drive an automobile in "spurts," we might conclude that there are those who handle religion in the same manner. Rather than sustain a good enthusiastic speed, the tempo is erratic. Our faith should not be viewed as a novelty. It needs ever to be a wholesome part of us. We have known young converts to be very enthusiastic as they obeyed the gospel and then later see that enthusiasm fail. If their conception of the truth was proper and adequately balanced, shouldn't they have grown and developed rather than to have failed? As was stated earlier, perhaps their enthusiasm was not grounded in faith as it needed to be from the beginning. And then there are those who let Satan come into their lives and rob them of their faith and enthusiasm.

A life in which enthusiasm for the truth is sustained is a thing of beauty to behold. On the other hand, it is a pathetic thing to view a life that demonstrates no enthusiasm or has lost enthusiasm that once was a part of that life. The church at Laodicea was inspected by the Lord and found to be lukewarm. True zeal was not a part of their activities. Jesus called upon this church, "As many as I love, I rebuke and chasten: be zealous therefore, and repent" (Rev. 3:19). Whether we be few or many, enthusiasm for the truth should characterize the true followers of Jesus Christ. How about your enthusiasm?

Except A Man Be Born Again

To many people, the subject of the new birth is a deep mystery. To them it is a theme that can neither be explained nor understood. As a religionist, they talk much about being born again and advocate the necessity of the new birth, but their conclusion is that the subject is beyond man's comprehension or something better felt than told. In John 3:3, Jesus said, "Except a man be born again, he cannot see the kingdom of God" and in verse 5, "Except a man be born of water and of the Spirit, he cannot enter into the kingdom of God." No one is a citizen of the kingdom of God without being born again. If it is not understandable how men are born again, then it must follow that men are in the kingdom without knowing how they enter or became citizens. This is absurd and involves sheer nonsense! The word of God reveals in understandable fashion the truth that we know regarding the new birth.

This man, Nicodemus, was a descendant of Abraham and doubtlessly considered that earthly ancestry would give him citizenship in the kingdom of God. He recognized and confessed that Jesus was a teacher come from God, but Jesus told him, "Except a man be born again, he cannot see the kingdom of God." More than recognition and confession is required of a man in being born again. The thing that seemed to puzzle this ruler of the Jews was how he could be born when he was old. "Can he enter the second time into his mother's womb, and be born?" As he viewed birth, he could only comprehend the physical birth. The expression "being born again" is a figurative expression. When one becomes a new creature spiritually, this process is called a birth. In other places in the Bible, the change is called conversion, creation, or forgiveness of sins. To be saved, or to become a Christian, is what Jesus meant by being born again!

The kingdom that the new birth places one into is the kingdom concerning which Daniel prophesied (Dan. 2:44), the kingdom that John saw as being at hand (Matt. 3:2), the kingdom of which the brethren at Colosse were citizens (Col. 1:13), and the Hebrew writer said that they had received (Heb. 12:28). The Christians at Colosse were in the kingdom (Col. 1:13) and they were also a part of the body, the church (Col. 1:18). This kingdom of God, the church of Christ, had its beginning on Pentecost day in Acts 2. Peter spoke of people being born again by the incorruptible seed, the word of God (1 Pet. 1:22-23). If they were born again, they were in the kingdom of God. If the kingdom of God doesn't exist, then no new birth exists. The two are not to be separated.

The two factors of the new birth are water and Spirit. There are not two births mentioned, but one, which involves the two factors "of water and of the Spirit." Some people say, "I do not know what it means, but I know it does not mean water." On occasions John 7:38 is suggested to show that this is not literal water. John 7:38 reads: "He that believeth on me, as the scripture hath said, out of his belly shall flow rivers of living water." Certainly this refers to figurative language! Surely no one is so naïve as to think literal rivers of water are to flow out of his belly. However, in John 3:5, there is no reason to conclude that the water is figurative. If water doesn't mean water in this verse, what does it mean? Some people want to make the water refer to the physical birth. In natural birth the element is known as "amniotic fluid," not water! Furthermore, Nicodemus was aware of the circumstances of a physical birth. Others have said, "water seems to mean word." If it means word, why doesn't the passage read word?

Why such an effort to change water from being water? You guessed it! Myriads of religious people do not want baptism to be essential. Though some are quite inconsistent in their reasoning, yet nearly all scholars understand that the word "water" refers to baptism. Albert Barnes, a noted Presbyterian, labors to prove that water in John 3:5 is referring to baptism and then before his comments are concluded, states that baptism is not essential. Baptism is the only religious act in the New Testament in which water is used (Acts 8:36-38). Furthermore, it establishes baptism to be immersion. A thing cannot be born of that which is smaller than itself (Col.1:18).

"Born of the Spirit" refers to the inward, or spiritual, change that takes place by the Holy Spirit. The Spirit operates upon the human heart through the agency of the word (Jas. 1:18). One is born again by following the Spirit's instructions. Hence, one "born of water and of the Spirit" is an individual who believes in Christ, repents of his sins, and upon a confession of faith in Christ is baptized in water for the remission of his sins. The new birth is explained by numerous passages in the New Testament. Notice Acts 2:36-41; 1 Peter 1:22-23; Acts 18:8; 1 Corinthians 4:15. These passages emphasize that the believer is baptized that he might be born again.

Excuse Making

This is what the Scriptures reveal: "They all with one consent began to make excuse" (Luke 14:18). Three men are set forth as excuse makers. "The first said unto him, I have bought a piece of ground, and I must needs go and see it: I pray thee have me excused. And another said, I have bought five yoke of oxen, and I go to prove them: I pray thee have me excused. And another said, I have married a wife, and therefore I cannot come" (Luke 14:18-20). Mind you, they were not invited to a dull, dry, or stupid lecture, but they were invited to a feast.

These three men are not said to have had excuses, but they all with one consent began to "make" excuse. Their action suggests that they manufactured one for the occasion. The piece of ground, five yoke of oxen, and the man's bride would doubtlessly still be there after the feast had been attended. These things were simply used as a "scapegoat" for the men not doing what they didn't want to do! Excuses are as old as men. Actually they are nothing more than dressed up and camouflaged lies! Adam started the race off in the excuse making business when he tried to justify himself in his fall. "The woman thou gavest me," he said (Gen. 3:12). He laid the blame first on her and then on God! God had given Adam the woman. Adam would charge the blame to God. The majority of the excuses that men offer ultimately make God the offending party and the reason for man's failure to do right.

We hear people at times say, "I just can't understand the Bible." To say that you, as a normally intelligent person, can't understand the Bible is to say that God gave you an impractical and unreasonable book. By making such a statement, God is made the offending party. He gave us the Bible and told man to read it with understanding (John 8:32; Eph. 5:17). It is just another excuse that sinful man has come up with to deter him from bearing his responsibility in doing what the Bible has for him to do. Again, individuals say, "We can't all see the Bible alike." This is another excuse that places the blame on God. Is it reasonable to conclude that God created man, gave him the Bible, told him to read it, and then commanded that we be one when he knew this was impossible? It is an insult to God to say that we can't all see the Bible alike. The Corinthians were admonished to "speak the same thing, and that there be no divisions among you; but that ye be perfectly joined together in the same mind and in the same judgment" (1 Cor. 1:10). Men may never see the Bible alike, but it is certainly no fault of God. Remember this: When a man stands before God, he will not be making excuses. He will be receiving the due reward for his deeds of excuse making, of dodging and lying about why he never obeyed the gospel of Christ, and why he never lived in service to God.

Some years ago, I received a clipping from a newspaper which was entitled, "No Excuses." The writer had lifted an article from a church bulletin entitled, "No Excuse Sunday" (source unknown). The purpose of the article was to show how this church could eliminate all the excuses that so many of the members made for not being faithful in attending the services. It read like this:

> To make it possible for everyone to attend church on Sunday we are going to have a "no excuse Sunday" every Lord's Day. Cots will be placed in the foyer for those who say Sunday is my only day to sleep in. Murine will be available for those with tired eyes from watching television late on Saturday night. We will have hard hats

for those who say the roof will cave in if I ever came to church. Blankets will be furnished for those who think the building is too cold and fans for those who think it is too hot.

We will have hearing aids for those who think the preacher speaks too softly and cotton for those who say he preaches too loudly. Score cards will be available for those who wish to list the hypocrites present. There will be TV dinners for those who cannot go to church and cook dinner also.

A deacon will be available to escort those to the lake and through the woods who wish to seek God in nature. Finally the auditorium will be decorated with Christmas poinsettias and Easter lilies for those who have never seen the auditorium without them. Can we count on you? Since you are without an excuse, we will look for you and yours this Lord's Day?

The above constitutes a satire on excuses from a denominational church's viewpoint. You might say such is very ridiculous (and you would be right), but have you considered how truly ridiculous our excuses are for not doing what God would have us do?

Faith That One Has

Faith in the Lord Jesus Christ is a very personal matter. Every individual must believe for himself. No one can believe for another. The Bible definitely instructs its readers as to how faith is derived. "So then faith cometh by hearing, and hearing by the word of God" (Rom. 10:17). "And many other signs truly did Jesus in the presence of his disciples, which are not written in this book: but these are written, that ye might believe that Jesus is the Christ, the Son of God; and that believing ye might have life through his name" (John 20:30-31). Just as surely as the Bible reveals how faith comes; it also reveals things that may happen to an individual's faith. The faith that one has may be . . .

Increased. This is what every child of God should desire to do with his faith. It should be encouraging to all who believe to know that their faith can be increased. After hearing their master relate that they should forgive one seven times in a day if he repents and desires forgiveness, The apostles said unto the Lord, "Increase our faith" (Luke 17:5). Faith may be increased as it is derived by studying the word of God! Paul wrote to the Corinthians, ". . . but having hope, when your faith is increased, that we shall be enlarged by you according to our rule abundantly" (2 Cor. 10:15). He knew that their faith could be increased or augmented. He was thankful to God for the brethren at Thessalonica "because that your faith groweth excceedingly" (2 Thess. 1:3). We need to work at constantly increasing our faith. Are we doing this?

Perfected With Works. James denotes thirteen verses in the second chapter of James to teach that faith without works is dead. "Yea, a man may say, Thou hast faith, and I have works: show me thy faith without thy works, and I will show thee my faith by my works" (Jas. 2:18). We need to perfect faith by doing the works that God has ascribed for us to do. "Thou believest that there is one God; thou doest well: the devils also believe, and tremble" (v. 19). To profess to have faith and be void of works is to be no better than the devils, for "the devils also believe, and tremble." Paul wrote to the Galatians: "For in Jesus Christ neither circumcision availeth anything, nor uncircumcision; but faith which worketh by love" (Gal. 5:6). We must do more than believe. We must have a faith that works and one that works by love. Are you perfecting your faith with works by love?

Added To. Christians are to grow. To grow and to keep from being failures, there are principles that they are to add to their faith. Peter speaks of these in 2 Peter 1:5-7: "And besides this, giving all diligence, add to your faith virtue; and to virtue, knowledge, and to knowledge, temperance; and to temperance, patience; and to patience, godliness; and to godliness, brotherly kindness; and to brotherly kindness, charity." These graces or principles are to be added to our faith. We should constantly labor in developing these in our character and adding such to our faith. "For if these things be in you, and abound, they make you that ye shall neither be barren nor unfruitful in the knowledge of our Lord Jesus Christ.

But he that lacketh these things is blind, and cannot see afar off and hath forgotten that he was purged from his old sins" (vv. 8-9). Blind Christians are the ones who have not added these to their faith. How well do you see?

Made Shipwreck. Thus far we have spoken of those things that may happen to our faith from a beneficial standpoint. But there is another side of the matter. Just as surely, the Bible teaches that we can lose faith or make shipwreck of it. Concerning Hymenaeus and Alexander, Paul wrote, "Holding faith, and a good conscience; which some having put away, concerning faith have made shipwreck" (1 Tim. 1:19-20). As we picture a derelict ship fastened on a coral reef, we can visualize what happened to the faith of Hymenaeus and Alexander and what can also happen to our faith. We need to keep working and studying lest we run aground in this "sinful and perverse generation." Paul knew this could happen to his faith. He wrote, "But I keep under my body and bring it into subjection: lest that by any means, when I have preached to others, I myself should be a castaway" (1 Cor. 9:27). Don't let it happen to you! There is perhaps nothing more pathetic and more tragic than a shipwrecked faith.

Kept Unto Death. This is what every individual should desire to do and must do in order to have heaven at the end of the way. Paul wrote, "I have fought a good fight, I have finished my course, I have kept the faith: henceforth there is laid up for me a crown of righteousness, which the Lord the righteous judge, shall give me at that day: and not to me only, but unto all them also that love his appearing" (2 Tim. 4:7-8). It is a beautiful thought when one thinks of souls keeping a strong faith unto death. We should all labor to do so! What else is more important? "Be thou faithful unto death, and I will give thee a crown of life" (Rev. 2:10).

Father, Forgive Them, For They Know Not What They Do

The human race is accustomed to striking contrasts. The pauper and millionaire pass each other on the street. The bridal veil and the shroud touch each other. The life of Christ presents some striking contrasts. Jesus was a child of poverty in Mary's arms, yet he was the object of God's love and the stars were but dust beneath his feet. He was a man of sorrows and acquainted with grief, yet all things were created by him and for him (Heb. 2:10). We see the suffering Savior praying for the cup to be removed, yet a few weeks before God had said: "This is my beloved son, in whom I am well pleased, hear ye Him" (Matt. 17:5). All the contrasts that are presented do not show the Savior in a more glorious point of view than when he prayed on the cross, "Father, forgive them; for they know not what they do."

Wherein lies the contrast? Not in the principle of prayer. It was not unusual for Christ to pray. He began his ministry with prayer (Luke 3:21) and ended it with prayer (Luke 24:50-51). He prayed before selecting the apostles (Luke 6:12). He taught his disciples to pray (Matt. 6:9-16) and the whole of John 17 is the prayer of the Lord in the night that he was betrayed. But the most sublime of all his prayers is the prayer from the cross. The circumstances are such as to make us surrender body, soul, and spirit to his service. He was not an intruder on earth. Christ was sent by a merciful Father to save a lost and ruined, wrecked and recreant race. He had gladly come. He was glad especially to do anything that the tide of sin might be stayed. His earthly pilgrimage (one third of a century) had been a life of purity, love divine. The spirit of partisan prejudice had planned for his destruction in a way that would give him the most intense misery. He had been tried before Pilate. He had been dragged up Golgotha and nailed to the cross. The great surging mob was reviling him and sneering at his claims to be divine. Though there was sympathy from the material universe, there was no sympathy from the angry mob. Breath that might have been spent in pleading for himself or his friends was used by Christ in praying for his murderers. These words were probably the first of his utterances from the cross: "Father, forgive them; for they know not what they do."

Lessons From These Ten Words

A Beautiful Instance of Human Magnanimity. Magnanimity is defined as "a spirit enabling one to disdain meanness and revenge." Conscious of his innocence, unrewarded, unappreciated—what wonder if, under such conditions, all the kindliness of his nature had turned to bitterness? What prompted him to pray this prayer? Why didn't he wreck vengeance on this mob? Was it because the Scriptures must be fulfilled? Such was conceivable in the garden (Matt. 26:53-54) but he is in a dying condition now and it only remained for him to cry aloud and give up the ghost that all be over. We must look to one reason—he was filled with divine love for others.

Man Is Accountable To God Though Acting In Ignorance. "They know not what they do," yet they needed forgiveness. Ignorance of physical laws does not exempt the transgressor from injuries. God holds every accountable being answerable to his spiritual laws (Matt. 15:14; Acts 3:17; 17:30). If ignorance is excusable why did Jesus ask forgiveness for those who through ignorance did what they did? Furthermore, if ignorance is excusable, why bother to teach individuals the truth? Why endeavor to carry the gospel to those who have never heard it? The Scriptures have concluded all under sin (Gal. 3:22). This should refute the idea of sincerity and honesty making the deed of no importance.

A Beautiful Example of His Own Lofty Doctrine. Jesus taught his disciples to pray for those who despitefully use you (Matt. 5:44). Our Lord was consistent in that he practiced what he taught. "The former treatise have I made, O Theophilus, of all that Jesus began both to do and teach" (Acts 1:11). The greatest leaders never bade men to do that which they were not willing to do themselves. Jesus is the greatest of all leaders. He practiced what he taught.

It Is The Father Who Forgives, Who Answers Prayers. Was this prayer answered? Were these people forgiven? Certainly Jesus was one whom the Father would hear! If not, then there is no need for us to pray. But when was it answered? At the cross? The resurrection? His ascension? No, not at these events or times! They were forgiven conditionally as they obeyed the gospel of Christ. They were forgiven in answer to Christ's prayer as they met the conditions of forgiveness in God's will as preached in Acts 2:38-41.

Give Us An Understanding Heart

Solomon, the son of David, had become king of Israel and sat upon the illustrious throne of his father. In 1 Kings 3, the Lord appeared unto Solomon in a dream and said, "Ask what I shall give thee" (v. 5). Solomon realized the great responsibility that lay before him in being king over Israel. It would appear that he felt an immense need in fulfilling the task and recognized a certain unworthiness in adequately serving as king. Thus, he asked of the Lord, "Give therefore thy servant an understanding heart to judge thy people. That I may discern between good and bad: for who is able to judge this thy so great a people?" (v. 9). This pleased the Lord. Solomon had not asked for long life, riches, or the life of his enemies. He was granted his request and was given a wise and understanding heart. Along with this, he was also given riches and honor for which he did not ask.

Solomon realized he needed an understanding heart. This is something that the Lord's people need throughout their lives. Solomon was not the only one who needed an understanding heart. The request for an understanding heart should be included in our prayers to our Father. We need an understanding heart regarding . . .

Ourselves. We all have weaknesses and temptations of which we need to be aware. There is ever the need to evaluate such things and not let them control our lives. We should profit from the mistakes we have made and not practice the same things again. "Examine yourselves, whether ye be in the faith; prove your own selves. Know ye not your own selves, how that Jesus Christ is in you, except ye be reprobates?" (2 Cor. 13:5). The word "reprobates" conveys the thought of one failing the test. We need to examine, prove, and know our own selves in being faithful in Christ and not failing the test. "But let every man prove his own work, and then shall he have rejoicing in himself alone, and not in another" (Gal. 6:4).

Others. So many problems arrive in our lives because we fail to understand other people. We need to develop an understanding heart regarding the weaknesses of others. We may never walk in their shoes, but we can strive to feel as though we do. Families and churches have been torn asunder because individuals failed to have an understanding heart of others. "Let nothing be done through strife or vainglory; but in lowliness of mind let each esteem other better than themselves. Look not every man on his own things, but every man also on the things of others. Let this mind be in you, which was also in Christ Jesus" (Phil. 2:3-5). There are few passages in the Scriptures which are more beautiful than these verses. The emphasis in these verses is focused upon others. Lord, give us an understanding heart in the proper regard and treatment of others! How can one obey Galatians 6:1-2 if there is not an understanding heart of the conditions and problems of others? How can one have the mind of Christ and not strive for an understanding heart regarding others?

The Lord's Will. "Wherefore be ye not unwise, but understanding what the will of the Lord is" (Eph. 5:17). The Lord's will regarding our salvation is revealed in the Scriptures. It can be understood and we have the responsibility of understanding and obeying it. Our hearts need to rejoice in following the Lord's will and be filled with the confidence that God would have us to realize. Yet, there are those who have been taught for years who still evidence the lack of an understanding heart concerning the Lord's will. Their ignorance is greater than their knowledge. This is largely due to a lack of study of God's word and meditation upon it (2 Tim. 2:15). We need to make the proper application of truth to our lives and defend it with an understanding heart.

Discerning Good and Evil. Solomon requested an understanding heart that he might discern good and bad (1 Kings 3:9). This quality was very important to a king who would reign with dignity and honor. As children of God, we certainly confront occasions where such discernment is needed. There are times when the distinction between good and evil is not as obvious as on other occasions. We are taught to "let love be without dissimulation. Abhor that which is evil; cleave to that which good" (Rom. 12:9). The understanding heart is needed that we might distinguish between that which we are to abhor from that which we are to cleave. Paul's prayer for the Philippians involved discernment. "And this I pray, that your love may abound yet more and more in knowledge and in all judgment (discernment, NAS); that ye may approve things that are excellent; that ye may be sincere and without offence till the day of Christ" (Phil. 2:9-10). Yes, Solomon needed the understanding heart and we sorely need it every day that we live!

Giving God Our Best
(Genesis 22:1-19)

Here is something that most of us have never really tried — giving God our best! Abraham is an outstanding example of one who truly gave God his best, the offering of his son. Abraham had experienced trials before, but none was as severe as this! "Take now thy son, thine only son Isaac, whom thou lovest, and get thee into the land of Moriah; offer him there for a burnt offering upon one of the mountains which I will tell thee of" (Gen. 22:2). The long delay of the fulfillment of the promise regarding Isaac was not easy to endure, but these trials were light and insignificant as compared to this one.

God called for Abraham's best. There were many difficulties connected with this command. God had never before demanded a human sacrifice. Abraham had to weigh the possible misunderstanding of his neighbors. What type of a father would offer his own son? Remember also that he was a stranger in this land. The command was opposed to the feeling of humanity—shedding the blood of man's son—every instinct of his nature cried out in protest. Abraham was not called upon to offer Ishmael. Such, no doubt, would have constituted second best. God called upon Abraham to offer his best.

In spite of the cost, Abraham gave God his best. To comply with God's command would possibly cost him his domestic comfort. How would this father explain such to his wife and Isaac's mother, Sarah? From a human observation, it cost him his hopes. With Isaac, the long promised seed gone, how could he become the father of a great nation and through him all nations of the earth be blessed? Yet, Abraham did not hesitate. He made no excuses. He offered no alibis, but arose early and went to God's appointed place and entered upon this trying ordeal. "By faith Abraham, when he was tried, offered up Isaac: and he that had received the promises offered up his only begotten son, of whom it was said, That in Isaac shall thy seed be called: accounting that God was able to raise him up, even from the dead; from whence also he received him in a figure" (Heb. 11:17-19). We should well remember that such deeds of faith were written for our learning. "For whatsoever things were written aforetime were written for our learning, that we through patience and comfort of the scriptures might have hope" (Rom. 15:4).

As Abraham was called upon to give his best, God calls upon his people in this age to give their best. He wants the best of their . . .

Love. "Thou shalt love the Lord thy God with all they heart, and with all thy soul, and with all they mind. This is the first and great commandment" (Matt. 22:37-38). Again, "He that loveth father and mother more than me is not worthy of me: and he that loveth son and daughter more than me is not worthy of me" (Matt. 10:37). If there is any meaning to words, it is very definite from these words that God is saying that he will not take second best. He wants the very best of our love.

Gifts. Under the Old Covenant and particularly in the days of Malachi, weak and sickly animals were offered upon the altar to Jehovah. Such were not acceptable with God. They were robbing God! "Will a man rob God? Yet ye have robbed me. But ye say, Wherein have we robbed thee? In tithes and offering" (Mal. 3:8). Christians are not under the law of tithing as found in the Old Testament. They have this commandment: "Upon the first day of the week let every one of you lay by him in store, as God hath prospered him" (1 Cor. 16:2), "as he purposeth in his heart, so let him give; not grudgingly, or of necessity: for God loveth a cheerful giver" (2 Cor. 9:7). Furthermore, God's people are called upon to "present your bodies a living sacrifice, holy, acceptable unto God" (Rom. 12:1). If you retain the belief that God will accept just anything or second best today, you are definitely operating under a strong delusion.

Labors. "Therefore, my beloved brethren, be ye steadfast, unmovable, always abounding in the work of the Lord, forasmuch as ye know that your labor is not in vain in the Lord" (1 Cor. 15:58). Scraps from the tables of our pleasure seeking activities will not suffice with the Lord. "Seek ye first the kingdom of God and His righteousness" (Matt. 6:33).

Abraham discovered that what one places on God's altar is not lost. Not a hair of Isaac's head was harmed and Abraham received children as numberless as the stars of heaven. Christians need to faithfully realize that what we place on God's altar is not lost. So many of us never receive God's best because we have never given him our best (2 Cor. 9:6).

Have I Become Your Enemy?

The spiritual condition of the churches of Galatia was not very commendable. Paul marveled that they had so soon been removed from the truth (Gal. 1:6-9). He accused them of being bewitched that they should not obey the truth (Gal. 3:1). These Galatians had become desirous of again keeping the ordinances of the Law of Moses. Paul showed the error of such by stating that justification was not by the works of the law (Gal. 2:16), that the law was a schoolmaster to bring us to Christ (Gal. 3:24), and that the law was a yoke of bondage—liberty was in Christ (Gal. 5:1). Their fickle conduct prompted him to say that he was afraid of them. He feared that his labor in teaching them had been in vain and that they would look upon him as their enemy because he told them the truth in these matters (Gal. 4:8-16).

To be considered an enemy is usually because one is set to do another harm. An enemy is one who usually is intent upon doing harm to another. However, there are times when we are mistaken as to just who is our friend or enemy. The drunk might deem one his enemy who takes the bottle from him and refuses to let him drink more. Isn't such a one trying to help rather than injure the drunk? At the time it would be difficult for the drunk to be aware that he was being befriended! We recall the account of a very strong man riding in the wagon and forcing a woman of frail statue to follow along attempting to catch hold of the wagon. The weather was freezing! The scene was cruel! How could a man be so inconsiderate and heartless as to permit a woman to run along behind the wagon while he rode and drove? A viewer doubtlessly would classify the man as the woman's enemy, but that was not the truth. In love for the woman and cognizant of her condition, he was forcing her to exert herself to keep the circulation as it should be in her body lest she freeze to death. He actually was jeopardizing his life for her preservation. Who are our friends? Who are our enemies? Think! Consider the end in view before we jump at improper conclusions.

Many times when the truth is presented, people consider the one presenting the truth as their enemy. Religious truth affects people this way more than in other fields. Ahab had this attitude toward Elijah (1 Kings 21:18-20). The same Ahab said of Micaiah, "Did I not tell thee that he would prophesy no good concerning me, but evil?" Since the Jewish leaders looked upon Jesus as their enemy, "they tried to stone him" (John 8:59; 10:31). We have modern

Ahabs today! People who look upon truth speakers as enemies. Some are very complimentary of lessons until their religious sins are exposed. Then they become "modern Ahabs" viewing the speaker as an enemy. Members of the church have been known to adopt such attitudes. As long as others agree with them, they speak well of the speaker, but when they disagree or differ, they brand them an enemy. The truth hurts, but what profit is there for us to brand the truth bearer as our enemy. Nature is not all roses and lilies. Nettles and thorns also exist. In the realm of spiritual truth, there are things unpleasant that need to be spoken. John the Baptist preached unpleasant truth to Herod (Matt. 14). The doctor who diagnoses must speak about terrible diseases. The truth speaker is our best friend. "Faithful are the wounds of a friend; but the kisses of an enemy are deceitful" (Prov. 27:6).

Here are things that follow or are indicated when we consider the truth speaker as our enemy:

Implies a grave departure from the truth. The pain shows there is something wrong within. The Galatians were spiritually diseased. The truth would have us appreciate those who speak it rather than hold them in contempt.

Shows one to be foolish. Truth is not the less true because we are blind to it. The revelation of its existence is not the creating of it. We can't stop the hurricane by becoming angry at the barometer. Paul called the Galatians foolish (Gal. 3:1).

Proves one to be unjust. If we are what we should be, why do we object to the truth being spoken? The only way to be justified before God is by obeying and loving the truth. When one becomes angry at truth and brands the truth speaker an enemy, it is a definite evidence of a lack of justice in his life. The faithful servant, like his master, will wish nothing but good to those whose guilt he denounces.

Shows one to be ungenerous. It is always a thankless task to tell unpleasant truth. It would have been much more pleasant for Paul to have retained his popularity at the expense of the churches' welfare.

His soul's welfare and their spiritual welfare were far greater than a desire for pleasantness. How about you? Do you count one an enemy who tells you the truth?

Having the Preeminence

Jesus Christ, as God's only begotten Son, and as the Redeemer of men, has been so honored by the Father that in all things, in all spheres, in all times, he should have preeminence. Preeminence is the "quality or state of being preeminent." Preeminent is defined as "eminent above others; prominent; superior; esp. in excellence." Colossians 1:15-19 suggests and reveals several principles and areas in which Christ has the preeminence. Appreciation and respect for these are important regarding our eternal salvation. Who can ever hope to be saved without recognizing the preeminence of Christ? From Colossians 1:15-19, we observe his preeminence.

In Power. "For by him were all things created, that are in heaven, and that are in earth, visible and invisible, whether they be thrones, or dominions, or principalities, or powers: all thing were created by him, and for him" (v. 16). It pleased God that "by" him, "through" him, "in" him, and "for" him were all things brought into existence, and without him was not anything made (John 1:3). By him also he made the worlds (Heb. 1:2). Think of it! This is the same Christ by whom, through whom, in whom, and for whom, God is now seeking to save sinners for the glory of his Name. "For it became him, for whom are all things, and by whom are all things, in bringing many sons unto glory, to make the captain of their salvation perfect through sufferings" (Heb. 2:10).

In Birth. "Christ is the firstborn of every creature" (v. 15). Christ could say, "I am Alpha and Omega, the beginning and the end" (Rev. 21:6). In verse 18, he is referred to as "the beginning, the firstborn from the dead." This has been called his second birth. Paul wrote in 1 Corinthians 15:23, "But every man is his own order: Christ the firstfruits; afterward they that are Christ's at his coming." The firstborn usually becomes the heir. God hath "appointed Him heir of all things" (Heb. 1:2). Now through the grace of God, we who obey the Christ are made "heirs together with Him" (Rom. 8:15-17). His preeminence in birth brings hope and assurance to those who walk in his steps.

In Likeness. "Who is the image of the invisible God" (v. 15). Angels are doubtlessly holy, many of his people in every age have been godly, but Christ alone in his essential character was the "express image of his person." "Who being the brightness of his glory and the express image of his person, and upholding all things by the word of his power, when he had by himself purged our sins, sat down on the right hand of the Majesty on high" (Heb. 1:3). He could say, "He that hath seen me hath seen the Father" (John 14:9). Also, "I and my Father are one." We need continually to read the Gospels in this light.

In Authority. "And he is before all things, and by him all things consist" (v. 17). The law of gravitation as an ordinance of God has a mighty balancing effect in holding material things together. But this law has no influence over heavenly things. Concerning matters of a spiritual nature, Jesus said, "All power (authority) is given unto me in heaven, and in earth" (Matt. 28:18). These are the words of Christ as Matthew recorded the Great Commission. Christ has the right to direct. In all things concerning our soul's welfare, we need to be concerned with what Christ authorizes. The authority is his! The cancer of so many religionists today is that they profess to submit to the authority of Christ but in actuality do only those things that are convenient for them. We need ever to recognize his preeminence in authority and continually do whatsoever he commands for us to do (Matt. 17:5). "Then cometh the end, when he shall have put down all rule, and all authority and power. For he must reign, till he hath put all enemies under his feet" (1 Cor. 15:24-25). Christ now reigns and his preeminence is to be respected.

In the Church. "And he is the head of the body, the church: who is the beginning, the firstborn from the dead; that in all things he might have the preeminence" (v.18). Christ is the head of his body, the church. It is the head of the body, and not the hands, that does the thinking and planning. The church is to function as the head directs. In his word, we have his mind and will concerning the function/mission of the church. "Therefore as the church is subject unto Christ" (Eph. 5:24), the body is to be subjected to the head. What does the church of Christ teach regarding such and such? A quite common question! In essence, the church does not teach but is taught as it (the body) is subject to the head and the head is Christ. What Christ has taught is that which the body is to perform. How can one say Christ is truly the head with preeminence when the church engages in those things that the head has never authorized? May we always grant Christ the preeminence that he so richly deserves. Our soul salvation depends upon it.

He Preaches Like He Means It

This comment is one which has been made by some in their evaluation of a preacher and his particular lesson which they had heard. It is possible that some individuals did not mean it to appear so, but I definitely feel that such a statement is quite a compliment. Everything that a Christian is called upon to do should be done with meaning. To do something and not truly mean it is to border upon sheer hypocrisy! We should labor to leave the proper impression in the minds of individuals, the proper impressoin being that we mean what we do and say and desire for them to be impressed with the fact that we do mean it. Especially is this true in regard to preaching and teaching the word of God.

The comment, "He preaches like he means it" suggests that individuals have the impression that some preach and do not mean it. Perhaps such individuals might be referred to as "professionals"! This would be those who are preaching primarily for a living and preaching what pleases their hearers, treading ever so lightly lest they might arouse the fury of their worldly minded listeners. Jesus spoke of some, "Ye hypocrites, well did Isaiah prophesy of you, saying, This people draweth nigh unto me with their mouth, and honoreth me with their lips; but their heart is far from me" (Matt. 15:7-8). One can never please the Lord when his heart is far from him. Isn't this saying that the person does not really mean what he is saying or doing? Paul spoke of preachers: "Some indeed preach Christ even of envy and strife; and some also of good will; the one preach Christ of contention, not sincerely, supposing to add affliction to my bonds: but the other of love, knowing that I am set for the defense of the gospel" (Phil. 1:15-17). It is hard to conceive of a man preaching "Christ even of envy and strife" as one who would over a period of time impress his hearers as a preacher meaning what he was preaching. It must be a horrible feeling for a man to preach something that he does not mean or believe! He is to be pitied in more ways than one. If he continues in such, he is going to jeopardize his soul's salvation and be miserable as long as he has any conscience that is awake to right or wrong. Paul admonished Timothy saying, "Take heed unto thyself, and unto the doctrine; continue in them: for in doing this thou shalt both save thyself, and them that hear thee" (1 Tim. 4:16).

Why shouldn't a man mean what he preaches in the truth? It involves the greatest principle that man will ever confront, the salvation of his soul. If this doesn't warrant meaning, then please tell me, what does? "For what shall it profit a man, if he shall gain the whole world and lose his own soul? Or what shall a man give in exchange for his soul? Whosoever therefore shall he ashamed of me and of my words in this adulterous and sinful generation; of him also shall the Son of man he ashamed, when he cometh in the glory of his Father with his holy angels" (Mark 8:36-38). To be ashamed of Christ and his words may account for our lack of meaning in our actions! Let's say what we mean and mean what we say!

He Received Orders From His God

Several years ago, the above words, were the explanation of Wayne Chenault's shooting to death Mrs. Alberta King and a deacon in an Atlanta Baptist church. Wayne Chenault was without a doubt a deranged and misled person. He possessed a warped and perverted concept of religion. I believe these observations go without question, but there is yet a sobering aspect to his contention that "he received orders from his God" to do what he did.

Myriads today believe that God personally speaks to individuals other than through his divine word. Multitudes still contend for latter-day revelations from the Lord. They do not believe that God only speaks to man through the Scriptures. How could people who believe that God directs and moves individuals apart from his word be able to say that he didn't receive such orders? Perhaps such people would explain it away with the contention that God would never order or direct anyone to do anything as immoral as killing innocent people. This reasoning has merit to it, but still where is the authority for believing that God speaks to anyone today other than through his revealed word in the Scriptures? To believe in latter-day revelations is to place one in situations where it is difficult to know what is true. Through history, it is often observed that horrible deeds have been committed on the basis of individuals contending that the Devil made them do it or by obeying the direction from God. The Devil cannot make anyone do anything without man helping, and the Lord only speaks to man through his word, which certainly does not advocate such deeds of sinful violence. Therefore, it is a very dangerous concept to think of God speaking to man other than through his word. Untold damage has been done to religious thought by men holding this concept. They might not make a practice of killing on this pretence, but every manner of false practice has been adopted by some fanatic crying, "God spoke to me and told me to do it."

If God speaks to man apart from his word today, then certain things must follow. We observe a few of these:

God respects persons. Would he not be a respecter of persons when he reveals to one what is not made known to others? The Scriptures contend that God is not a respecter of persons (Acts 10:34-35; Rom. 2:11). By speaking through his word in the Scriptures, every accountable individual has the same opportunity to hear and know. In such a manner, he reveals himself without respecting any man's person or granting anyone an advantage above another individual. All men have equal access to his revealed word!

God acts contrary to his word. The Scriptures reveal that in these last days, God speaks to man through his Son (Heb. 1:1-2). Christ is heaven's last argument (Heb. 12:25). 1 Corinthians 2:9-13 is an outstanding passage in revealing how God speaks to man today. Paul contends that the Spirit searched the deep things of God and revealed what he found to the apostles and the apostles spoke these things to men. Hence, the word of the Lord reveals what God desires for man to know regarding his will. In this manner, God speaks to man!

His word is not final authority. This is a very obvious conclusion if God is revealing his will separate and apart from his word. Stating it in another way, if God grants men authority to do certain deeds not revealed in the word, then the word can never be final authority. The sober Bible reader is aware of numerous passages that teach that the word does constitute final authority. John 12:48, Galatians 1:6-9, and 1 Timothy 1:3 are a few of these. These verses, as well as many more, point to the fact that final authority is determined in and by the word of God.

The claim of the Scriptures is misleading. What is the claim of the Scriptures? That they are perfect and able to make a person "thoroughly furnished unto all good works" (2 Tim. 3:16-17). If this be true, what need and value is there for any latter-day revelations? Colossians 2:9-10 and Psalm 19:7 also teach the perfection of God's word. How could such a claim be true if God is directing men to act apart from the directions in his word?

No true standard of right or wrong. God has given us that standard in his word (2 Tim. 3:16-17). What a man teaches is to be tried by the word of God (1 John 4:1). Paul speaks of some believing a lie that they might be damned "who believed not the truth, but had pleasure in unrighteousness" (2 Thess. 2:10-12). How could a lie be determined or how could one believe a lie, if there is no standard of right or wrong? Personal revelations defy the standard. God speaks through and only through his word.

He Stirreth Up the People

During the life of Christ and particularly those events that involved his trial and crucifixion, many false and unjust accusations were hurled against him. Though spoken in hatred and malice, some of the accusations were actually founded in truth and reflected complimentarily upon the accused. The language in Luke 23:5 is a good example of what we have in mind: "And they were the more fierce, saying, He stirreth up the people, teaching throughout all Jewry, beginning from Galilee to this place." Though the Jews spoke this in a derogatory fashion, it was nevertheless quite complimentary to the mission of Christ.

The Jews needed stirring up! They were walking in the traditions of men and had lost sight of true reverence and devotion to God. In no uncertain words, Jesus called this to their attention. "Howbeit in vain do they worship me, teaching for doctrines the commandments of men. For laying aside the commandment of God, ye hold the tradition of men, as the washing of pots and cups: and many other such like things ye do. And he said unto them, Full well ye reject the commandment of God, that ye may keep your tradition" (Mark 7:7-9). The people needed to be stirred into seeing their true condition before God that they might be led to repentance. His message was stirring! The enemies acknowledged that in their accusation and it was obvious that teaching was the stirring medium. It has been said that a man was never the same after coming in contact with Christ and his words of life. He either obeyed and became a disciple to follow Christ in love, or he departed in worldly sorrow destined to be hardened to the ways of the world. The rich young ruler could possibly be an example of this. Having come in contact with Christ and hearing the Lord tell him what he needed to do, "when the young man heard that saying, he went away sorrowful: for he had great possessions" (Matt. 19:22). The servant is not above his master! What was said of the lord in hateful accusation was said of the servants of Christ. "And when they found them not, they drew Jason and certain brethren unto the rulers of the city, crying These that have turned the world upside down are come hither also" (Acts 17:6). Though it was not meant to be, this was a great compliment to the servants of the Lord. By their teaching, the community was being stirred and disturbed. It was for their good! The society needed to be turned upside down that the corruption, filth, and iniquity might be purged from the lives of the people. This required distinct and specific preaching.

The truth stirs people today! People need stirring as in the days of Christ and his apostles. It shouldn't greatly bother a servant of God to hear that certain individuals are "shook up" after hearing a particular lesson. There are people who need to be disturbed that they might realize where they stand before God or see just what some of their conclusions do to the church and its mission as God gave it. The pitiful commentary on much of the preaching today is that it is so insipid, weak, and lifeless that there is nothing about the preaching to stir anyone. It should not be the intention of the preacher to personally offend anyone or delight in crudeness in preaching the truth. However, the discourse should be characterized with such plainness that the hearer can see himself as God sees him. We should always keep in mind that we are to please God rather than man. "For do I now persuade men, or God? Or do I seek to please men? For if I yet pleased men, I should not be the servant of Christ" (Gal. 1:10).

Many sermons, that so-called gospel preachers preach today, could well be preached in denominational churches without a stir of offense coming from them. I am not inferring that every sermon should stir the denominational people, but over a short period of time there should be sermons that convey distinct and specific truth that should do so. And I suppose an even more pathetic commentary is the fact that many in the church of the Lord today feel that inoffensive preaching is the type of preaching that is needed. Don't preach to stir individuals to see their sins and seek forgiveness before God, but rather preach lessons that will help them feel good and comfortable in their sins. Make people happy! That's the way to please people and be praised as a real preacher. Jesus stirred up the people and the apostles preached in such a manner that they were accused of turning the world upside down. They were concerned with reaching the souls of men that they might be saved. Believe me, preaching should never be for the purpose of personal glory or to simply get someone told, but where sin, false teaching, and complacency exist, let us continually place the word before people that they might be stirred up enough to do something about it!

Holding Traditions

What do you mean by traditions? How shall we define the word? There are various and sundry definitions of the word and the summary of these seems to be: "The handing down, delivery, transfer, transmission, giving over, conveyance of a story, beliefs, customs, law, teachings, ordinances, instructions, doctrines, precepts, from one source (God or men) to another, or from generation to generation by word of mouth or written, and the receiving of that which is handed down orally or written." There are different traditions spoken of in the Scriptures. Some are to be followed and others to be rejected. Those precepts that were spoken by the apostles involve God's truth and they are referred to as traditions. "Therefore, brethren, stand fast, and hold the traditions which ye have been taught, whether by word, or our epistle" (2 Thess. 2:15). Rather than to avoid traditions, Paul admonished brethren at Thessalonica to "hold the traditions." In the third chapter of this same epistle, brethren were commanded to withdraw from every brother "that walketh disorderly, and not after the tradition which he received of us" (2 Thess. 3:6). "Now I praise you, brethren, that ye remember me in all things, and keep the ordinances, as I delivered them to you" (1 Cor. 11:1). This is the reading in the King James Version. There are other versions that use the word "traditions" rather than "ordinances." Thus, we should be able to recognize that some traditions come from God, and are good and right, and are universally binding.

However, we seem to be living in an era when people speak derogatorily of traditions. I am a traditionalist and thoroughly believe that all people must be if they hope to live with God in eternity. The passages that have been related refer to the truth that the apostles spoke as being traditions. God's people are to hold the traditions that came from inspired men who had the authority of binding and loosing on earth. There are those who profess to be members of the Lord's church who crave new things and practices that are right in their own eyes. The teaching and traditions that have come from the apostles are not respected and revered as truth from God. The phrase "new hermeneutic" is being used by brethren in regard to the Scriptures. Though I may not understand a plausible definition of the phrase, it seems to involve doing whatever you want to do in religion and giving no respect for the truth of the Scriptures.

The Scriptures reveal that there are traditions which are contrary to God's law and should not be allowed to govern our activities. Paul wrote to the Colossians saying, "Beware lest any man spoil you through philosophy and vain deceit, after the tradition of men, after the rudiments of the world, and not after Christ" (Col. 2:8). We must be concerned about the traditions that we follow. There are traditions of men that lead us from Christ while there are traditions from the apostles that lead us to faithfulness in Christ. Paul spoke of "his being exceedingly zealous of the traditions of my fathers" (Gal. 1:14). He came to recognize that such were vain in obtaining salvation in Christ. Peter stated: "Forasmuch as ye know that ye were not redeemed with corruptible things, as silver and gold, from your vain conversation received by tradition from your fathers; But with the precious blood of Christ, as of a lamb without blemish and without spot" (1 Pet. 1:18-19). That which was delivered from the fathers was not to be recognized as the truth of God's word. The Scriptures reveal traditions that were not inherently wrong, but they are made wrong when they are bound on others or placed above God's law. We are speaking of many of the traditions that the Pharisees had adopted. "For laying aside the commandment of God, ye hold the tradition of men, as the washing of pots and cups: and many other such like things ye do. And he said unto them, Full well ye reject the commandment of God, that ye may keep your own tradition" (Mark 7:8-9). The traditions that have originated with men have no right to be bound upon men. They are without God's authority (Col. 3:17; 2 Cor. 5:7; 1 Pet. 4:11). They have no right to exist and will cause one's religion to be vain (Matt. 15:9).

The traditions that we are to hold are those practices that have been delivered by the Lord through the apostles. These were taught by word or epistle (2 Thess. 2:15). Such are not subject to change They have come from the Lord and are bound upon men forever. Baptism for the remission of sins (Acts 2:38), the Lord's supper on every first day of the week (Acts 20:7), giving of our means on the first day of the week (1 Cor. 16:1-2), singing and making melody in our hearts as the divinely authorized music (Eph. 5:19), the autonomy of the local church (1 Pet. 5:1-4); these are but a few of the things that might be termed traditions regarding the churches of Christ. But where did they originate? Not from men, but from the teaching of the apostles. These are traditions that we are to hold. When you are doing God's will and following the pattern of truth, there may be those who label you as a traditionalist. Be thankful that you can be and continue on!

How Can A Man Obey God?

There is absolutely no substitute for safety in religion. God requires man to obey him. "Not every one that saith unto me, Lord, Lord, shall enter into the kingdom of heaven; but he that doeth the will of my Father which is in heaven" (Matt. 7:21). In speaking of Christ, the Hebrew writer said, "though he were a son, yet learned he obedience by the things which he suffered; and being made perfect, he became the author of eternal salvation unto all them that obey him" (Heb. 5:8-9). There is no substite for obedience. Man should desire to know what God requires in proper obedience.

Here are a few thoughts that we should keep in mind in rendering obedience to God.

A commission to do a thing authorizes only the doing of the act specified. The doing of all other things is virtually forbidden. There is an old Latin maxim: "The expression of one thing is the exclusion of another." This principle was evident in the Old Testament: "What thing soever I command you, observe to do it: thou shalt not add thereto, nor diminish from it" (Deut. 12:32). The "it" was the thing emphasized! In the New Testament, this principle is ever so apparent. "Whosoever transgresseth, and abideth not in the doctrine of Christ, hath not God. He that abideth in the doctrine of Christ, he hath both the Father and the Son" (2 John 9). Man is not to design what he does in obedience to God.

The specification of one act is never respected when a substitute for it is rendered instead. God commanded Moses to speak to the rock to produce water. Among other things, Moses disobeyed by smiting the rock. This displeased God, because this act of substitution was an act of disobedience (Num. 20). To substitute is but to disobey! Numerous Old Testament examples are pathetic memorials of this principle. In the New Covenant, God specifies a burial in baptism, and this renders sprinkling or pouring only as disobedient substitutes (Rom. 6:4; Col. 2:12).

The extension or application of the law of God to others than to whom it was divinely given is never allowed in obedience. Noah was commanded to build an ark. For others to construe this command as applying to themselves is utterly ridiculous. But would you be amazed if some one today were to advocate it? Christ commanded the baptism of believers (Mark 16:15-16). This excludes the baptism of unbelievers and infants who are not capable of believing. God taught the Jews under the Law of Moses to keep the seventh day holy. Christians have not been given such a command (Col. 2:14-17). Those who are Sabbath observers today are making an application of a fulfilled law of God to others than to whom it was divinely given.

Obedience demands that the divinely specified purpose attend the divinely specified act. Peter not only commanded the people to be baptized, but also commanded them to be baptized "everyone of you in the name of Jesus Christ for the remission of sins" (Acts 2:38). It excludes baptism for any and all purposes other than to obtain the remission of one's sins, the salvation of one's soul. Paul had to rebuke the Corinthians for violating this principle when they did not evidence the proper purpose in eating the Lord's supper (1 Cor. 11:27-29).

Obedience demands that the divinely specified place be used when God specified such a place for acts of worship. Paul wrote "unto him be glory in the church" (Eph. 3:21). No physical place of worship is specified by God, but he does require the spiritual location of worship and that being in the church of his Son. Only those in Christ can approach God in acceptable worship in the name of Christ (Col. 3:17).

Obedience demands that the divinely specified time be respected without alteration or substitution when a certain time is given for doing God's service. "Upon the first day of the week" cannot mean that such acts specified for that time can be acceptably regarded on some other day. The disciples observed the Lord's supper and gave of their means upon the first day of the week (Acts 20:7; 1 Cor. 16:1-2). The first day of the week is the divinely specified time for such acts to be observed and to practice such at some other times is disobedience before God.

The divinely specified agent or means is to be used before obedience is acceptable when God specified an agent or means. "Making melody in your heart to the Lord" clarified the instrument with which melody is to be made in God's praise (Eph. 5:19; Col. 3:16). No mechanical substitute can suffice. Are we obeying God or just going through some form that pleases us?

How Close A Friend Are We To Jesus?

We speak of having friends and then we refer to some as being close friends. Disciples of Christ are friends of Christ. Jesus said, "Greater love hath no man than this, that a man lay down his life for his friends. Ye are my friends, if ye do whatsoever I command you. Henceforth, I call you not servants; for the servant knoweth not what the lord doeth: but I have called you friends; for all things that I have heard of my Father I have made known unto you" (John 15:13-15). We sing the very beautiful and meaningful song, "I'll be a friend to Jesus." Here are the lyrics of the second verse are: "The world may turn against him, I'll love him to the end, And while on earth I'm living, My Lord shall have a friend." Think of the times that we have sung these words. Did we really mean what we were singing? While professing to be a friend of Jesus, just how close a friend are we?

The True Friends Of Jesus ...

Keep His Commandments. Jesus associated friendship with his commandments. "Ye are my friends, if ye do whatsoever I command you" (John 15:14). Again, "If ye love me, keep my commandments" (John 14:15). Being a true friend of Christ involves keeping his commandments. Jesus asked, "And why call ye me, Lord, Lord, and do not the things which I say?" (Luke 6:46). We may deceive ourselves in thinking we are close friends of Christ by keeping a commandment or so, but Christ said "whatsoever I command you." We have no right to segregate or ignore any of his commands if we are true friends of Jesus.

Are Not Ashamed of Him. Remember the words of the song: "The world may turn against him, I'll love him to the end." The true meaning of these words leaves no place for being ashamed of Christ. "Whosoever therefore shall be ashamed of me and of my words in this adulterous and sinful generation; of him also shall the Son of man be ashamed, when he cometh in the glory of his Father with the holy angels" (Mark 8:38). True friendship and the feeling of shame are not compatible. Paul was a true friend of Christ when he wrote: "For I am not ashamed of the gospel of Christ" (Rom. 1:16). Again, "Be not thou therefore ashamed of the testimony of our Lord, nor of me his prisoner: but be thou partaker of the afflictions of the gospel according to the power of God" (2 Tim. 1:8). Whatever may occur, close friends of Jesus are not ashamed of Christ or his words!

Declare Themselves. This is a segment of not being ashamed of him. The true friends are on the Lord's side without any hesitation or embarrassment. The close friends of Jesus are not neutral or fence straddlers. They love the Lord and his word. "No man can serve two masters: for either he will hate the one, and love the other; or else he will hold to the one, and despise the other. Ye cannot serve God and mammon" (Matt. 6:24). Mr. Facing Both Ways is not a close friend of Christ. There are those who sing "I'll be a friend to Jesus" and keep loving the world and its affections. Of these, James wrote these piercing words: "Ye adulterers and adulteresses, know ye not that the friendship of the world is enmity with God? Whosoever therefore will be a friend of the world is the enemy of God" (Jas. 4:4). Where do we stand regarding Christ and his doctrine? How often do we tell others of our wonderful friend and what he means to us?

Rejoice In Spiritual Matters. Being a friend of Jesus, we are fond of the things of which he is fond. This involves doing the will of his Father and being spiritually minded. Paul speaks of the two minds saying, "For they that are after the flesh do mind the things of the flesh; but they that are after the Spirit the things of the Spirit. For to be carnally minded is death; but to be spiritually minded is life and peace" (Rom. 8:5-6). It is the spiritually minded who are close to the Lord and have true friendship. "But his delight is in the law of the Lord; and in his law doth he meditate day and night" (Ps. 1:2). Periods of worship are not boredom, but they are occasions of joy to the close friends of Jesus. They have David's attitude: "I was glad when they said unto me, Let us go into the house of the Lord" (Ps. 122:1).

Look Forward To Being With Him. Close friends have a desire to be together. There is sorrow that separation brings. The Scriptures speak of Christ's coming and what a blessing it will be to be his true friends. "Looking for that blessed hope, and the glorious appearing of the great God and our Saviour Jesus Christ" (Tit. 2:13). "Beloved, now are we the sons of God and it doth not yet appear what we shall be: but we know that, when he shall appear, we shall be like him; for we shall see him as he is" (1 John 3:2). By being close friends of Jesus, we can be preparing for his coming. We need to give prayerful consideration to what is involved in being a close friend of Jesus. The way some so-called friends act, he needs no enemies!

How Noble Are We?

"These were more noble that those in Thessalonica, in that they received the word with all readiness of mind, and searched the scriptures daily, whether those things were so" (Acts 17:11). "These" evidently has reference to the synagogue in Berea and "those" refers to those constituting the synagogue in Thessalonica (vv. 1, 10). The word "noble" can be used in regard to one's birth and heritage. However, here it conveys the thought of being noble-minded. W. E. Vine states that the word is a translation of the Greek word *eugenesteros* and he renders it more noble-minded. The statements that follow in verse 11 reveal some characteristics of those who are noble-minded in the sight of God. These were noble in that they were:

Free of Prejudice. The phrase, "in that they received the word with all readiness of mind," indicates that prejudice did not control their lives. They were ready to investigate and give consideration to what they heard. Readiness of mind is not a prejudicial mind! Jesus evaluated some by saying, "For this people's heart is waxed gross, and their ears are dull of hearing, and their eyes they have closed; lest at any time they should see with their eyes, and hear with their ears, and should understand with heart, and should be converted, and I should heal them" (Matt. 13:15). This is a prophecy from Isaiah 6:9-10 and stated in other places in the New Testament. Pre-judgment or prejudice closes the hearts of individuals to the truth and can certainly cause them to be lost in eternity. Noble-minded people endeavor to avoid prejudice and strive to be open-minded.

Not Gullible. The gullible person is ready to accept most anything without investigation. Their view of life involves pronouncing everything right without consideration for what is right or wrong. The Bereans were not gullible! They listened with unprejudicial minds "and searched the scriptures daily, whether those things were so." They wanted what was so! That which is so is that which is found in the Scriptures. The gullible person is ready to let some others think for him. Whatever the preacher says or some influential person relates is accepted with little, if any, investigation of the Scriptures. The gullible individual is not a noble-minded person. We can be deceived and everyone has the responsibility of knowing what is so and not gullibly accepting something that is false. "Prove all things; hold fast that which is good" (1 Thess. 5:21).

Energetic. The Bereans "searched the scriptures daily, whether those things were so." Energy is involved in searching the Scriptures. They examined what they heard in the light of what the Scriptures revealed. What Scriptures were available to them at this time? One must answer that the Old Testament Scriptures were available to them and this involved the Septuagint translation of the Hebrew into the Greek language. It would be supposition to contend that a quantity of the New Testament books were available at this period. They were faced with reading scrolls that were written on vellum or animal skins and doubtlessly necessitated considerable effort in searching them. Yet, they daily did this! There are some members of the church today who seldom read the Scriptures. To daily search the Scriptures is something that is foreign to their lives. In a time when the Scriptures are so conducive for reading, members of the church don't find time to do so on a daily basis. Mind you, this is when the Scriptures have been divided into books, chapters, and verses and most of our Bibles have a concordance and marginal notes that make the search much easier. The Bereans were void of these advantages, yet they asserted the energy in searching the Scriptures daily. How many members picked up one of the schedules for reading the Bible through in a year and are engaged in doing so? I have even known some who misplaced their Bible and didn't miss it for a week or so. Would you call such indifference as being noble-minded? So many have the problem of laziness when it comes to reading the Scriptures! We need to heed these admonitions: "Not slothful in business; fervent in spirit; serving the Lord" (Rom. 12:11). "And let us not be weary in well doing: for in due season we shall reap if we faint not" (Gal. 6:9).

Receptive. "Therefore many of them believed; also of honourable women which were Greeks, and of men, not a few" (v. 12). The noble-minded before God are obedient to what is so. What value is it, in the final analysis of life, if a person is free of prejudice, not gullible, and knows what is so in the Scriptures and refuses to obey the truth? These traits help us appreciate what is so that we might be obedient and have the blessings of the Lord. What good is it to know the Scriptures "from cover to cover" and still not obey the truth revealed there in? Jesus said, "And why call ye me, Lord, Lord, and do not the things which I say?" (Luke 6:46). How noble are we? Are we one of God's nobility? THINK!

I Am Not Ashamed

"For I am not ashamed of the gospel of Christ: for it is the power of God unto salvation to every one that believeth; to the Jew first, and also to the Greek" (Rom. 1:16). This is a very familiar verse to Bible readers. It suggests the theme of the Roman letter, establishing that the gospel of Christ is God's power to save! Paul was contemplating a trip to Rome for the purpose of preaching the gospel. He had preached in some of the great political and religious centers of the world and had not been ashamed to preach the gospel wherever he had gone. He desired for the brethren in Rome to know that in this the greatest of all cities in this age of the world, he still would not be ashamed of the gospel of Christ. His words to the Roman saints should be of great encouragement for Christians today. His feelings should be our feelings in this age. We must never be ashamed of the gospel of Christ.

Perhaps one of the great failures of man is that he has never consistently learned of what he should be ashamed. So many times man is not diligent in being ashamed of what he should be ashamed; on the other hand, he is sometimes ashamed of the things that he should never even think of being ashamed. When one knows of what an individual is ashamed, he has a fairly accurate commentary on that individual's attitude of life. As a child of God, of what are you ashamed? Perhaps it will help us know ourselves better as we ask ourselves concerning what we are ashamed of.

Some Things For Which We Should Be Ashamed

Our Past Life. Before becoming a Christian, we were in sin. We committed things of which now we have been forgiven. Of these ungodly acts, we should naturally be ashamed. On occasions, we have heard professed Christians boast of their sinful and wild life before obeying the gospel. Are people truly converted to Christ who manifest such an attitude? Paul had much to forget in his past life (1 Tim. 1:13-15). The fact that he said he wasn't ashamed of the gospel possibly implied that there were things in his life of which he was ashamed.

Commiting Sin. As a Christian, we are to follow faithfully Christ. We should be ashamed of ourselves when we do anything contrary to the will of the Lord. We are to strive continually unto perfection and view sin as a shameful thing, regardless of how the world may justify such deeds. "For the wages of sin is death" (Rom. 6:23).

Fellowshiping Darkness. "And have no fellowship with the unfruitful works of darkness, but rather reprove them. For it is a shame even to speak of those things which are done of them in secret" (Eph. 5:11-12). The Christian has a twofold obligation toward the works of darkness. We are not to fellowship such from the negative view, and from the positive side, we should reprove them. It is a shameful thing to give encouragement to a false practice or any acts of immorality. "Unfruitful works of darkness" refer to anything that is incompatible with the teachings of Jesus Christ, the light of the world. "Be ye not unequally yoked together with unbelievers: for what fellowship hath righteousness with unrighteousness? And what communion hath light with darkness" (2 Cor. 6: 14). God calls upon his people to "be ye separate."

Our Lack of Knowledge. "Awake to righteousness, and sin not; for some have not the knowledge of God: I speak this to your shame" (1 Cor. 15:34). For some not to have the knowledge of God was a shameful thing. Paul said, "I speak this to your shame." Doubtlessly, they were not novices! They had "sufficient" time to develop in knowledge. The shameful thing was that they had not grown. There are so many in the church today who have not developed in knowledge. They seem to know little more now than they did when they obeyed the first principles. Some of them are so unconcerned with their condition that they never consider it to be shameful. Perhaps if they had some shame regarding the matter, they would set about to apply themselves so that knowledge might be developed. "Study to show thyself approved unto God, a workman that needeth not to be ashamed, rightly dividing the word of truth" (2 Tim. 2:15).

Neglecting the Church. Jesus loved the church enough to die for it. We ought to love it enough to support it and place it first in our lives. We should be ashamed to neglect the church in any respect. What if every member were like me—what type of a local church would it be? It is shameful how little some attend; how little some give; how little some work. Are they ashamed? Evidently not! They go right on in the same attitude. May the Lord help us never to be ashamed of the gospel of Christ. At the same time, may he help us to be ashamed of the things that we should be and to do something about them.

I Don't Care

This is a phrase that most of us use quite often. Hardly a day goes by but what we use this phrase. As free moral agents, we have the prerogative to make such an evaluation of things that we confront. We can care or not care! The freedom of choice is usually granted to us. It might be good for all of us to give careful consideration to what is involved when we say, "I don't care." Our lives are regulated by the things for which we care or do not care. Unfortunately, the majority of individuals do not care for things of a religious nature. They do not care to hear about spiritual matters and deem such as being foolishness. Their cares are for the things of this world. They give little regard for the word of God and care not for what is found in the Scriptures. The mercy and goodness of God means nothing to them. The death of Jesus for their sins goes without concern in their lives. How sad it is, but "I don't care" is their reply. Heaven will be the abode of those who cared enough to respond to the love of God in doing his will. Perhaps the rich man in Luke 16 had the don't care attitude in life. After death, he lifted his eyes in hell "being in torments." In hell he manifested care that was too late for the saving of his soul. "For what shall it profit a man, if he shall gain the whole world, and lose his own soul? Or what shall a man give in exchange for his soul?" (Mark 8:36-37).

Have you ever heard people say, "I don't care" what others think? Such a statement needs considerable thought! Christians should be concerned about others and should want all people to think properly with their affections on things above. We should rejoice when people think in keeping with the mind of Christ and be grieved when thoughts are to the contrary. The "I don't care" attitude is contrary to the doctrine of Christ. It condones and sanctions sins with no real concern for trying to do something about the evil in the world.

Are you concerned about how others feel about you? Do you take the "I don't care" approach regarding how people look upon your life? Christians are to evaluate their influence very highly and try to influence others for good. We are to preach the truth and live it before those who are not Christians. This subject came up in a Bible class some years ago and while discussing the value of preaching the truth to others, an individual stated that she didn't care how the hearers felt about her. If our hearers reject the word of God, we should feel sadness. She later qualified her statement by adding that she was not putting the feelings that hearers would have for her above telling them the truth. I have no problem with that! Paul asked the Galatians, "Am I therefore become your enemy, because I tell you the truth?" (Gal. 4:16). I believe Paul was concerned about how they felt about him, but not to the refusal of telling them the truth that they needed to hear.

"Is it nothing to you, all ye that pass by, behold, and see if there be any sorrow like unto my sorrow, which is done unto me, wherewith the Lord hath afflicted me in the day of his fierce anger" (Lam. 1:12). The city of Jerusalem had been ravaged and lay in destruction. The city is personified and is portrayed as speaking as a human. Is there no one who cares? When you pass by and behold the ruins, is it nothing to you? The city was crying for care. The church of the Lord needs people who care about following the pattern that God has given for the church. Every digression and innovation should be viewed with sorrow. There is no time to adopt the "I don't care" attitude and approach. If the church is to continue as a bulwark of faith, there must be those who care enough to defend the truth and cry out against perversions of truth. In many respects, we are those who have been benefited because others have cared. Preachers and brethren cared enough in the restoration years of the 1800s to help us appreciate and understand many things that their faithful labors left us as a heritage. We may not be able to accomplish what we desire, but we can always keep caring. The old "I don't care" approach can defeat almost anything! There is no place for such in the hearts of those who have a desire for heaven.

When one really considers the thought, he is led to see that in all things there should be care. As a Christian, I should be concerned about what I think, say, and do. In like manner, I should care about others and the lives they live. Certainly I have more control over my own life than the lives of others, but that does not eliminate my responsibility in being concerned for them. "Look not every man on his own things, but every man also on the things of others. Let this mind be in you, which was also in Christ Jesus" (Phil. 2:4-5). Do you ever recall Jesus Christ evidencing the "I don't care" attitude? He cared for mankind and that is why we can have a hope of eternal life. I care what you think! I would like to think that every reader could find profit in this short article!

I Don't Feel Good

This is a statement that is common to our vocabulary. It is frequently made, and so many times it is the truth. Most of us have aches and pains which keep us from feeling as good as we would like to feel. I suppose there are degrees of how well a person feels. Some individuals feel much worse on occasions than others. I recall on one occasion asking a class of individuals if there were those who could truthfully say that they felt good. One of those present raised her hand. How truly blessed that person was in being able to say that she felt good!

The statement "I don't feel good" is made on occasions for an excuse in not performing certain tasks. It seems to be one of the favorites that members have for not being present at some of the worship services. The truthfulness of their statement is not being questioned! No one has a right to say that the person is not speaking the truth when saying, "I don't feel good." No one can actually say that he knows how someone else feels. Paul's statement in 1 Corinthians 2:11 should be considered when we think of this: "For what man knoweth the things of a man, save the spirit of man which is in him? Even so the things of God knoweth no man, but the Spirit of God." It would appear that most of us do the things that we really desire to do. There are exceptions, but the things that lie within our capabilities, we make a part of our lives. Our feelings do not prevent us from doing what we really love to do. When we say, "I don't feel good" and offer this as an excuse for not participating, is this something that we really love to do? There have been members who attend services at times when they really do not feel good. It is obvious that they do not feel good! Yet, they are there because they love God and want to worship him. Again, I recall speaking to an individual regarding her health before the service began. Her reply was much like this: "I'm certainly not feeling good, but I feel as good here as I would at home and here is where I desire to be." Her statement has stuck with me through the years and her convictions were of the nature that make a church strong.

It is quite possible that some who excuse their absence by saying, "I don't feel good" never use such sentiment to keep them from going on a vacation when the time comes. Let some planned sporting event or some family gathering that folks enjoy be on the agenda. Are they usually neglected because one is not feeling good? Do we not carry our feelings with us and keep the appointments? How many who were not feeling good enough to be at service on Sunday absent themselves from their work on Monday? Yes, there are some, but others carry their aches and pains on with them to work on Monday. One party mentioned that the difference was that he was thinking of his much-needed payday and being faithful to his employer. In like manner we should be thinking about our faithfulness in pleasing God. This is more important than those things of a temporal nature that we have the tendency to exalt above the spiritual.

Some months ago, I read an article in which the author contended that some of the greatest things accomplished by man were done by those not feeling good. It went on to say that if they had waited for the good feelings, the feats would doubtlessly have never materialized. People void of good health kept on working and looking to the goal. They didn't let their feelings defeat them or keep them from reaching the goal that they had in mind. Think about the suffering and agony that Jesus experienced in dying for us. "Let this mind be in you, which was also in Christ Jesus: Who being in the form of God, thought it not robbery to be equal with God: But made himself of no reputation, and took upon him the form of a servant, and was made in the likeness of men: and being found in fashion as a man, he humbled himself, and became obedient unto death, even the death of the cross" (Phil. 2:5-8). Jesus didn't let the suffering and horror of crucifixion keep him from doing the will of his Father. "I have glorified thee on the earth: I have finished the work which thou gavest me to do" (John 17:4). When we assemble and observe the Lord's supper, we are to do so in remembrance of Christ. We are to discern his body and his death for us. Yet, at times we say I won't be there to commemorate his death, "I don't feel good." In comparison with what he has done for us, shouldn't we be ashamed to let our feelings keep us from doing what Christ would have us to do.

I can hear it now. Having read thus far, some will be prone to say that the author expects us to be at service even if the paramedics have to bring us. He is saying that IV tubes might be hanging from our bodies; nevertheless, we should be at worship. Such is not the theme of this article. Most people know this is not so, but some that excuse themselves by saying "I don't feel good" when they can do most everything else, might use such to cover their lack of spirituality. I don't particularly feel good, but I still was able to write this.

If You Can't Convert, Join Them

All my life, I have heard the expression, "If you can't beat them, join them." I have no idea where the expression originated, but it has certainly been around for a long while. Most of the time, it would appear those uttering the words are using them in a humorous manner. However, such is not always the case. It becomes a decision of life by many individuals. As you know from the title, we have changed the expression to read "convert" rather than "beat." It was not a typographical error, as we are often prone to make, but just a little different slant on the expression. Believe it or not, there are members of the body of Christ who have been faithful through the years and have faithfully opposed false teaching who are now endorsing what they once opposed. They have worked diligently in times past in trying to convert others to Christ, but now accept what they once condemned as unscriptural practices. They evidently have adopted the view, "If you can't convert them, join them." This is extremely disheartening, but how else can you account for the turn about in their actions? There are reasons and explanations that possibly account for such actions.

Some children of God let themselves become weary in well doing. We read of a football coach who gave as his explanation for leaving the coaching profession that he was simply "burnt out." It just could be that this is what has happened to individuals who once contended for the faith. They have let themselves become weary of well doing or "burnt out." In more than one place, the Scriptures warn that such can happen. "And let us not be weary in well doing: for in due season we shall reap, if we faint not" (Gal. 6:9), and again, "But ye, brethren, be not weary in well doing" (2 Thess. 3:13). Other versions speak of not losing heart rather than not being weary in well doing. If this cannot happen to Christians, there would be no value in the warning that these Scriptures present.

I recently spoke with a faithful gospel preacher regarding a brother who through the years stood faithful against all false teaching. He has now become engrossed with the unity-in-diversity concept. We both found it hard to believe that this brother would endorse such teaching. We both felt that this one has just become tired of fighting for the truth and now has joined in malignant unity those that he couldn't convert. We need to keep studying, praying, working, and keeping our eyes on the Lord that this will not happen to us.

There are those who are strongly affected by numbers. They see liberal churches "bursting at the seams" and they think of the much smaller numbers in churches striving for the faith. Though they have taught that truth is more important than numbers, they nevertheless let themselves become affected by numbers. They couldn't convert the liberals and now fellowship those they once opposed. Wonder what Noah might say to such individuals? He was a preacher of righteousness and only eight souls were saved in the ark when the floodwaters came (Gen. 7:23). It is evident that he did not convert those in the world, but neither did he join them. Paul stated, "I have planted, Apollos watered; but God gave the increase" (1 Cor. 3:5). We need always to remember that the increase comes from the Lord. Let us keep on striving to convert, but whether or not we are successful, never let us turn from the faith in joining unscriptural practices.

We have already used the phrase "unity-in-diversity" in this article. It involves fellowshipping those who practice and teach things which we do not view as right, yet for peace and harmony, we accept such. Isn't this concept fostered by the spirit that, if we can't convert or change them, we should therefore just join them in condemning nothing and accepting most everything? Brethren are perverting Romans 14 to help them fellowship and join those whom they feel they cannot convert. God does not expect any of us to convert everyone with whom we might differ. Jesus did not do so and neither did the apostles or disciples of the Lord. Though we are not expected to convert everyone, we are to keep trying and always contend for the truth. God expects us to stand for the truth and have convictions that will stand. Faithful men of God are those who stand for the truth "and have no fellowship with the unfruitful works of darkness, but rather reprove them" (Eph. 5:11).

There are brethren and churches that are losing heart in preaching the simple gospel of Christ. They are actually apologizing for the truth being preached. If there is any conviction in them, it is manifested in condemning faithful servants of God for preaching the truth. Many of these brethren and churches have in years past displayed faithfulness to the plea of truth, but now it is different. They find it more convenient to join what they feel they can not convert. This is a disgrace to Christ and true righteousness. May God help us all to keep on doing right regardless what others might do!

I'm Sorry

These words are often spoken. Perhaps a day does not go by but that we utter this expression. We commonly make mistakes or blunders that should not cause us to rejoice. There is no time for a Christian to rejoice in hurting any individual. As one meditates upon such deeds, sorrow should prevail in our hearts and we need to be ready to say "I'm sorry." It is good for us to feel and express the sentiment of sorrow for misfortunes that we might bring upon others.

The expression should be spoken with sincerity. It is easy to say things that are spoken without the true meaning being involved. Jesus said of some, "This people draweth nigh unto me with their mouth, and honoureth me with their lips; but their heart is far from me" (Matt. 15:8). We need to say what we mean and mean what we say. It is convenient for people to use this expression to merely relieve them from the consequence of their deeds. When they say "I'm sorry," the expression does not actually come from the heart and their actions later evidence this to be true. Recently, I was confronted with a person who felt that I had made a mistake. Though it was not really something of great significance, I stated that I was sorry for what had occurred. His reply was, "That doesn't cut it." He felt some compensation should accompany the expression and he was possibly within his rights to say so. One of the better ways to suggest our sincerity is to endeavor to show that our deeds are in accord with saying "I'm sorry." An individual said he was sorry for his failure to produce as a partner in a project. He was told that in the dictionary "sorry" is just a little before "spit" and "spite." Though this can be carried to extremes, fruits of sorrow were evidently what he was expecting to accompany the expression.

Paul wrote of sorrow in 2 Corinthians 7: "For though I made you sorry with a letter, I do not repent, though I did repent: for I perceive that the same epistle hath made you sorry, though it were but for a season. Now I rejoice, not that ye were made sorry, but that ye sorrowed to repentance: for ye were made sorry after a godly manner, that ye might receive damage by us in nothing. For godly sorrow worketh repentance to salvation not to be repented of: but the sorrow of the world worketh death" (vv. 8-10). These verses reveal different categories of sorrow. There is godly sorrow and sorrow of the world. Godly sorrow worketh repentance to salvation. The sorrow of the world worketh death. Godly sorrow is after a godly manner and can produce repentance. The sorrow of the world worketh death that certainly is not pleasing in the sight of the Lord. When we say "I'm sorry" are we expressing godly sorrow or sorrow of the world?

There are examples of these sorrows in individuals depicted in the New Testament books. The rich young ruler came to Jesus and asked what he should do to inherit eternal life. Jesus told him to keep the commandments. He related that these he had kept from his youth. His next question was, "What lack I yet?" Jesus said unto him, "If thou wilt be perfect, go and sell that thou hast, and give to the poor, and thou shalt have treasure in heaven: and come and follow me. But when the young man heard that saying, he went away sorrowful: for he had great possessions" (Matt. 19:20-22). Yes, he experienced sorrow, but it was sorrow of the world. He was not ready to pay the cost of discipleship. These worldly possessions meant more to him than the blessings available in following Jesus.

Actually, he said "I'm sorry" to Jesus, but I'm keeping what I have rather than obeying your commandments. Perhaps Judas Iscariot would fall under this category of sorrow. The account in Matthew 27:3-5 suggests that he experienced sorrow regarding his betrayal of Jesus. His sorrow literally worked death as he "departed, and went and hanged himself" (v. 5).

Godly sorrow involves being sorry for one's sins. The sinner comes to acknowledge that the will of God has been violated and the Lord's forgiveness is needed. Such an attitude motivates one to repent and conform to God's requirements. No one becomes a Christian without experiencing godly sorrow. On the day of Pentecost in Acts 2, there were those pricked in their hearts. They were sorry for their part in crucifying the son of God. They asked what to do that they might call on the name of the Lord and be right in the sight of God. They were told to repent and be baptized in the name of Jesus Christ (v. 38). With godly sorrow in their hearts, it was no problem in gladly receiving the word and being baptized. (v. 41). So many today are sorry, but it is not godly sorrow that worketh repentance. When one has done wrong, it is good to hear the person say "I'm sorry." But is it sorrow because one has been caught in the wrong and nothing more than sorrow of the world? Or is it, sorrow of a godly manner that leads one to repent of the wrong to be right in the sight of the Lord? We need to prayerfully think on these things!

Inconsistency Can Be Over Emphasized

There are some legitimate principles that are derived from one being consistent in truth. Certainly consistency is a jewel and that which is greatly desirable. We should always make an effort to practice what we preach. We should be active in living in accord with the truth that we believe and have professed. Christians should abhor inconsistency and make a diligent effort throughout life to be free of such. There is little to be admired in the life of an individual who is grossly inconsistent. However, in our condemnation of inconsistency, let's be careful not to overemphasize the subject. It needs to be kept in its proper and rightful perspective.

Inconsistency Is Overemphasized

When one believes or uses it to void truth. The word of God determines or establishes truth in religion. Christ said that his Father's word is truth (John 17:17). The fact that an individual professing to follow God's word does not live in accord with it does not change the truth. Jesus said, "Heaven and earth shall pass away, but my words shall not pass away" (Matt. 24:25). Man's hypocritical actions are not going to make the word of God any less the truth. Yet, it appears at times some people feel that, if they can find an inconsistency in some one who knows the truth and teaches it to others, then that inconsistency destroys or voids the truth that is taught. A hypocritical life may blind others from recognizing truth, but it doesn't lessen our obligation to obey it and live consistent with it. One may preach that it is sinful to commit adultery and then while teaching it, practice adultery. Such a sinful life cannot be influential for the truth, but it does not make void the truth. It is still the truth that men sin in committing adultery and "they which do such things shall not inherit the kingdom of God" (Gal. 5:19-21). Paul wrote of the Cretians, "They profess that they know God; but in works they deny him, being abominable, and disobedient, and unto every good work reprobate" (Tit. 1:16). Are we to conclude that their inconsistency made it wrong for men to profess to know God? Certainly not! Their inconsistency did not destroy the weight of truth. Jesus said of the scribes and Pharisees, "All therefore whatsoever they bid you observe, that observe and do; but do not ye after their works, for they say, and do not" (Matt. 23:3). They were alerted to be aware of inconsistencies, but not to over emphasize them.

When one uses it to justify his own sins. It seems to be a common practice with some to pick out an inconsistency in some individual and use such to justify his own failure before God. The

Bible would have us understand that every man shall bear his own burden (Gal. 6:5). The inconsistent, hypocritical action of another certainly gives us no license to sin or justify our failure before God. If this were true, then why bother with knowing what God's will is toward us? Just wait for the inconsistency of some brother and dwell on such for justification of our sins. Now, it may sound ridiculous and truly it is as far as the word of God is concerned; however, this must be what some believe by what they say concerning inconsistencies of others. If a person is guilty of not practicing what he professes, we ought to exhort and admonish such a one without attempting to use his inconsistencies as a form of exemption for our own irregular actions. There are hypocrites in the church! This is the same old cry that some have made time and time again. Perhaps at times they are right, but God will deal with the hypocrites in the church and such will not justify any man from not obeying the gospel and living a faithful life in Christ.

When one permits such to lessen his zeal for the Lord's work. Christians are to be zealous of good works. "Who gave himself for us, that he might redeem us from all iniquity, and purify unto himself a peculiar people, zealous of good works" (Tit. 2:14). Christ is the perfect example that we are to follow. He lived a beautiful consistent life. Whatever men might do or might not do, we still have Jesus to follow who never failed anyone desirous of doing God's will. Men seem to forget this and take their eyes off the Christ. They observe the inconsistencies of men and find themselves losing interest in the Lord's cause. Peter was inconsistent. Paul wrote, "But when Peter was come to Antioch, I withstood him to the face, because he was to be blamed. For before that certain came from James, he did eat with the Gentiles: but when they were come, he withdrew and separated himself, fearing them which were of the circumcision. And the other Jews dissembled likewise with him; insomuch that Barnabas also was carried away with their dissimulation" (Gal. 2:11-13). Paul rebuked Peter in helping him overcome this weakness. However, there is no evidence of such causing Paul to lessen his zeal for doing right. May we abhor inconsistencies, but never to the extent of perverting or over emphasizing the meaning of the word.

Is It A Sin To Change In Religion?

When one considers this question, it is like various other questions that one faces. Before a plausible and scriptural answer can be given, one needs to know what the change is that a person considers in religion. The question from an open standpoint might be well answered "Yes" and "No." Certainly, it is no sin to change in religion when one considers that becoming a Christian in itself is the greatest of changes. When one is converted, he has been affected by change. In obedience to the gospel, one has changed his heart, will, allegiance, and state to conform to Christ. Faith changes the heart (Acts 15:9); repentance affects the will (Matt. 21:28-30); confession involves our allegiance (Rom. 10:10); and baptism changes our state (Gal. 3:26-27; 1 Pet. 3:21). Sin is a transgression of law. The unconverted individual is the one in sin. If he is to be pleasing unto God, he must change or be converted to Christ in obedience to the gospel of Christ. The book of Acts abounds in relating cases of religious individuals who changed in religion. Among these were the devout Jews in Acts 2, the Ethiopian eunuch of Acts 8, Cornelius and his household in Acts 10, and Lydia in Acts 16. All of these were religious, but they changed from religious error to the truth. When the truth was preached to them, they did not hesitate to change in religion! They did what many need to do today and that is to change from a false religion to the acceptance of the truth. Truth saves while error condemns!

After becoming a Christian, one must continue in following the truth. There have been those who have changed from truth to error. Paul speaks of Demas, "For Demas hath forsaken me, having loved this present world" (2 Tim. 4:10). Here is an example of it being sinful to change in religion. It appears that Demas changed from the love of Christ to the love of this present world. Peter speaks of some, "For if after they have escaped the pollutions of the world through the knowledge of the Lord and Saviour Jesus Christ, they are again entangled therein, and overcome, the latter end is worse with them than the beginning. For it had been better for them not to have known the way of righteousness, than, after they have known it, to turn from the holy commandment delivered unto them" (2 Pet.2:20-21). Having been converted, they ceased to follow the truth. They sinfully changed in religion from truth to error.

The Christian should always be ready to give up any false view in order to accept that which is the truth. Over the years, many of us permitted ourselves to be deceived in thinking that many of the innovations and brotherhood schemes were in harmony with the Sriptures. Seeing that these projects were unscriptural, the only course left for a true disciple of Christ to follow is to change and accept the truth. To continue in error would be to practice sin. It would be sinful not to change. Yet, in some circles, brethren seem to feel that, if a man changes his views, he is wrong. It is never wrong to change from error to truth. It is always wrong to change from truth to error.

I hear brethren boasting that they stand now where they have always stood. Well and good, if they have always stood in the truth. With some of these, it is not well and good for even now they are not contending for the truth. They cannot give one book, chapter, and verse for what they are teaching. Some of us have had to make changes. It was a shame that we were wrong and deceived, but there is no shame in making a change to accept the truth. A Christian should always be open minded enough to investigate and, if wrong, to change. We should always be able to give the authority for our change. Some change for convenience's sake and not for conviction. When asked for the word of God for their position, they are not able to give it. Pride, convenience, and prestige are motivating principles that lead men to change from truth to error. The love of the world gets them as it did Demas. All the "Demas's" are not dead by any respect.

There are brethren today in congregations in which the truth is not being preached or practiced. Error exists and yet they continue on! They belittle denominational people for not changing from error to truth and yet they continue right on in error themselves. Evidently, they feel people will speak of them as being fickle or double minded if they change. The devil has such a hold on them that they believe if is sinful to make a change. But change they must if a home in heaven will be their eternal abode. When you are found to be wrong, don't be afraid to change from error to truth. A change from error to another form of error will not be the answer. It takes truth to save and we should "buy the truth, and sell it not" (Prov. 23:3).

Job's Wife

A great deal is related in the Scriptures regarding the value of a wife. "And the Lord God said, It is not good that the man should be alone, I will make him an help meet for him" (Gen. 2:18). "Therefore shall a man leave his father and his mother, and shall cleave unto his wife: and they shall be one flesh" (Gen. 2:24). In praising a wife, the writer of Proverbs stated in generalization: "Whoso findeth a wife findeth a good thing, and obtaineth favor of the Lord" (Prov. 18:22). Again, he asked the question: "Who can find a virtuous woman? For her price is far above rubies. The heart of her husband doth safely trust in her, so that he shall have no need of spoil. She will do him good and not evil all the days of her life" (Prov. 31:10-12).

It is *often* said that behind every good man there are two good women—his mother and wife. There have been exceptions to this statement, but generally it is true. Job had a wife. The first two chapters of Job revealed the calamities that befell this righteous man who "was perfect and upright, and one that feared God, and eschewed evil" (Job 1:1). Satan said that Job would curse God to his face if his substance were taken from him. God told Satan, "all that he hath is in thy power; only upon himself put not forth thy hand. So Satan went forth from the presence of the Lord" (Job 1:12). In swift successions, Job's possessions were taken from him and his seven sons and three daughters were killed, but Job did not curse God as Satan said he would. "In all this Job sinned not, nor charged

God foolishly" (Job 1:22). Satan did not give up and still contended that Job could be moved to curse God. "And Satan answered the Lord, and said, Skin for skin, yea, all that a man hath will he give for his life. But put forth thine hand now, and touch his bone and his flesh, and he will curse thee to thy face. And the Lord said unto Satan, Behold, he is in thine hand; but save his life. So went Satan forth from the presence of the Lord, and smote Job with sore boils from the sole of his foot unto his crown" (Job 2:4-7). But Job had a wife! He had been deprived of his possessions and children. The boils evidently were causing him to suffer tremendously, but his wife had not been taken from him. What we know of Job's wife is found in Job 2:9-10: "Then said his wife unto him, Dost thou still retain thine integrity? Curse God, and die. But he said unto her, Thou speakest as one of the foolish women speaketh. What? Shall we receive good at the hand of God, and shall we not receive evil? In all this did not Job sin with his lips." From these two verses, we concluded that Job's wife recognized the existence of God, served Satan's cause, felt that sins were punished by afflictions, emphasized this present life, didn't do her husband's thinking, and all in all, she spoke foolishly.

Wives have been known to offer splendid suggestions to their husbands. The wife of Pilate did so as we read in Matthew 27:19: "When he was set down on the judgment seat, his wife sent unto him, saying, Have thou nothing to do with that just man: for I have suffered many things this day in a dream because of him." To curse God is never splendid advice! Whether conscious of it or not, Job's wife was an ally of Satan. Some years ago, while teaching a ladies' Bible class, I spoke concerning Job's wife and made the observation that, in her direction to her husband, she was serving Satan's cause. One of the ladies vehemently defended her actions. She felt Job's wife could not bear to see him suffer any longer. Her heart went out to him and felt he would be better off if he were dead. I tried to help her see that she was calling upon her husband to curse God and that was exactly what Satan was saying that Job could be led to do. Perhaps the lady had a point in thinking Job would have been better dead than to live in the condition he was in. On occasions, we have said of individuals who were suffering so tremendously that they would be better off if they were dead. This should only be said of those who are God's children and those who could die in the Lord (Rev. 14:13). Never could it be said of those who would curse God and die. I tried to help the lady see that her conclusion was wrong, but I never seemed to convince her. She continued to make a case for Job's wife and could not see her as serving the cause of Satan by telling her husband to curse God and die. What if Job had listened to his wife and done what she said? Who would have been right in what they said about the faith of Job? Would it have been God or Satan?

It is good for husbands to accept suggestions and advice from their wives, but we need to see that our actions are in keeping with the will of God. Job retained his integrity and told his wife that she spoke as one of the foolish women when she told him to curse God and die. The book of Job ends in a beautiful way. Faithful Job's possessions were restored twofold and he again had seven sons and three daughters. Nothing more is mentioned of Job's wife. Do you suppose she ever admitted that she spoke as one of the foolish women?

Jonah, The Man Who Tried the Impossible

"But Jonah rose up to flee unto Tarshish from the presence of the Lord, and went down to Joppa; and he found a ship going to Tarshish: so he paid the fare thereof, and went down into it, to go with them unto Tarshish from the presence of the Lord" (Jon. 1:3). When one thinks of the book of Jonah, he usually thinks of the big fish that swallowed him. Many people consider the book simply a big fish tale. The book has been ridiculed by skeptics and modernists as being a religious novel rather than consisting of historical truth. The basis of their ridicule is centered around the great fish swallowing Jonah. What's so astonishing here? "The Lord had prepared a great fish to swallow up Jonah. And Jonah was in the belly of the fish three days and three nights" (Jon. 1:17). This appeared to be a special fish; however, it would appear that some species of whales that now exist could possibly swallow a man. Is the ridicule and unbelief due to the record stating that Jonah lived three days and nights in the fish's belly? If one can believe that God created the world in the miracles of Genesis 1, why should his sustaining Jonah's life in the belly of a great fish be considered incredible? In other words, if one accepts the miracles of creation, what problem should there be in accepting an isolated or special miracle as found in the book of Jonah or any other book of the Bible? The Bible is so developed that one cannot reject a part without reflecting upon the whole. In the account before us, Jesus placed certification on the book of Jonah and its contents by saying, "for as Jonah was three days and nights in the whale's belly; so shall the Son of man be three days and nights in the heart of the earth" (Matt. 12:40). Consistency demands that we take both accounts as truth or reject both as false!

There is much more in the book of Jonah than the story of a man being swallowed by a great fish. It represents the exploits of a man who tried the impossible. What was the impossible? Disobeying God? No! For a man is a free moral agent who has the ability to refuse or accept the will of God. The impossibility is that Jonah tried to flee from the presence of God and his responsibility to God. God is everywhere (Acts 17:27-28; Ps. 139:7-9). Our responsibility to his will is just as necessary in one place as another. Whether in Joppa, the belly of the great fish, or Tarshish, Jonah could not flee from God's presence. God ordered Jonah to Nineveh. He fled in the opposite direction. The devil will help those who try to flee from God. There was a ship to Tarshish with room for Jonah and Jonah had the fare for the voyage.

Why did Jonah attempt to side step his responsibility and flee from God? We do not know a great deal regarding his background. He was a Hebrew, the son of Amittai. We do not know where he lived or where he was when God appeared to him giving him the call to go and preach to Nineveh. Let us suggest some possible explanations as to why at first he went the wrong way and became such a backslider that even the great fish could not stomach him. "And the Lord spake unto the fish, and it vomited out Jonah upon the dry land" (Jon. 2:10).

May have felt that he was unequal to the task. From a human standpoint, to go and preach to Nineveh was quite a big order. Many of us would quake at such an assignment. There are many less assignments today that, if we aren't careful, we will find ourselves pleading that we can't do them.

May have felt that he had been doing enough. We hear individuals today intimate such when called upon to work in the kingdom of God. The attitude of some people is to let someone else do the work. Friend, someone has to do it if it is to be done! What if all people had such an attitude? Would anything be accomplished?

May have considered the task too unpleasant. At times, it is a very unpopular thing to tell people of their sins and their doom. There are preachers today who do not do so because they are afraid to do it! John the Baptist was beheaded because he dared to accuse Herod of wrongdoing (Matt. 14).

May have been prejudiced. Jonah, being a Hebrew, may have had some prejudice in preaching to Nineveh, a Gentile city. Who wants to preach to those Gentiles? This may have been his attitude. Prejudice may have existed and it is even more implied by Jonah's anger after the Lord had spared the city when Nineveh repented. Prejudice certainly keeps people from fulfilling their obligations before God!

Perhaps he felt that he did not have the time, talent, or resources that were essential to the job. Such, at least, are the excuses of many in our time. God would not have called him to perform the task if Jonah were not able to perform the task or lacked tools in doing it. It is fatal to say "No" to God! There are two courses available to us today—downward to Tarshish or upward to Nineveh. Jonah renounced his first decision and obeyed God. He turned from Tarshish and fleeing from God to Nineveh and duty. Are we trying the impossible in fleeing from God and our responsibility to him?

Just A Christian

The greatest thing that anyone can ever do is to become a Christian. When one fails to become a Christian and live faithfully in Christ, that person has failed in life. Whatever else he might accomplish is insignificant to his failure in becoming a Christian. We are prone to believe that many people make light of the value of being a Christian. We wonder at times if some professed Christians actually realize what it means to live the life of a Christian. The word "Christian" is found three times in the KJV of the New Testament. It is to be found in Acts 11:26, 26: 28, and 1 Peter 4:16. A Christian has put on Christ. Paul informed the Galatians: "For ye are all the children of God by faith in Christ Jesus. For as many of you as have been baptized into Christ have put on Christ" (Gal. 3:26-27). Surely no one will affirm that one is a Christian who has failed to "put on Christ." When one has enough faith in Christ to repent of his sins and, upon a confession of faith in Christ, to be baptized for the remission of sins, that individual has put on Christ—he has become a Christian (Mark 16:16; Acts 17:30; 22:16; Rom. 10:10; 6:3-4).

Though the word "Christian" is abused by many religionists in our time, those who truly love the Lord should do all in their power to keep the word and all it stands for consistent with the oracles of God. We feel on occasions that there are individuals who actually use the word in a plea for neutrality. When some issues come up that face us in contending for the truth, some find it convenient to say that they are "neither—nor." They are just Christians! On the surface, that might sound wonderful and it might even touch the hearts of the more unassuming. But let us go a little deeper. Shouldn't a Christian above all be ready to stand for the truth and have convictions that he is prepared to defend? When a decision involving truth or error arises, can we ignore standing for the truth and exerting an influence for truth by saying, "We are just Christians and want no part of it"? A Christian is called upon to study and determine what the truth is upon every subject that might affect his soul and the purity of the Lord's church. Peter wrote to Christians, "But sanctify the Lord God in your hearts: and be ready always to give an answer to every man that asketh you a reason of the hope that is in you, with meekness and fear" (1 Pet. 3:15). It should not be considered embarrassing or offensive when some one calls upon Christians to express their convictions on matters affecting their soul salvation.

The majority of the denominational church members would say that they are Christians. To state that they are, does not make it so! The Christian is one who is obedient to Christ (Heb. 5:8-9) and not to some man-made church and doctrine! When a member of the Christian Church professes to be a Christian, is it wrong to ask that one of his view concerning instrumental music? Certainly not! But according to some of our brethren, when one says, "I'm just a Christian," that takes care of the whole matter and exempts one from any personal stand. Actually, in the true meaning of what is involved in being a Christian, it obligates a person to be prepared to give an answer for his convictions and all he believes. The true and faithful Christian says that he is a Christian and then is ready to take a stand for all the truth of the word of God.

It is regrettable that problems and issues arise among the Lord's people wherein members are divided. No one who has the spirit of Christ should rejoice in this! However, we should always remember that this is not something new. The early church in the days of the apostles had its problems and there were definite issues that had to be faced. Professed Christians were then called upon to express their convictions. Matters arose wherein for some to say "we are just Christians" did not altogether convey their stand on a particular subject. For example, in Acts 15, we note that there were some teaching that, except the Gentile Christians be circumcised after the manner of Moses, they could not be saved. Some teaching was affecting the church! Paul and Barnabas "had no small dissension and disputation with them." They expressed themselves as Christians against such false teaching. They did not rest upon the fact that they were Christians and that such within itself would convey their convictions.

Brethren, we need to be careful and not to pervert the beautiful word "Christian" by making it represent neutrality. The Lord's side exists and we need to be a part of it in every decision that is to be made. Jesus said, "He that is not with me is against me; and he that gathereth not with me scattereth abroad" (Matt. 12:30). Think on these things!

Lord, Increase Our Faith (1)
(Luke 17:5)

Christ had previously spoken in reference to offenses and forgiveness (vv. 1-4). The disciples most likely considered these commands to be difficult. They asked for an increase of faith that they might follow the teachings of Christ. This was a request that their faith might be increased. We could hardly deem such as prayer for faith as some have desired to make their request teach. "Increase" is defined as "to become greater; to grow; augment." "Faith" might be defined as "taking hold on God, on Christ, on the Holy Spirit, on the promises with all the heart, mind, and strength" or "taking God at His word."

Faith is something that can be increased. This is quite evident from the request of the disciples. The disciples recognized that they had need of more faith. Faith is increased in the manner or same channel in which it is derived. "So then faith cometh by hearing, and hearing by the word of God" (Rom. 10:17). In requesting that their faith be increased, could not the disciples have been asking Christ to teach them more that such an increase might materialize? Paul's prayer for the brethren at Thessalonica: "We are bound to thank

God always for you, brethren, as it is meet, because that your faith groweth exceedingly" (2 Thess. 1:3). Peter admonished Christians to add to their faith (2 Pet. 1:5-8). How thankful we should be that faith is something that can be added to or increased!

The request of the disciples should be our sentiment and desire. When commandments appear difficult, rather than manifesting a spirit of giving up or rebellion, we should, as the disciples of old, desire that our faith be increased that we might be obedient in all things. Many realize their lack of faith. Some are indifferent and unconcerned. They really see no need of any more faith as their religion is so superficial and they see no reason of drawing any closer to God. They are satisfied in their indifference and unconcern. We are thankful to God that all are not of such sentiment. There are yet those who are interested in increasing their faith and growing before God.

Why Should Disciples Desire To Increase Their Faith?

To Hold What We Have. If we fail to increase, we will soon be decreasing. God's law of disuse is quite applicable. "For unto every one that hath shall be given and he shall have abundance: but from him that hath not shall be taken away even that which he hath" (Matt. 25:29). The greatest assurance of retaining is to be constantly adding. Faith can certainly be lost (1 Tim. 1:19-20).

To Remain True to the Faith and the Commandments of the Lord. The root of indifference is a lack of faith. Those who increase their faith are unlikely to depart or abandon the faith. God's power to keep us is dependent upon our faith. "Who are kept by the power of God through faith unto salvation ready to be revealed in the last time" (1 Pet. 1:5). As one works at increasing his faith, he is lessening the possibility of his being untrue to the truth that is in Christ Jesus.

To Accomplish Greater Things For Christ. Our lack of faith keeps us from doing much. The faithless report of the ten spies and like sentiment of the people of Israel caused God to decree that they would wander in the wilderness until that generation perished (Num. 13). Through faith the land could have been taken, but the people were afraid of the inhabitants of the land. The one talent man was afraid and buried his talent. Lack of faith produces fear that motivates us to reject the beauty and simplicity of God's commandments, which have been designed for our ultimate happiness. We are very prone to limit our faith in God. We are far more inclined to talk of faith in the Lord rather than demonstrate such by faithful labor of love. "And the Lord said, if ye had faith as a grain of mustard seed, ye might say unto this sycamine tree, Be thou plucked up by the root, and be thou planted in the sea; and it should obey you" (Luke 17:6).

To Fortify Ourselves Against Obstacles and Problems That Arise. Events arise that try our faith. Those with little faith often lose it all. Death of loved ones, sickness, and failures in life are parts of the scene of life. We need to increase our faith to have a reserve for such times so that we don't charge God foolishly.

Lord, Increase Our Faith (2)

In the last article we began the study of the request that the disciples made of the Lord, "Lord, increase our faith." Space permitted us to note that faith is something that can be increased and the sentiment of the disciples in this incident should be our sentiment as we confront some commands of the Lord that seem to be more difficult than others. The remaining portion of the article dealt with reasons why we should desire to increase our faith. To hold what we have, to remain true to the faith, to accomplish greater things for the Lord, and to fortify ourselves against obstacles and problems that arise were mentioned. In this article we will be endeavoring to answer the question, "How may we increase our faith?"

This is a question that is often in the minds of sincere individuals. They have come to realize the value of having faith and are cognizant of the fact that their faith needs to increase. They view the exploits of others who demonstrate more faith than they possess and find themselves desirous of being like them. Regarding this question, "How may we increase our faith?" we make the following observations:

Not by some miraculous means. This seems to be what many are seeking. When they think of religion, their minds run in the channel of the mystical and miraculous. This is their conception of religion as a whole. They have been taught that faith can be received in a miraculous way and in a similar manner, it can also be increased. Nothing is any further from the truth! The answer to this question is so simple that it is hard for some to actually grasp. I am pleased to give the prescription, but the results cannot be promised unless one takes it according to directions.

By feeding our faith. Faith grows as it starts. "So then faith cometh by hearing, and hearing by the word of God" (Rom. 10:17). "And many other signs truly did Jesus in the presence of his disciples, which are not written in this book: but these are written, that ye might believe that Jesus is the Christ, the Son of God; and that believing ye might have life through his name" (John 20:30-31). The word of God is food for our faith. The more food we consume the greater probability of our faith being increased. "And now, brethren, I commend you to God and to the word of his grace, which is able to build you up, and to give you an inheritance among all them which are sanctified" (Acts 20:32). One must be careful to keep a pure diet. Peter supplied the answer: "Wherefore laying aside all malice, and all guile, and hypocrisies, and envies, and all evil speaking, as newborn babes, desire the sincere milk of the word, that ye may grow thereby" (1 Pet. 2:1-2). Along with the proper diet, the food must be consumed properly. A proper consumption of spiritual food involves persistence, regularity, and liberality. We must be determined to receive the word of God often and not be afraid to eat a goodly amount of it. Our physical health is in many respects dependent upon our bodies absorbing food persistently, regularly, and liberally. The same is so regarding our spiritual health. If people didn't feed their body more than they feed their faith, they wouldn't have strength to complain about not receiving joy from spiritual endeavors as some do. Food for our faith comes from reading the word, and attending services where the word is preached and in the classes where it is informally discussed. Show me a person who persistently neglects these and I will show you one who is virtually starving his faith!

By exercising our faith. Food without exercise causes a sluggish, unhealthy body. This is equally true in the spiritual realm. We need to give our faith something to do. The Hebrew writer stated, "For every one that useth milk is unskillful in the word of righteousness: for he is a babe. But strong meat belongeth to them that are of full age, even those who by reason of use have their senses exercised to discern both good and evil" (Heb. 5:13-14). Observe in particular the phrase, "who by reason of use have their senses exercised to discern both good and evil." In exercising they had developed and grown to the extent of being able to absorb strong meat that belonged to them of full age.

We exercise our faith in worship, prayer, teaching, and helping others. The teacher in preparing lessons oftentimes gains more than the pupils who hear such. We need to put the word of God to a practical test (Matt. 6:33; Phil. 4:13). This is wonderful exercise. It is the simple answer, but quite profound!

Lot's Wife

In one of the shorter verses of the New Testament, Jesus said, "Remember Lot's wife" (Luke 17:32). One is not able to remember her name or genealogy. These have not been revealed or made known for our remembrance. In fact, we are limited in our knowledge of things to remember concerning the wife of Lot. With the exception of this statement in Luke 17, our knowledge of Lot's wife must be gathered from the events stated in Genesis 19. Regarding the wicked city of Sodom, the two angels told Lot, "For we will destroy this place, because the cry of them is waxen great before the face of the Lord; and the Lord hath sent us to destroy it" (Gen. 19:13). Lot was told, "Arise, take thy wife, and thy two daughters, which are here; lest thou be consumed in the iniquity of the city" (v. 15). The command was given, "Escape for thy life; look not behind thee, neither stay thou in all the plain; escape to the mountain, lest thou be consumed" (v. 17). When the Lord rained upon Sodom and Gomorrah brimstone and fire, Lot's wife "looked back from behind him, and she became a pillar of salt" (v. 26). Only Lot and his two daughters were saved when the city of Sodom was destroyed with fire and brimstone. We are to remember that Lot's wife perished although she:

Was the Wife of a Righteous Man. Peter speaks of Lot as being just and righteous (2 Pet. 2:7-8). The righteous obey the commands of the Lord and that was what Lot did. His wife disobeyed in looking back upon the city of Sodom in its destruction. Righteousness is an individual responsibility. One cannot be righteous for another. Paul wrote, "For every man shall bear his own burden" (Gal. 6:5). Lot's wife had the responsibility of obedience in the same respect as Lot and his two daughters did. The righteousness of one may influence others for good, but it does not obey for them.

Was Warned of Her Danger. "And it came to pass, when they had brought them forth abroad, that he said, Escape for thy life; look not behind thee, neither stay thou in all the plain; escape to the mountain, lest thou be consumed" (Gen. 19:17). The warning was plain and definite. It was made known to her as it was to Lot and his two daughters. She had no ground to plead ignorance. In like manner, there are warnings that Christ has given us which must not be ignored. "Therefore we ought to give the more earnest heed to the things which we have heard, lest at any time we should let them slip. For if the word spoken by angels was stedfast, and every transgression and disobedience received a just recompence of reward; How shall we escape, if we neglect so great salvation. . ." (Heb. 2:1-3). She was warned and we are warned regarding what the Lord expects of us (Acts 3:22-23).

Made Some Effort to Be Saved. It would appear that she along with Lot and her two daughters had departed from Sodom. The wording in verses 16-17 make this known: ". . .the Lord being merciful unto him: and they brought him forth, and set him without the city. And it came to pass, when they brought them forth abroad. . . ." We need to start the effort in being saved and continue in the effort. So many start the race, but they fail to run the race. "And Jesus said unto him, No man, having put his hand to the plough, and looking back, is fit for the kingdom of God" (Luke 9:62). Wouldn't it be wonderful if all who had started were continuing faithful? Our church buildings could hardly contain the attendance!

Committed But One Sin. "But his wife looked back from behind him, and she became a pillar of salt" (Gen. 19:26). The command was "look not behind thee." Lot's wife disobeyed by looking back upon the burning city of Sodom. In doing so she was turned to a pillar of salt. It may be that sentiment motivated her to look back. She was thinking of loved ones and friends who were perishing in the city. Whatever prompted her to look back is immaterial. She looked back and disobeyed the command of God. Someone may say, "I know she committed other sins," but where does one read this in the word of God? It must be in the "second chapter of Jude" for it is not stated in the Scriptures that we have in the canon of the Bible. Another says, "I just can't believe one sin can cause a man to be lost." How many sins are charged against Simon in Acts 8 that prompted Peter to say that his money perished with him? I read where he sinned by the thought of his heart, thinking he could buy the power of laying on of hands from the apostles. There are so many today who are determined to make the Bible read as they want it to read rather than accept what is said. "For whosoever shall keep the whole law, and yet offend in one point, he is guilty of all" (Jas. 2:10). We can get "so smart" that our thoughts are above God's rather than his being above ours (Isa. 55:8-9). We need to seriously remember Lot's wife in the above respects!

May As Well Say Or Do It As To Think It

Have you ever heard someone make such a statement? I have! In fact it is quite often quoted. "You may as well go ahead and say or do it as to think it in your heart." I have often wondered about the merits and truthfulness of such a statement. Somehow the statement doesn't seem to ring true in the complete light of God's dealings with man. Let's examine a few principles that might help in determining whether or not the statement is true. We appreciate the fact that:

Man is accountable for his thoughts. "Keep thy heart with all diligence; for out of it are the issues of life" (Prov. 4:23); "for as he thinketh in his heart, so is he" (Prov. 23:7). "But those things which proceed out of the mouth come forth from the heart; and they defile the man. For out of the heart proceed evil thoughts" (Matt. 15:18-19). Peter told Simon, "Repent therefore of this thy wickedness, and pray God, if perhaps the thought of thine heart may be forgiven thee" (Acts 8:22). Christians are admonished to bring "into captivity every thought to the obedience of Christ" (2 Cor. 10:5). We can certainly sin in thought. We must repent of evil thoughts. Thoughts in a sense control our entire life! Please appreciate such, but is this the answer to our search? Is it as evil to think something as to say or do it? Many people have made the statement. I have heard it all my life. But let's notice further . . . .

An individual's thoughts are his own. In plainer words, we are saying that what a man thinks affects only himself. When he puts the thoughts into action by words or deeds, then others are affected. You may ask for an illustration. Jesus said, ". . . whosoever looketh on a woman to lust after her hath committed adultery with her already in his heart" (Matt. 5:28). This is sin! And granted that lust involves the thought of his heart, it constitutes sin in thought. But such usually affects only one! Let the sinful deed also be committed and then someone else is involved. A young maiden may be deprived of chastity. A home may be destroyed as husband or wife yield to temptation that forever casts a dark suspicion over their fidelity one to another. Have you stopped to think of this when you condoned the statement that "you may as well say or do it as to think it"? We have given an illustration to show that this is not so and many more illustrations could be given. Furthermore . . .

Thoughts void of deeds involve less agony of correction. Evil thoughts must be repented of! Certainly we are aware that these are not condoned by the Lord and man must confess and forsake them to have mercy of the Lord. Repentance of an evil thought would appear to be easier than the thought expressed in word or deed. One may become angry and experience an evil thought but he has enough control to keep from executing his emotion. Is he to be classed on the same level as the one who goes ahead and commits the deed? We are cognizant of the statement of John: "Whosoever hateth his brother is a murderer and ye know that no murderer hath eternal life abiding in him" (1 John 3:13). This verse may be taken to mean that the act is no worse than thinking it. However, John is demonstrating the value of love of brethren and the horribleness of hate. Here is proof again of our accountableness for our thoughts and emotions but not the evidence that the deed is no worse than the thought. David experienced an evil thought toward Bathsheba—the deed was committed and it led to the death of Uriah. Wouldn't it have been easier to have had only the thought to repent of rather than the adulterous act and death of Uriah? That's the point we are trying to make! David said, ". . . and my sin is ever before me" (Ps. 51:3).

Possibly there are men who make such a statement as the one we are examining without stopping to consider the consequence. They do it largely in ignorance. Others, no doubt, have a more sinister motive. They seek self-justification of their deeds. They desire to make it appear that the deed is no worse than the thought in an effort to cover their sinful deeds. They reason that individuals have sinful thoughts and those who have sinful thoughts are just as guilty as those who commit sinful acts. I fail to find this in keeping with scriptural conclusions. Let's be fair with ourselves and above all fair with God and his word. What do you think about it?

Mind Your Own Business

I have always enjoyed listening to the songs by Hank Williams. On one of the tapes, there was a song entitled, "Mind Your Own Business." One of the lines of the lyrics went like this: "If you mind your own business, you won't be minding mine." There was another phrase that said, "If you mind your own business, you'll be busy all the time." Listening to these lyrics, brought to my mind a couple of passages from the New Testament. Paul wrote in 1 Thessalonians 4:11: "And that ye study to be quiet, and to do your own business, and work with your own hands, as we commanded you." Peter had this to say: "But let none of you suffer as a murderer, or as a thief, or as an evildoer, or as a busybody in other men's matters." It is obvious from these verses that a Christian is to take care of his own business and not be a busybody in other men's matters.

Being a busybody has brought about hard feelings and even division among God's children. The commands to abstain from being a busybody are as definite as any of the commands that God calls upon his people to obey.

Like all other commands that God has given, the subject of busybodies can be misunderstood and abused. There are those who feel that anytime a person becomes involved in the affairs of others he becomes a busybody. Perhaps this is the reason why some Christians seem to ignore trying to help others—they do not want to be branded as a busybody. But how can we do what God desires of us without becoming involved in the affairs of others? "Brethren if a man be overtaken in a fault, ye which are spiritual, restore such an one in the spirit of meekness; considering they self, lest thou also be tempted" (Gal. 6:1). How can one truly recognize when one is overtaken in a fault without becoming involved in the lives of others? James wrote, "Brethren, if any of you do err from the truth, and one convert him; let him know, that he which converteth the sinner from the error of his way shall save a soul from death, and shall hide a multitude of sin" (Jas. 5:19-20). The question is similar to what we have already asked. How can one convert a sinner from the error of his way without becoming involved with the one who needs to be converted? When one does become involved and the sinner is brought back to the Lord, the work is wonderful and receives praises of friends and loved ones of the converted sinner. On the other hand, when the effort does not produce desired fruit and the sinner resents what was done for him, don't be surprised if those trying are labeled as busybodies.

Being concerned for the spiritual welfare of others should be recognized as the business of Christians. The word of God does not speak of a busybody as being one trying to help others in spiritual matters. There are so many who want to do their thing without anyone saying anything to them about it. They don't want to be bothered and when something is done to try to help them see the error of their way, they view those who try to help as busybodies.

I can't fully agree with the lyrics of the Hank Williams song that was mentioned in the beginning of this article. "If you mind your own business, you won't be minding mine." Christians are to be their brother's keeper. They have the obligation to mind their own business which involves trying to be helpful in the business of others. It would appear that the busybody whom the word of God condemns is the person who becomes involved in matters that are not of any spiritual significance.

There are number of examples that might be cited to illustrate such. I recall a wedding ceremony where the photographer took pictures during the ceremony. One of the witnesses became upset at his doing so and voiced derogatory remarks. When it was mentioned to me, my reply was, "It is their wedding and they can have what they want so long as it is not sinful." Photographers have asked me beforehand about this very thing and I have told them to see the couple who is to be married. It is their wedding and their business. I sometimes call my wife "mother." Actually, she is not my mother, but what sin have I committed in calling her mother? A lady had something to say about it and I simply told her it was none of her business. Some children call their parents by their first names. They do not refer to them as Mother or Daddy. That has always been unusual to me, but that is their business and who am I to be involved in something that does not involve sin or spiritual matters?

It is a sad state of affairs when Christians will not try to help those in the body of Christ to be faithful to the Lord. Such an attitude and disposition is so contrary to the life of Christ. Christ became involved for us. He gave his very life that we might be saved. If we are to follow the example of Christ, we will never be afraid to help others though we might be called busybodies. It just might be that, in order to cover our spiritual laziness and apathy, we hide behind the word "busybody." We do not want to be looked upon as a busybody and so we go right on refusing to become involved and continuing to neglect our responsibilities one to another.

Misrepresentation

In John 21:18-19, Jesus related to Peter by what death he should glorify God. "Then Peter, turning about, seeth the disciple whom Jesus loved following; which also leaned on his breast at supper, and said, Lord, which is he that betrayeth thee? Peter seeing him saith to Jesus, Lord, and what shall this man do? Jesus saith unto him, If I will that he tarry till I come, what is that to thee? Follow thou me. Then went this saying abroad among the brethren, that that disciple should not die: yet Jesus said not unto him, He shall not die; but, If I will that he tarry till I come, what is that to thee?" (John 21:20-23). What Jesus said regarding John was misrepresented! The saying went abroad among the brethren that was a misrepresentation of what Jesus had said.

It has been said that when a person is misrepresented it is either due to the one responsible being either green or mean—"green" referring to ignorance and "mean" to intentionally desiring to harm the person who is misrepresented. Misrepresentation can do a great deal of harm to those who are misrepresented. If Jesus were misrepresented, his disciples are not above the master and not immune to such happening to us today.

Those who professed to be the Lord's disciples should be very careful to avoid misrepresenting anyone. We certainly do not crave misrepresentation of our beliefs, and we should not be reckless in quoting the position of others. "Therefore all things whatsoever ye would that men should do to you, do ye even so to them: for this is the law and the prophets" (Matt. 7:12). When one follows this rule given by Jesus, he finds no room for misrepresenting what others teach or for what they stand. "For by thy words thou shalt be justified, and by thy words thou shalt be condemned" (Matt. 12:36). We need to guard our words and be careful of what we say lest we be found sinning against others by falsely representing the position they assume. Remember that this can be done by being green or mean!

While viewing this subject of misrepresentations, another thought comes to mind. Individuals have cried, "I have been misrepresented" when actually such has not occurred and they give no proof of such happening. Their position will not stand the test of truth and they camouflage such by feigning to being misrepresented. On more than one occasion, I have encountered the scenario when those who cried misrepresentation, were offered a piece of paper and a good writing pen with the request that the position they hold be stated. *They never did it!* Yet, they continued to tell brethren that they were being misrepresented. I do not have confidence in a person who will not state what he believes on any given subject. If he is preaching the truth and believes he is doing so, what does he have to hide? The problem is that there are those who desire to please all and to protect their position so they keep on speaking about being misrepresented. I recall years ago that brother N. B. Hardeman at Freed-Hardeman College made the observation: "When asked what you believe on any Bible subject, one can state it plainly on a penny postcard and still have plenty of room to also include a wholesome greeting to the party who requested it." That was a good while ago when one thinks of a penny postcard being used. Believe me, there are those who do not stand for the truth and they continually cry misrepresentation when such is not the case. The thing bothering them is that they are being represented accurately and they are not ready to acknowledge it.

We come to another consideration regarding this subject. Some years ago, a congregation or so, prepared questionnaires regarding various Bible subjects and mailed them to the preachers that they supported and others who were scheduled to come for meetings. This was not done as a brotherhood project! The questions were asked of those with whom the congregations had personal contact regarding financial support and preaching in gospel meetings. They were simply asked what they believed and preached on certain subjects. I may have been partially responsible for one of these churches becoming involved with the questionnaires. While laboring with the Pruett and Lobit congregation in Baytown, Texas, there were reports regarding some of the thirty preachers that we were helping support as to what they were preaching or not preaching on various subjects. Some time later the questions were mailed to these preachers regarding their positions. They were simple questions which involved a simple yes or no. At that time, I had left Texas and was being partially supported by the Baytown church. I received one of the questionnaires myself and it took me about ten minutes to answer the questions. Most all of the preachers had no problem with the questions. However, there were a few who cried, "The church has drafted a creed" and we condemn such as unscriptural. When is it a church creed when a preacher is asked what he believes on any subject? I was honored to be asked the questions and give the answer that no one could misunderstand my position on any of these subjects. Others possibly didn't want any part of it because it smoked out their positions and eliminated them from being able to cry: "I've been misrepresented"!

More Than a Bumper Sticker

There are people who will stick most anything on their automobiles. Some of these stickers are of a vulgar nature and convey the hearts of individuals who would publicize such filth. There are also some that are quite decent and bring a smile to our faces. Another popular category are those that are religious in nature. I followed a van last week that had a number of stickers pasted on the large rear window. I remember some of them: "JESUS IS LIFE," "I LOVE JESUS," "JESUS SAVES," and some others, but I do not recall the wording. One must acknowledge that, if you are prone to display something on your automobile, these signs are far better than something that is of a vulgar and filthy nature.

However, as I followed this vehicle that certainly advertised Jesus, the thought came to my mind if the one responsible for these signs really believed what was on them? Take the one that read, "I LOVE JESUS," do you suppose the one who placed it there really loves Jesus as Jesus directs and expects of his followers? In other words, it is one thing to declare something and, on the other hand, a different thing in being genuine in our declaration. It is quite easy to say "I LOVE JESUS" and not be consistent with what Jesus would have us to do in demonstrating that love. Jesus said, "If ye love me, keep my commandments" (John 14:15). Again in the same chapter, "He that hath my commandments, and keepeth them, he it is that loveth me: and he that loveth me shall be loved of my father, and I will love him, and will manifest myself to him" (John 14:23). Numerous other passages could be related which definitely teach that the love of Jesus and his commandments are inseparable. We truly show our love for Jesus in keeping his commandments. It is good for people to say that they love Jesus, but such love is of no value and quite empty if the love is not proven by doing what Jesus authorizes. "And why call ye me, Lord, Lord, and do not the things which I say?" (Luke 6:46). The real meaning of our love for Jesus is in declaring it and demonstrating what we declare by our obedience to what he commands of us.

I have known some folks who were very affluent in saying that they loved Jesus, but when their life and actions were viewed in the light of what Jesus wants men to do, they even became offended by it being mentioned to them. When it came to the subject of obedience in baptism, they didn't believe it was necessary and scoffed at the idea of such being a part of loving Jesus. What did Jesus say about the subject? Listen: "And he said unto them, Go ye into all the world, and preach the gospel to every creature. He that believeth and is baptized shall be saved; but he that believeth not shall be damned" (Mark 16:15-16). These are the words of Jesus whom people say they love. Yet, how many truly believe what Jesus said and obey what he says? I do not know who the people were in the van that had these signs. I am not attempting to determine what they had done or not done in obeying Christ, but I would strongly be of the opinion that many would scoff at the idea that their loving Jesus involved obedience to what he says in Mark 16:16. Many other commands of the Lord could be stated which require the obedience of man in showing love for him. All of us who profess to know the Lord must be careful in doing and respecting all that he says and not just a part of it.

How about the purity of our lives? Do we love him enough to keep ourselves pure? Those who truly love the Lord will strive to abstain from every appearance of evil and not fashion their lives after the pursuits of the world (1 Thess. 5:22; Rom. 12:1-2). How about our giving to the Lord? It is easy for some to profess that they love Jesus and give only the scraps of their prosperity to him. Concerning the matter of contributing, Paul reminded the Corinthians that their giving was "proof of the sincerity of their love" (2 Cor. 8:9).

Yes, our love for Christ involves keeping his commandments from sincere hearts *and such involves far more than posting bumper stickers!* How about giving as we are prospered? Love is not just a command, but all that he commands us. Yes, it will take far more than a bumper sticker to give us a heavenly home!

More Than Teaching

It is very difficult to overemphasize the value of teaching the truth to an individual. The very heart of the religion that Jesus presents to the world rests upon teaching. One is drawn to Christ through instruction. "No one can come to me, except the Father which hath sent me draw him: and I will raise him up at the last day. It is written in the prophets, And they shall be all taught of God. Every man therefore that hath heard, and hath learned of the Father, cometh unto me" (John 6:44-45). As the passage clearly states, the drawing is not one of a miraculous process, but through a person being taught and learning of God. Where teaching has not been administered, drawing power has not been administered. In the great commission according to Matthew, Jesus pointed to teaching as a prerequisite for being saved and to the need of continued teaching of the saved regarding all things that Jesus had for them to observe. "Go ye therefore, and teach all nations, baptizing them in the name of the Father, and of the Son, and of the Holy Ghost: Teaching them to observe all things whatsoever I have commanded you: and lo, I am with you alway, even unto the end of the world. Amen" (Matt. 28:19-20).

We need teaching and we need a great deal of it. It might be truthfully said that no one outgrows the need for teaching. On occasions, we say of some one that by the actions of that person it is evident that he needs teaching. I would suppose that all of us at one time or another have made such a statement. It could possibly be that the thing responsible for the person failing God was not in the lack of teaching, but a failure to manifest in his life what is to accompany or follow teaching. There are those who have been taught. They can relate God's instructions or his will toward them. They need something more than teaching. They possibly need . . .

To apply the teaching to themselves. So many hear the word, but they never seem to apply it to their own lives. Teaching that is of profit must be applied. When the Bereans were taught the word, ". . . they received the word with all readiness of mind, and searched the scriptures daily whether those things were so" (Acts 17:11). Jesus condemned the Scribes and Pharisees for failing to make proper application to themselves (Matt. 23:29-33). We need to examine our hearts with what is being taught (2 Cor. 13:5).

Obedience to the truth that is taught. To be obedient to Christ, one must be taught what Christ expects in obedience. However, one may be taught and never obey the truth. There are those who stubbornly defy what the truth directs them to believe and do. Jesus said of some, "For this people's heart is waxed gross, and their ears are dull of hearing, and their eyes they have closed; lest at any time they should see with their eyes, and hear with their ears, and should understand with their heart, and should be converted, and I should heal them" (Matt. 13:15). Effort had been made to instruct these people that they might obey the truth. They needed to open their hearts to the truth taught and conform their lives to the precious word of God. Teaching had been exerted upon them. They weren't lacking in being taught. They lacked, as so many lack today, obedience to what had been taught them. James calls upon us to be more than hearers. We are to be doers of the word. "But be ye doers of the word, and not hearers only, deceiving your own selves. For if any be a hearer of the word, and not a doer, he is like unto a man beholding his natural face in a glass: For he beholdeth himself, and goeth his way, and straightway forgetteth what manner of man he was. But whoso looketh into the perfect law of liberty, and continueth therein, he being not a forgetful hearer, but a doer of the work, this man shall be blessed in his deed" (Jas. 1:22-25). There is certainly no profit in hearing only! Those who were baptized on Pentecost day in Acts 2 were those "that gladly received His word" (Acts 2:41). We need an obedient reception of the truth that has been taught us.

Conviction for the truth taught. Conviction requires courage and effort. It is not by following the course of least resistance. The failure of some is not due to a lack of teaching. It stems back to a lack of conviction for the truth that they have been taught. One may be able to quote the Bible from Genesis through Revelation, but what good is it to his soul salvation if he doesn't make an application of it to himself in obeying the truth and having enough conviction to stand for it in love? Paul said with conviction, "I am set for the defence of the gospel" (Phil. 1:17). He wasn't sitting on the fence. He was set for a *defence* of the gospel. It is highly possible that individuals excuse themselves and others for their lack of convictions by saying that they need teaching. If one means that they need teaching to develop convictions, we find no particular argument with that conclusion. However, there are some who have been taught the truth from their youth who have no convictions for it. May we never minimize teaching! We need more and more teaching, but may we also appreciate the fact that there are other factors and principles that must accompany and follow teaching.

Narrow Mindedness (1)

The enemies of Christ have continually hurled epithets at Christ and his followers. Jesus was called a Nazarene (Matt. 2:23). Paul was called a babbler (Acts 17:18) and "a ringleader of the sect of the Nazarenes" (Acts 24:5). When Paul referred to the resurrection of Christ, Festus called him mad (Acts 26:24). The Jews referred to the church as "the sect . . . everywhere spoken against" (Acts 28:22). We shouldn't marvel when the epithet of narrow-mindedness is hurled at the Lord's people today. Epithets have been a very common thing from the Lord's enemies! To be called narrow-minded may be actually a compliment in disguise. In religion there seems to be an insatiable lust for broad-mindedness. A person who maintains some limits on how broad he is willing to be in religion is often frowned upon. It is strange that it should be this way in religion when such is not so in other fields of endeavor. There is no room for broad-mindedness in the field of chemistry, music, mathematics, biology, athletics, or mechanics. In all of these fields there are formulas and equations, etc. that the participants must definitely respect. To broaden out is but to invite impending failure and consequent disaster. All the broadness in the world cannot change the truth that 2 + 2 = 4.

But let us notice: There is a sense in which Christians should be as broad as the universe in our religious thought:

Our love should be for all men—never selfish. "But I say unto you, Love your enemies, bless them that curse you, do good to them that hate you, and pray for them which despitefully use you, and persecute you" (Matt. 5:44). "As we have therefore opportunity, let us do good unto all men" (Gal. 6:10). "For if ye love them which love you, what reward have ye? Do not even the publicans the same?" (Matt. 5:46).

We should have a deep yearning to see all men saved. Our view should be in accord with God's will "who will have all men to be saved, and to come unto the knowledge of the truth" (1 Tim. 2:4). Paul wasn't narrow-minded in this respect. His heart's desire and prayer to God for his countrymen were that they might be saved (Rom. 10:1). The anger of Jonah when Nineveh was spared after the city had repented could have easily been attributed to his narrow-mindedness concerning salvation. Christians must have a deep yearning to see all men saved. Any attitude contrary to this borders upon the spirit of narrow-mindedness.

We should realize that the doctrine of Jesus Christ, the gospel of Christ, and the church of Christ are for all men. No individual has a monopoly on the truth. The truth of the word of God is available to all. Christ died for all. "But we see Jesus, who was made a little lower than the angels for the suffering of death crowned with glory and honor; that he by the grace of God should taste death for every man" (Heb. 2:9). By the grace of God, Jesus tasted death for every man. We need to keep this truth just as broad as the truth states it. Furthermore, the gospel of Christ is for all men. Christ directed his apostles: "Go ye into all the world, and preach the gospel to every creature" (Mark 16:15). Paul said of the gospel: ". . . it is the power of God unto salvation to every one that believeth; to the Jew first, and also to the Greek" (Rom. 1:16). God sent a vision to Peter while Peter was on the house top in Joppa to help him comprehend this broadness and defeat a narrow-minded concept concerning the gospel (Acts 10, 11). Even later on, one is led to conclude that Peter was too narrow when he refused to eat with the Gentiles when the Jews were present. For this dissimulation, it was needful for Paul to withstand Peter to the face because he was to be blamed (Gal. 2:11-14). When we restrict the gospel, we are only condemning ourselves (Gal. 1:6-9).

We should realize that every command of God for this age is to be obeyed. It is possible to set aside one or two commandments from the Lord and exalt these to heaven while neglecting some others. The Christian's thinking is to be broad in obeying everything that God has for him to obey. "What will thou have me to do?" Not just a portion of God's will but all of it. This broadness should always be in our hearts! "For whosoever shall keep the whole law, and yet offend in one point, he is guilty of all" (Jas. 2:10) "For this is the love of God that we keep his commandments: and his commandments are not grievous" (1 John 5:3). The passage emphasizes commandments—not one commandment or so!

Narrow Mindedness (2)

In the last article we suggested that the Lord's people should not marvel when the epithet of narrow-mindedness is hurled at them. Epithets have been a very common thing from the Lord's enemies. We proceeded to emphasize that in religion there seems to be an insatiable lust for broadness. Though there is no room for such broadness in fields like chemistry, music, etc., yet there is a great craving for such an approach in the world's thinking regarding religion. The remaining portion of the article was used to point out principles in which Christians should never be narrow-minded, but should be as broad as the universe in their religious thought. Our love should be for all men; we should have a deep yearning to see all men saved; we should realize that the doctrine of Jesus Christ, the gospel of Christ, and the church of Christ are for all men; and that we should realize that every command of God for this age is to be obeyed. In this issue we desire to note and consider just why it is that Christians are at times called narrow-minded. We approach the subject in an effort to determine the answer by asking a few questions:

Is it because of nonconformity to the world, hence transformation of life, is the real work of a Christian? If so, should one "broaden out" and yield to the world to avert this epithet? To do so would deny the prerogative of Christ to set the standard for his followers, "who gave himself for us, that he might redeem us from all iniquity, and purify unto himself a peculiar people, zealous of good works" (Tit. 2:14). "And be not conformed to this world: but be ye transformed by the renewing of your mind, that ye may prove what is that good, and acceptable, and perfect will of God" (Rom. 12:2). If consecration makes us narrow, let us hasten to be such. Peter refers to Christians who had old friends who doubtlessly viewed them as being narrow: "For the time past of our life may suffice us to have wrought the will of the Gentiles, when we walked in lasciviousness, lusts, excess of wine, revellings, banquetings, and abominable idolatries; wherein they think it strange that ye run not with them to the same excess of riot, speaking evil of you" (1 Pet. 4:3-4). Would you suggest that they go back to walking in lasciviousness, lusts, etc. to avoid the epithet of narrow-mindedness?

Is it because of devotion to principle rather than looseness of ideals? If so, great men of God whose praises have been sung for many generations must be branded as narrow-minded. Elijah who challenged the false prophets of Baal (1 Kings 18:21), Daniel who refused to defile his body with the king's meat and wine (Dan. 1:8), and Stephen who died with prayer on his lips for his murderers (Acts 7)—these must then be branded as narrow-minded fanatics, while such wicked characters as Jezebel and the Herods must be idealized as being broad minded heroes. Are you ready to accept such a view? I certainly hope not!

Is it because one puts duty to God before self-interest? If so, then Abel, Moses, and Joseph, who put duty to God before their own interests, must be classified as narrow minded. On the other hand, Cain, Absalom, and Judas who placed self-interests before

God's will and being righteous, must be viewed as broad-minded heroes! If putting God first brands us narrow, may God help us to be narrow always.

Is it because one contends for the faith once delivered unto the saints? Then, the apostles were narrow. Peter and John were narrowest of all when they said, "Whether it be right in the sight of God to hearken unto you more than unto God, judge ye. For we cannot but speak the things which we have seen and heard" (Acts 4:19-20). On the other hand, those who persecuted them were broad-minded. The faith once delivered includes: Christ the way (John 14:6), true worship (John 4:24; Matt. 4:10; Acts 2:42), true gospel (Gal. 1:6-9), the true church (Matt. 16:18; 15:13; Eph. 5:23-27). In a summary it includes the "ones" stated in Ephesians 4:4-6: one body (church), one Spirit, one hope, one Lord, one faith, one baptism, and one God and Father of all. If contending for these makes one narrow, how can one be true and do otherwise? May their tribe definitely increase.

If for these reasons enumerated, one is called narrow, then one should consider himself happy to be so reproached for the name of Christ. "So serve I the God of our fathers" should be our reply. Pray for those who use such an epithet in an effort to do you harm. "Ye have heard that it hath been said, Thou shalt love thy neighbor, and hate thine enemy. But I say unto you. Love your enemies, bless them that curse you, do good to them that hate you and pray for them which despitefully use you, and persecute you" (Matt. 5:43-44).

Necessary Inference and Authority

Through the years that I have preached the gospel, I accepted the fact that authority is determined by three things. The three considerations are expressed command, approved example, and necessary inference. Any one of these principles revealed in the Scriptures can, within itself, grant one the authority to act and stand approved of God. For many years, it appeared that brethren accepted this approach to determining how the New Testament teaches authority. However, in recent years, there have been those who have challenged such conclusions and are prone to call them man-made traditions that have been adopted rather than the truth.

    To ignore these principles as constituting authority can cause devastating circumstances in accepting the pattern of truth in the New Testament. We illustrate this thought by viewing the subject of the Lord's supper. Jesus said, "This do in remembrance of me" (1 Cor. 11:24-25). Thus, we have a command to observe the Lord's supper. The authority to eat the Lord's supper comes by a direct command from our Lord. When are the disciples of the Lord to observe the Lord's supper? This authority comes by *apostolic example* or approved example from the apostles. Acts 20:7 reveals that Christians met on the first day of the week to break bread or to observe the Lord's supper. "And upon the first day of the week, when the disciples came together to break bread, Paul preached unto them, ready to depart on the morrow; and continued his speech until midnight." The apostle Paul met with them at Troas and added his approval of the meeting to break bread on the first day of the week. If this verse does not tell us when the Lord's supper is to be observed, I know of no other passage that does. If this example does not constitute authority for meeting on the first day of the week, where is authority for doing it any other time? The Lord's supper represents the most important memorial ever known to man. Does it seem plausible that God would leave the followers of his Son without knowledge of when this memorial is to be observed? Certainly not! He has given the answer and authority by approved example as noted in Acts 20:7. Not everything we do by divine authority can be found in expressed commands. The ambassadors of the Lord, with the authority to bind and loose, spoke and acted officially for the Lord and this is the realm of authority evidenced in their examples. Paul commanded the Corinthians to keep the "ordinances as I have delivered them to you" (1 Cor. 11:2). He wrote the Philippians, "Those things, which ye have both learned, and received, and heard, and seen in me, do: and the God of peace shall be with you" (Phil. 4:9).

Now, our attention is given to *necessary inference*. Though a passage may not spell out the truth, there is the inference of particular truth being conveyed in the passage. By command, we have authority for observing the Lord's supper and by approved example we have authority for observing it on the first day of the week. We learn the frequency of the observance of the Lord's supper by necessary inference. This means that the plain language used necessarily means that they met as often as the first day of the week came to break bread or observe the Lord's supper. Once again, if Acts 20:7 doesn't teach us when to observe the supper, what passage does? In like manner, if Acts 20:7 doesn't reveal the frequency of the observance, what passage does? Are we to conclude that we have no authority for the frequency? Some preachers scoff at the authority of necessary inference. We have known some to say that necessary inference is authoritative only when there is a commandment for the practice. Such is absurd—when a commandment exists, that authorizes the practice within itself without any other consideration.

One of the distinctions of the church of Christ from denominations is the observance of the Lord's supper on each first day of the week. Brethren, this is determined by necessary inference and when one rejects such as authority, he has no grounds for partaking of the Lord's supper on each first day of the week. Then, adopt the denominational practices of eating it monthly, quarterly, or yearly. Attacks are being made upon those who advocate the authority of necessary inference. We quote the words of one who professes to be a gospel preacher: "Anyone that teaches that necessary inference is equal in any way to commandments and examples in establishing a principle as doctrine, is a heretic. They are teaching their own will and opinions and claiming it is of God. No different than any denomination." This same person has circulated letters asking preachers to labor to have fellowship concerning the things that have divided churches through the years. His attitude toward necessary inference would suggest grave difficulties in having the fellowship which he says he craves. The Jews were commanded to observe the Sabbath Day, to keep it holy. That meant every Sabbath Day, as regularly as it came. The first day of the week means every first day of the week!

Nor Charged God Foolishly

"There was a man in the land of Uz, whose name was Job; and that man was perfect and upright, and one that feared God, and eschewed evil" (Job 1:1). This verse is the opening statement of the book of Job. "And there were born unto him seven sons and three daughters. His substance also was seven thousand sheep, and three thousand camels, and five hundred yoke of oxen, and five hundred she asses, and a very great household; so that this man was the greatest of all the men of the east" (Job 1:2-3). From these verses, it is quite evident that Job was a very prosperous man having been greatly blessed of the Lord.

God asked Satan if he had considered his servant Job, "that there is none like him in the earth, a perfect and an upright man, one that feareth God, and escheweth evil." Satan's reply was that God had built a hedge or protection about Job and actually Job had never been tried. Satan argued that, if this substance of prosperity be taken from Job, he would curse God to his face. In proving Satan to be wrong, God permitted Satan to have power over all that Job had. In swift succession, all of Job's possessions were taken from him. The Sabeans fell upon the oxen and asses and took them away; fire fell from heaven and burned up the sheep; the Chaldeans fell upon the camels and carried them away. Mind you all of this happened in one day and this isn't all! While Job was receiving word of the Chaldeans taking away his camels, a servant informed him that a great wind from the wilderness smote the house in which his sons and daughters were eating and drinking and they were all dead. "Then Job arose, and rent his mantle, and shaved his head, and fell down upon the ground, and worshiped, and said, 'Naked came I out of my mother's womb and naked shall I return thither:

the Lord gave, and the Lord hath taken away; blessed be the name of the Lord'" (Job 1:20-21). The chapter ends with the beautiful statement: "In all this Job sinned not, nor charged God foolishly" (Job 1:22).

This was a statement of great faith and trust in the Lord. It would have been so easy for Job to have charged God foolishly. As one reads this account, he is almost amazed that Job did not bring some foolish accusation against God. The circumstances were conducive for one of less faith to have uttered foolish charges against God. We repeat the commentary of Job's actions: "In all this, Job sinned not, nor charged God foolishly."

In our hours of trial, we are tempted to charge God foolishly. Rather than do as Job did when sore trials come, we are apt to:

Become Impatient. During such impatient moods, we do and say things that ordinarily we would not have said or done. Even John the Baptist sent messengers to the Christ questioning if he were the Christ or should they look for another. Perhaps John in the trials of prison life, felt that Jesus had delayed in his work and the development of his mission (Matt. 11:1-6). "Take, my brethren, the prophets who have spoken in the name of the Lord, for an example of suffering affliction, and of patience. Behold, we count them happy which endure. Ye have heard of the patience of Job, and have seen the end of the Lord; that the Lord is very pitiful, and of tender mercy." We need to learn to wait on the Lord and not become impatient. During such impatient times, we are prone to charge God foolishly for what is happening.

Become Rebellious. When trials come, we may find ourselves rebelling against the will of God on the basis of thinking that others are just as well off who never make any efforts to obey him. An element of bitterness prevails in the hearts of some when severe trials befall them. They reason that it doesn't pay to serve God or that God doesn't reward those that are his. They adopt the foolish resignment: "Let us eat and drink; for tomorrow we die." Trials have their purposes! There were purposes in the trials of

Job! Job didn't rebel against God and he was convinced in the end "that the Lord is very pitiful, and of tender mercy." He had sons and daughters and his possessions were restored twofold. How foolish rebellion is!

Question God's Love. How many times have you heard someone say when trials come upon him that God must not love him? We seem to think that the only evidence of love is the bestowing of good things. A father loves his child when he properly disciplines the child. At the time, the child may question that such is a token of a father's love, but with maturity, he learns to appreciate that discipline and love are closely associated. Trials can be "more precious than of gold that perisheth" (1 Pet. 1:7). We must have enough faith and conviction not to question God's love when trials come upon us in life. We must not charge God foolishly!

Not Far From the Kingdom of God

In the days of Christ on the earth, there were people who were definitely nearer to the kingdom of God than others. This is evident from the words of Jesus spoken to the scribe in Mark 12:24. He had acknowledged that Jesus spoke the truth by stating what was the first and second commandment of all. "And when Jesus saw that he answered discreetly, he said unto him, Thou art not far from the kingdom of God." The man was not in the kingdom for it had not been established at this time! Yet he was not far from the kingdom in some respect. We would conclude that Jesus recognized a disposition in this man that would be an asset in obeying the will of the Father in becoming a citizen of the kingdom that then was "at hand" and soon to be established. Hence, having developed this disposition or attitude, he was nearer in becoming a citizen of the kingdom than those who had not. He displayed attributes that would be prerequisites of obedience for those entering the kingdom of God.

The kingdom of God is available to men now. It came into existence on that memorable Pentecost Day recorded in Acts 2. This was the right time and place prophesied in the Old Testament Scriptures regarding the beginning of the kingdom of God. A kingdom necessitates having a king, laws, subjects, and territory. All these existed as the events in Acts 2 unfolded. Later on, Paul wrote to the Colossians, "Who hath delivered us from the power of darkness, and hath translated us into the kingdom of his dear Son" (Col. 1:13). The Hebrews were reminded, "Wherefore we receiving a kingdom which cannot be moved, let us have grace, whereby we may serve God acceptably with reverence and godly fear" (Heb.12:28). It is obvious from these Scriptures, and numerous others that could be mentioned, that the kingdom of God or his church has been established and we have the privilege of being citizens therein. Many are not in the kingdom, yet of these some are nearer citizenship than others. In their lives, they manifest a spirit and attitude that is essential to anyone becoming a citizen in the kingdom much as Christ recognized in this scribe. What are some of the attributes that would make one "not far from the kingdom of God"?

This scribe appeared to be teachable! He didn't manifest the "know it all" spirit. He readily acknowledged what Jesus said to be the truth and in a discreet manner. No one can enter the kingdom without being taught (Matt. 28:18-20). Teaching is the very foundation of Christianity. When a man will not listen and does not have a teachable spirit, he is a long way from the kingdom of God. And that is just where so many are today! Jesus said of his contemporaries, "For this people's heart is waxed gross, and their ears are dull of hearing, and their eyes they have closed: lest at any time they should see with their eyes, and hear with their ears, and should understand with their heart, and should be converted, and I should heal them" (Matt. 13:15).

A spirit of humility brings one nearer to the kingdom. The principle of humility underlines the beatitudes that Jesus spoke in Matthew 5:1-12. It is the right attitude. The acts of obedience appeal to the humble rather than to the proud. The proud in heart are far from the kingdom. "And Jesus called a little child unto him, and set him in the midst of them, and said, Verily I say unto you, Except ye be converted, and become as little children, ye shall not enter into the kingdom of heaven" (Matt. 18:2-3). In most cases, the child is teachable and has a humble concept of life whereby he can be led.

The scribe showed discretion. "And when Jesus saw that he answered discreetly." Discreet is defined as follows: "Possessed of or showing discernment or good judgment in conduct and esp. in speech; prudent; circumspect." He considered loving God and his neighbor as himself to be more than all whole burnt offerings and sacrifices. He had a true conception of the objective of life and the real principle of true religion. Worldly wisdom did not control his thinking. Such is not true of many today! They glory more in their burnt offerings and sacrifices of human wisdom than they do in loving God and keeping his commandments. "For this is the love of God that we keep his commandments: and his commandments are not grievous" (1 John 5:3). True discretion is needed to enter the kingdom of God and those who lack such are a long way out as far as the kingdom of God is concerned. Man needs to realize his lost condition and start preparing for eternity by obeying Christ and becoming a citizen in his kingdom. Possessing the right attributes may constitute us near the kingdom, but nearness is not in! One can be near and never enter in. We must obey the gospel of Christ to come into the kingdom (Mark 16:16; Acts 2:41; Rom. 10:16).

Not Good If Detached

Did you ever notice on various tickets or on many coupons, "Not good if detached"? The coupon or ticket was made of the same material as the rest of the ticket, printed with the same ink on the same press, and kept in the same office. But it was not good if detached. Its usefulness was dependent upon its relation to the rest of the ticket.

Of how much worth is a church member detached from the rest of the church? How much fruit can a branch have detached from the vine? How good is a hand detached from a body? A Christian is one who stays with the rest of the congregation. He cannot serve God acceptably apart from it. Did you ever notice how quickly a banana gets skinned after it leaves the bunch? All who profess to follow Christ are to stay near to the Lord and others who are striving to faithfully follow Christ. Peter followed afar off and denied his Master. We need closeness rather than detachment. Remember the admonition from the Hebrew writer: "Forsaking not the assembling of yourselves together" (Heb. 10:25).

Offended In Christ

"And blessed is he, whosoever shall not be offended in me" (Matt. 11:6). These were the concluding words that Jesus spoke to two of John's disciples when they had come to him with the question "Are thou he that should come, or do we look for another?" Jesus knew the possibility of people being offended in him. It was true then and it continues to be true now. To be "offended" is defined as "to cause to feel hurt or resentful; annoy; to displease." The prophet Isaiah predicted that Christ would be "for a stone of stumbling and for a rock of offense to both the houses of Israel, for a gin and for a snare to the inhabitants of Jerusalem" (Isa. 8:14).

He who came to bring life was to many the most offensive person who ever lived. He was constantly the victim of resentment. Many of his own had no place for him in their lives. "He came unto his own, and his own received him not" (John 1:11). To many, his origin on earth was offensive. Some were offended at what he did. Others were offended at what Christ said (John 6:60-61, 66-69). The resentment continued to increase and culminated in his crucifixion.

People continue to be offended in Christ. At his birth, there was no room for him in the inn. The "no vacancy sign" continues to be prevalent today in the lives of many offended in Christ. There are those who read the Bible and behold accounts of individuals showing resentment toward Christ. They find themselves saying, that had we been living then, we would have acted differently; yet, they permit themselves to be offended at times in more drastic ways than those about whom they read in the word of God. Why is this so? Why is it that anyone would be offended in Christ? We suggest:

He Stressed the Spiritual above the Temporal. To deny the importance of the material antagonizes a great many people in our time. He emphasized the futility of riches by saying "a rich man shall hardly enter into the kingdom of heaven" (Matt. 19:23). He stressed the supremacy of the soul over the body. "For what is a man profited, if he shall gain the whole world, and lose his own soul? Or what shall a man give in exchange for his soul?" (Matt. 16:26). By teaching that spiritual ties are stronger than fleshly ties, he continued to place the spiritual above the temporal and in so doing offended people who gloried in strong fleshly bonds. "He that loveth father or mother more than me is not worthy of me: and he that loveth son or daughter more than me is not worthy of me" (Matt. 10:37). As these principles are taught today, those who glory in the material and temporal values are often offended in Christ. Such was so in the days that Jesus lived on this earth and such is so in the attitudes of many in our time. Human nature is one thing that has suffered little change.

Christ Contradicted the Popular Religions of His Day. He would not leave the popular religions alone. He charged the Scribes and Pharisees with making void the word of God with the commandments of men, being hypocrites, and indulging in vain worship (Matt. 15:3-9). Upon being informed by his disciples that these people were offended in him, he replied, "Every plant, which my heavenly Father hath not planted, shall be rooted up. Let them alone: they be blind leaders of the blind. And if the blind lead the blind, both shall fall into the ditch" (Matt. 15:13-14). No one should conclude that it was the intention of Christ to offend these people. He was endeavoring to help them by exposing what was wrong with their teaching and practices. However, when they were offended at the truth which he taught, there was no apology offered by the Lord. He referred the disciples to the consequences of those who are offended at the truth. It should not be the intention of a faithful preacher of God's word to personally offend his listeners. On the other hand, no preacher should apologize to anyone who has become offended at the truth which Christ has given to be preached. To do so is to place the disciples above the Master.

Christ Exalted Simple Things. The very essence of his religion is simplicity. The Lord used weak and foolish things to confound the wise and mighty (1 Cor. 1:26-29). This simplicity is offensive to some. His simple teaching involved the church that he died to establish. In this age of modern thinking, many become offended when they hear that Jesus only built one church and that salvation is to be found therein (Eph. 1:22-23; 4:4; Acts 2:47). To preach that water baptism is essential to salvation is also offensive to many (Mark 16:16; 1 Pet. 3:21). They have been reared on a diet of faith alone and deceived into thinking that such will save souls. Practically everything that Jesus taught has constituted grounds for offence to some individuals. To be offended in Christ is a very fatal thing. What hope can we have to live in heaven with Christ if we have become offended by him in this life? We must not let it happen if we hope to live with him in eternity!

Our Calling

"I press toward the mark for the prize of the high calling of God in Christ Jesus" (Phil. 3:14). Much is said in the Scriptures regarding the calling mentioned in this verse. We deem a lesson of this nature valuable because it affects our salvation. Anything involving our souls is valuable and worthy of prayerful consideration. Though much is stated regarding the subject, there still exists considerable confusion over the subject. Many have not found peace before God because they have missed the simplicity of the subject. At times members of the church are not well enough established in the subject that they might give a plausible explanation to others

(1 Pet. 3:15). This subject also constitutes an outstanding difference between denominational churches and the church of Christ. We at times need a lesson to renew our allegiance to this calling. It represents such obligations as require strong allegiance.

The Scriptures designate this calling as being a "high calling" (Phil. 3:14). There is nothing higher for man! It involves the highest and holiest of honors ever conferred upon man. Paul said, "I count all things loss for the excellency of the knowledge of Christ Jesus my Lord" (Phil. 3:8). This calling is a holy calling. "Who hath saved us, and called us with an holy calling, not according to our works, but according to his own purpose and grace, which was given us in Christ Jesus before the world began" (2 Tim. 1:9). He who calls is holy and man is called to a holy way of life. We do not merit this call. It is not according to our works or design, but according to God's purpose and grace. This calling is also designated as being heavenly. "Wherefore, holy brethren, partakers of the heavenly calling, consider the Apostle and High Priest of our profession, Christ Jesus" (Heb. 3:1). Those who make it possible are from heaven. If we accept the call and work worthily, heaven shall be our eternal home. The calling is as lofty as heaven itself.

The subject involves: (1) How God calls; (2) How we accept or answer the call; (3) The calling or profession that is the consequence of this calling.

How does God call man or how is this call extended to man? At times, God has called man directly or personally for a particular work. Such a call was given to Moses (Exod. 3:10), Jonah (Jon. 1:1-2), and Paul (Acts 26:19). In all these calls, God respected man's volition. Man could have refused, but in doing so, one could not be pleasing unto the Lord. These direct and personal calls were not unto salvation or the call itself did not constitute salvation. So many contend that a direct call is needed for salvation. Such was never so! The Scriptures reveal how God calls us to this heavenly calling: "whereunto he called you by our gospel, to the obtaining of the glory of our Lord Jesus Christ" (2 Thess. 2:14). God does the calling. The medium is the gospel of Christ. The end is the obtaining of the glory of our Lord Jesus Christ. Where the gospel is preached, there goes the call of God. The gospel of Christ is the power of God unto salvation (Rom. 1:16). The call is given in the gospel message. The failure with most people is that they have not realized that they have been called through the gospel!

How does one accept this call? Man must realize that he is being called. So many hear the gospel and never realize any obligation to it. Man accepts the call by obeying the conditions of the gospel (Mark 16:15-16; Acts 2:38). A good example of God's call and man's acceptance is found in Acts 8:26-39. The angel of the Lord tells Philip where to go to find one who needs to hear the gospel of Christ. Philip preaches Jesus to this officer of Queen Candace of the Ethiopians. "And as they went on their way, they came unto a certain water: and the eunuch said, See, here is water; what doth hinder me to be baptized? And Philip said, If thou believest with all thy heart, thou mayest. He answered and said, I believe that Jesus Christ is the Son of God. And he commanded the chariot to stand still: and they went down both into the water, both Philip and the eunuch; and he baptized him. And when they were come up out of the water, the Spirit of the Lord caught away Philip, that the eunuch saw him no more and went on his way rejoicing." Jesus was preached to the eunuch and this involved the call of God to salvation. In his obedience, this man accepted the call of God and became a part of that high, holy, and heavenly calling which is available to man today. Circumstances may differ, but the how of the call and acceptance remains until time shall be no more.

What is involved when this call is accepted? We are called to be saints (1 Cor. 1:2). Members of the church of Christ are the called of Jesus Christ (Rom. 1:6). We are to walk worthy of the vocation wherein we are called (Eph. 4:1). We are exhorted to make the calling sure (2 Pet. 1:10). Have you responded to God's call in the gospel? Are you faithful to your calling?

Our Double Life

This subject may imply to most people a very undesirable condition. Generally we think of a double life as a Dr. Jekyll and Mr. Hyde affair or one who plays two roles in life much on the basis of hypocrisy or being two-faced. The Scriptures certainly condemn such a life. James wrote that "a double minded man is unstable in all his ways" (Jas. 1:8; 4:8). "Not double-tongued" is one of the negative qualifications expected of deacons (1 Tim. 3:8). Every Christian is to view a double life with detest and abstain from being a part of anything resembling it. However, there is a double life of duty that we are to follow in being pleasing to God. This double life involves things that pertain to God and those things involving evil. With the same zeal and loyalty we must respond to each responsibility even though each obligation is opposite to the other in object and action. This double duty falls under the general heading of positive and negative actions. Some may refer to it as being contradictory. In a sense, such may be true, but our duty toward each principle is certainly not!

Observe A Few of These Principles Involving This Double Life

We must remember and forget. There are things that the Christian is called upon to remember while on the other hand there are things that he must forget. Hence, he has the double life of remembering and forgetting! Peter stated, "This second epistle, beloved, I now write unto you; in both which I stir up your pure minds by way of remembrance: that ye may be mindful of the words which were spoken before by the holy prophets, and of the commandment of us the apostles of the Lord and Saviour" (2 Pet. 3:1-2). We are ever to remember the commandments of the Lord and give heed "lest at any time we should let them slip" (Heb. 2:1). We are to remember them which have the rule over us (Heb. 13:17), as well as many other principles that are emphasized in the word of God. On the other hand, there are things that the Christian is called upon to forget. Paul wrote, "But this one thing I do, forgetting those things which are behind, and reaching forth unto those things which are before" (Phil. 3:13). Consider the things Paul forgot: A noble ancestry (Phil. 3:5), a respectable religion (Phil. 3:3-6), his personal accomplishments—moral, intellectual, and political. He did not allow the memory of these things to breed vanity in his soul. Think of his injuries! There were stripes, bruises, imprisonments, false charges, etc. He allowed none of these things to discourage him; he harbored no malice. He was called upon to forget his mistakes. He had persecuted the Lord's church. The memory of his sins, which had been forgiven, did not thwart his onward march "toward the mark for the prize of the high calling of God in Christ Jesus." At times we are guilty of remembering the things we should forget and on the other hand, forgetting the things we should remember. Such can mar our happiness here and lessen our hope of eternal life.

We must run and stand. The writer of Hebrews admonished Christians saying, ". . . let us lay aside every weight, and the sin which doth so easily beset us, and let us run with patience the race that is set before us, looking unto Jesus the author and finisher of our faith" (Heb. 12:1-2). The life of a Christian is pictured in the Bible under the figure of a race in which we are to faithfully run. Such involves all the activities in which the Christian is to engage and the race is not concluded short of death (Rev. 2:10). On the other hand, we are admonished to stand as regarding principles of faith. "Watch ye, stand fast in the faith, quit you like men, be strong" (1 Cor. 16:13). Regarding the warfare of the Christian, Paul wrote, "Wherefore take unto you the whole armor of God, that ye may be able to withstand in the evil day, and having done all, to stand. Stand therefore, having your loins girt about with truth" (Eph. 6:13-14). It is obvious from the Scriptures that we have the obligations both to run and stand as pertaining to this double life.

We must love and hate. There are many passages in the word of God which teach the importance of love. There is love for God (Matt. 22:37), love for brethren (1 Pet. 1:22-23), and love for the truth (2 Thess. 2:10). Love is even personified in 1 Corinthians 13.

Certainly no one who knows anything about the Scriptures will deny the importance of love. But in the emphasis upon love, some seem to forget that there is also the admonition to hate. Notice: "Let love be without dissimulation. Abhor that which is evil; cleave to that which is good" (Rom. 12:9). "Abhor" is defined as "to shrink from in fear, disgust, or hatred." So many appear to be so wrapped up in love that they forget to hate that which is evil. Deliver me from the man who loves everything and finds no place to hate. Jesus commended the church at Ephesus: "But this thou hast, that thou hatest the deeds of the Nicolaitans, which I also hate" (Rev. 2:6). Jesus hated the deeds of the Nicolaitans and he calls upon his disciples to hate the deeds of false teachers (Ps. 119:104). Both love and hate are to be a part of the well balanced life of double duty. How is your life?

Our Likes and Our Dislikes

"Like" as used in this sense is defined as "a favorable feeling; preference." There are many things about our lives that are shaped by what we have grown to like or dislike. We generally do what we like and refrain from doing what we dislike. Such things, in turn, have a great bearing upon molding our character for good or bad. The very heart of training children is that the parents help them to like what is good and dislike evil. "Abhor that which is evil; cleave to that which is good" (Rom. 12:9).

There are realms of activity wherein what a person likes or dislikes has little bearing upon the destiny of a man's soul. We have in mind man's preferences in colors, transportation, living conditions, etc. So much freedom has been granted us in these pursuits and items similar to them, that man has developed the conception that his likes and his dislikes are to govern all that he does.

People have incorporated this philosophy into the realm of religion or faith with God. So many today have as their standard of authority simply that which they *like or dislike*. What they like they approve as right and what they dislike they approve as wrong. Does man have this prerogative before God? Isaiah wrote, "For my thoughts are not your thoughts, neither are your ways my ways, saith the Lord. For as the heavens are higher than the earth, so are my ways higher than your ways, and my thoughts than your thoughts" (Isa. 55:8-9). Again, from Jeremiah, "O Lord, I know that the way of man is not in himself: it is not in man that walketh to direct his steps" (Jer. 10:23). If a man were permitted to do or follow what he likes or dislikes in religion, why then have the word of God? The Scriptures reveal the mind of God and what is right in matters that affect our souls. 1 Corinthians 2:6-13 reveals how God reveals his will to man.

> But as it is written, Eye hath not seen, nor ear heard, neither have entered into the heart of man, the things which God hath prepared for them that love him. But God hath revealed them unto us by his Spirit: for the Spirit searcheth all things, yea, the deep things of God. For what man knoweth the things of a man, save the spirit of man which is in him? Even so the things of God knoweth no man, but the Spirit of God. Now we have received, not the spirit of the world, but the spirit which is of God; that we might know the things that are freely given to us of God. Which things also we speak, not in the words which man's wisdom teacheth, but which the Holy Ghost teacheth; comparing spiritual things with spiritual.

Now notice the order: The Holy Spirit searched the things of God; the Spirit revealed these things to the apostles or inspired men; those inspired by the Holy Spirit spoke the things revealed to them and when those to whom they spoke or wrote heard these things, they received God's will or what he expected of man to be pleasing to him. Thus by reading the Scriptures, man comes to know what God likes and what is expected of man to be saved. The same thought is conveyed in 2 Timothy 3:16-17: "All scripture is given by inspiration of God, and is profitable for doctrine, for reproof, for correction, for instruction in righteousness. That the man of God may be perfect, throughly furnished unto all good works." We are to follow the word of God whether we like it or not! This is the only way we can ever hope to be pleasing before the Lord. Perhaps the Galatians were accepting what they liked in disregard for what God had given them to do. This prompted Paul to write:

> I marvel that ye are so soon removed from him that called you into the grace of Christ unto another gospel: Which is not another; but there be some that trouble you, and would pervert the gospel of Christ. But though we, or an angel from heaven, preach any other gospel unto you than that which we have preached unto you, let him be accursed. As we said before, so say I now again, if any man preach any other gospel unto you than that ye have received, let him be accursed" (Gal. 1:6-9).

They may have liked or preferred another gospel, but they would be accursed in accepting anything other than the gospel that Paul preached which had been given him by the revelation of Jesus Christ (Gal. 1:11-12).

There are members of the church of Christ who still haven't learned that what they like and dislike does not constitute authority. We have known some members to leave a congregation because they didn't like some things that were being scripturally practiced. They went to where they could find what they liked. What God likes or what is found in the Scriptures becomes secondary to what they like. The subordination of women to men, the lack of church sponsored social activities for their families, the practice of discipline, preaching that condemns—these things and others have affected the likes and dislikes of individuals to govern their lives. There may be numbers of things that I do not like about what God says, but really what difference does this make in the matter? God says do it and that is the thing that must matter if we are to be pleasing to him to enter heaven.

Paul's Secret of Success

"Brethren, I count not myself to have apprehended: but this one thing I do, forgetting those things which are behind, and reaching forth unto those things which are before, I press toward the mark for the prize of the high calling of God in Christ Jesus" (Phil. 3:13-14). In these verses, it might be said that Paul is revealing the secret of his life, telling us what made him the kind of man he truly was. As we observe these verses and the thoughts revealed therein, the secret of lasting success is unveiled to those who are desirous of knowing them. What are these principles?

A Sense of Personal Unworthiness. "Brethren, I count not myself to have apprehended" or "to have laid hold of the prize." Paul was quick to admit that he was not perfect (v. 12). Though a faithful and devoted servant of Jesus Christ, he was painfully aware of his own weakness. "But I keep under my body, and bring it into subjection: lest that by any means, when I have preached to others, I myself should be a castaway" (1 Cor. 9:27). Humility is necessary in the area of spiritual success. Personal improvement is impossible to the man who does not see his mistakes and mourn over them. So many of us see the mistakes of others, but we fail to realize our own mistakes and be cognizant of personal unworthiness. The thing that may hinder some from true success and happiness is that they fell in love with themselves too early in life.

Singleness of Purpose. "This one thing I do." There is immense power in the concentration of purpose. The rays of the sun when diffused are relatively impotent, but if focused, these rays would burn the world. In like respect, steam when diffused is powerless, but when concentrated, steam can move the giant locomotive. Faithful Daniel exhibited singleness of purpose: "But Daniel purposed in his heart that he would not defile himself with the portion of the king's meat, nor with the wine which he drank: therefore he requested of the prince of the eunuchs that he might not defile himself" (Dan. 1:8). A life divided in purpose is a weak life, continually the victim of circumstances. "A double-minded man is unstable in all his ways" (Jas. 1:8). Do we simply play at being a Christian or has it become the purpose of life with us? "No man can serve two masters" (Matt. 6:24).

Forgetting the Past. "Forgetting those things which are behind." The runner has no time to focus his eyes over his shoulder to mark the steps already trodden. "No man . . . looking back, is fit for the kingdom of heaven" (Luke 9:62). If the things behind cannot make us better, if possible, they should be remembered no more. The apostle has a number of things that he was called upon to forget:

1. A noble ancestry (Phil. 3:5). When he became a Christian, he left kindred behind. Of fleshly attainments, he said, "But what things were gain to me, those I counted loss for Christ" (Phil. 3:7).

2. A respectable religion in which he profited above many of his equals in his own nation (Gal. 1:14). The Jews' religion was venerated with traditions of ancient worthies, but when the call came Paul "was not disobedient to the heavenly vision" (Acts 26:19). He had personal accomplishments that were moral, intellectual, and political, but he did not allow the memory of such to breed vanity in his soul. "Forgetting those things which are behind"—these things were insignificant as compared to blessings in Christ Jesus. ". . . I have suffered the loss of all things, and do count them but dung, that I may win Christ" (Phil. 3:8).

3. His miserable mistakes. He had persecuted Christ's church. He had consented unto the death of the first martyr in the church, faithful Stephen. The memory was there! But he did not allow the memory of such deeds, which now in Christ had been forgiven, to thwart his onward progress in Christ. Who has done more against the truth than Saul of Tarsus? Yet, later, who did more for the truth than Paul, the apostle of Christ? Think of his stripes, imprisonments, and often persecutions! He allowed none of these to discourage him from his singleness of purpose in serving the Lord. He evidenced no bitterness or malice toward those who had mistreated him, but wrote of vengeance belonging to the Lord (Rom. 12:19).

The Spirit of Progress. "I press toward the mark for the prize of the high calling of God in Christ Jesus." From the beginning, God has wanted man to move forward. Even the position of the eyes in front and not in the back of our bodies is evidence of this. We are to exert ourselves in pressing onward in doing those things that are pleasing in the sight of God. We need to keep in mind that movement is to be toward the goal revealed in the Scriptures. We can find ourselves pressing for modernism and liberalism. Movement in the wrong direction and for the wrong thing is not proper progress. Do we desire spiritual success? Think on these things!

Personalities

Have you ever heard some observer commenting upon certain difficulties that churches and individuals experience as the problem being a matter of personalities? Those who are aware of certain situations must admit that the expression or its counterpart is often the summation that some have. Just what does a person mean by the expression "a matter of personalities"? Unless I fail to understand their meaning, they are saying that the problem or problems are due to the feelings that persons have toward one another. Factors such as envy, revenge, or resentment are responsible for their actions. In accrediting the problem to personalities, they are eliminating doctrinal issues or making it quite evident that doctrine is not involved.

For a good while, certain thoughts have been in my mind regarding this subject which I believe all who desire to be right before God should seriously meditate upon. Consider the following:

Personalities Involved Do Not Eliminate the Possibility of Doctrine Also Being Involved. For an example, in Galatians 2:11-13, one reads of Paul standing before Peter to his face and telling him that he was to be blamed. Peter had eaten with the Gentiles when the Jews were not present; but when the Jews were present, Peter declined to do so. Here were persons definitely involved, as in most all matters of religion, but the matter also involved doctrine. At a very crucial time in the church regarding some matters, Peter was evidencing respect of persons and committing dissimulation, and as a follower of the doctrine of Christ, Paul was obligated to rebuke him. How easy it might have been for an observer, or particularly one hearing the matter second or third handed, to say that Paul was acting upon the basis of personalities or personal feeling toward Peter rather than his being motivated by doctrine. It is a serious and unjust thing to accredit any rebuke or problem that arises to it being a matter of personalities with no consideration for higher motives being involved—namely, following the doctrine of Christ. Friends of Peter might have suggested to Peter that Paul was a little jealous of him and was just endeavoring to find fault. It happens in our time! Some make it a matter of personalities!

One Should Not Attempt to Evade Responsibilities By Conveniently Crying Personalities. It is understood by those who respect the word of God that a man of faith is definitely to declare himself in matters of faith, but such is not so regarding personalities. This is the out for some! They render the problem as a matter of personalities and ignore what they call doctrinal matters to keep from having to be either/or. Elders have been known to find this convenient to save face without having to take a stand. Why should they be involved when it is only a matter of personalities? So they go on their merry way still as great stalwarts of the faith. Preachers have relied upon "personalities" to relieve them of dealing with some congregational problems. A matter of personalities doesn't keep them from holding meetings anywhere or endorsing any congregation. See how convenient this thing works! It's a great help in evading responsibilities and saving face!

Fairness Should Be Manifested When Advocating Personalities. I know of a situation existing in a congregation where the elders said that the problem was a matter of personalities between the preacher and certain members. The preacher denied such and contended that, at least on his part, it was over the teaching of Christ that some members would not accept. To evade really dealing with the contentious members and upholding the preacher, they persisted in saying that it was a question of personalities, let them smooth it out themselves. A short time later, the elders had a run in with some of the same members. You guessed it—the matter then was no longer over personalities, but doctrine. What had changed? Not the issues, but simply the shoes. They were on the elders' feet this time rather than on the preachers'.

Matters of personalities do at times exist and even these must be properly dealt with. It is certainly sinful for envy, jealousy, and resentment to exist among members and congregations. However, we need to be careful and use caution in advocating that something is solely a matter of personalities. It could be that we are simply making a cowardly approach rather than a scriptural evaluation of the situation. When you are on the battle line of truth and doing all in your power to contend for the faith, would you appreciate someone saying that your actions were matters of personal dislike toward some individuals with whom you were dealing? Think brethren and be careful!

Persuading Men

"Knowing therefore the terror of the Lord, we persuade men; but we are made manifest unto God; and I trust also are made manifest in your consciences" (2 Cor. 5:11). The words "reason" and "persuade" are very similar in meaning. In fact, "reason" is defined as "to talk persuadably." Throughout God's dealings with men, he has not chosen to compel or force men to obey him. He has on the other hand chosen to persuade men to do his will through the instrumentality of men preaching to men. By such a procedure, the free moral agency of man is respected. Isaiah admonished his people saying, "Come now, and let us reason together, saith the Lord" (Isa. 1:18-20). Under the New Covenant, Paul reasoned and persuaded men, as did the other faithful preachers of God's word. "And he reasoned in the synagogue every sabbath, and persuaded the Jews and the Greeks" (Acts 18:4) In this particular passage, the words "reasoned" and "persuaded" are both found and are indicative of the approach Paul used upon the minds of men. Before Felix, Paul "reasoned of righteousness, temperance, and judgment to come" to such an extent that "Felix trembled, and answered, Go thy way for this time; when I have a convenient season, I will call for thee" (Acts 24:25).

Two Schools of Thought Regarding Who Is to Be Persuaded

Some religionists seem to feel that God, Christ, and the Holy

Spirit must be persuaded to save. This is the basis of the mourner's bench and the theory of praying so long and loud that God will finally be persuaded to accept the poor sinner. Why persuade God, Christ, and the Holy Spirit? They are ready to save! Consider these passages: Acts 10:34-35; Romans 10:13; Revelation 22:17; 2 Peter 1:3. What more could be done for the sinner? It is absurd and foolish to think of having to persuade someone to do something when he is already willing to do it!

Preachers persuading men to obey the gospel of Christ. God, Christ, and the Holy Spirit have made salvation available to men. It is now the obligation of man to obey the truth and become Christians. Preaching has the objective of teaching men this truth and persuading them to obey the gospel that they might be saved (Rom. 1:16). Paul was trying to persuade Agrippa to become a Christian. At least, this was the conclusion Agrippa reached when he said, "Almost thou persuadest me to be a Christian" (Acts 26:28). Whatever Agrippa may have meant by the statement, he understood who was persuading whom.

What Are Principles of Persuasion to Be Used in Admonishing Men to Obey Christ?

The value of a man's soul—uncertainty of life. "For what shall it profit a man, if he shall gain the whole world, and lose his own soul?" (Mark 8:38). The only way for a man to save his soul is by obeying the gospel of Christ. God is "not willing that any should perish, but that all should come to repentance" (2 Pet. 3:9). He has done what is needed for man's salvation that his soul might be saved. Friend, have you considered the real value of your soul? Can't you be persuaded to obey the gospel that your soul might be saved? The liberal tendency is to persuade men upon the principles that the church needs you or it would be wonderful for you to be united in religion with your wife, etc. Such considerations were not the approach of persuasion that the men of God made in the New Testament times. These men of God awakened men to the thought that they were lost and persuaded them to do something about it on the basis of the value of one's soul.

The terror of the Lord. "Knowing therefore the terror of the Lord, we persuade men" (2 Cor. 5:10). The terror of the Lord is a definite principle of persuasion. The Bible reveals the goodness and severity of God (Rom. 11:26). The terror of the Lord doubtlessly must refer to the punishment of those who disobey God. Knowing this to be the fate of the disobedient, Paul exerted all the power of his being in persuading men to obey the gospel and escape the terror, the wrath, or severity of God (2 Thess. 1:7-9). Much of modern preaching ignores the terror of the Lord. "We don't want to frighten people" is the philosophical concept of preaching of our time. The terror of the Lord motivates men to preach the truth and is ever a truthful consideration for persuasion. Help us to treasure it!

The love of Christ. "For the love of Christ constraineth us" (2 Cor. 5:14). This love motivates men to preach and it persuades men to obey. If Christ loved us enough to die for our sins, shouldn't we love him enough to obey his gospel that we might be saved (Rom. 5:8)? "We love him, because he first loved us" (1 John 4:19). With these considerations, what more do we need to be persuaded to obey the gospel of Christ and become a Christian. God is ready to save you! Are you ready to be saved?

Placing the Proper Emphasis

Numerous demands are made upon our time and energy as Christians. For us to do everything we wish to do or people might expect us to do is virtually an impossibility. Failure at times to properly realize this has caused some faithful children of God intense emotional strain. We are obliged, therefore, to select, to eliminate. The things that should be eliminated are things of secondary importance. We should select things of prime importance and work to eliminate from our lives things that are minor. Rather than do this, we often find ourselves "majoring in the minor" or emphasizing the things that are of little importance to the neglect of the truly great matters.

One of the purposes of revelation is to establish the right order of things or to place the emphasis where it belongs. Jeremiah wrote: "O Lord, I know that the way of man is not in himself: it is not in man that walketh to direct his steps" (Jer. 10:23). The commonest sin is the sin of misplacing the emphasis, of making secondary things primary, or making primary things secondary. Lot pitched his tent toward Sodom in the choice that was granted to him. As events materialized, he barely escaped with his life. In our failure to emphasize proper things, we can surely find ourselves pitching our tents toward a Sodom of spiritual destruction. We need to accept the divine order and make first things first (Matt. 6:33). A Christian once remarked, "Before conversion, it was I not God; at conversion, it was God and I; after conversion and growth it is God not I."

What Things Are of Prime Importance? Where Should the Emphasis Be Placed?

God's kingdom and his righteousness before material things. Our interest in the kingdom or church should be paramount. For it Jesus died; it is his body, his bride; for it he will come again. Christ's kingdom will endure (Heb. 12:28). Material substances will perish. Emphasis should be placed upon those things that endure rather than upon the perishing material. Jesus asked, "For what shall it profit a man, if he shall gain the whole world, and lose his own soul? Or what shall a man give in exchange for his soul?" (Mark 8:36-37). There are entirely too many professed Christians who are too busy seeking material gains to make the kingdom of God and his righteousness first in their lives! They have confused making a living with the obsession of "living it up"!

Righteousness before money making or the love of money. Principle is more important than gain. The rich young ruler in Matthew 19 failed to place the proper emphasis where he should have. He placed his riches and material substances before following the Christ and true righteousness. Money will be left behind. We can't take it with us. Paul wrote, "For we brought nothing into this world, and it is certain we can carry nothing out" (1 Tim. 6:7). How foolish it is for one to make money-making or the love of money the primary emphasis in life. The Lord spoke of such a one saying, "Thou fool" (Luke 12:20). The wise emphasize righteousness or laying up for themselves treasures in heaven (Matt. 6:19-21).

Following Christ before or above all other things. In Luke 9:59-62, we read of two men who reversed the divine order. They misplaced the proper emphasis: "And he said unto another, Follow me. But he said Lord, suffer me first to go and bury my father. Jesus said unto him, let the dead bury their dead: but go thou and preach the kingdom of God. And another also said, Lord, I will follow thee; but let me first go bid them farewell, which are at home at my house. And Jesus said unto him, No man, having put his hand to the plow, and looking back, is fit for the kingdom of God." These men made the mistake of placing good things before the best things. For one to bury his father; for one to desire to tell them at his home goodbye—these are good things. But oftentimes the good becomes the worst enemy of the best. We find ourselves emphasizing the good and placing secondary the best. To preach the kingdom of God and be a fit subject in his kingdom are far greater things than what these men had placed first.

If we expect to be with God in heaven, we must begin here by laying stress upon heavenly principles. We must understand where the proper emphasis belongs and start placing it there. This is not a popular subject and it even becomes offensive to some to hear it mentioned. However, much is said in the Scriptures regarding the subject and it behooves all of us to respect its value. "If ye then be risen with Christ, seek those things which are above, where Christ sitteth on the right hand of God. Set your affection on things above, not on things on the earth" (Col. 3:1-2). What is your emphasis?

Playing Fair (1)

"Receive us; we have wronged no man, we have corrupted no man, we have defrauded no man" (2 Cor. 7:2). In using these words, Paul was exhorting the Corinthians to receive him and his fellow workers in the bond of fellowship. He wanted them to know that they would not be mistreated. He was asserting that they would be fair in their dealings with them. Parents often admonish their children to play fair with their playmates. This advice or direction should not be limited to the playing of children. Christians, above all, should be given to fair play. We are thinking of "fair" as "characterized by frankness; honesty; impartiality; or just." It is a consoling thought to know that one is doing business with a person who will play fair. On the other hand, who desires transactions with an individual who will not play fairly? It is certainly a very disturbing thing to hear of professed Christians having a reputation of not playing fair in their dealings with others.

What causes people to be unfair? Behind our actions, there are reasons or explanations that account for them. Here are some explanations for unfairness:

Pride. Such is defined as "inordinate self-esteem; conceit." Some folks think so much of themselves that they can't bring themselves to deal honestly with others. They can't think of their being wrong at anytime. A proud look is an abomination to the Lord. "Pride goeth before destruction, and a haughty spirit before a fall" (Prov. 16:18).

Envy. Envy is defined as "intolerant rivalry." Think about how unfairly Joseph was treated by his brothers. "And the patriarchs, moved with envy, sold Joseph into Egypt" (Acts 7:9). When the Israelites said, "Saul hath slain his thousands, and David his ten thousands," it was too much for Saul. "And Saul eyed David from that day and forward" (1 Sam. 18:7-9). He dealt very unfairly with David, accelerating his own downfall before God. No one can deal dishonestly with man and still be right with God.

Prejudice. "Prejudice" may be defined as "to prejudge; to judge without or before the facts have been gathered." It is founded in ignorance and continues to exist in ignorance. Prejudice caused the Jews to be unfair with Stephen in stoning him to death (Acts 7:57-58). It is the lock on the door of the closed mind, the ignorance we usually mistake for reason, the first enemy of information and progress. It is intellectual stigmatism, a perfect combination of conceit and ignorance. Prejudice never saved a soul or settled any question in the light of truth and justice. It is the defense of the devil, the shell of a petrified mind, and the ceiling on understanding. Prejudice keeps individuals from playing fair with God and man!

Covetous. We view covetousness as being "inordinate desire of something which belongs to another." A covetous individual will stoop to most anything to obtain his objective. So completely can covetousness control an individual that Paul was directed to write that it is idolatry (Col. 3:5; Eph. 5:5). Fairness is not in the vocabulary of the covetous individual. In seeking his goal, he is unconcerned about his treatment of others. Be not deceived, the covetous person shall not inherit the kingdom of God (1 Cor. 6:10).

Love of Authority. In writing unto the well-beloved Gaius, John stated, "I wrote unto the church: but Diotrephes, who loveth to have the preeminence among them, receiveth us not. Wherefore, if I come, I will remember his deeds which he doeth, prating against us with malicious words: and not content therewith, neither doth he himself receive the brethren, and forbiddeth them that would, and casteth them out of the church" (3 John 9-10). Here was an individual who loved the preeminence. His love of authority forbade him to receive the brethren. Such led him to deal unfairly with these brethren.

Ignorance and Unbelief. In describing his life before becoming a Christian, Paul stated, "who was before a blasphemer, and a persecutor, and injurious: but I obtained mercy, because I did it ignorantly in unbelief" (1 Tim. 1:13). In ignorance and unbelief, he had persecuted Christians. His ignorance and unbelief led him to be very unfair just as it has done to many through the ages. Ignorance is not excusable! Whether in ignorance or under knowledge, it is quite sinful to refuse to play fair in all phases of life.

Christians need to hold this principle in reverence: "Therefore all things whatsoever ye would that men should do to you, do ye even so to them: for this is the law and prophets" (Matt. 7:12).

Playing Fair (2)

In the last article we discussed a number of reasons why people refuse to be honest and play fair in life. Space would not permit us to complete the study regarding this subject. We continue with some observations regarding with whom we should be fair. We believe this to be a vital subject! Some individuals have the conception that they can be fair with someone or something and this alone constitutes them as being a fair person. Such reasoning conveys a gross misconception of our responsibilities to the relationships of life. Actually, it would be rather difficult to find an individual that, at one time or another, didn't demonstrate fairness to someone in life. Christians need to be fair with all and not feel that fairness to one or so covers the unfairness manifested to others. We are aware of the fact that it is perhaps easier to show fairness to some than it is to others, but the difficulty does not exempt one from the obligation that he has before God and man to be fair in his dealings.

With Whom Should We Be Fair?

With God. When the subject of fairness is considered, there are multitudes who never consider that God is to be treated fairly. God, who should be our first concern, is at times completely ignored. People seem to feel that they can treat God anyway and still be fair-minded individuals. Paul wrote that the Gentiles were not fair with God, "Because that, when they knew God, they glorified him not as God, neither were thankful" (Rom. 1:21). Jeremiah lamented the unfairness of the people of God in his day saying, "For my people have committed two evils; they have forsaken me the fountain of living waters, and hewed them out cisterns, broken cisterns, that can hold no water" (Jer. 2:13). Fairness with God demands that we love him (Matt. 22:37), wholeheartedly obey him (Rom. 6:17-18), worship him (John 4:23-24), and give him the glory that he deserves (1 Cor. 10:31).

With Christ. Jesus said of some, "They hated me without a

Speaking Truth in Love

cause" (John 15:25). Saul of Tarsus dealt unfairly with the Christ and was asked on the Damascus road, "Saul, why persecutest thou me?" (Acts 9:4). Saul was persecuting Christ's body, the church. Fairness with Christ involves faithful obedience to his words of life. The principle of shame has caused men to play unfairly with Christ. Concerning such, Jesus said, "Whosoever therefore shall be ashamed of me and of my words, in this adulterous and sinful generation, of him also shall the Son of man be ashamed, when he cometh in the glory of his Father with the holy angels" (Mark 8:38).

With Self. This suggests an area where some never think of being fair. We need to be fair with ourselves that we can be fair in dealing with others. Fairness with self involves examining self to see that we are what we ought to be and not some hypocrite. "Examine yourselves, whether ye be in the faith; prove your own selves. Know ye not your own selves, how that Jesus Christ is in you, except ye be reprobates?" (2 Cor. 13:5). We are taught not to deceive ourselves. When we let that happen, we are refusing to be fair with ourselves. "For if a man think himself to be something, when he is nothing, he deceiveth himself. But let every man prove his own work, and then shall he have rejoicing in himself alone, and not in another" (Gal. 6:3-4). A person who thinks more highly of himself than he ought to think is not dealing fairly with himself. God would have all men to properly evaluate their lives on the basis of the Scriptures (Rom. 12:3).

With Family. Selfishness exists in some families to the extent that fairness with one another does not exist. Families need to heed Paul's admonition: "Look not every man on his own things, but every man on the things of others" (Phil. 2:4). Proper support from the head of the family is only fair (1 Tim. 5:8). Every member is obligated to follow a clean life that no shame falls upon the family. Consideration, love, and faithfulness are all to be a definite part of one being fair with his family. Cheating in unfaithfulness leaves bitterness and scars that are hard to overcome.

With the Church. If we are fair with the church, we have learned

Pollution—A Grave Concern

We are hearing a great deal about pollution control. It would appear that the American people are awakening to the need for anti-pollution laws which would help to keep our air, water, and environment clean. Practically every newspaper has some article dealing with the subject of pollution. Even some political candidates have made the theme of pollution the main platform of their campaign. Perhaps this awakening is long over due. Many of our natural resources have taken a tremendous beating due to the ravages of pollution. Webster defines pollution as "to make unclean, impure, or corrupt; define."

As we have definitely stated, it is well and good to place emphasis upon pollution in areas that affect our physical welfare. But what about the sphere of spiritual pollution? Here is an area that is far more important; yet many people seem to ignore it completely. In his second epistle, Peter wrote, "For if after they have escaped the pollutions of the world through the knowledge of the Lord and Saviour Jesus Christ, they are again entangled therein, and overcome, the latter end is worse with them than the beginning" (2 Pet. 2:20). In this verse, Peter speaks of pollutions of the world that Christians had escaped in their obeying the gospel of Christ. He points them to the fact that through unfaithfulness to the will of God they could permit themselves to be entangled again in these pollutions and be overcome in them. Such could affect their lives to such a magnitude that "the latter end is worse with them than the beginning." Other translations render the word translated "pollutions" in the King James Version as "contaminations" or "defilements."

Wouldn't it be wonderful if people would become as concerned over spiritual pollutions as so many have awakened to environmental pollutions? We are even aware of the fact that some who profess to be Christians seem to be relatively unconcerned about pollution of their souls. We must continually fight this pollution or find ourselves "again entangled therein, and overcome."

Pollution Which The Christian Must Fight

The Heart. The wise man wrote, "for as he thinketh in his heart, so is he" (Prov. 23:7). "Keep thy heart with all diligence; for out of it are the issues of life" (Prov. 4:23). Jesus stated, "Blessed are the pure in heart: for they shall see God" (Matt. 5:8). Peter speaks of both Jew and Gentile "purifying their hearts by faith" (Acts 15:9). Obedient faith in Christ can keep our hearts free of contamination and filth of pollution. We must continue in this faith to keep pollution out of our hearts.

The Home. Unscriptural marriages and divorces have polluted many homes. Such has become so common that many homes are hardly worthy of the designation. The teaching of Christ regarding marriage and divorce is being disregarded and supplanted by lust and the philosophy, "why, everyone is doing it"! Christians need to stand firm for the truth regarding the sanctity of the home and be free of this pollution that undermines the very heart of society and nations. Jesus stated that the only cause for divorce and remarriage is fornication (Matt. 19:3-9). Look about and observe how lightly some professed Christians view this truth. Furthermore, in many homes the father is not recognized as the head of the wife and the children are not being trained in the proper manner before God (Eph. 5:23-26; 6:1-4). The majority may not desire that such be called pollution, but what else is it when the truth of God's word is so degraded and abused? The truth evidently has become too "old-fashioned" for some so-called "Christians."

Morals. It is almost unbelievable that the practices that now exist in the present world were almost unmentionable a decade or so ago. Pre-marital relationships have always been practiced to an extent, but now we find even religious people and churches recognizing such relationships as not being sinful but admirable in some incidents. Same sex marriages are being considered as honorable by the legislators in some of our states. The word "fornication" has become a forgotten word in many pulpits and its meaning has been made a point of jest. Members of families where the parents profess to be members of the Lord's church have acknowledged that fornication was permitted in their home. And these same parents have blamed other members of the church for their children not being spiritually minded! Paul admonished the Corinthians to "flee fornication" (1 Cor. 6:18). This is an admonition for all who respect the will of God. God's people need to stand firm for the truth and not let such moral degradation pollute their personal lives. We need an anti-pollution tag before it becomes too late!

Providing Things Honest

In the confused standards of society in which we live, it is apparent, in many respects, that honesty has become a forgotten virtue. On every hand we read of corruption and graft in places of leadership and authority, the very places where great emphasis should be placed upon honesty! With such an environment, it is no wonder that the younger generation is maturing with the perverted conception that to be honest is to be a "square"! Perhaps this age is comparable to the time when the ancient philosopher walked about in daylight with a lighted lantern hoping to be able to find an honest man.

The Lord's people must not be lacking in honesty! There may be a gross amount of dishonesty in the world, but let's not overlook the fact that Christians are not to be of this world. The religion that Christ has given emphasizes the virtue of honesty. Paul wrote, "Provide things honest in the sight of all men" (Rom. 12:18). Again, "providing for honest things, not only in the sight of the Lord, but also in the sight of men" (2 Cor. 8:21). Among those things that Christians are to think upon is "whatsoever things are honest" (Phil. 4:8). We are to pray "for all that are in authority; that we may lead a quiet and peaceable life in all godliness and honesty" (1 Tim. 2:2). Peter admonished Christians to abstain from fleshly lusts, which war against the soul, "having your conversation honest among the Gentiles" (1 Pet. 2:11-12). As we contemplate honesty, we need to be honest with everyone and all things. Some may be alert in manifesting honesty to some people and things and at the same time neglect the others.

We Need To Be Honest

Toward God. Some folks never think about being honest toward God. They actually have no conception of what honesty toward God involves. Honesty toward God means that we place him first. His commandments are not to be neglected. We are not to rob him (Mal. 3:8-9). Some men would never think about robbing or lying in reference to men. They are honest with men and yet have no hesitation in withholding from the Lord that which is rightfully his. Are we truly obeying his commandments (1 John 5:3)? Are we giving as we should (Matt. 6:33; 1 Cor. 16:1-2)? Examination may reveal that we have become cheats as far as responding wholeheartedly to the will of the Lord.

Toward the Church. The local church of which I am a member has the right to expect certain things of me. Faithfulness to God necessitates my being a part of a faithful congregation. That congregation has a right to expect that I live a clean, pure life, that I support the work of the church, and that I cooperate with others who are endeavoring to do the will of the Lord in that local church. The principle of honesty demands that I do so. How can I be honest with myself, God, and man and not endeavor to bear my responsibilities as a member of the church of the Lord? What if every member of the church were like me? Would the cause of the Lord be flourishing? We have nothing to hide or conceal. Nothing has been done in a corner! Honesty does not hide or conceal the facts. Are you being honest toward the congregation?

Toward Self. One of the most miserable of people is the character who knows that he has not been honest with himself. He cannot be right in heart and be dishonest with himself. When we deceive ourselves we are actually being dishonest with self. Paul wrote, "For if a man think himself to be something, when he is nothing, he deceiveth himself. But let every man prove his own work, and then shall be have rejoicing in himself alone, and not in another.

For every man shall bear his own burden" (Gal. 6:3-5). Men are prone to blame others for their situations and attempt to justify themselves when the root of their problem lies in the fact that they have been dishonest. They have done what they know to be wrong. The only way to correct it is to repent and return to God in God's appointed way.

Toward Others. "Provide things honest in the sight of all men" (Rom. 12:17). ". . . that ye may walk honestly toward them that are without, and that we may have lack of nothing" (1 Thess. 4:12). How can we ever expect to influence anyone for good and not be honest in our words and deeds? "Therefore all things whatsoever ye would that men should do to you, do ye even so to them: for is the law and the prophets" (Matt. 7:12). Let's all be honest with one another—that is certainly what we desire of others!!

The following story is a good example of what effect dishonesty can have upon one's influence. "After attending a church service a dentist said to the preacher, 'I cannot attend this church again.' When the preacher asked why, the dentist said, 'One of your members was singing praises to God through teeth she refused to pay for.' Unpaid bills can bring shame to God and his work." Heaven is for honest people—just how honest are you?

Refreshing Christians

The word "refreshing" is defined as "to restore strength, spirit, etc." It is opposed to stale or stagnant. The word "refreshing" is used in the Scriptures to describe some Christians. Paul uses the word several times and it appears to be also peculiar to his writings. There are some Christians in whose presence we feel uncomfortable. Like a wintry blast, they seem to chill us through and through. On the other hand, there are those in whose presence we find sunshine and genuine delight. As water refreshes the thirsty, food the hungry, sleep the weary, and air the suffocating, there are Christians who refresh the souls of others. Who wants to be considered stale and stagnant? We should have a definite desire to be looked upon as refreshing! Paul evaluated Philemon in these words: "For we have great joy and consolation in thy love, because the bowels of the saints are refreshed by thee, brother" (Phile. 7).

Let us notice other Christians who refreshed Paul. In so doing, we can learn what is expected of us in refreshing Christians.

They were praying Christians. This is evident from what one reads in Romans 15:30-32: "Now I beseech you, brethren, for the Lord Jesus Christ's sake, and for the love of the Spirit, that ye strive together with me in your prayers to God for me; that I may be delivered from them that do not believe in Judea; and that my service which I have for Jerusalem may be accepted of the saints; that I may come unto you with joy by the will of God, and may with you be refreshed." This language was written by Paul before he went to Rome. In it he requested their prayers to the end that he and they might be refreshed. The prayers of saints are refreshing to the weary worker in the kingdom of God. Paul was desirous of their prayers for him. This was foremost in his mind at such a time. Christians are refreshing to fellow workers in the vineyard of the Lord when they pray for them and are not ashamed to let them know about it. If we aren't careful, we can become so self-centered that we pray only for our needs without concern for anyone else. We hardly refresh ourselves, let alone any of our brethren!

They were optimistic Christians. This thought is suggested by Paul's words in 1 Corinthians 16:17-18: "I am glad of the coming of Stephanas and Fortunatus and Achaicus: for that which was lacking on your part they have supplied. For they have refreshed my spirit and yours: therefore acknowledge ye them that are such." Evil tidings concerning the brethren in Corinth had reached the ears of the apostle. These things had depressed his soul, but the coming of these brethren refreshed him. Perhaps, they presented the bright side of a dark picture. The optimist brightens while the pessimist dampens. One has defined an optimist as "a person who finds a worm in the morning and anticipates fish for dinner." When the pessimist thinks he is taking a chance, the optimist feels he is grasping an opportunity. The optimist looks upon life as an unexpected dividend; the pessimist, as a note coming due. We are not to discolor the situation and deny facts, but all things considered, Christians have every right to be optimistic. "What shall we then say to these things? If God be for us, who can be against us? He that spared not his own Son, but delivered him up for us all, how shall he not with him also freely give us all things? Who shall lay any thing to the charge of God's elect? It is God that justifieth. Who is he that condemneth? It is Christ that died, yes rather, that is risen again, who is even at the right hand of God, who also maketh intercession for us" (Rom. 8:31-34). Optimism is catching and it is a very refreshing thing as compared to pessimism.

They were responsive Christians. We note this thought from 2 Corinthians 7:13: "Therefore we were comforted in your comfort: yea, and exceedingly the more joyed we for the joy of Titus, because his spirit was refreshed by you all." Hearing of the sins of the Corinthians, Paul sent them a letter by Titus calling the congregation to repentance. The church had responded in proper repentance and Paul sent them another letter in which he related how their response had been refreshing. Perhaps nothing refreshes Christians more than seeing those who need to repent respond to the will of God. It is never refreshing to see people give a deaf ear to the word of God. Our faith should never waver when people reject the word of God. It is still God's word and just as powerful as it ever was. However, what a refreshing thing it is to see people obey and respond to the truth as they should. Such adds emphasis to the glorious fact that the word of the Lord lives and abides forever.

Let's give heed to being refreshing Christians. This certainly means that we fervently pray for workers in the kingdom, that we are filled with optimism, and that the word "quit" is not a part of our vocabulary as we continue to be diligent doers of his word.

Regarding Love

Without love, we are nothing (1 Cor. 13:1-3). This is the great theme of the New Testament. It is hard to overemphasize the value of love, yet, it can be done. On occasions, we are aware of brethren making the following observations: "If there had been more love, the division over institutionalism, co-operation, and the social gospel would have never occurred." Some are also making this observation in reference to the differences that have arisen over the unity-in-diversity issue. They are contending that love would have prevented any division that has affected the church concerning these and other matters. I have no problem with such observations if love for the truth is the love that is involved. When all brethren love the truth and sincerely endeavor to accept nothing but the truth, doctrinal differences that result in division can be avoided. However, it is evident that not all brethren will love and accept the truth on some matters of faith. Paul wrote of those perishing, "because they received not the love of the truth, that they might be saved" (2 Thess. 2:10). Love of the truth will encourage servants of the Lord to preach it and exhort all men to follow it. Unfortunately, there are those who are determined to follow things that are not in the pattern of truth, and they resent being told of their sins. I have come to conclude that, when brethren say that love would have prevented the divisions among us, they are thinking of their definition of love which says to leave them alone and still fellowship them in whatever they do. Paul wrote, "And have no fellowship with the unfruitful works of darkness, but rather reprove them. For it is a shame even to speak of those things which are done of them in secret" (Eph. 5:11-12). This is truth! Love of the truth would have disciples of the Lord practicing the truth, rather than advocating an umbrella of love that ignores it.

"But speaking the truth in love, may grow up into him in all things, which is the head, even Christ" (Eph. 4:15). The truth is to be spoken in love. The speaker has the responsibility of speaking the truth in love. The verse does not say "speak lovingly," but speaking in love for the truth and the souls of those who hear the message. Perhaps, those who cry that love would have prevented the divisions, dwell on the manner of the presentation. Every preacher should give thought to his manner of presenting the word of God, but what right does anyone have to say that such is greater than the truth? There is no indication of such in the Scriptures. The parable of the sower places the failure on the hearts of the hearers. Failure is not accredited to the seed sown or the manner of the sower sowing the seed (Luke 8).

There are things that love covers. This is brought to our attention in 1 Peter 4:8: "And above all things have fervent love for one another, 'for love will cover a multitude of sins'" (NKJV). This appears to involve our dealings with one another or things that affect our personal lives. There are things that we are to ignore that would otherwise lead to ill feelings and sin. But does this authorize love overlooking sinful practices that have led to division in the Lord's church? A positive answer places the thought in contradiction with what is stated in Ephesians 5:11-12. The tendency of some individuals is to place the blame for every failure on those laboring to practice the truth rather than on those who will not accept it. Their commentary is that, if there had been more love in those teaching and more love in ignoring some practices, then the division could have been averted. All the love in the world is not going to result in some people accepting the truth whereby brethren can walk together with them in truth.

"So there was a division among the people because of him" (John 7:43). "Because of him" refers to the greatest individual that has ever lived, Jesus Christ. Are we prepared to say that the lack of Christ's love resulted in the division? God forbid! There were those accepting the claims of Christ and there were those who had not the love of the truth in their hearts. When Paul warned Timothy concerning Alexander, the coppersmith, was he lacking in love to do so? "Alexander the coppersmith did me much evil: the Lord reward him according to his works: Of whom be thou ware also:

for he hath greatly withstood our words" (2 Tim. 4:14-15). This difference was a love problem! Alexander did not have the love of the truth in his heart to walk in truth and refrain from doing evil. The beloved apostle John had lack of fellowship with Diotrephes. "I wrote unto the church: but Diotrephes, who loveth to have the preeminence among them, receiveth us not" (3 John 9). This was another love problem. Diotrephes had the love of preeminence rather than a love for the truth. Are we to conclude that John was lacking in love when he wrote this of Diotrephes? There is nothing that will take the place of love of the truth. When we have it in our hearts, we can walk with God and walk with those of like precious faith. "Can two walk together, except they be agreed?" (Amos 3:3).

Rejoice in the Lord Always (1)

(Phil. 4:4)

To rejoice in the Lord is a command that many times is overlooked even by those who appear somewhat zealous in obeying other commandments found in the Scriptures. This command is not optional, but quite imperative. Christians cannot disregard it and be true to the Lord. How many sermons have you heard concerning this text? In stressing other commands, here is one that is often overlooked. Let us notice some facts about this command:

A Discriminating Command

The phrase "in the Lord" refers to relationship. Those "in the Lord" are those who have obeyed the gospel and put on Christ (Gal. 3:26-27). Christians are "in the Lord" and are to rejoice in him. The blessings of Christ are with them (Eph. 1:3), and they have reason to rejoice. In regard to the Lord of what does an alien sinner have to rejoice? He has none of the spiritual blessings that are in Christ for he has not obeyed the gospel of Christ (Rom. 6:17-18). There are some things in which it is vain to rejoice and the Christian should beware of these things.

In the flesh. In this same book, Paul wrote, "For we are the circumcision, which worship God in the spirit, and rejoice in Christ Jesus, and have no confidence in the flesh" (Phil. 3:3). Concerning confidence in the flesh he further wrote: "But what things were gain to me, those I counted loss for Christ" (Phil. 3:7).

In the wisdom of the world. "Where is the wise? Where is the scribe? Where is the disputer of this world? Hath not God made foolish the wisdom of this world? For after that in the wisdom of God the world by wisdom knew not God, it pleased God by the foolishness of preaching to save them that believe" (1 Cor. 1:20-21).

In one's own righteousness. "Not by works of righteousness which we have done, but according to his mercy he saved us, by the washing of regeneration, and renewing of the Holy Ghost" (Tit. 3:5). The prophet Isaiah referred to the righteousness of man "as filthy rags" (Isa. 64:6). We need to work God's righteousness (Acts 10:34-35; Rom. 10:1-3).

We Are To Rejoice In Those Things Which Pertain Unto the Lord

In the truth concerning him. Having the promise of God that sins were forgiven, the eunuch went on his way rejoicing (Acts 8:39). In personifying love, Paul spoke of it as pertaining to truth, "rejoiceth not in iniquity, but rejoiceth in truth" (1 Cor. 13:6). "I have no greater joy than to hear that my children walk in truth" (3 John 4). When the truth is preached, the people of God should rejoice. Whatever pertains to truth should be an element of rejoicing with the children of God.

In the hope God instills in his children. Hope is a very precious thing! Paul wrote that Christians "are saved by hope" (Rom. 8:28). The apostle spoke of himself saying that he was "in hope of eternal life, which God, that cannot lie, promised before the world began" (Tit. 1:2). Hope is dependent upon the promise of God. Through God's word and the promises therein, hope is instilled in the heart of the obedient child of God. This hope, the Hebrew writer refers to "as an anchor of the soul, both sure and steadfast" (Heb. 6:19). In this hope there is ever reason for rejoicing. Troubles and sorrows may arise, but in the midst of these, the Christian still has a foundation of rejoicing in the hope of eternal life. While hope is a precious thing, the absence of hope is a very dismal condition. Before obeying the gospel of Christ, the Ephesians were described by these words: "That at that time ye were without Christ, being aliens from the commonwealth of Israel, and strangers from the covenants of promise, having no hope, and without God in the world" (Eph. 2:12). But read the following verse and see their basis of rejoicing: "but now, in Christ Jesus, ye who sometime were far off are made nigh by the blood of Christ." Now they had hope and reason for rejoicing. Have you obeyed the gospel that you might have hope and reason for rejoicing in the Lord (Mark 16:15-16)?

In the fact that the disciples' names are written in heaven. The seventy returned to the Lord with joy over the fact that the devils were subject unto them through the Lord's name. Jesus replied, "Notwithstanding, in this rejoice not, that the spirits are subject unto you; but rather rejoice, because your names are written in heaven" (Luke 17:20). Here is mentioned grounds for perverted rejoicing and grounds for true rejoicing. They were not to rejoice that the devils were subject to them but that their names were written in heaven. Our names are written in heaven or in the book of life as we obey the gospel of Christ (Acts 2:38-41; Phil. 4:3; Heb. 12:23). Let's rejoice in these things.

Rejoice in the Lord Always (2)

We can think of no lesson or theme that is more worthy of consideration than that of rejoicing in the Lord. This is a command that many times is overlooked. By the actions of some who profess to be Christians, one is led to wonder if such people are aware that Paul wrote, "Rejoice in the Lord always: and again I say, Rejoice" (Phil. 4:4). The burden of the last article was to emphasize that this is a discriminating command. The place of rejoicing is "in the Lord" and only those who have obeyed the Lord have a reason for rejoicing in him (Acts 8:37). Men have abused the principle of rejoicing by undertaking to rejoice in things that are not compatible with the teaching of Christ. For Christians to rejoice in the flesh, in the wisdom of the world, or in their own righteousness is for them to rejoice in vain things. Of what should Christians rejoice? We endeavored to emphasize that their rejoicing should be in the truth concerning the Lord, in the hope that the Lord instills in children of God, and in the fact that the names of his disciples are written in heaven (Luke 17:20). We proceed in this lesson to note from Philippians 4:4 that this is . . .

A Perpetual Command

Always. The joy of a Christian is not something akin to a mood or temperament that comes and goes with changing winds, but a perpetual spring. The epistle to the Philippians has been termed the epistle of joy. Some seventeen times, the words "joy," "rejoice," or "rejoicing" are found in this four-chapter epistle. Where was the apostle when he wrote it? He was in Rome as a prisoner for preaching the gospel of Christ (Phil. 1:12-13). Yet, he wrote of contentment and joy under such trying circumstances! When should the Christian rejoice?

Whether in prosperity or in adversity, rejoice. "Yea, and if I be offered upon the sacrifice and service of your faith, I joy and rejoice with you all. For the same cause also do ye joy, and rejoice with me" (Phil. 3:17-18).

Whether amid friends or shut up in prison, rejoice. As we have already noted, this letter which is dominated by joy was written by Paul, the prisoner. Concerning the preaching of Christ, he wrote: "What then? Notwithstanding, every way, whether in pretense, or in truth, Christ is preached; and I therein do rejoice, yea, and will rejoice" (Phil. 1:18). Paul could even rejoice when there were those preaching Christ of contention, not sincerely, supposing to add affliction to his bonds. Christ was being preached and that was the thing that prompted rejoicing in the apostle.

Whether in sickness or in health, rejoice. When in sickness, there is the Christ to help us bear the pain and suffering; the great physician is ever concerned with the suffering of his people. When in health, there should be rejoicing for the health that affords us energy to be active in his service. There are faithful saints who rejoice in the Lord in the time of sickness to such an extent that in our health, we feel almost ashamed that we do not evidence more rejoicing.

Whether favored by men or persecuted by them, rejoice. "Blessed are ye, when men shall revile you, and persecute you, and shall say all manner of evil against you falsely, for my sake. Rejoice, and be exceeding glad: for great is your reward in heaven: for so persecuted they the prophets which were before you" (Matt. 5:11-12). When the apostles were beaten for preaching in the name of Christ, "they departed from the presence of the council, rejoicing that they were counted worthy to suffer shame for his name" (Acts 5:41). When we do God's will, we have his assurance that he is with us. Why shouldn't we rejoice whatever the circumstances may be?

Whether in life or in death, "rejoice in the Lord." It was the writer of this epistle who wrote, "For to me to live is Christ, and to die is gain." The life that one lives in the Lord is preparing him for the appointment of death. There is rejoicing in the death of faithful saints. For them "to die is gain." They depart to be with Christ. "And I heard a voice from heaven saying unto me, Write, Blessed are the dead which die in the Lord from henceforth: Yea, saith the Spirit, that they may rest from their labours; and their works do follow them" (Rev. 14:13).

Keeping this command to rejoice in the Lord brings many gratifying results. It helps to cure dissensions when they exist among God's children. Perhaps Euodias and Syntyche needed more rejoicing in the Lord to help them be of the same mind in the Lord (Phil. 4:2). Rejoicing in the Lord can put to death murmuring. Rejoicing and murmuring are not done at the same time. In many respects, rejoicing will preserve health and one's efficiency. Our personal attraction will be enhanced and our religion will radiate a wholesome influence upon the lives of others. We need to rejoice more in the Lord!

Reverence For God

Acceptable service to God must be with reverence and godly fear. "Wherefore we receiving a kingdom which cannot be moved, let us have grace, whereby we may serve God acceptably with reverence and godly fear" (Heb. 12:28). Reverence for God should be everywhere. The pathetic note is that it is usually a scarce article. We speak of reverence for our country, the flag, the aged, various memorials, and for the dead. Consideration should be given to these, but above all, there should be reverence for the Living God. Just what is reverence? "Honor and respect felt or manifested—profound respect mingled with love and awe" (Webster). It is closely akin to honor, respect, and admiration and even includes these thoughts. There must be a difference between worship and reverence. We are taught to worship God and him only (Matt. 4:10). Pertaining to the relationship between husband and wife, Paul admonished the wife to reverence her husband (Eph. 5:33). As one considers these two passages, he can see that there must be a difference between worship and reverence. We might conclude that reverence is a requisite or essential of worship and that one cannot worship acceptably without reverence.

Why Should Reverence For God Be Above All?

He is the Creator (Gen. 1:1; 2:7). The creature should certainly fear, love, and respect his Creator, but that is not always true (Rom. 1:25). Man has at times made a miserable failure of his mission in glorifying God (Isa. 43:7).

Man is dependent upon God as a guide (Jer. 10:23). God who is so good to supply us with such means of guidance should be an object of our deepest reverence. Men should show great honor and respect to those who guided them to safety and greatly helped in making them what they are today. Think what God has done for his children!

God is the father of our spirits. As the father of our spirits, he rightly deserves our reverence (Heb. 12:9). God has made our bodies and is father of spirits. Both body and spirit must unite in reverential service to him.

How May We Show Our Reverence For God?

Reverence his name. The word "reverend" is only found once in the King James Version of the Bible and when it does appear, it has reference to God (Ps. 111:9). It is a lack of reverence for God to refer to any man as "Reverend." We reverence his name by not using it in a vain way. God's name is to be hallowed and not used in vain (Matt. 6:9). It is never right or proper to use profanity or even the euphemistic by-words such as "gosh," "golly," "gee," "lordy," which are corrupted forms of God's name. His name should never be used in any light, useless, or flippant way. (Eph. 4:29; 5:3-4).

Reverence his word. One cannot reverence God and disrespect his word. He who reverences the word will not wrest or pervert the Scriptures to his own destruction (2 Pet. 3:16). "... but to this man will I look, even to him that is poor and of a contrite spirit, and trembleth at my word" (Isa. 66:2). So many in the Lord's church appear to have lost the proper reverence for his word. Their attitude betrays them!

Reverence his commandments. We can't reverence the person and scoff at his word and the commandments that we are to obey. "For this is the love of God, that we keep his commandments: and his commandments are not grievous" (1 John 5:3). When we wholeheartedly obey, we are proving our love for the Lord and manifesting reverence for his commandments. It is the curse of inconsistency to contend that we have reverence for God and then refuse to do what he has for us to obey.

Reverence the worship of God. To enter the court of praise with fear and devotion, respect and love are the highest thoughts of reverence. In every service, we should understand that we are in the presence of God. An ideal assembly is mentioned in Acts 10:33: "Now therefore are we all here present before God, to hear all things that are commanded thee of God." Generally speaking, our actions depict the feelings that are in our hearts. Outward signs are indications of inward feelings. Talking, laughing, and unnecessary gestures in the services do not depict an atmosphere of reverence. A visitor at a particular service was quoted as saying that the service had more of a circus atmosphere than that of worship to God. With proper preparation and thought, things that tend to disturb the spirit of reverence in the worship, could be easily eliminated. Some may deny the fact that they lack reverence, but it is hard to convince others that they possess it by their conduct in the assemblies. God knows our hearts. We cannot deceive him! We must possess proper reverence for God if we hope to enter heaven.

Right and Wrong

Few words in our vocabularies are more often used than the words "right and wrong." These words or their equivalents are used by all persons in all nations. Though the words are frequently used, there is a great difference when deciding what is right and what is wrong. Ancient Sparta encouraged theft and approved of it as being right. We have read where Plato recommended the murder of weak and sickly children and even speaks of drunkenness at the feast of Bacchus as being proper and quite praiseworthy. Contrary to the views of our society, the Stoics commended suicide as a cardinal virtue. The ancient philosophers generally disregarded the obligation of marriage. We might mention a number of other incidents of individuals approving as right principles that others generally view as wrong. Man needs a standard to determine right and wrong. As a farmer estimates by a half-bushel and a merchant by means of a yard-stick, so mankind needs the proper standard to determine what is right and what is wrong. "O lord, I know that the way of man is not in himself: it is not in man that walketh to direct his steps" (Jer. 10:23).

Will the Standard be One's Conscience? Conscience is defined as the "faculty, power, or inward principle which decides as to the character of one's actions, warning against and condemning that which is wrong, and approving that which is right." Conscience plays an important part in an individual's life, but it is not the position of conscience to determine what is right or wrong. One's conscience will accuse or convict (Rom. 2:15; 9:1). When we do what we believe to be right, conscience will approve of our actions as being right. On the other hand, when we fail to do what we believe to be right, conscience will warn and condemn us for our actions. Saul of Tarsus had his conscience set with the Law of Moses and he felt it was right for Christians to be persecuted which he did with "all good conscience before God" (Acts 23:1). His conscience did not make his improper knowledge right. The standard for right and wrong can never be one's conscience. Conscience must have the standard on which to function. It is not the prerogative of conscience to determine this standard!

Will the Standard be Expediency? "Expediency" is defined as "apt and suitable for the end in view. The doing or consideration of what is selfish rather than what is right or just; guided by self-interest." There are those who contend that happiness is our being's end and aim. Anything, in their estimation, that will bring happiness is therefore right. Such a view very definitely sanctions and encourages selfishness. There is more involved in right and wrong than what affects one individual. Furthermore, man in himself is not capable of knowing what will bring or produce happiness. He may think that he is capable, but his history of tragic failures cries to the contrary. Expediency can never be the proper standard for right and wrong. It involves such things that are too high and complex for finite reasoning.

Will the Inspired Scriptures be the Standard? They were definitely given for this exalted purpose! Paul informed Timothy, "All scripture is given by inspiration of God, and is profitable for doctrine, for reproof, for correction, for instruction in righteousness: that the man of God may be perfect, throughly furnished unto all good works" (2 Tim. 3:16-17). The Scriptures reveal the mind of God (1 Cor. 2:9-13). They have been given "for instruction in righteousness." Those things approved by the Scriptures are right. On the other hand, any practice or principle that is not approved by the Scriptures is wrong. The proper standard for right and wrong must come from without man. Jeremiah emphasized this by stating "that the way of man is not in himself: it is not in man that walketh to direct his steps" (Jer. 10:23). If for no other reason, conscience and expediency must be rejected as the standard for right and wrong due to the fact that they are from within man and not guidance from without. As the Psalmist wrote, "Thou shalt guide me with thy counsel, and afterward receive me to glory" (Ps. 73:24). The Lord guides men in the right way and that way is revealed in the Scriptures which man is rightly to divide or handle aright. "Study to shew thyself approved unto God, a workman that needeth not to be ashamed, rightly dividing the word of truth" (2 Tim. 2:15).

When anyone affirms something as being that which is right in the sight of God, for it to be so, he must be able to prove it by the word of God (1 Thess. 5:21). Any teacher of God's word should reverence this principle. Something may appear to be good and men may like it that way, but where does the God of heaven say it is right? Remember, "There is a way which seemeth right unto a man; but the end thereof are the ways of death" (Prov. 14:12).

Salvation to the Uttermost (1)

"And they truly were many priests, because they were not suffered to continue by reason of death: but this man, because he continueth ever, hath an unchangeable priesthood. Wherefore he is able to save them to the uttermost that come unto God by him, seeing he ever liveth to make intercession for them" (Heb. 7:23-25). This is one of several passages in the book of Hebrews which shows contrast between the eternal and unchangeable priesthood of Christ and the ministries of the earthly priests of the Levitical priesthood. The earthly priests were mortal men, but not so with Christ for "he ever liveth"—"he hath an unchangeable priesthood." That Jesus Christ is able or has the power to save is the theme of the entire New Testament (Matt. 1:21; Luke 19:10; Heb. 5:8-9).

This passage affirms that Christ is able to save "them to the uttermost that come unto God by him." What is the meaning of the word "uttermost"? Webster defines the word as "situated at the farthest point; most extreme, distant." The word is translated from a Greek word, *panteles* which suggests perfect, complete. Williams in the *New Testament in the Language of the People* renders the phrase, "to save completely." The idea stressed in the text is complete and perfect salvation provided through Jesus Christ.

Several assertions are found in the clause. "He is able to save to the uttermost."

From the Uttermost Depth of Depravity. There is no degree of guilt from which he cannot save. ". . . he that cometh to me I will in no wise cast out" (John 6:37). The chief of sinners may and can obey his gospel and be saved from his sins. Paul referred to Christ as coming "into the world to save sinners; of whom I am chief" (1 Tim. 1:15). Christ reaches down to the lowest and can lift to heights of purity and glory. In 1 Corinthians 6:9-11, the apostle reminds the Corinthians, "Know ye not that the unrighteous shall not inherit the kingdom of God? Be not deceived: neither fornicators, nor idolaters, nor adulterers, nor effeminate, nor abusers of themselves with mankind, nor thieves, nor covetous, nor drunkards, nor revilers, nor extortioners, shall inherit the kingdom of God. And such were some of you: but ye are washed, but ye are sanctified, but ye are justified in the name of the Lord Jesus, and by the Spirit of our God." Such were some of the Corinthians, but they had obeyed the gospel and Christ had saved them from the depth of these sins. Don't ever be guilty of saying of anyone that he is too evil to be saved! The gospel of Christ is a powerful thing and Christ can save from the uttermost depth of depravity!

To the Uttermost Limit of Time. His saving power continues undiminished by the lapse of time. "Jesus Christ the same yesterday, and today and for ever" (Heb. 13:8). Many systems have had a brief day of power and have passed away. Jesus Christ has not lost one jot or one tittle of his power to save. His saving arm extended to the transgressions of the Old Covenant and it extends forward till time shall be no more (Heb. 9:15). Christ is heaven's last argument and his saving power is to the uttermost limit of time.

To the Uttermost Completeness. This wasn't to be found under the first covenant. "For the law made nothing perfect, but the bringing in of a better hope did; by the which we draw nigh unto God" (Heb. 7:19). There was a remembrance again made of sins every year under the law (Heb. 10:3). In the New Covenant under Christ the Scripture says, "and their sins and iniquities will I remember no more. Now where remission of these is, there is no more offering for sin" (Heb. 10:17-18). Socialism may put a new coat on a man, but Jesus Christ can put a new man in the coat (2 Cor. 5:17). Christ can fully restore our lives to purity, beauty, and joy. He saves to the uttermost completeness as men faithfully continue in his truth.

To the Uttermost Degree of Man's Need—Last Limit of Life. Down past the last trying temptation, Christ is able to save. "For we have not a high priest which cannot be touched with the feeling of our infirmities; but was in all points tempted like as we are, yet without sin. Let us therefore come boldly unto the throne of grace, that we may obtain mercy, and find grace to help in time of need" (Heb. 4:15-16). Christ saves through the last trying experience—even death itself! He knows our needs and is both willing and able to save those who come unto God through him. He is able to save from sin here and from eternal destruction in the world to come. Have you obeyed his gospel (Mark16:16)? Are you faithful in Christ?

Salvation to the Uttermost (2)

> And they truly were many priests, because they were not suffered to continue by reason of death: but this man, because he continueth ever, hath an unchangeable priesthood. Wherefore he is able to save them to the uttermost that come unto God by him, seeing he ever liveth to make intercession for them (Heb. 7:23-25).

In the last article from this text in Hebrews 7 we dealt with what is the meaning of salvation to the uttermost and pointed out some of the things involved in Christ saving to the uttermost. From the uttermost depth of depravity, to the uttermost limit of time, to the uttermost completeness, and to the uttermost degree of man's need were the factors mentioned in his saving to the uttermost.

We will not take the time and space in this article to review these points, but rather consider the ground of his ability to save "them to the uttermost that come unto God by Him."

The ground of his ability to save to the uttermost is found in the expressions "because he continueth ever" and "he ever liveth."

The great glory of the faith that a Christian has is that he has a living Savior. "I am he that liveth, and was dead; and, behold, I am alive for evermore, Amen; and have the keys of hell and of death" (Rev.1:18). The priests of the Law of Moses were not suffered to continue by reason of death. In contrast, this man (Jesus Christ) because he continueth forever, hath an unchangeable priesthood.

Much emphasis is placed upon what Christ has done for the redemption of man. It is proper and right that such be emphasized, but let's not forget what Christ is doing for us. We have a living Savior and it is most vital to our eternal salvation that, as a living Savior, he works for the redeemed. Christ as our living Savior never grows weary, is never moody, is never out of patience with us, but is ever aware of our needs as he sits on the right hand of the throne of God. God's people sin (1 John 1:8-10). We need forgiveness to stand justified from our sins. This forgiveness is made possible through him that "ever liveth."

The Method of His Work

"To make intercession for them." As we have already stated and endeavored to emphasize, Christ is now doing something for us. Being clothed in power and authority, he is on the right hand of God to intercede for those who come to God by him. Perhaps no writer speaks of this more than John who says, "But if we walk in the light, as he is in the light, we have fellowship one with another, and the blood of Jesus Christ his Son cleanseth us from all sin" (1 John 1:7). Again, "My little children, these things write I unto you, that ye sin not. And if any man sin, we have an advocate with the

Father, Jesus Christ the righteous" (1 John 2:1). Christ spent his life on earth in the interest of men. He continues to devote himself to the same cause! "Who is he that condemneth? It is Christ that died, yea rather, that is risen again, who is even at the right hand of God, who also maketh intercession for us" (Rom. 8:34). His intercessory work is made available to his people as they comply with the conditions in his word.

The Condition of Obtaining "Salvation to the Uttermost"

Christ saves to the uttermost those "that come unto God by him." This involves a daily delight rather than an occasional privilege. "That come unto God by him" implies reverence for him, confidence in him, and obedience to him. As those who have obeyed the gospel of Christ (Mark 16:16) and have become Christians, we have the privilege of coming unto God through Christ. He intercedes for those who come unto God by him. This is why Christians are to strongly believe in prayer and "pray without ceasing" for it is in prayer that we make our desires and wants known. Christians are priests and Christ is their high priest. "But this man, because he continueth ever, hath an unchangeable priesthood" (Heb. 7:24).

Christ's saving power is complete in every detail. He died that we might have the atonement for sin and that our sins might be forgiven. He lives that he might intercede for us as we approach the throne of grace coming unto God by him. "Seeing then that we have a great high priest, that is passed into the heavens, Jesus the Son of God, let us hold fast our profession. For we have not an high priest which cannot be touched with the feeling of our infirmities; but was in all points tempted like as we are, yet without sin. Let us therefore come boldly unto the throne of grace, that we may obtain mercy, and find grace to help in time of need" (Heb. 4:14-16). May we ever rejoice that Christ can save to the uttermost.

Scornful Laughter

When Jesus came to the house of Jairus, a ruler of the synagogue, he found that the ruler's gravely ill twelve-year-old daughter had died. "And all wept, and bewailed her: but he said, Weep not; she is not dead, but sleepeth. And they laughed him to scorn, knowing that she was dead" (Luke 8:52-53). As he did in speaking of the death of Lazarus in John 11, Jesus on this occasion referred to death as sleep. This the people did not comprehend and they laughed him to scorn or laughed in a scornful manner. Others versions state that they simply laughed at him, while some of the editions of the NKJV speak of them ridiculing Jesus.

Laughter has its place in the lives of human beings. The writer of Proverbs stated, "A merry heart maketh a cheerful countenance . . . but he that is of a merry heart hath a continual feast" (Prov. 15:13, 15). Though laughter is not stated as being a part of the merry heart, there is reason to think that it is a part of it. We are speaking of laughter that is wholesome and grounded in good taste. It has been said that laughter is an index of a person's heart. What prompts one to laugh reveals what is in one's heart. Laughter that is uttered by the faithful in Christ should be prompted by things that are decent and righteous in the sight of the Lord. Scornful laughter or ridicule of individuals should not be a part of the Christian's demeanor. All who profess to follow Jesus should give serious thought to what causes them to laugh. Personal ridicule of others has no place in the lives of those truly striving to follow Christ. We are called upon to stand for the truth and oppose those who teach contrary to it. This we can do with all boldness without resorting to ridicule of individuals with whom we differ.

Some weeks ago, I received an e-mail of a particular politician's profile being shown in likeness to the profile of Frankenstein. People may oppose certain politicians regarding their political views. They have a right to do so, but what need is there for the ridicule of the physical features of the individual? Is this showing good taste and being Christ like? What do people hope to gain by such tactics? Some time ago, I told a joke which dwelled upon the physical looks of a certain lady official. At the end, some laughed, but one person told me that the lady looked as well as she could and I had no right to make fun of her appearance. Her rebuke stung me, but I had it coming. She was right and I have profited from the rebuke in resolving to be more careful when referring to the features of others. But let us notice . . .

Though a victim of being laughed to scorn, such did not prove Jesus to be false. Notice what followed: "And he put them all out, and took her by the hand, and called, saying, Maid, arise. And her spirit came again, and she arose straightway: and he commanded to give her meat" (Luke 8:54-55). Jesus had said, "she is not dead, but sleepeth." He raised the maid to life demonstrating that his words were true. The scornful laughter directed toward him did not keep his words from being the truth.

Though laughed to scorn, the ridicule did not defeat Christ's purpose. He did what he intended to do. The maid was raised from the dead. The laughter did not deter Jesus from his purpose. We may at times feel the sting of scornful laughter, but that should never keep us from doing what is right. Insecure people ridicule! On the other hand, those who are faithful endure the ridicule and keep on fulfilling the purpose that God has for them in life.

Scornful laughter is manifested by some today when they hear the truth. They delight in ridiculing the speaker. Rather than investigating what is spoken, they find refuge in laughing to scorn the one who has spoken the truth. All the scorn that people can muster is not going to make the truth any less the truth. It didn't when they laughed at Jesus and it is not going to do it in our time. The Scriptures speak of one church and one faith (Eph. 4:4-6). Men may ridicule the thoughts, but such is not going to change the truth. Men may call members of the body of Christ narrow minded and ridicule them for following the pattern that is in God's word. All the ridicule in the world is not going to make that which is wrong right in the sight of God. Peter wrote, "baptism doth also now save us" (1 Pet. 3:21). The laughter of ridicule may come and be hurled at those who believe and obey this truth. It may be called "water salvation" and those obeying such as being "water dogs," but the truth of Peter's words still stands. There is no Bible subject but what some people abuse it and ridicule those who stand for the truth involved. We should be ready to expect and accept such. The disciple is not above his master! They ridiculed Jesus and we can expect the same.

In the long run, the scornful laugher is the one that will be hurt the most. He may receive satisfaction at the time by ridiculing the speaker of truth, but what about that which awaits all men? How much scornful laughter will be evidenced in the Day of Judgment? "For we must all appear before the judgment seat of Christ; that every one may receive the things done in his body, according to that he hath done, whether it be good or bad" (2 Cor. 5:10). There may be things taught in the religious world that appear very ridiculous as compared to the truth revealed in the Scriptures. Let us oppose these things by the Scriptures and not find ourselves in the position of those who ridicule others in laughing them to scorn. Let us look upon the things of others (Phil. 2:3-5).

See That Ye Refuse Not Him That Speaketh

"See that ye refuse not him that speaketh: for if they escaped not who refused him that spake on earth, much more shall not we escape, if we turn away from him that speaketh from heaven" (Heb. 12:25). He that "speaketh from heaven" is the Christ (Heb. 1:1-2). It is possible for men to refuse him; this is implied in the admonition. It is even possible for Christians to refuse him—this admonition was addressed primarily to them.

How May People Refuse Him That Speaketh From Heaven?

By refusing to listen. Some literally "turn away from him." They do not read the Bible or listen to a gospel sermon. They are comparable to those to whom Jesus referred in Matthew 13:15: "For this people's heart is waxed gross, and their ears are dull of hearing, and their eyes they have closed; lest at any time they should see with their eyes, and hear with their ears, and should understand with their heart, and should be converted, and I should heal them."

By listening with no intention of obeying. There are some who are like the Athenians. They listen for curiosity's sake but with no intention of obeying (Acts 17:18). They do not make the personal application of seeing themselves as God sees them. Dear reader, it is not the hearing alone, but the hearing and obeying that counts. Jesus asked, "And why call ye me, Lord, Lord, and do not the things which I say?" (Luke 6:46).

By rejecting the gospel and the gospel preacher when he speaks the truth. Israel rejected God when they rejected Samuel. When the people desired a king to rule over them, God told Samuel, "Hearken unto the voice of the people in all that they say unto thee: for they have not rejected thee, but they have rejected me, that I should not reign over them" (1 Sam. 8:7). When Christ sent out the preachers under the limited commission, they were assured, "He that heareth you heareth me; and he that despiseth you despiseth me; and he that despiseth me despiseth him that sent me" (Luke 10:16). Have you ever despised some preacher who spoke the truth of God's word to you? Did you realize that you were also despising Christ, "the author and finisher of the faith" (Heb. 12:2)?

By trying to be neutral. A failure to accept him after hearing his truth is to reject him. "He that is not with me is against me; and he that gathereth not with me scattereth abroad" (Matt. 12:30). To profess neutrality regarding Christ is to be guilty of disobedience. It is a refusal of him that speaks from heaven.

Why Do People Refuse Him?

We have noticed the "how" and now the "why." We may not be able to give all the answers to why people refuse him, but here are a few obvious ones.

Some trust in their own goodness. They are self-righteous to such an extent that they see no need for Christ. They feel sufficient within themselves. Paul spoke of his countrymen, "For I bear them record that they have a zeal of God, but not according to knowledge. For they, being ignorant of God's righteousness, and going about to establish their own righteousness, have not submitted themselves unto the righteousness of God" (Rom. 10:1-2).

Some trust in their own wisdom. Feeling themselves "superior" they do not "condescend" to the teaching of the Bible. Such is foolishness to them. Paul wrote of such saying, "For the Jews required a sign, and the Greeks seek after wisdom: but we preach Christ crucified, unto the Jews a stumblingblock, and unto the Greeks foolishness; but unto them which are called, both Jews and Greeks, Christ the power of God, and the wisdom of God. Because the foolishness of God is wiser than men; and the weakness of God is stronger than men" (1 Cor. 1:22-25).

For fear of the world, some refuse him. They fear losing their social, business, or religious standing. Such was true while Jesus was on earth, "Nevertheless among the chief rulers also many believed on him; but because of the Pharisees they did not confess him, lest they should be put out of the synagogue: for they loved the praise of men more than the praise of God" (John 12:42-43). The praise of men still means more to some in our day than the praise of God.

Many trust the future. Procrastination cries "tomorrow" but means "never." There are those who intend to obey some day! But when? They keep on refusing him that speaketh from heaven. It is a serious thing to refuse him that speaks from heaven. Have you considered just how serious it really is (Heb. 10:28-31)? Today is the day of salvation.

Self-Pity

Self-pity is defined as "pity for oneself; especially a self-indulgent dwelling on one's sorrows or misfortunes." It is a very easy thing to give over to our feelings and find ourselves feeling so sorry for ourselves that our former effectiveness no longer exists. Sympathy is a wonderful virtue. A Christian should develop a sympathetic understanding toward his brethren and his fellowman. Paul wrote, "Rejoice with them that do rejoice and weep with them that weep" (Rom. 12:15). But if one isn't careful, he can overdo sympathy toward someone to the extent, as in self-pity and sympathy craving, one can virtually give up. This is the worst thing that can happen to anyone as far as this world is concerned. As we keep moving along, there is hope that things may improve and strength can be gained. But not so when one possesses a "give up" spirit. In essence, we become our own worst enemy. We get to the point that we can't see the forest for the trees. We defeat ourselves and become tools of Satan who wants all of God's children to become engrossed with self-pity to the extent that they give up the faith.

Problems of life are not limited to just a few. All of us have obstacles to overcome. Peter wrote, "Beloved, think it not strange concerning the fiery trial which is to try you, as though some strange thing happened unto you" (1 Pet. 4: 12). Some seem to think that they are the only ones who have any problems. They let their problems control their lives to such a degree that they lose sight of the joy that Christians are to experience. Men of faith have had to suffer but where is there any evidence that they reduced them to a life of self-pity?

Who was tried any greater than Job? It would seem that if anyone, from a physical standpoint, had a right for self-pity, it would be Job. Though he earnestly contended that his calamities were not due to any sins he had committed, where is there any indication that he was driven to self-pity? "Take, my brethren, the prophets, who have spoken in the name of the Lord, for an example of suffering affliction, and of patience. Behold, we count them happy which endure. Ye have heard of the patience of Job, and have seen the end of the Lord; that the Lord is very pitiful, and of tender mercy" (Jas. 5:10-11).

Self-pity can deprive an individual of patience and endurance that he must have to continue faithful in the Lord. Again, where does one find self-pity governing the life of the apostle Paul? He suffered greatly and defended his apostleship by pointing to these things in 2 Corinthians 11:23-29. Yet, he spoke of such matters as follows: "For our light affliction, which is but for a moment, worketh for us a far more exceeding and eternal weight of glory; while we look not at the things which are seen: but at the things which are not seen: for the things which are seen are temporal; but the things which are not seen are eternal" (2 Cor. 4:17-18). Self-pity focuses upon the things that are seen rather than on the things that are not seen!

I once knew a preacher who labored in a very difficult field. When he was inclined to feel sorry for himself and became "blue," he followed the practice of making a determined effort to go out and teach someone the truth. In the process of so doing, he lost sight of himself and the self-pity that he was building in his mind. I have recalled his statement through the years and his approach to combating self-pity has been very helpful. "Let nothing be done through strife or vainglory; but in lowliness of mind let each esteem other better than themselves. Look not every man on his own things, but every man also on the things of others. Let this mind be in you, which was also in Christ Jesus" (Phil. 2:3-5). Self-pity is closely associated with selfishness that can be overcome by looking on the things of others rather than always thinking of self. In trying to teach someone the truth, one can get his mind off himself and his problems. In the case that I mentioned, the effort of trying to teach someone was actually therapy to this preacher. From various circles one hears of therapy in our society. There are programs of physical and mental therapy that individuals participate in for the purpose of "snapping them out of it." But what about spiritual therapy? There are those who need to snap out of it and stop emphasizing self-pity. We need to keep looking to Christ and trusting his word. "I can do all things through Christ which strengtheneth me" (Phil. 4: 13). This is a declaration of faith and not a cry of self-pity!

It is possible for congregations to be governed by self-pity. Congregations have suffered for contending for the faith and later that is all the members can talk about. Rather than reaching forth for those things that are before them, they are engrossed in self-pity and barely make an effort "in keeping house for the Lord." All members should make a prayerful effort in trying to teach someone the truth. It can keep us from being engulfed in self-pity. I saw a man sitting in a wheelchair hoeing weeds out of the grass. The man had no legs, but he wasn't defeated. He was still in there pitching—self-pity hadn't made him useless!

Set For the Defence of the Gospel

(Phil. 1:17)

While a prisoner of Rome, the apostle Paul wrote this letter to the church at Philippi. He speaks of those events involving his imprisonment as having "fallen out rather unto the furtherance of the gospel" (Phil. 1:12). The furtherance of the gospel referred to the facts that Christ was manifested in the palace and brethren (many of them) had gained strength by Paul's example. They were "much more bold to speak the word without fear" (Phil. 1:13-14). Two classes of preachers were motivated by Paul's bonds. Some preached Christ of envy and strife, of contention, not sincerely, supposing to add afflictions to Paul's bonds. On the other hand, there were those who preached Christ of good will and of love "knowing that I (Paul) am set for the defence of the gospel." Just who these were who preached of envy and strife we might not know. It has been suggested that these were of the Judaizing party who were desirous of exalting their ideas and depreciating the influence of Paul. Whoever they were, they did preach Christ and, though it was done in envy and strife, Paul could rejoice that his Savior was preached (v. 18). They preached the facts, commands, and promises of the gospel, but with the wrong motives. This certainly does not justify denominational preaching. Denominational preachers do not preach Christ which involves preaching the facts, commands, and promises of the gospel. Yes, they may preach the man but not his plan. To preach Christ is to preach the man and his plan (Acts 8:5, 12, 35-38). Furthermore, as a Christian, Paul never rejoiced when false doctrine was taught and for him to have done such would have been very inconsistent with his character. Yet, regarding this teaching, Paul wrote, "notwithstanding, every way, whether in pretense, or in truth, Christ is preached; and I therein do rejoice, yea, and will rejoice" (v. 18). Truth was preached and Paul rejoiced in the fact that it was. This text offers no solace or refuge for false doctrine!

For a preacher to be saved, he must preach the truth and live in keeping with the truth (1 Tim. 4:16). Envying is a work of the flesh and they which practice such shall not inherit the kingdom of God (Gal. 5:21). Paul was not saying that these who preached with envy and strife were justified before God. He was not advocating that they would be saved in such conduct. He was saying that they preached the truth that could save others and in this he rejoiced. False teaching from the most pious can never save anyone!

Let us now observe the phrase "I am set for the defence of the gospel." We will be noticing particular truth connected with the words "set," "defence," and "gospel."

Emphasis now is on the word "set." To be "set" is equal to being ready. We use the expression "all set" in this sense. Hence, Paul was ready, "all set" for the defence of the gospel. There were certain things involved in this statement, "I am set." He knew the gospel. One cannot defend a principle that he does not know. He believed in the gospel. One is not expected to defend something in which he does not believe (2 Tim. 1:12). He possessed the necessary equipment for the defence. There are tools associated with being set for a given task (Eph. 6:10-17). He was also filled with courage to meet the task (Phil. 4:13).

The attention now is on "defence." The gospel is something that must be defended. There are always opponents of the gospel seeking to pervert it (Gal. 1:6-7). God uses men in defending his gospel. It is no reflection on God or the gospel that it needs defending by men. Every Christian should recognize the obligation to defend the gospel. If Christians will not rise to the occasion of defence, then who will? If we are not set for the task, who will be?

The "gospel" is that which needs defending. What is the gospel of Christ that is to be defended? It literally means the good news or glad tidings that have come due to the death, burial, and resurrection of Christ (1 Cor. 15:1-4). Furthermore, it is God's worded grace. No one can truthfully separate the gospel from the grace of God (Gal. 1:6; Acts 20:24). It is God's power to save (Rom. 1:16-17). The call of God is in the gospel (2 Thess. 2:13). The gospel of Christ can and must be obeyed (1Pet. 4:17-18).

God's people need to be set at all times to defend the purpose of the gospel (Rom.1:16) along with its scope (Acts 10:34-35), its facts (1 Cor. 15:1-4), its commands (Mark 16:16; Acts 2:38; 18:8), and its promises (Acts 2:38; 1 John 2:25). May the Lord help all of us who wear his name to stay set for a defence of the gospel. We have known those whose favorite expression was that they were "set for a defence" but when it really came to the conflict they would "set on a fence." What about you? Are you ready to defend the gospel?

Set Thine House In Order: For Thou Shalt Die and Not Live

This announcement is from 2 Kings 20:1 and was made to King Hezekiah when he was dangerously ill. In answer to his prayer, fifteen years were added to his life (v. 6). This text furnishes us with a theme for profitable consideration and meditation.

"Thou Shalt Die"
Though this was spoken to an individual, it is universally true.

Death is a certainty! We are reminded of this by the obituary notices, the passing funeral processions, the cemeteries on the right and the left, and the statements from the word of God, "Wherefore, as by one man sin entered into the world, and death by sin; and so death passed upon all men for that all have sinned" (Rom. 5:12). "For as in Adam all die, even so in Christ shall all be made alive" (1 Cor. 15:22). Only one thing can prevent death and that is the coming of the Lord. Health, science, and cautious living can only postpone it. It comes to the righteous as well as the unrighteous, to youth as well as the aged. It will come through one of five avenues:

- **Disease:** The body is a target for such unseen foes.
- **Accident:** We live in a world of disorder and commotion. No position is absolutely sure.
- **Murder:** Perhaps we have made an enemy consciously or unconsciously, who may strike without warning.
- **Suicide:** Some people, during a crisis, lose their mental balance and take their own lives.
- **Decay:** The machine or old house will simply wear out. Paul spoke of the "the outward man perishing" (2 Cor. 4:16).

What Death Means

Death is a departure from this world—a severance of all earthly ties. The strongest of all earthly ties (the marriage tie) is broken at death.

Death is a forerunner of our appearance before the judgment seat of Christ. "For we must all appear before the judgment seat of Christ; that every one may receive the things done in his body, according to that he hath done, whether it be good or bad" (2 Cor. 5:10). "And it is appointed unto men once to die, but after this the judgment" (Heb. 9:27). Therefore, it is far more serious than a passing to nothingness.

A Fitting Command

"Set thine house in order." This phrase has a threefold significance:

Regarding material things. It would appear that Hezekiah was instructed to dispose of his earthly affairs—to make his will. We should endeavor to keep our business affairs in such a condition that, if we die without warning, there will be no difficulty, no expense to those we leave behind. It is also a good policy to leave some instructions with your loved ones about the funeral and burial arrangements you prefer.

Regarding human relationships. "Owe no man any thing, but to love one another: for he that loveth another hath fulfilled the law" (Rom. 13:8). There are houses that are badly in disorder as regarding this command to "owe no man any thing." We need to set our affairs in order and keep them that way. Hands should not be stained with ill-gotten money. "Recompense to no man evil for evil. Provide things honest in the sight of all men" (Rom. 12:17). We should hold no grudges; allow no grudges, if possible. "If it be possible as much as lieth in you, live peaceably with all men" (Rom. 12:18). Men may have proper regard for these human relationships and still lack a great deal in having set their house in order, for there is definitely the third relationship.

Regarding Divine Relationship. When we depart this world, we arrive in another. When we leave our fellow men, we go out to meet God. It is of the greatest importance that we be on intimate terms with God. We have known men to be careful with their will making, concerned about their human relationships, but abounding in apathy regarding this divine relationship. No one has set his house in order who has not obeyed the gospel of Christ (Mark 16:16; Acts 2:38). Furthermore, one who is not living faithfully in Christ has a house that needs setting in order. He needs to repent of his sins and pray God for forgiveness in the name of Jesus Christ. "Repent therefore of this thy wickedness, and pray God, if perhaps the thought of thine heart may be forgiven thee. For I perceive that thou art in the gall of bitterness, and in the bond of iniquity" (Acts 8:22-23). "If we confess our sins, he is faithful and just to forgive us our sins, and to cleanse us from all unrighteousness" (1 John 1:9).

Are you faithful in the Lord? Death is certain! We know not when it will come. We need to set our houses in order and keep them that way. Are you prepared to meet God? There are no preparations for death after death!

Some Works Revealed in the New Testament

There are very few subjects that seem to confuse some people more than the position of works as far as their salvation is concerned. Most denominationalists vehemently deny that works have anything to do with an individual's salvation. In fact, they contend in some instances that an effort to perform works will nullify one's salvation. Perhaps some of these have been affected by the teaching of Martin Luther in his denunciation of the works of Catholicism. Luther was right in contending that by such works one could not be justified, but rather than accept the New Testament teaching on the subject, he advocated another extreme—that one is saved *soli fidi* or simply by faith. In the reading of the Scriptures, we need to be careful not to accept something that has been placed in our minds by men and read the Scriptures to try to justify such.

There are religionists who make a difference concerning principles in the Bible when there is no difference, and then there are those who say no difference exists concerning certain subjects when a difference certainly exists. Following either one of these considerations, an individual is destined to accept error. We are aware of many who advocate that being saved and church membership are two different things, but the Bible does not make such a difference. "And the Lord added to the church daily such as should be saved" (Acts 2:47). This is just one of the many examples of making a difference where such does not exist. On the other hand, concerning the second fallacy, no difference is made in the minds of some concerning the subject of works when a definite difference is obvious to the open-minded reader of the word of God. Yes, works are condemned in the Scriptures, but what type of works are these? There are different types of works and not all works are of the same nature! Some read a passage where particular works are condemned and they ignorantly or dishonestly (mean or green) refer to such a passage to condemn all works. In the remaining space, let's notice a few of the different works that are revealed in the New Testament:

Works of the Law of Moses. "Knowing that a man is not justified by the works of the law, but by the faith of Jesus Christ, even we have believed in Jesus Christ, that we might be justified by the faith of Christ, and not by the works of the law: for by the works of the law shall no flesh be justified" (Gal. 2:16). The verse on three occasions speaks of "the works of the law." Paul is contrasting the system of works under the Old Testament or Law of Moses with the system of faith in Jesus Christ. Yet, religious teachers use such a verse to affirm that there are no works of any type that one is to perform in the system of faith to be justified. Romans 3:28 and 4:4-5 also refer to works of the Law of Moses and these verses are often quoted with the intention of showing that no works are to be performed in one being accepted of God in the New Covenant. Involved in their erroneous concept is that of seeing no difference where one exists. There are different types of works revealed in the New Testament!

Works of Man's Righteousness. "Not by works of righteousness which we have done, but according to his mercy he saved us, by the washing of regeneration, and renewing of the Holy Ghost" (Tit. 3:5). I would like to have a dollar for every time that I have heard this passage quoted in an effort to prove that man has no works to perform to be saved. But notice how the verse qualifies works! It speaks of works which we have done. By such works, man cannot be saved. He needs the mercy of God in the gospel of Christ. The passage condemns the moral man thinking he can be saved in his own goodness or works of righteousness which he is doing. So many believe that by being morally clean and reasonably honest that such assures them of salvation. This can never be "for all have sinned and come short of the glory of God" (Rom. 3:23). We need God's mercy in the gospel. Man can never originate a plan to remove one single sin. This is condemned in the verse, but works of all nature are not condemned. The verse is not to be understood as condemning what God has for one to do in obeying the gospel of his Son.

Works of God's Righteousness. Just as surely as the Bible condemns certain works, it also approves and sanctions certain others. In Acts 10:34-45, we read, "Then Peter opened his mouth, and said, Of a truth I perceive that God is no respecter of persons: but in every nation he that feareth him, and worketh righteousness, is accepted with him." What works are involved in one being accepted with God? The works of God's righteousness or the acts that he has ordained for one to perform in order to be accepted with him. God has authorized faith (John 6:29; Jas. 2:24), repentance (Acts 17:30; 2 Pet. 3:9), confession (Rom. 10:10), and baptism (Mark 16:16; 1 Pet. 3:21) for one to obey in working his righteousness to be saved. When one obeys such, he is not working man's righteousness, but the righteousness of God. Be not deceived!

Staying in the Boundary

"Whosoever transgresseth, and abideth not in the doctrine of Christ, hath not God. He that abideth in the doctrine of Christ, he hath both the Father and the Son" (2 John 9). This passage emphasizes the value of staying in bounds. Generally, we recognize the value of staying in bounds in regard to athletic contests, international relations, and property surveys. Even more emphasis should be given to recognizing the spiritual boundary that is determined by the doctrine of Christ. This passage mentions two possible classes of people: Those who "hath not God" and those who "hath both the Father and the Son." Humanity cannot escape being in one or the other of these two classes. Infants and unaccountable beings "hath God." Accountable beings who abide not in the doctrine of Christ "hath not God." Those who abide in the doctrine of Christ "hath both the Father and the Son." The phrase "hath God" refers to being in the favor of God or one who has the blessings that God offers in his spiritual realm. This passage is wrought with both hope and fear (Eph. 2:12-13). What we do toward Christ is also done toward God (Eph. 1:3). To transgress and not abide in the doctrine of Christ is to lose God (1 John 3:4).

What does it mean to transgress? The Greek word which is translated in the KJV "transgresseth" literally means "to progress." The meaning is this: Whosoever becomes progressive and abides not in the doctrine of Christ has not God. Men often boast that they are progressive. Progress is good only when it is in the direction of Christ and not away from him (Phil. 3:14). In some matters, it is far preferable to be non-progressive, particularly, in not going beyond what the Lord has said. The weight of this verse is this: When one progresses or goes beyond what Christ and his apostles taught, he has not God. We must appreciate the value of staying in the boundary!

What is the doctrine of Christ? Other versions render this phrase "the teaching of Christ." It involves those precepts and commandments of the Lord which he taught and those given through those whom the Holy Spirit inspired to teach the truth in this dispensation. We need to appreciate that the gospel of Christ is the doctrine of Christ (Rom. 6:17-18). The apostles' doctrine is also the doctrine of Christ (Acts 2:42; Matt. 18:18). The apostles taught what Christ through the Holy Spirit moved them to teach (John 16:13; Acts 2:4; Gal. 1:11-12). When the word "doctrine" is used in the plural, it refers to other doctrines than the doctrine of Christ (Matt. 15:9; 1 Tim. 4:1). Christ has doctrine—not doctrines! There are not doctrines for men to abide in, but there is the doctrine of Christ that we must abide in to have both the Father and the Son. "To abide in the doctrine" simply means to respect and stay in the bounds of the teaching of Christ. It is only as we stay in bounds that we can show respect to the authority of Christ, principles of faith, and the silence of the Scriptures. Respect for this principle of staying in the boundary or abiding in the doctrine of Christ helps to explain many of the features of the church of Christ. It explains:

Lack of authoritative value of the Ten Commandments in this age. The Ten Commandments were given under the Law of Moses. Jesus fulfilled that law (Matt. 5:17-18). We can't abide in Christ and follow something that he fulfilled (2 Cor. 3; Col. 2:14-

17). We need to concentrate upon what Jesus authorized and obey his commandments (Heb. 5:8-9).

Why hearing, faith, repentance, confession, and baptism are preached as terms of salvation. These are commands which constitute steps that Jesus authorized, and they are found in the doctrine of Christ (Mark 16:16; Acts 2:38; 8:37). To add or take from these commands is to fail to abide in the doctrine of Christ. Remember those who fail to abide in the doctrine of Christ have not God!

The Lord's supper being observed weekly. By apostolic example and necessary inference, we conclude that such is authorized in the Scriptures (Acts 2:42; 20:7). If it is not to be observed on the first day of each week, when is it to be observed? Where is the authority for any other day or time?

The absence of mechanical instruments of music in worship. There is no authority for mechanical instruments of music in worship in the doctrine of Christ. Jesus authorized singing and when we practice that, we are abiding in the doctrine of Christ (Eph. 5:19; Col. 3:16).

The absence of observance of holy days. Paul wrote that he was afraid of those who observed special holy days (Gal. 4:10-11), and that no man had the right to judge another in respect of a holy day (Col. 2:16). The observance of humanly devised holy days is not in the doctrine of Christ. We need to stay in the boundary. Our soul salvation depends upon our doing so. Let us rightfully respect this thought and always abide in the doctrine or teaching of Christ!

Strong in the Lord

Finally, my brethren, be strong in the Lord, and in the power of his might (Eph. 6:10).

This admonition is found near the conclusion of Paul's beautiful epistle to the Ephesians. Verse 10 is followed by principles that enumerate the armour of the Christian that are necessary in his being strong in the Lord. It appears that man has a natural desire to be strong. Perhaps it goes without saying that no one desires to be weak. Though men almost universally have a desire for strength, the object of one's strength often varies. With some it is a quest for physical strength (1 Tim. 4:8). With others, it may be a longing for financial strength and they sell their soul in pursuit of it (Mark 8:36-38). Still with others, there is the craving for intellectual strength and recognition (Eccl. 12:12). These do not constitute the true objective of strength. The greatest strength is to be strong in the Lord. This is the very thing that so many ignore and for which they have little regard. Several admonitions in the New Testament are noted regarding this subject: "Watch ye, stand fast in the faith, quit you like men, be strong" (1 Cor. 16:13). Again, "Thou therefore, my son, be strong in the grace that is in Christ Jesus" (2 Tim. 2:1).

Why Should One Be Strong in the Lord?

To meet our enemy. "Be sober, be vigilant; because your adversary the devil, as a roaring lion, walketh about, seeking whom he may devour" (1 Pet. 5:8). There must be strength to resist the devil (Jas. 4:7).

To preach the gospel and contend for the faith. Paul wrote, "I am set for a defence of the gospel" (Phil. 1:17). To be set for a defence requires a great deal of strength. This explains why some do not contend for the faith. Weakness prevails in them rather than strength in the Lord to do what true disciples should be doing.

To live acceptably and overcome. "For whatsoever is born of God overcometh the world: and this is the victory that overcometh the world, even our faith" (1 John 5:4). The world is overcoming us or we are overcoming the world! To overcome the world requires faith that involves being strong in the Lord.

What Is Required in Developing Strength?

All strengths have basically the same requirements for development. Spiritual strength is no exception. Growth is required (1 Pet. 2:2; 3:18). This growth is made possible by food (Matt. 4:4), exercise (2 Tim. 4:8), cleanliness (2 Cor. 7:1), proper surroundings (1 Cor. 15:33), time (Heb. 5:11-14), and the armour previously mentioned in Ephesians 6:14-18. These principles cannot be ignored if an individual expects to be strong in the Lord. Be concerned enough to read these Scriptures and meditate upon their significance.

When Is One Strong in the Lord?

When the Lord's will is supreme in his life. He has obeyed the gospel and in so doing has put on the Lord (Gal. 3:26-27). Throughout his activities he recognizes that the Lord's ways and thoughts are as much higher than his as the heavens are higher than the earth (Isa. 55:8-9). He prays to God "not my will, but thine be done" and consistently patterns his life after the beautiful sentiment. He doesn't have to know "the why" of everything that God authorizes, but is content to do what God says and believes that he says what he means and means what he says.

When he is weak. Paul wrote this paradox: "Therefore I take pleasure in infirmities, in reproaches, in necessities, in persecutions, in distresses for Christ's sake: for when I am weak, then am I strong" (2 Cor. 12:10). This seems contradictory, but that is the feature of a paradoxical statement. Weak in the eyes of the world are the commandments of God. "But God hath chosen the foolish things of the world to confound the wise; and God hath chosen the weak things of the world to confound the things which are mighty" (1 Cor. 1:27). Men consider men weak when they manifest a need and dependence upon God. By worldly standards, religion is effeminate. It is good for the wife and kids, but not for the worldly strong. In view of this concept, Paul relates, "for when I am weak (by man's standard in doing what God authorizes) then am I strong" (before God and the spiritually minded people in that the world has been defied with its strength).

The arrogant and proud will never be strong in the Lord. When one is so strong that he can't see himself a sinner, that one is weak before God and he is a great distance from being strong in the Lord. We must never withhold from God if we hope to be strong in the Lord. The Macedonians had the right concept of strength: they "first gave their own selves to the Lord, and unto us by the will of

God" (2 Cor. 8:5). What about you? Are you ready to pay the price to be strong in the Lord?

Stubbornness Is As Iniquity and Idolatry

"For rebellion is as the sin of witchcraft, and stubbornness is as iniquity and idolatry." These words were spoken by Samuel to King Saul in 1 Samuel 15:23. The Lord had directed Saul to utterly destroy the Amalekites with all that they had and with their king. "Now go and smite Amalek, and utterly destroy all that they have, and spare them not; but slay both man and woman, infant and suckling, ox and sheep, camel and ass" (1 Sam. 15:3). Saul had disobeyed by sparing King Agag and the best of the flocks and herds. "But Saul and the people spared Agag, and the best of the sheep, and of the oxen, and of the fatlings, and of the lambs, and all that was good, and would not utterly destroy them: but everything that was vile and refuse, that they destroyed utterly" (1 Sam. 15:9). God had said "utterly destroy." Saul had disobeyed the Lord. To partially obey the commandment of the Lord is but to disobey! When Samuel confronted Saul regarding his disobedience, he spoke of stubbornness. Therefore, among other things, we conclude that Saul's failure in doing the Lord's command was due to his stubbornness. Stubborn is defined as "fixed, unyielding, obstinate."

Stubbornness can be so great that it can be a form of idolatry in a person's life. This is what our text states. "For rebellion is as the sin of witchcraft, and stubbornness is as iniquity and idolatry" (1 Sam. 15:23). It shouldn't be difficult for us to comprehend how stubbornness can be idolatry. A man by stubbornness refuses God's directions toward him. He sets his desire and will against God. Such means more to him than pleasing God in obedience. Hence, his will is fixed, unyielding and obstinate against God. This is stubbornness which is idolatry. Man's will and way mean more to him than doing the will of God.

Stubbornness can be a very obnoxious characteristic. It was that way in the life of Saul. But Saul isn't alone! We have known individuals who actually admitted that they were too stubborn to change their positions though they knew such to be false. This is very pathetic and tragic! They admit knowing the truth and being too stubborn to do anything about it. Their will and position is more important to them than the will of God and the truth. Such stubbornness is that which Saul possessed and it is iniquity and idolatry. Stubbornness can keep us from being reasonable and open minded in dealing with the Scriptures. It moves us to protect our view of the Scriptures without concern for what is right.

Perhaps in all of us there are traces of stubbornness that we need to properly evaluate. With caution, it might be an admirable thing and even a virtue when channeled in the truth. Paul wrote that he was "set for a defence of the gospel" (Phil. 1:17). He had a fixed, unyielding position as far as the gospel was concerned. In a very critical time in the early church, there were those who wanted Paul to circumcise Titus. Paul replied, "To whom we gave place by subjection, no, not for an hour; that the truth of the gospel might continue with you" (Gal. 2:5). Though it might not be termed stubbornness, Paul concluded 1 Corinthians 15 with this beautiful admonition: "Therefore, my beloved brethren, be ye stedfast, unmoveable, always abounding in the work of the Lord, forasmuch as ye know that your labour is not in vain in the Lord" (v. 58). We must always strive to be stedfast and unmoveable in following the truth and never in something that might be in rebellion to God.

How wonderful it would be if all of God's children were as unmoveable in following and defending the truth as some are stubbornly opposed to it. The children of Israel were not permitted to enter the promised land. In their wanderings, the bones of that generation bleached the wilderness. In hope of the following generation, the Psalmist wrote, "And might not be as their fathers, a stubborn and rebellious generation; a generation that set not their heart aright, and whose spirit was not stedfast with God" (Ps. 78:8). There is no place in heaven for those who are stubbornly opposed to God's will and refuse to obey it. Idolaters cannot inherit the kingdom of heaven (1 Cor. 6:9; Gal. 5:20). When we fail to do what God directs us to do, we may be governed by stubbornness that "is as iniquity and idolatry."

Take Ye Away the Stone

Jesus was in Galilee when he received word of the sickness of Lazarus. He abode two days before departing to Bethany. He knew that Lazarus was dead before reaching Bethany. Lazarus had been dead for four days and was buried in a cave "and a stone lay upon it." Jesus commanded the stone to be taken away and offered a prayer of thanksgiving. "And when he thus had spoken, he cried with a loud voice, Lazarus, come forth. And he that was dead came forth, bound hand and foot with graveclothes; and his face was bound about with a napkin. Jesus said unto them, Loose him, and let him go" (John 11:43-44).

This command "Take ye away the stone" suggests some forceful lessons of divine truth. Let us notice:

Jesus is pleased to associate individuals with himself in his divine work. Christ chose to give those who were also concerned with the matter something to do. A word from Jesus could have no doubt removed the stone as easily as a word from Christ raised Lazarus to life. Careful reading of the Bible will reveal that the Lord gives men something to do when his work concerns them (John 9:7; Luke 17:14; 2 Cor. 6:1; Rom. 1:16-17; Mark 16:15-16).

There is a sphere for human agency in connection with the divine economy. God seeks to bless man but with man's co-operation. There is the human as well as the divine side of salvation (Heb. 11:6; Acts 2:40; Phil. 2:12). The use of human agency in the divine economy does not limit the power of God nor does it subtract from the glory of God. It manifests it! There are two hurtful extremes that we must avoid, the one being that God does it all and the other being that we do it all. Remember, Jesus said, "Take ye away the stone."

Where human power is sufficient, divine power will not be put forth or, God does not do for man what he can do for himself. God has done for man what man could not do for himself. He has given his Son to die for the sins of mankind. He has made possible a plan of salvation and revealed in his word how man can receive this salvation. Yes, he has given the gospel with its facts, commands, and promises, but man must believe these facts and obey the commands in order to appreciate the promises. Some evidently must expect God to do it all! God will never do man's part for him. Forcing man to do his will would destroy man's free will along with his responsibility and accountability. Christ raised Lazarus from the dead, but he required others to remove the stone and grave clothes.

Christ required the stone to be removed before he began his work. Such suggests that there are some things in our lives which must be removed before we can expect the blessings of the Lord. What might be some stones which need to be removed before we can receive the blessings of the Lord? Consider the following:

Stone of ignorance. Jesus said, ". . . if ye continue in my word, then are ye my disciples indeed; and ye shall know the truth, and the truth shall make you free" (John 8:31-32). Ignorance enslaves men! It is the truth that enables one to be free. Christ offers freedom through knowledge of the truth. One must remove the stone of ignorance to have this freedom in Christ. Again, "No man can come to me, except the Father which hath sent me draw him: and I will raise him up at the last day. It is written in the prophets, And they shall be all taught of God. Every man therefore that hath heard, and hath learned of the Father, cometh unto me" (John 6:44-45). Teaching, hearing, and learning are necessities in one being drawn to the Father.

Stone of prejudice. This is one of the darkest of principles. Perhaps one should even apologize for referring to prejudice as a principle. There is never a man so blind as the man who does not want to see! Men have been known to make up their minds before any investigation is made. There are even those who condemn investigation as being unfair. Their minds are fixed like concrete and they oppose anything which would disturb the "tranquility" of their fixed mind. How unlike the noble Bereans are they! "These were more noble than those in Thessalonica, in that they received the word with all readiness of mind, and searched the scriptures daily, whether those things were so" (Acts 17:11). The Bereans were being fair! The stone of prejudice did not block them from the blessings of the Lord. Stones of self-esteem, indifference, along with all things out of harmony with God's will, might be mentioned. These stones must be removed if we are to be right with the Lord. We must not let anything hinder us from obeying his commands and continuing faithful to him. Christ said, "Take ye away the stone."

Teachers of God's Word

There is always a demand for qualified teachers. In a local congregation, there is almost a perpetual seeking for teachers to be in the particular classes. Teaching is the very heart of the religion of Jesus Christ (John 6:44-45; Matt. 28:19). The salvation of one's soul is dependent upon that one being taught the word of God. Christians are those who have been taught. They have obeyed "that form of doctrine delivered them" (Rom. 6:17-18) and are rejoicing in the promise of God that their sins have been forgiven. Having received this joy, why shouldn't they desire to teach this truth to others? How can one truly say that he loves the truth and doesn't desire to teach others concerning it? I have said on many occasions that one of the real tests of a man's conversion being real and true is his attitude toward others who have not obeyed the word of God. When one appears docile and indifferent toward trying to teach loved ones, friends, or acquaintances the truth, who can say that he deems it important and as valuable as the Bible reveals that it is? The Christian is to greatly consider others (Phil. 2:3-5) and no greater consideration can be given to others than the thought of teaching them the truth.

Nevertheless, teachers appear to be hard to come by. At times it often reaches the low level of extreme urging and pleading for some to teach. Invariably, it has come down to who will do it regardless of other considerations or qualifications. Brethren, these things ought not so to be! But this being true at times, what accounts for it? Isn't it basically due to the attitudes that members have toward teaching? What are some of these attitudes?

There Are Those With . . .

Ability and knowledge but no desire. These are not novices! They have been sufficiently schooled in the truth to teach others. They have the ability to do so and in past times when their love was greater, they adequately demonstrated their ability in teaching. What has happened? The desire has gone! Let someone else do it. They are content to sit back and be a back seat member rather than use their ability and knowledge for the glory of God. Perhaps, to be a teacher of the Bible has become entirely too commonplace for them. The glory of man's achievements has thwarted their evaluation to the extent that desire has gone. In the light of what Jesus taught in the parable of the talents (Matt. 25:14-30), this constitutes a very serious attitude that can cause one to lose his own soul.

Reasonable desire but lack of knowledge. From our conversion, we are to "grow in grace, and in the knowledge of our Lord and Saviour Jesus Christ" (2 Pet. 3:18). It is understandable that young converts need growth before assuming a responsible teaching role. The desire will prompt them to knowledge as time goes one. However, there are those who have had the time and yet they lack knowledge to be dependable teachers. The Hebrew writer describes some: "For when for the time ye ought to be teachers, ye have need that one teach you again which be the first principles of the oracles of God; and are become such as have need of milk, and not of strong meat" (Heb. 5:12). There are those who are babes in Christ and then there are those who might be termed "spiritual runts"! In respect to time, they have had sufficient time to add knowledge, but they have neglected to do so and have not spiritually developed. How long is it proper to refer to them as babes? Hosea wrote, "My people are destroyed for lack of knowledge, because thou has rejected knowledge, I will also reject thee" (Hos. 4:6). Lack of knowledge is certainly a detriment to a program of teaching and causes individuals to fail God's work and his purpose in them.

Knowledge and ability but no consecration. We mean by this that there are those who know and can do it but they will not live it. They are so grossly inconsistent with the truth that they are not "meet for the master's use" (2 Tim. 2:21). I have known of individuals who were capable of teaching a good lesson from the word of God; however, that was about the only time they would be present. Time after time they would prove themselves unfaithful by failing to assemble with the saints. Surely, no one could contend that such people are "meet for the master's use." They need to listen to themselves and start practicing what they preach. Their knowledge and ability in being used as teachers of God's word is to no avail until faithfulness becomes a part of their lives. "Thou therefore which teachest another, teachest thou not thyself?" (Rom. 2:21). May God help us to be diligent and zealous teachers of his word. May we always count it a great honor and privilege to serve in such a capacity and keep ourselves "meet for the master's use."

Tekel

The fifth chapter of Daniel reveals the great feast that King Belshazzar of Babylon made for a thousand of his lords. During the course of this feast there "came forth fingers of a man's hand and wrote over against the candlestick upon the plaister of the wall of the king's palace: and the king saw the part of the hand that wrote" (v. 5). Having seen this, the king was terrified. He sought his wise men to read the writing and give the interpretation thereof. They were not able to do so and it was the queen who suggested that there was a man in the kingdom who would be able to read the writing and give the interpretation. Then was Daniel brought before the king and consented to "read the writing unto the king, and make known unto him the interpretation" (v. 17). Daniel made known the writing: "And this is the writing that was written, *mene, mene, tekel, upharsin*" (v. 25). The word *tekel* was interpreted, "Thou art weighed in the balances, and art found wanting" (v. 27).

Belshazzar was not the only man ever weighed in the balances. Nor was he the last man to come up short after being weighed. Judas was weighed in the balances and found wanting. He made a choice between Christ and thirty pieces of silver and was found with a deficit in love, honesty, unselfishness, and loyalty. Paul said of one of his companions in the work of truth: "Demas hath forsaken me, having loved this present world" (2 Tim. 4:10). Demas was weighed by the temptation of the world and was caught with a shortage of consecration and with a vanished sense of fairness and dependability. John wrote a letter to the "well beloved Gaius" and said, "I wrote unto the church; but Diotrephes, who loveth to have the preeminence among them, receiveth us not" (3 John 9). Diotrephes was found lacking in the valuable principles of humility and hospitality.

Others have been weighed in the balances and did not come up short. Abraham was weighed to see whether he loved his son, Isaac, more than he loved God. He was told to offer up Isaac as a burnt offering unto God (Gen. 22:2). While he was in the very act of obedience, God said, "Now I know that thou fearest me" (Gen. 22:12). Abraham was not found wanting when "God did tempt (try) Abraham." Time after time was Jesus weighed in the balances and every time he was approved of God. "Then was Jesus led up of the Spirit into the wilderness to be tempted of the devil" (Matt. 4:1). He withstood the temptations as one faithful in his loyalty to God and his word, fit to be the Savior and example for mankind.

Peter said, "Think it not strange concerning the fiery trial which is to try you" (1 Pet. 4:12). We are being tested, weighed in the balances, every day that we live. Every invitation to worship God is a test of our love for him in comparison with our love for pleasures, family, or business in the world. Every appeal that the world makes to us to violate our conscience is a test to see whether we fear the censure of God or the world. It is a proof as to whether we had rather follow the tide of public sentiment and opinion rather than the express will of God.

When we stand before the rows of magazines to select something to read at the newsstand, we are in the balances, being weighed. How do we measure up? Does our mind feast upon the sensual, lewd, sordid, and evil things to be had there, or do we seek that which is clean and beneficial? We are weighed by the associates we pick, by the conversations in which we participate, by the TV programs we observe, by the opportunities to save the lost that we either use profitably or let slip uselessly by. Character, love for the truth, the church, the God of heaven, our stedfastness in prayer—all of these are weighed out in the hard times and the easy times of life.

Church problems also serve as balances to test members. I still contend that they determine who is on the Lord's side. In fact, Paul wrote, "For there must be also heresies among you, that they which are approved may be made manifest among you" (1 Cor. 11:19). Look about and behold the multitudes engrossed in the sins of liberalism. They have been weighed and found wanting in the love and devotion for God's pattern of truth found in the New Testament.

Our manhood and worthiness in parenthood is determined by our faithfulness in bringing up our children in the nurture and admonition of the Lord (Eph. 6:4). If the Lord's day finds us not bringing our little ones to be taught and encouraged in the right way, and if it does not find us setting a worthy example before them in worship and devotion, we can mark it well that we are "weighed in the balances and found wanting." It is not going to be a pleasant thing to be found with a deficit at the Day of Judgment.

Tell Us Plainly

And it was at Jerusalem the feast of the dedication, and it was winter. And Jesus walked in the temple in Solomon's porch. Then came the Jews round about him, and said unto him, How long dost thou make us to doubt? If thou be the Christ tell us plainly (John 10:22-26).

The Jews surrounded Christ seeking a request. "If thou be the Christ, tell us plainly." The request was probably prompted by extreme perfidiousness. Christ's replied, "I told you, and ye believed not: the works that I do in my Father's name, they bear witness of me" (v. 25). Jesus had told some directly that he was the Christ, including the blind man (John 9:37) and the Samaritan woman (John 4:26). The works that he performed were the greatest answer. A reference to these works was the answer sent back to John the Baptist when from prison he had sent two of his disciples to inquire, "Art thou he that should come, or do we look for another?" (Matt. 11:2-6). Nicodemus, a ruler of the Jews, knew that Jesus was "a teacher come from God" on the basis that "no man can do these miracles that thou doest, except God be with him" (John 3:2). John sums up the book bearing his name saying, "And many other signs truly did Jesus in the presence of his disciples, which are not written in this book: but these are written, that ye might believe that Jesus is the Christ, the Son of God; and that believing ye might have life through his name" (John 20:30-31). These Jews had abundant evidence upon which to believe that Jesus was the Christ. They were without excuse! We have abundant evidence in the Scriptures available to us to truly believe that Jesus is the Christ, the Son of the Living God. But some mourned then and some lament in our day, "How long dost thou make us to doubt? If thou be the Christ tell us plainly."

Several Insolent Insinuations Were Made In This Request
Insinuated that Jesus was making them to doubt. Jesus doesn't make one to doubt. Christ came to make faith possible. Men are prone to doubt when they lack faith. Christ came to bring peace and serenity not doubt and fear (John 7:17). To continue in a state of doubt is to be miserable (Rom. 14:23). When we doubt, examination should be made of self rather than accusing Christ of

making us doubt. Peter doubted when he took his eyes off the Lord and saw the boisterous winds (Matt. 14:31).

Insinuated that Jesus was withholding from them, desiring that they should beg of him "how long." Christ came to give, not to withhold. He wants all to know him as the Christ—to honor and obey him as Christ that he might give them rest. He hasn't withheld, he invites (Matt. 11: 28-30; John 5:40).

Insinuated that his teaching had been ambiguous, that his previous work and teaching had proven nothing. "Tell us plainly" as though he had not told them. They were attempting to place the responsibility of unbelief on Jesus. One of the oldest excuses for failure is to accuse the teacher of being ambiguous, not teaching plainly. Others had believed on Christ. It was evidently plain enough for them. These insinuations were directed as reflections upon Christ. Excuses today that men give are in like manner reflections upon Christ and God. Men say that the way of the Lord is not plain enough. In so doing, upon whom are they reflecting? They are endeavoring to exempt themselves from not following the truth by saying it is not plain enough for them to obey. In so doing they are placing the blame on Christ whether conscious of it or not. Jesus said, "I told you, and ye believed not" (v. 25). Something more than a lack of plainness accounted for their unbelief. What was it? Others had heard and believed!

Wherein Was the Root of Their Unbelief?

Jesus gave the explanation: "But ye believe not, because ye are not of my sheep." They didn't possess those dispositions of teachableness and humility which are conducive to discipleship. They were "far from the kingdom" (Mark 12:34). They were not willing to make the sacrifices of pride, money, comfort, and prestige that it took to follow the Christ. To such people, regardless of how plain the teaching, it is never plain.

Jesus Has Spoken Plainly

Jesus speaks plainly in the Scriptures concerning the matters of our soul salvation. Yet men still contend it is not plain enough for them to believe. Jesus has given plain answers to the following questions: What must I do to be saved (Mark 16:16)? Is the church essential to salvation (Acts 2:47)? What name must I wear (Acts 11:26)? What is baptism (Rom. 6:3-4)? What is its purpose (1 Pet. 3:21)? What about the music question (Eph.5:19)? We have only mentioned a few! These Jews made insolent insinuations in an effort to excuse their unbelief of truth. Are you doing the same? Such can be very tragic! Jesus will also speak plainly in the Day of Judgment!

That's Not My Thing

 This is a phrase that we often hear and even find ourselves using on occasions. It would appear to be a slang expression stating that we do not relate to certain situations and actually do not desire to have any part of them. In many respects, it may be uttered to say that we are closing the door of our involvement in certain undertakings or pursuits. I suppose all of us can relate to this evaluation and on occasions have honestly and sincerely made this statement. When I think of this loud rap music that seems so common in our communities, I have no problem in saying, "that's not my thing." The disturbance that rap music makes even causes me to wish that it were pronounced a violation of our civil law. However, such must be "the thing" of others for they persist in engaging in it. When I behold men wearing necklaces and earrings, I find myself saying once again "that's not my thing." I am content to leave that with the women, but it is obvious, to wear necklaces and earrings, is "the thing" of many males in our society.

 We could continue to relate numerous other observations that might be classified as "that's not my thing." They might often fall into the category of indifference and personal preference of the individual. However, the thing that becomes alarming and has dire ramifications is when this is the sentiment of individuals involving matters of their souls. When trying to encourage some to continue attending the worship services and eventually obeying the gospel, their explanation for not doing so was, "That's not my thing." It is not my purpose to degrade those who have made such a statement. I am not questioning their honesty or sincerity! They probably meant what they said, but think about what is involved in what they said.

They Have Said . . .

It Is Not My Thing To Please God. God would have every man to do his will. When one does as God directs, he is pleasing him. Jesus said, "Not every one that saith unto me Lord, Lord, shall enter into the kingdom of heaven; but he that doeth the will of my Father which is in heaven" (Matt. 7:21). So many seem intent upon pleasing themselves and doing "their thing" rather than pleasing God in obeying his will. Jesus pleased his Father when he prayed, "O my Father, if it be possible, let this cup pass from me: nevertheless not as I will, but as thou wilt" (Matt. 26:39). If we have any hope of living with God in eternity, we must learn to be pleasing to him while we sojourn on this earth. This view is definitely "the thing" of those who have any hope of heaven.

It Is Not My Thing To Truly Follow Jesus. Jesus said, "If any man will come after me, let him deny himself, and take up his cross, and follow me" (Matt. 16:24). There is self-denial and a cross to bear when one follows the Lord. This does not come easy and it certainly is not "the thing" that attracts the average religionist. They want to talk about believing in Christ in their own way that does not involve any element of sacrifice. It is not "their thing" to obey the gospel and dedicate their lives to the Lord. There used to be a hair crème commercial on TV that featured the thought that a little dab would do you. This sentiment has been incorporated into religion with people thinking that a little dab will do them. They are far removed from the spirit manifested by Paul, "I am crucified with Christ: nevertheless I live; yet not I, but Christ liveth in me: and the life which I now live in the flesh I live by the faith of the Son of God, who loved me, and gave himself for me" (Gal. 2:20). It might be said that so many do not want to be void of religion, but they certainly do not want to be overloaded with it. It is not "their thing" to really get involved in faithfulness to the Lord.

It Is Not My Thing to Be Stedfast in True Worship. Worship to them is a matter of their own design. They do what comes natural with them and resent anyone telling them to the contrary. The present evil world holds such fascination for them, that the worship of God finds little significance. Perhaps some of the special days that men have originated for worship appeal to them, such as Christmas, Easter, and other "holy" days that have been created in man's imagination. But it is not "their thing" to obey Christ and be faithful in worshiping God in his appointed way. "But the hour cometh, and now is, when the true worshippers shall worship the Father in spirit and in truth: for the Father seeketh such to worship him. God is a Spirit: and they that worship him must worship him in spirit and in truth" (John 4:23-24). This is what happened when the Lord's church came into existence, "And they continued stedfastly in the apostles' doctrine and fellowship, and in breaking of bread, and in prayers." Here were people concerned with what the Lord would have them do rather than saying, "that's not my thing." It is a sad thing when individuals view God's word and say "that's not my thing"! In essence, they are saying heaven is not for me and eternal punishment will be my fate.

That's The Way It Was

History does not lie! Historical facts greatly affect our lives and we must learn in life to accept them. In other words, I am trying to say that no one can change the facts of history. There are things in history of which we are greatly thankful. On the other hand, some things exist that are not so honorable and bring shame as we view them. Two centuries ago, slavery abounded in various sections of this country. Generally speaking, the institution of slavery was not an honorable society in the history of this country. In defense of it and state's rights, eleven states seceded from the union. The Civil War was fought in which, until recently, more lives of Americans were lost than in all this country's wars combined. These are historical facts! That's the way it was and no man can change them. For years and years, segregation existed that was a horror to the lives of many people. For people with respect for God and human dignity, it was nothing for which to be thankful. But it's history and that's the way it was. Many other things could be mentioned to support the thought that we might profit from history, but we certainly can not change what occurred. That's the way it was!

The movie, "The Passion of Christ," vividly portrayed the death of Christ and the place that the Jews had in crucifying Jesus. There were cries from the Jewish communities that their part in the crucifixion was exaggerated. They viewed the film as being anti-Semitic and prejudicial to the Jewish race. Other classes of people have also taken this view in exonerating the Jews. I recall some years ago that the Episcopalian hierarchy made a declaration that the Jews were not responsible for the death of Jesus. The Pope of Rome has even uttered sentiments of this nature! After viewing Mel Gibson's production, Paul Harvey seemed to have exempted the Jews by stating that the human race, as a whole was guilty of the death of Jesus. But what does history reveal concerning the matter? Believe me, the historical account in the Scriptures constitutes as good a historical record as any source available to the human mind.

From the very beginning of his ministry, the Jews sought to kill Jesus. Luke 4 reveals that after reading from Isaiah 61:1-2 and saying that this Scripture was fulfilled in him, they sought to cast him down headlong from the brow of the hill where they had led him. John 5 gives the account of Jesus visiting Jerusalem during one of the feasts of the Jews. He healed an impotent man on the Sabbath day, which infuriated the Jews. "And therefore did the Jews persecute Jesus, and sought to slay him, because he had done these things on the Sabbath day" (John 5:16). Other scenarios similar to these are mentioned by the gospel writers which reveal the efforts of the Jews to kill the Christ. "He came unto his own, and his own received him not" (John 1:11). His own (the Jewish people) as a majority did not receive him as their promised Messiah. Prompted by their leaders, they were soon destined to cry for his crucifixion.

When Jesus was arrested and tried in the mockery of a trial before the Jewish tribunal, they needed the help of the Romans for the death penalty to be pronounced. The Romans had taken this authority from the Jews. This caused them to take Jesus to Pilate, the Roman Governor, for a sentence of death. Pilate recognized that Jesus was innocent. When Pilate asked the Jews who would they choose to be released unto them, "they said, Barabbas. Pilate saith unto them, What shall I do then with Jesus which is called Christ? They all say unto him, Let him be crucified. And the governor said, Why, what evil hath he done? But they cried out the more, saying, Let him be crucified" (Matt. 27:21-23). "Then answered all the people, and said, His blood be on us, and on our children" (Matt. 27:25). It is apparent that Roman authorities administered the actual execution. But listen to what Jesus said to Pilate regarding his sentence of crucifixion: "Thou couldest have no power at all against me, except it were given thee from above: therefore he that delivered me unto thee hath the greater sin" (John 19:10). The Jews were the ones who had delivered Jesus to Pilate and had demanded of him that Jesus be executed. After the death of Jesus and on that memorable Pentecost Day recorded in Acts 2, Peter reminded the Jews that "devout men, out of every nation under heaven" (Acts 2:5) "have taken, and by wicked hands have crucified and slain" Jesus (Acts 2:23). Speaking to the Jews in Acts 3, Peter uttered these forceful words: "But ye denied the Holy One and the Just, and desired a murderer to be granted unto you; And killed the prince of life, whom God hath raised from the dead; whereof we are witnesses" (Acts 3:14-15).

These considerations are historical facts. There is as much evidence that the Jews killed Jesus as there is that the holocaust occurred in Hitler's time. Both Jews and Gentiles can obey the gospel and be saved. The unfortunate consideration is that so few have faith in Christ to obey him (Mark 16:16)!

The Balance of Life

"And he saith unto them, Take heed what ye hear, With what measure ye mete, it shall be measured to you; and unto you that hear shall more be given" (Mark 4:24). In life there is always a balance. A man's "getting" will in most cases be determined by his "giving" which is the truth conveyed in this passage from the words of Christ.

This is true of study. The more study a man is prepared to give to any subject, the more he will get from it. Subjects give pleasure and satisfaction in proportion to the effort that we are prepared to spend upon them. This is especially so in regard to the study of the word of God. Some people study so little of the word of God that it actually constitutes only a bore to them. They put so little effort into their study that it is no wonder that they receive so little satisfaction. As one gives time and determined effort in study, he can expect to receive in proportion to these efforts. We need to effectually heed the admonition of Paul to Timothy: "Study to show thyself approved unto God, a workman that needeth not to be ashamed, rightly dividing the word of truth" (2 Tim. 2:15). Peter admonished children of God saying, "And beside this, giving all diligence, add to your faith virtue, and to virtue knowledge" (2 Pet. 1:5). He closes his writings with, "But grow in grace, and in the knowledge of our Lord and Saviour Jesus Christ. To him be glory both now and for ever. Amen" (2 Pet. 3:18).

This is true of worship. The more we bring to the worship the more we will get from it. When we come to the services, there are at least three wrong ways in which we may come. *We may come entirely to get.* If we come in that way the likelihood is that we will criticize and find fault with practically everything involved in the items of worship. We will likely find ourselves regarding the whole service as a performance laid out for our special entertainment. We must come to give! We need to take into consideration that worship is an individual act in paying homage to God, and that each of us can contribute something to it. If we ask, not, "What can I get out of this service?" but, "What can I contribute to this service?" we will in the end get far more out of it than if we simply came to take. *We may come without expectation.* Our coming may be the result of habit and routine. Our attendance may be simply part of the timetable into which we have divided the week. But after all, we come to be in the presence of God, and when we meet God great blessings are available for the true worshiper. Think of the great expectation that Cornelius and his household had. "Now therefore are we all here present before God, to hear all things that are commanded thee of God" (Acts 10:33). *We may come without preparation.* It is easy to leave for the worship with no preparation of mind or heart at all. It is easy to do that for often it is a rush to get there at all. It is quite obvious that some come without Bibles and equally obvious that others never give any evidence of having studied the Bible lesson before coming. How can any of us expect to receive from that of which we are giving so little? Remember Jesus said, "with what measure ye mete, it shall be measured to you" (Mark 4:24).

This is true of personal relationships. One of the great acts of life is that we see our own reflection in other people. If we are cross and irritable and bad-tempered, we will likely find other people equally unpleasant. If we are critical and faultfinding, the chances are that we will find other people the same. If we are suspicious and distrustful, the likelihood is that others will be so to us. If we wish others to love us, we must first learn to love. The man who would have friends must show himself friendly. As one has said, "It was because Jesus believed in men that men believed in Him." "A man that will have friends must shew himself friendly: and there is a friend that sticketh closer than a brother" (Prov. 18:24).

There are many unhappy people in this world and even in the church of our Lord. Much of it is due to the unbalanced life that they are living. Expecting to receive without giving is not the balance of life. It would be good for all to take a personal inventory of self in regard to this principle. However, I am afraid that some have lived so unbalanced for so long that they will not exert the effort and energy to do so. They expect it for nothing!

The Christian and Pressure

We live in a pressure filled world. The pressure that we are referring to is defined as "a compelling influence; constraining force: as, social pressure" (Webster's *New World Dictionary*). Often some one speaks of another as being under pressure and that such accounted for his behavior that was not in keeping with the will of Christ. I firmly believe that anyone who endeavors to do right is faced with considerable pressure to do otherwise. It is not simply that such people have pressure placed on them and others are permitted to go free. If we are endeavoring to follow Christ, all of us face pressure. The problem evolves around whether or not we are strong enough to resist the pressure. We are thankful to say that some Christians are strong enough to endure and they joyfully bring forth fruit to perfection. On the other hand, there are others who wither under the pressure and fall away from the hope of eternal life. The Parable of the Sower suggests the feature of pressure and reveals failures along with the honest heart of success. Friend, don't think you are the only one who has to face pressures of life. We all have them. Some magnify them and make them worse than common, while other faithfully cope with the problem in the confidence that they can do all things through Christ who strengthens them. But let us notice a few of the pressures a Christian faces in his activities. He faces pressures to:

Conform To This World. The world is about the Christian. He is in the world, but is not to be of the world. The world doesn't desire for anyone to differ with it. This difference in righteousness condemns the world (Heb. 11:7). Hence, there is the continual pressure for Christians to be immodest, indecent, and immoral as the world is. The cry of truth rings out! "And be not conformed to

989 - You Are my All in All

Wednesday Night	Song Leader	Opening Prayer	Closing Prayer
9/7/2016	P Porter	M Carter	M Gorham
9/14/2016	T Reed	C Boss	G Wright
9/21/2016	D Carter	C Waller	C Boss
9/28/2016	D Wall	J Cooper	K Baker

this world: but be ye transformed by the renewing of your mind, that ye may prove what is the good and acceptable, and perfect will of God" (Rom. 12:2). After some have left the world in becoming Christians, the pressure is there to return. "Wherein they think it strange that ye run not with them to the same excess of riot, speaking evil of you" (1 Pet. 4:4). Pressure comes from sinful companions who want the Christian to be back with them and above all, not to condemn them. Yes, there is continual pressure to conform to this world—to give in a little here and a little there and before long to stand for nothing.

Be Dishonest In Business. Businessmen are constantly faced with this pressure. Around them are unscrupulous individuals who are ready to lie and cheat for the almighty dollar. On occasions, they are tempted to be as unscrupulous as some of these competitors. Pressure is upon them to be like others who might be dishonest in business. They get to thinking that such is necessary in this "dog eat dog" world of survival. Especially does one face such thoughts when it is evident that sales have taken a dip and expenses, etc. are rising with the present inflation. God would have his children to defy such pressure. His children are to "provide things honest in the sight of all men" (Rom. 12:17). In writing to the Corinthians, the apostle admonished them to receive him and his co-workers on the beautiful basis that "we have wronged no man, we have corrupted no man, we have defrauded no man" (2 Cor. 7:2). There may have been pressure to do the contrary, but they had not yielded. They may not have been the most prosperous in the eyes of the world, but they could live with themselves for they were honest with themselves and others. Jesus stated, "Therefore all things whatsoever ye would that men should do to you, do ye even so to them: for this is the law and the prophets" (Matt. 7:12). When we follow this rule, there is no room for dishonesty. Certainly, no one would have others treat him that way. In like manner, the Christian must not yield to pressure to be dishonest with anyone regardless of the circumstances. We need always to let our light shine and there is no light in dishonesty!

Compromise the Truth. Truth is not to be compromised. Christians do not determine truth. God has determined such and revealed it in his word. As God's children, we have the blessed privilege of following truth, but never of changing or compromising it. However, there is the pressure on Christians for them to compromise their convictions in the truth. Epithets of narrow-mindedness and "squares" are hurled at them and some yield to the pressure by compromising their convictions. An unbelieving husband attacks the convictions of his wife by saying, "If you love me, you will go with me and forget about worship this once." The pressure is on! Who will win? So many times the truth does not! Jesus said: "He that is not with me is against me" (Matt. 12:30). Compromise in one thing and it is much easier to do it again and even in a more devastating manner.

Christians, don't let the pressure destroy your convictions!

The Church's Responsibility

The following request has been received: "I would love to have your concise thoughts regarding one aspect of withdrawal, namely the church's responsibility when a member moves to an unfaithful congregation." Having some knowledge of the situation that prompted this question, I would conclude that by "unfaithful" we are referring to a congregation which supports institutions and unscriptural cooperation, along with practices of a social gospel. The practice of any one of these categories would be sufficient to classify a congregation as unfaithful. There are other practices that would classify a congregation as being unfaithful, but we are focusing upon what, through the years, has been designated as liberalism. It is good to know that there are still brethren who are discerning enough to realize that unfaithful churches do exist. By what is being said by some today, I have been prone to believe that they no longer view any congregation as being unfaithful. They no longer speak of the pattern of truth in the New Testament and do not condemn these liberal views as being departures from the truth. The truth regarding these practices needs to be continually taught. I have said that, if we do not continue to teach the error of such, there will be a generation developing that, with what little they know of liberalism, will deem the division over church support of human institutions as some personal squabble in which their parents or grandparents became involved. I made this observation in a recent sermon and a brother commented that it was already happening. Such thinking was already in the hearts of some in the present generation.

Years ago, I was involved in supporting the Herald of Truth radio program. I can remember taking the pilot film to congregations and showing them the arrangement that I felt was doing good in spreading the gospel. In fact, the congregation where I preached was committed to sending support to the Highland Avenue congregation in Abilene, Texas which sponsored the program. While reading the *Woods-Cogdill Debate* in Birmingham, Alabama, I came to see how such was contrary to the word of God. As a penitent individual, I started speaking out against the unscriptural arrangement and calling upon brethren to stand in the truth. This brought about having meetings cancelled and alienation from members of my fleshly family. Heartaches and tears followed, but truth is to be obeyed and we cannot control the consequences that develop.

In answer to the question regarding what responsibility a church has to a member who moves to an unfaithful church, we need to think upon certain principles. Is it a sin to engage in such practices as we know as liberalism? Such practices are not found in the pattern of truth. Paul wrote, "And have no fellowship with the unfruitful works of darkness, but rather reprove them" (Eph. 5:11). Again he said, "Wherefore come out from among them, and be ye separate, saith the Lord, and touch not the unclean thing: and I will receive you" (2 Cor. 6:18). It is obvious from these passages, that Christians are not to fellowship sinful practices, but rather reprove them and be separate from those who would engage in sinful endeavors.

Are individuals sinning who are bidding Godspeed to such unscriptural practices? Will such individuals be lost who die as members of these unfaithful congregations? It appears that many brethren feel that they will not be lost in fellowshipping these unscriptural practices. I even hear of preachers who profess to be conservative making such conclusions. Thus, when a member gets unhappy with the truth being preached on these matters and becomes identified with an unfaithful church, the brethren where he or she left do nothing about it due to their believing that people are alright in these churches. Brethren, what's it all about? If people are saved in practicing these things, why the pain, sorrow, and tears that faithful brethren have had to endure through the years in opposition to such practices? These matters are critical and they affect one's soul salvation. If they aren't, then many of us have misjudged others and our work in opposing such has been in vain.

When a member moves to an unfaithful church, he is moving into sin. With proper exhortation and concern, this is to be pointed out to the individual who contemplates doing such. When such fails and the party moves to the unfaithful church, appropriate discipline is to be executed as in dealing with any impenitent brother who will not be faithful to God's pattern of truth. Believe me, there are brethren who scoff at this answer because they do not really believe that members of an unfaithful church will be lost. I firmly believe that this is the core of their objection to any disciplinary action being taken.

Other brethren want no part of censuring the moving brother because they don't believe a church can withdraw from one who "supposedly" withdraws himself. They talk about the autonomy of the church and feel that they have no responsibility in the matter. This does not violate autonomy! The church is simply finishing the work of trying to save a brother who departs from the truth and their fellowship. Shouldn't there be love enough for his soul to try to help him? What is the purpose of any proper discipline other than that of trying to save the soul of the one engaging in sin? If one is not to be disciplined, what shall be the attitude of his brethren in the congregation he left? Shall they eat with him or keep company with him as before? Discipline will settle the answer to such questions (2 Thess. 3:14-15). This again suggests why some scoff at the idea of any form of discipline being exerted. They do not want any situation to arise that would keep them from eating or keeping company with those who have gone to unfaithful churches. THINK!

The Confession of An Extremist

An extremist is defined as "1. a person who goes to extremes. 2. A supporter of extreme doctrines or practices." For extremities to exist in any field of endeavor, there must be other views in which comparisons are made. When the position of so many individuals is considered and compared, I must confess that I am to be classed as an extremist. In fact,

I Am So Extreme That I Believe . . .

The Scriptures Are Perfect. "All scripture is given by inspiration of God, and is profitable for doctrine, for reproof, for correction, for instruction in righteousness: That the man of God may be perfect, thoroughly furnished unto all good works" (2 Tim. 3:16-17). The Scriptures are able to make a man perfect. Is it plausible to conclude that something imperfect is able to accomplish this? Peter wrote, "According as his divine power hath given unto us all things that pertain unto life and godliness" (2 Pet. 1:3). Furthermore, I am extreme enough to believe that the Scriptures are to be man's critic rather than fallible man placing himself as the critic of the Scriptures. Furthermore, I'm so extreme that I believe:

God's Word Is To Be Obeyed. There are those who talk about believing God's word, but they inconsistently refuse to obey what it says. This brings to one's mind the words of Jesus, "And why call ye me, Lord, Lord, and do not the things which I say?" (Luke 6:46). The love of God and his commandments are not to be separated. "For this is the love of God, that we keep his commandments: and his commandments are not grievous" (1 John 5:3). Men may cry legalism when one preaches obedience, but Jesus is the "author of eternal salvation unto all them that obey him." Hence, in comparison to the liberal views that grace nullifies obedience, I confess that I am an extremist in rejecting their views. Furthermore, I am so extreme that I believe:

God Means What He Says. Paul wrote, "Now these things were our examples, to the intent we should not lust after evil things, as they also lusted" (1 Cor. 10:6). He was speaking of the children of Israel with whom God was not well pleased and overthrew them in the wilderness. The people had been warned, but they persisted in their murmuring and disobeying God. As they were sentenced to wander for years in the wilderness, it was apparent that God meant what he had told them. Examples abound in the Old Testament Scriptures which are written to teach that God means what he says and says what he means. After all the teaching that some people have received, they seem not to believe that God means what he says. I recall a member of the church speaking of her neighbor who had not been baptized into Christ and died without obeying the gospel. Her comment went something like this: "I know he did not obey the gospel, but he was a good neighbor and I believe God has a place for him in heaven." Here was a lady who had known the truth from childhood and yet she was saying that in the final analysis, God doesn't mean what he says. When Jesus said, "He that believeth and is baptized shall be saved," according to her concept, he really didn't mean what he said and one may ignore it along with other commandments and find a place in heaven. Furthermore, I'm so extreme that I believe:

Being A Christian Is Great Joy. Though there are restraints to accept and a price to pay in being a Christian, these things are light in comparison to the joy of walking with Jesus. Some professed followers of Christ seem to be duty bound rather than appreciating the joy of doing the Lord's will. David expressed his feelings toward worship by saying, "I was glad when they said unto me, Let us go into the house of the Lord" (Ps. 122:1). Do we have the sentiment of gladness or is it some unpleasant duty for us to perform? While he was a Roman prisoner, Paul spoke of joy some seventeen times in writing the book of Philippians. "Rejoice in the Lord always: and again I say, Rejoice" (Phil. 4:4). Joy is spoken of as a fruit of the Spirit (Gal. 5:22). Do you view one as an extremist who really receives joy in doing the will of God? Believe me there are those who actually experience this joy!

All the Truth Is To Be Taught. It is possible for individuals to adopt the view that they can hear and follow a portion of the truth and still be right with God. The writer of Proverbs wrote, "Buy the truth and sell it not" (Prov. 23:23). We are to buy all of it! Paul assured the Ephesian elders, "Wherefore I take you to record this day, that I am pure from the blood of all men. For I have not shunned to declare unto you all the counsel of God" (Acts 20:26-27). When I endeavor to preach all the truth, I must confess I am an extremist as compared to the practices of so many today.

The Culprit

Webster defines the word "culprit" as "1. One accused of or charged with a crime. 2. One guilty of a crime or fault." The definition given seems to be simple enough and one would think there would be no problem in making identification of the culprit. This, however, is far from being so! We are living more and more in a society that sympathizes with the guilty and labels the culprit as one who would bring the criminal to justice. Think of the times that we have viewed a story on television concerning a Robin Hood type thief who has boldly taken from others. We are influenced by his charm and find ourselves hoping his flight will not be apprehended by the law. We are so influenced that the culprits in our minds become those who are enforcing the law and seek to inflict justice upon the one breaking the law. This may not always be the case, but so often such sentiment exists that demonstrates that we do not at all time recognize the definition of culprit.

Just who is the culprit is not plain with some members of the church. There are those who adopt the idea of condoning most everything in the activities of the church. When someone is concerned enough to speak out against such practices, asking for the scriptural authority of such, he is branded as the culprit. We have seen this develop so many times in the thinking of brethren regarding the church's work in fields of benevolence and co-operation.

With some, if you keep your mouth shut and roll with the tide, you are the hero. Rock the boat with objections and plead for staying with the pattern of truth and you become the culprit. Many seem never to realize that their innovations and unscriptural practices have divided the church. They are determined to place the blame on those who object and plead for authority for their projects.

In 1 Kings 21, we read of Naboth the Jezreelite. He owned a vineyard that king Ahab desired. The king desired the vineyard because it was near his house. He offered Naboth a better vineyard or the worth of it in money. Naboth's reply was, "The Lord forbid it me, that I should give the inheritance of my fathers unto thee" (v. 3). Under the law of Moses, the inheritances were to remain with the family and it was God's will that forbade Naboth to give up his inheritance. Ahab was unhappy about the matter and his wife, Jezebel, took over. She sent letters to the elders in the name of the king that called upon evil men to stone Naboth to death. Such was accomplished and the death of Naboth was due to his having what a king wanted. Naboth respected God's will and died because he refused to give up his inheritance. Later Jezebel told her husband to go up and take his vineyard. The Lord was aware of these events. He directed Elijah to go and speak to Ahab saying, "Thus saith the Lord, Hast thou killed, and also taken possession? And thou shall speak unto him, saying, Thus saith the Lord, In the place where dogs licked the blood of Naboth shall dogs lick thy blood, even thine. And Ahab said to Elijah, Hast thou found me, O enemy?" (vv. 19-20). Who were the culprits in this scenario? As one respects the word of God, it would be obvious that it was Ahab and Jezebel with those who did her bidding. But if this occurred in our time, don't be surprised to hear those condemning Naboth for not taking the good offer from Ahab. Who was he to refuse a king's fair offer? The word of God means little to some people. They are more concerned about human relationships and refuse to admire one who respects the word of God as the faithful Jezeelite, Naboth, did. Again, Ahab definitely viewed Elijah as the culprit who dared to relate his doom. The definition of who is the culprit on many occasions is not so fixed in the hearts of men. Let individuals violate the rights of others and still there are those who will not view them as the culprits.

"Brethren, if a man be overtaken in a fault, ye which are spiritual, restore such an one in the spirit of meekness; considering thyself, lest thou also be tempted" (Gal. 6:1). There are occasions when those overtaken in a fault will make it known and seek the help of others. Such is not always the case! Others do not realize their being overtaken in a fault, and in order to follow God's directions to restore such a one, information is needed. When simple questions are asked about the spiritual lives of individuals, there are those who view those asking as being the culprits. Where is the passage that condemns one asking about another when trying to help that person? Paul wrote, "Look not every man on his own things, but every man also on the things of others" (Phil. 2:4). How can we look upon the things of others without having information regarding them? When things work out well and people are restored, what you did was alright and you are appreciated. But when the erring refuse to be restored, there are those who resent the efforts and make a culprit of those asking about them in order to help them. Perhaps the reason some refuse to work at helping others is due to the fact that they do not want to be unjustly labeled culprits. But whom do we desire to please, God or men?

The Fears of Paul

One of the sad commentaries on the lives of many is that they fear the things that should not be feared and ignore the fears that are of value and warrant our consternation. Jesus spoke of such when he said, "And fear not them which kill the body, but are not able to kill the soul: but rather fear him which is able to destroy both soul and body in hell" (Matt. 10:28). The life of the apostle Paul emphasizes a proper attitude and conception of fear. Paul had fears for himself and fears for others, but they were not concerning the material and trifling matters that so often perplex us.

What were his fears? Regarding his entrance among the Corinthians, he wrote, "And I, brethren, when I came to you, came not with excellency of speech or of wisdom, declaring unto you the testimony of God. For I determined not to know any thing among you, save Jesus Christ, and him crucified. And I was with you in weakness, and in fear, and in much trembling" (1 Cor. 2:1-3). What constituted his fear? In what was he afraid? Not of man or material matters! If so, he did not believe what he wrote. Viewing Paul as the writer of Hebrews, we note that he said, "Let your conversation be without covetousness; and be content with such things as ye have for he hath said, I will never leave thee, nor forsake thee. So that we may boldly say, The Lord is my helper, and I will not fear what man shall do unto me" (Heb. 13:5-6). When Paul spoke of his entrance among the Corinthians, I understand that his fear involved his being faithful to the will of God and fear that the Corinthians might completely reject the overtures of mercy in the gospel of Christ, which was the only hope of their salvation. This was often the state of his mind. He feared lest he should at anytime become unfaithful and so grieve the Spirit of God or that, having preached the truth to others, they might reject the will of God preached to them. Such a view seems consistent with the truth and what he wrote regarding the subject of fear. This conception of fear should be prevalent in every servant of the Lord, but often it is tragically ignored.

Paul expressed fear toward the Galatians. "Ye observe days, and months, and times, and years. I am afraid of you, lest I have bestowed upon you labour in vain" (Gal. 4:10-11). We lack definite information as to what days, months, etc. that they were observing. There is the possibility that these observances were involved with following the Law of Moses or the Old Covenant, but it is apparent that such observances were not authorized by the Lord. Observing such depicted a spirit of novelty and innovation in their hearts that led Paul to fear they had not made a complete surrender to the will of God. When a disciple of the Lord craves special services and religious observances of days that the Lord has never authorized such as Christmas, Easter etc., it is a thing to be feared—fear for what such a spirit can do to the church and the souls of those who are possessed by it. Paul desired for his converts to be true and not worldly minded so that his labor might not be in vain.

Again, to the church at Corinth, he wrote, "But I fear, lest by any means, as the serpent beguiled Eve through his subtilty, so your minds should be corrupted from the simplicity that is in Christ" (2 Cor. 11:3). The commandment of God to Adam was plain and simple. "And the Lord God commanded the man, saying, Of every tree of the garden thou mayest freely eat: But of the tree of the knowledge of good and evil, thou shalt not eat of it: for in the day that thou eatest thereof thou shalt surely die" (Gen. 2:17-18). The serpent tempted Eve and corrupted her mind by his subtilty so that she disobeyed the will of God. She ate of the forbidden fruit "and gave also unto her husband with her; and he did eat" (Gen. 3:6). In like manner, God's will for the Corinthians was equally simple and plain; yet, Paul feared that Satan would corrupt their minds from this simplicity that is in Christ and they might become unfaithful to the Lord.

One's mind today can certainly be corrupted from the simplicity that is in Christ. The fear of Paul toward those in the church at Corinth should be the fear that we have today, and there is much evidence or grounds for such fear. When brethren desire to socialize the gospel and contend that there are Christians in all denominations, when they advocate that there is no need for authority for what they do, when they deny that there is a pattern for benevolence and place more emphasis upon the institutions of men than upon the church of the Lord doing its work—then brethren, it is high time to fear that their minds have been corrupted from the simplicity that is in Christ.

Paul preached his fears! These fears need to be preached now! To do so, one is often referred to as "a brotherhood straighten outer." So be it—for somebody certainly needs to straighten it out with some bold and forceful gospel preaching. The same was doubtlessly said of Paul and other faithful men who dared to express their fears.

The Curse of Meroz

"Curse ye Meroz, said the angel of the Lord, curse ye bitterly the inhabitants thereof; because they came not to the help of the Lord, to the help of the Lord against the mighty" (Judg. 5:23). Jabin, the Canaanite king, had been mightily oppressing Israel for twenty years. Deborah was a prophetess in Israel during at least a portion of this time. Deborah delivered Jehovah's commandment to Barak, but Barak refused to go unless Deborah would go with him. She agreed and the army was assembled. The battle resulted in the complete defeat of the forces of Sisera, the captain of Jabin's army. The closing part of the narrative tells of Sisera's flight and death at the hands of Jael. Deborah's victory song followed and in the midst of it the words of the text are found.

What was Meroz? No other mention of it is in the Bible. The curse, as was with Chorazin in Matthew 11:21, preserves them from oblivion. Meroz evidently was a village somewhere in the vicinity of the Kishon River. The inhabitants of this village, for some reason, failed to respond to the call of Jehovah and were accordingly made the victims of the curse of the Lord.

What Was the Sin of Meroz?

Neglect of a plain and positive duty. "They came not to the help of the Lord." This implies that an invitation was given and that they were without excuse. We are led to conclude that the inhabitants were neutral and useless at this critical time. They are remembered, not because they conspired to betray, but because they failed to assist in a time of crisis. What if all villages had been like Meroz? What would have happened to the struggle for freedom? Everything might have depended on them! If it had been that way, where would victory have been? It was as much to their advantage to respond as was Napthali and Zebulun. As in our age, so many want the blessings of the Lord, but they are not ready to pay the price for them.

It was the sin of inactivity. The question concerning the curse of Meroz involves a vital principle. People in every community are to the Lord's work what the inhabitants of Meroz were to it then. Innocence of positive guilt is not enough to secure us from condemnation. Christ emphatically taught against "the sin of Meroz" in Matthew 25. The foolish virgins, the one talent man, and those in the judgment scene who did not help those in need were obviously guilty of the sin of neglect or inactivity. There are members of the Lord's church who follow in the steps of Meroz by neglecting the Bible study on Sunday morning, the evening worship, and service on Wednesday evening, as well as many other endeavors. It is a very common error for people to suppose that they are blameless so long as they do not commit evil. The Christian is to accent the positive and abstain from that which is wrong. The Christian also is to be concerned with an energetic exercise of charity (Jas. 1:27). "Therefore to him that knoweth to do good, and doeth it not, to him it is sin" (Jas. 4:17). It might be, in some respects, better to have some faults and much useful service than to be faultless and useless. Members of the church who will fail to make heaven will probably do so more on the basis of the sin of Meroz than the commission of heinous crimes.

Why Did Meroz Refuse the Call?

No reason is assigned! The tragedy is that they refused regardless of the reason. We might suggest a few possible reasons:

God does not really need help—he can give victory anyway. True! But does he will to excuse on this ground? Can we be excused from duty by pleading too much reverence or too much faith to do what he commands? Our love for God is determined by keeping his commandments (1 John 5:3).

We are obscure; others can do better; we won't be missed. What if all had such an attitude? God has always used obscure things to accomplish great things (1 Cor. 1:27-28).

Fear or actual cowardice could have caused Meroz to refuse to participate. Peace at any price is not taught in the Bible. Right is higher than peace (Rom. 12:18; Jas. 3:17). He who fears to offend the wicked is not right before God. The fearful shall not inherit heaven (Rev. 21:8; Matt. 25:15).

Indolence or mere laziness regarding the call of God. Israel was awake, but not enough to move sleeping Meroz. No zeal for the glory of God, no sympathy for others bearing the burden could pierce their heartless selfishness.

Whatever the reason, they failed to respond. They suffered the curse. Let us take heed!

The Day Which the Lord Hath Made

"The stone which the builders refused is become the head stone of the corner. This is the Lord's doing; it is marvelous in your eyes. This is the day which the Lord hath made; we will rejoice and be glad in it" (Ps. 118:22-24). A more beautiful prophetic description of the coming of Christ and the blessings of salvation through Christ could not be put in poetic or prophetic verse. The day, which the Lord hath made, must refer in some way to the life of Christ. When we observe religionists emphasizing certain days and classifying them as holy in memory of Christ, true disciples need to think soberly upon the day that the Lord hath made and scripturally regard it. But what is this day of which the Psalmist spoke in which we should rejoice and be glad? What is the emphasized day in our Lord's life?

It is not his birth. The event is marvelously described but the day is not mentioned in the Scriptures. If there were no other events in his life other than his birth, of what would we have to rejoice and be glad? Surely there is a day connected with salvation fulfilling the prophecy of David.

It is not his baptism. Again, the event is mentioned in the gospels, but the day is not mentioned.

It is not his transfiguration. We read of the glorious event in Matthew 17:1-5, but the day is not mentioned. It would be unfair to say that this is the day that the Lord hath made. However, if one attaches special significance to his birth, which the divine pattern does not, why not select one of the 365 days of the year as the day of transfiguration and mark it with pageantry? There would be just as much Scripture for one as for the other!

It is not his crucifixion. The event is vividly described. Perhaps this event is nearer the fulfillment of the prophecy from Psalm 118 than the other days that have been mentioned, but the specific day is not mentioned. No power is to be found in a dead Savior. There must be another event with the day mentioned wherein we can rejoice and be glad!

What event was so important that the day might be named? Every one of the gospel writers refers to the first day of the week in reference to the resurrection of Christ (Matt. 28:1; Mark 16:2; Luke 24:1; John 20:1). We believe the Psalmist was speaking of the resurrection as the event and the first day of the week as the day that the Lord hath made. Jesus arose from the dead on the first day of the week. This is the Lord's doing. This is the day in his life which he made his own beyond all others. This event and the day are occasions for gladness and joy (Rom. 1:4; 2 Tim. 1:10). Christ referred to this prophecy in connection with his death and resurrection (Matt. 21:42). The birth of Christ from the tomb on the first day of the week is the birth of spiritual value that means so much to man (Col.1:18).

Is the first day of the week a holy day? It is not a holy day in the sense of the old Jewish Sabbath or Day of Atonement under the law. Much error has arisen by calling the first day of the week, the Christian Sabbath. The evening, in which Christ was betrayed, he kept the last Holy Day ever kept by faith (Gal. 4:10-11; Col. 2:16). The first day of the week is not a hallowed space of time, but it does set time for very hallowed acts of divine service (Acts 20:7; 2 Cor. 16:1-2). When men set apart days as holy days, they are going beyond the doctrine of Christ (2 John 9) and are not restraining fleshly appetites though they profess to be spiritual.

How do we know that our first day is the same day as that on which Jesus arose? No need! God took care of this! Whatever happened to the calendar or weekly cycles, there will always be a first day of the week and this meets the divine specification. Had God said, "This selfsame day thou shalt observe throughout your generations," we could be confronted with grave difficulties. This he did not say, and we should be exceedingly thankful that he did not!

In what manner do Christians observe the first day of the week? We read in the word of God that the Lord's church assembled for worship upon that day (Acts 20:7). There are two items of worship that are peculiar to that day. We are speaking of the observance of the Lord's supper and the giving of our means as we have been prospered (Acts 20:7; 1 Cor. 16:1-2). The observance of the day is of extreme importance to the Christian and all should consider the spirit of the day (John 1:10).

Every December many religionists throughout the world will observe the fleshly birth of Jesus Christ. They view December 25th as a holy day. Such is without divine authority. We do not know on what day Christ was born. Furthermore, we are not taught by command, apostolic example, or necessary inference to observe such as a holy day. The true worshiper of God remembers Christ in worship on the first day of every week. This is the day that the Lord hath made and we need to respect his appointed way.

The Faith Which Was Once Delivered

"Beloved, when I gave all diligence to write unto you of the common salvation, it was needful for me to write unto you, and exhort you that ye should earnestly contend for the faith which was once delivered unto the saints" (Jude 3). These words from the one chapter epistle of Jude are very beautiful and present many wonderful lessons to those who would be governed by the will of

Speaking Truth in Love

God. It is our purpose to briefly observe some of these words and phrases with the hope of helping all of us appreciate the passage more. Notice now:

Beloved. This is the word Jude uses to address those to whom he was writing. They were his brethren in Christ. There was great affection in the use of the word among disciples long, long, ago. There was no impropriety in it then, and there is none now. Christians were taught to love one another with a pure heart fervently (1 Pet. 1:22). Jesus commanded love (John 15:12). If we love as we are taught in the word, the world might say, "Behold how they love one another!" When we depart from that blessed state of pure love, souls are bewildered in darkness where there should be light. We should read 1 Corinthians 13 to understand love and what true love does and does not do. Love among brethren is often a neglected subject.

Give All Diligence. Jude was writing by inspiration. If he gave all diligence under such circumstances, how much more important that we be diligent when we write or speak of spiritual things. None of us has been in danger of drowning in the floods of too much diligence regarding spiritual matters.

Common Salvation. Jude gave all diligence to write of the common salvation. Salvation in any sense is important! Salvation from perishing in a burning building or from a watery grave is extremely important. Jude was writing about another even more important, that being the one involving the soul. We use the words "common salvation" in two senses. We refer to things crude and cheap as being "common," and then "common" is used in a very honorable sense to depict things universally available to all. Jude was writing in the sense of universal application, the salvation which is extended to all or (and which) goes hand in hand with the great commission (Mark 16:15-16; Matt. 28:19). He was speaking of salvation belonging to all nations (Acts 10:34-35; Heb. 2:9-10; 5:8-9). Paul speaks of the common faith in this light (Tit. 1:4).

Needful For Me To Exhort You. Jude was writing in the earliest days of Christianity. Eyewitnesses to the Saviour's miracles were doubtless still living. There were those who had seen Christ face to face. Yet, there was also lukewarmness and prayerlessness. Christians needed to be exhorted. There were those who needed it then and there are those in our time who definitely need exhorting (Heb. 3:13; 10:25; 2 Tim. 2:4). When individuals become offended when exhorted, it is evidence that they need more than they are getting.

Contend. Webster defines "contend" as "to strive, to struggle." Jesus said, "Strive to enter in at the strait gate: for many, I say unto you, will seek to enter in, and shall not be able" (Luke 13:24). In 2 Timothy 2:23-26, Paul states that the servant of God is not to strive but be gentle unto all men, apt to teach. There is no contradiction here. They are referring to different types of striving. That strife which Paul forbids is bitter strife, contention. This is strife which heaven condemns. We are to contend for the faith in a manner benefiting the spirit of Christ, which is not bitter strife. This contending is to be done earnestly. Men and women are no less earnest in their pleadings though they are not rough in them. There have been those turned from a reception of the faith by the harsh and bitter contention of those who are supposedly contending for the faith.

For The Faith. Not for Judaism. Not for our whims, hobbies, systems, fancies, or fads, and not for any creeds, disciplines, confessions of faith or dogmas of men. Man cannot be contending for anything more modern than the book of Jude and use the verse as authority. The doctrine, the gospel of Christ, and the faith are synonymous terms revealed in the word of God. We are simply to take God at his word, believe what he says, do what he says and commands, and become what he requires.

Once Delivered. There are four divine assertions. It asserts the existence of an organized and formal body of truth under the title of "the faith" (Gal. 1:23; 1 Cor. 6:13). It asserts that this body of truth is complete and admits neither of change nor of addition (1 Cor. 11:25; Heb. 9:27-28). It lays the axe at any latter day revelations (Gal. 1:6-9). It asserts the authority due to the faith to be the authority of God. It was delivered (Luke 24:47; 2 Cor. 5:20; 4:1-7). Lastly, the text specifies the trustees, "the saints." The word refers to the whole company of the people of God, the church (1 Cor. 16:13). Let's appreciate the verse and earnestly contend for the faith, which was once for all delivered unto the saints.

Are you truly contending for the faith, as God would have you to do? Think!

The Few in Sardis

Sardis was one of the seven churches of Asia. When Jesus wrote unto the church at Sardis, he did not find their works perfect before God. However, he did say, "Thou hast a few names even in Sardis which have not defiled their garments; and they shall walk with me in white: for they are worthy" (Rev. 3:4). It would appear that he was saying that though the church, as a whole, was not acceptable, yet there were a few members who were. Through the years, I have heard numerous brethren use this passage to justify their staying in churches that no longer respected the pattern of truth and were engrossed in liberal practices. They admitted that these practices in the churches were wrong, but they could still worship and work with these brethren as the few in Sardis were evidently doing. They felt no constraint to leave and justified their membership on the basis of "a few names in Sardis which have not defiled their garments."

When this approach or argument was used, there were some other passages that came to my mind. One of these is found in Ephesians 5:11: "And have no fellowship with the unfruitful works of darkness, but rather reprove them." By their own admission, we have known of those staying in corrupt churches, admitting that works of darkness were being practiced. How could they continue in such and not violate the truth of Ephesians 5:11? Can one worship and work with a group and still say they are not fellowshipping those with whom they worship and work? There is also another passage that comes to my mind and that is 2 Corinthians 6:17: "Wherefore come out from among them, and be ye separate, saith the Lord, and touch not the unclean thing; and I will receive you." There were situations existing which were not pleasing to the Lord. The Corinthians were called upon to come out from among them and be separate. The weight of these two passages is certainly opposed to brethren staying in something that is not right in the sight of the Lord. I do not believe that the Scriptures contradict themselves. This being so, I feel we need to give some more thought to what might be involved in "a few names even in Sardis which have not defiled their garments." There may be some possible consideration that would harmonize these passages and not find them contradicting one another.

What did the Lord say was wrong with the church at Sardis? It seems to be found in these words: "I know thy works, that thou hast a name that thou livest, and art dead" (Rev. 3:1). The church was not active in doing what the Lord expected of them. It had the name of being alive, but it was dead. With this in mind, couldn't we say that the few who were walking with the Lord in white were active in doing while the others were dead or inactive? With most of the other churches addressed as the seven churches of Asia, there were things condemned in their practices that we could classify as doctrinal matters. In Sardis, such is not definite! I can relate to individuals staying in situations involving deadness and being active enough to be referred to as walking with the Lord in white. This thought comes to my mind when I confront harmonizing what is said here in regard to other passages in the Scriptures which call upon God's children to come out from among corrupt practices and have no fellowship with them. Think about the absence of what we might call corruption of God's pattern of truth.

As a whole, the church at Sardis was dead and needed to repent. We are not justifying deadness in any church, but we are suggesting that there are circumstances that members of a church can be classified as worthy while others are far from it. The condition of one's heart might be used as an example. Regardless of how sound a church is, can one say that all of the members have a pure heart and conscience before God? I hardly think so! In like manner, on a personal basis, isn't it possible for the majority to have impure hearts and a few to be to the contrary? The Lord knows as he knew the condition of the church at Sardis. With this personal viewpoint in mind, I could see how the passage could be harmonized with those passages that appear to be contradictory.

I suggest another possible explanation. This explanation involves the time element. Members recognize the corrupt situations in the church of which they are a member. They seek time before fellowship no longer exists. They are the few who hope to save the whole church by staying with them for a while longer, hoping to be able to teach those who need it and save the church. The Lord was calling upon the Sardis church to repent and warned them that, if they would not watch, he would come upon them as a thief in the night. In his own words, a time element was extended. Perhaps such is available for the few to teach and plead with those in error to be right with the Lord. Please note that I am simply offering some possible explanations to harmonize the Scriptures that have been mentioned. The pitiful thing regarding the time element is that so many never leave the corrupt churches regardless of how much time is afforded them. So many say, "I will be here a little longer in hope of teaching these people." The majority who say this usually keep on staying and do not have the conviction to come out from among them and take a definite stand for the Lord's truth.

Whatever might be your view regarding the few in Sardis, the definite truth of Ephesians 5:11 and 2 Corinthians 6:17 will meet us in the judgment of God. I do not profess to know all that was intended in Revelation 3:4, but I am confident it is not intended to violate the truth of plain definite passages from God's word. Let us labor to be those who have not defiled our garments and continue to walk in white without corrupting our souls in fellowshipping false practices.

The Fine Art of Forgetting

Like many other words, the word "forget" has more than one shade of meaning. It has been said that forgetting is one of the fine arts of living at one's best. It is to this view, rather than to the inability to retain in the memory a name, date, or a fact, that reference is made in this particular article. We might say that the art of forgetting means character asserting itself or, to express it in another view, it is the blue pencil of wisdom cutting out unnecessary words from the text of one's living. The right kind of forgetting determines what thoughts will be permitted to remain in one's heart. ". . . for as he thinketh is his heart so is he" (Prov. 23:7). In many respects, all the virtues, vices, and qualities of mental and moral life may be defined in terms of forgetting and remembering.

The apostle Paul had things to forget! He had things to cut out from the text of his life. Hear him in Philippians 3:13-14: "Brethren, I count not myself to have apprehended: but this one thing I do, forgetting those things which are behind, and reaching forth unto those things which are before, I press toward the mark for the prize of the high calling of God in Christ Jesus." As one approaches a New Year and closes out an old one, it is a good reminder to take an inventory of some things he should be forgetting and things to be remembered. The art of forgetting is often abused! Instead of benefiting by the faculty of forgetting, the memory sometimes hoards the things that ought to be discarded and diligently treasures the things that need to be forgotten.

When contemplating things to be forgotten, there are always the things that should never be forgotten. Our debts of gratitude fall under this heading. What we owe to God is often forgotten! It seems incredible that the children of God should forget his blessings, but that appears to be the characteristic of so many. "Can a maid forget her ornaments, or a bride her attire? Yet my people have forgotten me days without number" (Jer. 2:32). "Bless the Lord, O my soul, and forget not all his benefits" (Ps. 103:2). Why do we so easily forget the benefits of God? Perhaps, it is because we have grown accustomed to them and we refuse to count our blessings as we should. We have grown to take for granted the wonderful blessings of God without giving him the thanks that is due. What would happen if the stars should cease to shine for ten years and then suddenly flash again? Would we think more of the benefits of God? One week of illness is usually fresher in our memory than fifty-two weeks of unbroken health. We should never forget our debts of gratitude toward our fellow men. As the butler forgot what Joseph requested of him, men forget their obligations to their fellow men. "Yet did not the chief butler remember Joseph, but forgat him" (Gen. 40:23). Paul spoke of being a debtor to all men. "I am a debtor both to the Greeks, and to the Barbarians; both to the wise, and to the unwise. So, as much as in me is, I am ready to preach the gospel to you that are at Rome also" (Rom. 1:14-15). Paul did not forget his debt!

There Are Things That We Should Forget

Our Injuries. The sense of injury is ever aggravated and intensified by remembrance. Such remembrance can breed bitterness! If we continue to think of our injuries, a spark is likely to be fanned into a flame, and behold how great a matter a little fire kindles. To remember injuries keeps us continually ruffled and feverish; fills the soul with heaviness and gloom; takes away sunshine and sours our personality; and even the Lord is eclipsed. Who is it that can't think of some injury? But why dwell upon them and let them deprive us of the joy of living the life of a faithful Christian?

The Past that Hinders. There is the past that profits and the past that hinders. Philippians 3:13 does not mean that we are to be ungrateful and not profit from the past. Some people unwisely remember their sins that have been forgiven in obedience to the gospel. They dwell upon such and it causes them to be retarded in the service of the Lord. Who is there that has not failed one time or another? But why dwell upon our failures? If we need to make something right, do what is needed to make it right in keeping with the Lord's will. Then go on in faithful service and growth in the Lord's kingdom. It is useless to brood over the ruins of one's happier days. There are duties yet to be performed and the doing of them will bring more happiness. We ought to forget the lower for the higher, or the claims of earth and self, for the claims of Christ (Col. 3:1-3). May we train ourselves to forget the needless things and cherish in proper remembrances the things that are needful.

The Grace of God That Brings Salvation

For the grace of God that bringeth salvation hath appeared to all men, teaching us that, denying ungodliness and worldly lusts, we should live soberly, righteously, and godly, in this present world (Tit. 2:11-12).

From this passage, I note the following things regarding the grace of God: (1) it brings salvation; (2) it has appeared to all men; (3) it is a teaching instrument; (4) it teaches one from a negative and positive viewpoint how to live in this present world; (5) what it teaches constitutes definite requirements that man is to accept if he is to be benefited by the grace of God. So many marvel about the grace of God, but how many of these are ready to accept the simple facts stated in Titus 2:11-12? It appears that we live in an age when men view God's grace as an umbrella that covers everything without men having to comply with the conditions in God's will. Without the grace of God none of us would have the hope of eternal salvation. Paul states in the parenthetical expression that "by grace ye are saved" (Eph. 2:5). However, the Scriptures do not state that men are saved by grace; *alone* or *only* by grace. "For by grace are ye saved through faith; and that not of yourselves: it is the gift of God" (Eph. 2:8-9). By one's obedient faith, he has access into the grace of God whereby he is saved. "By whom we also have access by faith into this grace wherein we stand, and rejoice in hope of the glory of God" (Rom. 5:2). Yet, so many seem to expect the grace of God to do it all without their having to have the faith to comply with the conditions stated in God's will. We have mentioned what grace does, but we also need to be aware of what grace does not do. **Grace Does Not . . .**

Circumvent Jesus Christ. "For the law was given by Moses, but grace and truth came by Jesus Christ" (John 1:17). The Scriptures do not separate grace from Jesus Christ. What one does or authorizes, the other does. Speaking of Christ, Paul said, "In whom we have redemption through his blood, the forgiveness of sins, according to the riches of his grace" (Eph. 1:7). What Jesus teaches regarding redemption and forgiveness of sins is according to his grace.

Ignore the Gospel. Paul speaks of "the ministry, which I have received of the Lord Jesus, to testify the gospel of the grace of God" (Acts 20:24). The gospel of Christ is of the grace of God. The gospel and the grace of God are also not to be separated. We note this from Galatians 1:6-7: "I marvel that ye are so soon removed from him that called you into the grace of Christ unto another gospel. Which is not another: but there be some that trouble you, and would pervert the gospel of Christ." What the gospel does, the grace of God does! The gospel of Christ is not some mystical catch-all and neither is the grace of God.

Nullify Obedience. It seems some believe that the grace of God saves them without obedience to God's word. It is God's unmerited favor that grants us the privilege of obeying that we might be saved. When one contends that grace nullifies his need for obedience, how can there be proper value to statements emphasizing obedience? Jesus is the author of eternal salvation to those who obey him (Heb. 5:8-9). In a book where perversions are given concerning grace, Paul speaks of those becoming servants of righteousness by obeying that form of doctrine delivered to them (Rom. 6:16-18). Our love for God is determined by keeping his commandments (1 John 5:3). Obedience is one of the key words in the New Testament. If grace nullifies obedience, why is there so much said of the value of obedience in God's word? It may be argued that one cannot obey God's commandments and one needs grace to suffice for his inability to obey. John wrote that his commandments are not grievous (1 John

5:3). There are no grounds in the Sriptures for a person contending that the commandments are beyond man's ability to obey. The true grace of God involves respecting his commandments and obeying from the heart the things commanded of us. We can faithfully do what God expects of us and there is no need to advocate grace doing something that is not taught in the Sriptures. "Blessed are they that do his commandments, that they may have right to the tree of life, and may enter in through the gates into the city" (Rev. 22:14).

License to Sin. Some hold the view that, after a person becomes a child of God, grace unconditionally covers sins that one commits. Such unconditional cleansing is not taught in the Sriptures. When a child of God sins, he is commanded to follow the law of pardon to the erring child. Peter told Simon to repent and pray that he might be forgiven. John wrote, "If we confess our sins, he is faithful and just to forgive us our sins, and to cleanse us from all unrighteousness" (1 John 1:9). If grace unconditionally covers sins, why would there be any need to confess our sins? Be thankful for the grace of God, but beware lest you abuse its true meaning and purpose!

The "It" of God

The little word "it" is such a small word but so very important regarding the will of God toward man. It was quite important under the Old Covenant. "What thing soever I command you, observe to do *it*: thou shalt not add thereto, nor diminish from *it*" (Deut. 12:32). The "it" constituted God's command. It was to be observed without addition or subtraction. By so doing God was pleased and the obedient were blessed of God. Herein authority was exerted and recognized!

Occasions abound in the Old Testament Scriptures of those who failed to observe and respect God's "it" toward them. Saul was directed by God through Samuel to utterly destroy the Amalekites with their flocks and herds (1 Samuel 15). Saul failed in observing the command of God by sparing King Agag and the best of the animals. The bleating of the sheep and lowing of the oxen testified to the fact that the "it" had been disobeyed by Saul. His failure to obey resulted in his being rejected of God and the kingdom being taken from him.

Faithful Moses fell victim to the "it" of God at the desert of Zin (Num. 20). The children of Israel were again murmuring for the lack of water. God told Moses "to speak unto the rock before their eyes," but Moses smote the rock twice. He failed to observe the "it" and in his disobedience God decreed, "Because ye believed me not, to sanctify me in the eyes of the children of Israel, therefore ye shall not bring this congregation into the land which I have given them" (Num. 20:12). God accredited his failure "Because ye believed me not." Had Moses believed God as he should have, he would have obeyed the command of God as "it" was given to him.

The "it" was the defeat of Nadab and Abihu. In Leviticus 10:1-3, these two sons of Aaron "offered strange fire before the Lord, which he commanded them not." God had directed them in what to do, but they had done contrary to "it" and offered that which God had not commanded. "And there went out fire from the Lord and devoured them and they died before the Lord." God meant "it" as h said "it".

These things were written for our warnings and admonitions (1Cor. 10:21; Rom. 15:4). The Lord expects the observing of his "it" in this age. "For if the word spoken by angels was stedfast, and every transgression and disobedience received a just recompense of reward; How shall we escape if we neglect so great salvation" (Heb. 2:2-3). Though "the law was given by Moses, but grace and truth came by Jesus Christ," grace does not nullify the importance of obedience to any command from God. Quite the contrary, obedience complements grace and affords us the spiritual blessings that are in Christ Jesus. Paul often spoke of the grace of God in the Roman letter and was quite definite as to how the saints at Rome had been benefited by the grace of God. Listen: "But God be thanked, that ye were the servants of sin, but ye have obeyed from the heart that form of doctrine which was delivered you. Being then made free

12:32). The "it" constituted God's command. It was to be observed without addition or subtraction. By so doing God was pleased and the obedient were blessed of God. Herein authority was exerted and recognized!

Occasions abound in the Old Testament Scriptures of those who failed to observe and respect God's "it" toward them. Saul was directed by God through Samuel to utterly destroy the Amalekites with their flocks and herds (1 Sam. 15). Saul failed in observing the command of God by sparing King Agag and the best of the animals. The bleating of the sheep and lowing of the oxen testified to the fact that the "it" had been disobeyed by Saul. His failure to obey resulted in his being rejected of God and the kingdom being taken from him.

Faithful Moses fell victim to the "it" of God at the desert of Zin (Num. 20). The children of Israel were again murmuring for the lack of water. God told Moses "to speak unto the rock before their eyes," but Moses smote the rock twice. He failed to observe the "it" and in his disobedience God decreed, "Because ye believed me not, to sanctify me in the eyes of the children of Israel, therefore ye shall not bring this congregation into the land which I have given them" (Num. 20:12). God accredited his failure to lack of faith saying, "Because ye believed me not." Had Moses believed God as he should have, he would have obeyed the command of God as "it" was given to him.

The "it" was the defeat of Nadab and Abihu. In Leviticus 10:1-3, these two sons of Aaron "offered strange fire before the Lord, which he commanded them not." God had directed them in what to do, but they had done contrary to "it" and offered that which God had not commanded. "And there went out fire from the Lord and devoured them and they died before the Lord." God meant "it" as he said "it."

These things were written for our warnings and admonitions (1 Cor. 10:21; Rom. 15:4). The Lord expects the observing of his "it" in this age. "For if the word spoken by angels was stedfast, and every transgression and disobedience received a just recompense of reward; how shall we escape if we neglect so great salvation?" (Heb. 2:2-3). Though "the law was given by Moses, but grace and truth came by Jesus Christ," grace does not nullify the importance of obedience to any command from God. Quite the contrary, obedience complements grace and affords us the spiritual blessings that are in Christ Jesus. Paul often spoke of the grace of God in the Roman letter and was quite definite as to how the saints at Rome had been benefited by the grace of God. Listen: "But God be thanked, that ye were the servants of sin, but ye have obeyed from the heart that form of doctrine which was delivered you. Being then made free from sin, ye became the servants of righteousness" (Rom. 6:17-18). The form of doctrine stated in Romans 6:3-5 constituted the "it" of God that they had obeyed and granted them freedom from sin through the grace of God. Without obedience, the grace of God is in vain as pertaining to man's soul (2 Cor. 6:1).

Paul was very singular in his preaching when he declared to the Galatians that the gospel he preached was the only true gospel and those who preached any other were to be accursed (Gal. 1:6-9). Paul, speaking by the revelation of Jesus Christ (Gal. 1:11-12), said that this is "it" and there is not another. Men in all ages have rebelled at God's directions! They have replaced such with their own wisdom and have suffered the consequences of God's wrath. The tenor of our permissive generation is to view religion in a broad sense and be strongly opposed to anyone saying that this is "it." Men crave a form of freedom that licenses sin! They desire a freedom of expression wherein no one can say that this is "it" to the rejection of other concepts in religion. Men evidently find it exceedingly difficult to bring themselves to accept the singleness of truth or the "it" of God. Men crave the choice of religions with the church of their choice and the faith of their choice in defiance of the "it" of God (Eph. 4:4-6). They can't bring themselves to view God as being so narrow, as having arranged the "it" of truth to the rejection of other procedures that fit man's wisdom. Notice what Paul said of Christ and his church from Ephesians 5: Christ is "the savior of the body" (v. 23); Christ "gave himself for it" (v.

25); "might sanctify and cleanse it with the washing of water by the word" (v. 26). He was unashamed of the "it" of God! What about our attitude? Have we become bored and weary of hearing of the "it" of God or do we love "it" as we should?

The Judgment To Come

"And he commanded us to preach unto the people, and to testify that it is he which was ordained of God to be the Judge of the quick and dead" (Acts 10:42). The apostles profoundly respected the authority of Christ. They obeyed his commands. The text informs us that the apostles were commanded to do two things. They were to preach unto the people and to testify that Jesus is to be the judge of the quick and dead. "Testify" scarcely does justice to the original. The original word suggests "to make solemn, public affirmation; to declare earnestly, to urge and force." The judgeship of Christ was a capital item in the apostolic testimony. Christ is King, Lord, and Judge, and Christians dearly need to recognize this in their lives today! I call your attention to the subject at hand, his advent to judgment—his coming to reckon with every man. Consider:

The Certainty of a Future Judgment

Man's mental and moral constitution furnishes evidence of the judgment of God (Rom. 2:12-16). The apostle called conscience, "the law written in the heart" leading to the righteous judgment of God.

The justice of God requires that there be a day of judgment. Everywhere the laws of God and justice are being disregarded. It is apparent that iniquity, transgression, and crime run riot. If justice and judgment are the habitation of his throne, then there must come a day when his righteousness will be vindicated. If Thomas Jefferson could say, "I tremble for my country when I remember that God is just," every one may tremble for himself when he thinks of the day of judgment (Acts 24:25).

What says the word of God? Our Savior often speaks of the

judgment (Matt. 10:15; 11:22-24; 12:36, 42). Would Jesus speak of that which is never to be? The apostle Paul speaks of the appointed day (Acts 17:30-31; 2 Tim. 4:1; Heb. 9:27). The day is approaching and no power of man or angel can prevent its approach. To deny that such a day will exist is to deny the Bible!

The Judge

This is our Lord Jesus Christ. "For the Father judgeth no man, but hath committed all judgment unto the son" (John 5:22). "When the Son of man shall come in his glory, and all the holy angels with him, then shall he sit upon the throne of his glory" (Matt. 25:31). "He that rejecteth me, and received not my words, hath one that judgeth him: the word that I have spoken, the same shall judge him in the last day" (John 12:48).

Who Are To Be Judged?

Fallen Angels. ". . . and delivered them into chains of darkness, to be reserved unto judgment" (2 Pet. 2:4).

All men will be judged. The judgment will be universal. "For we must all appear before the judgment seat of Christ" (2 Cor. 5:10); "for we shall all stand before the judgment of Christ" (Rom. 14:10).

The Lord shall judge even his own people. "For we know him that hath said, Vengeance belongeth unto me, I will recompense, saith the Lord. And again, the Lord shall judge his people. It is a fearful thing to fall into the hands of the Living God" (Heb. 10:30-31). To fall into the Judge's hands is fearful because the judge is omnipotent. It is fearful because he is the searcher of every heart. It is fearful because the judge has power to destroy both body and soul in hell.

For What Are We To Be Judged?

Everyone will be judged individually! We will be judged for our works, deeds, conduct, and actions. The statement of our account will be revealed. God keeps a strict account of all we do. We may forget, but the Lord doesn't. His record is accurate and fair. How wonderful it is that the final judgment is with the Lord and not of men! ". . . that every one may receive the things done in the body, according to that he hath done, whether it be good or bad" (2 Cor. 5:10).

For our words we will be judged. "But I say unto you, That every idle word that men shall speak, they shall give account thereof in the day of judgment. For by they words thou shalt be justified, and by thy words thou shalt be condemned" (Matt. 12:36-37). Let us restrain our tongues from evil and pray God that he will set a watch upon our lips.

Our secret thoughts and purposes. Our hidden life must stand the scrutiny of the omniscient judge. ". . . in the day when God shall judge the secrets of men by Jesus Christ according to my gospel" (Rom. 2:16). "Let us hear the conclusion of the whole matter: Fear God and keep his commandments for this is the whole duty of man. For God shall bring every work into judgment, with every secret thing, whether it be good or whether it be evil" (Eccl. 12:13-14).

The solemn warning of the prophet Amos to the children of Israel resounds today: "Prepare to meet thy God, O Israel" (Amos 4:12). This meeting is coming and no one will be able to evade the meeting! Let's keep preparing to face the judgment!

The Land of Beginning Again

I wish that there were some wonderful place
Called the Land of Beginning Again,
Where all our mistakes and all our heartaches
And all of our poor selfish grief
Could be dropped like a shabby old coat at the door,
And never be put on again.

. . . .

For what had been hardest we'd know had been best,
And what had seemed loss would be gain
For there isn't a sting that will not take wing
When we've faced it and laughed it away,
And I think that the laughter is most what we're after
In the Land of Beginning Again.
Written by Louisa Fletcher.

Do these words of the poet express only a vain hope? There is much to make it seem that they do. Time cannot be turned back. We cannot relive yesterday. What has been done cannot be undone. One's hope for finding such a land indeed grows dim until one turns to the word of God wherein forgiveness is found.

One of the beautiful features of the gospel of Christ is that, to the obedient, it offers a land of beginning again. "Therefore if any man be in Christ, he is a new creature: old things are passed away; behold, all things are become new" (2 Cor. 5:17). One who is in Christ is a new creature. Through the promise of God, he is assured that his sins are forgiven and he now has a new existence in Christ Jesus. The Hebrew writer speaks of the blessings of the New Covenant: "This is the covenant that I will make with them after those days, saith the Lord, I will put my laws into their hearts, and in their minds will I write them; And their sins and iniquities will I remember no more. Now where remission of these is, there is no more offering for sin" (Heb. 10:16-18). The wonderful declaration is found in the words: "And their sins and iniquities will I remember no more." Doesn't this suggest a land of beginning again?

Paul describes this land of beginning again in the terms of putting off the old and putting on the new man. He wrote to the Ephesians: "that ye put off concerning the former conversation the old man, which is corrupt to the deceitful lusts; and be renewed in the spirit of your mind; and that ye put on the new man, which after God is created in righteousness and true holiness" (Eph. 4:22-24). He wrote the same consideration to the Colossians: "Lie not one to another, seeing that ye have put off the old man with his deeds: And have put on the new man, which is renewed in knowledge after the image of him that created him" (Col. 3:9-10). Through the power of the gospel of Christ, this putting off and putting on is available to man and lies within his ability to perform. There would be no true value to these words if this were not so. God makes available, but man must have the faith to follow God's word in being obedient to his commandments.

Many no doubt are in quest of happiness and thirst for a land of beginning again. The pathetic thought is that they shun him who can grant this desire. The land of beginning again is to be found in Christ. We put on Christ in obeying his gospel. "For ye are all the children of God by faith in Christ Jesus. For as many of you as have been baptized into Christ have put on Christ" (Gal. 3:26-27). As the obedient obeys the commands of Christ, he leaves the land of indecision and unrest to find a new existence in Christ. In the years that I have tried to preach the gospel of Christ, I have never felt I understood why so many fight obedience to Christ. It appears that there are those who think one is trying actually to victimize them when the truth is presented to them. They seem to fight with defiance doing what Christ would have them do. Christ offers so much and in comparison demands so little. It is hard to see why so many defy him when they can have the land of beginning again in Christ. Perhaps some expect salvation to fall from heaven and be bestowed upon them in some miraculous way without their having to give up anything of worldly value to have it. Evidently, being a Christian costs too much for them to pay and obedience is not in their vocabulary.

This land of beginning again is not only available to the alien sinner but also to the erring child of God. Those who have become unfaithful and for years have lived apart from following Christ can turn and find this land of beginning again. John wrote: "If we confess our sins, he is faithful and just to forgive us our sins, and to cleanse us from all unrighteousness" (1 John 1:9). This is God's promise to the penitent who will confess his sins and return in faithfulness to him. The words of the poet do not express a vain hope! There is definitely a land of beginning again in Christ Jesus! Let's never forget it!

The Marks of the Owner

From henceforth let no man trouble me: for I bear in my body the marks of the Lord Jesus (Gal. 6:17).

In the book of Galatians, Paul had been answering those who were questioning his apostleship and the authority by which he preached. Galatians 1:11-12 is a good example of his reply to them. "But I certify you, brethren, that the gospel which was preached of me is not after man. For I neither received it of man, neither was I taught it, but by the revelation of Jesus Christ." As he approaches the end of this epistle, it might appear that he uses a different approach. He had been thundering against the disputers of his authority. Now, he bares his arms and scarred bosom saying look on them and know I am a slave to Christ, having the right to speak as the representative of Christ. ". . . for I bear in my body the marks of the Lord Jesus." These words probably refer to the cruel custom of branding slaves, as we do cattle with initials or signs, to show ownership. No doubt Paul had physical scars as the results of the stonings and beatings that he had unjustly received at the hands of those who set themselves against the truth he preached. An almost identical thought is expressed in 2 Corinthians 11:23-28, as Paul sums up the tokens of his apostolic commission and his zeal for the Lord.

There are beautiful points to be considered in this phrase: "For I bear in my body the marks of the Lord Jesus."

Paul refers to himself as the slave of Christ. The word rendered "servant" in the King James translation (at least in the salutations of Romans, Philippians, and Titus) should more correctly be rendered "slave." There is much difference between a slave and a servant as we view the words. This metaphor asserts the most absolute authority on one hand and the claim of unconditional submission and subjection on the other. The slave belonged to his master; the master could do as he liked with him. All this is atrocious and blasphemous when it is applied to relations between man and man, but blessed and magnificent when applied to man and Christ. The Lord has absolute authority over us! We are to render utter, absolute, unquestioning, unhesitating, and unreserved obedience and submission. All of this is for our good for now and eternity! We are his slaves if we have any living relationship to Christ. This thought ever stresses the truth that disciples of Christ have no place for self-will, self-indulgence, murmuring, reluctance, or the assertion of any rights of his own as against the Master.

What is the basis of this metaphor? How do men acquire slaves? Chiefly by purchase! As Christians, we have been bought by Christ for his own. A number of passages teach this very thought, 1 Corinthians 6:19-20; 7:23; Titus 2:14; 1 Timothy 2:6. The only thing that gives a soul the right to have authority over another is that it has yielded itself to the soul which he controls. Christ gave himself for us! He has the right to possess! Rather than slavery to Christ being degradation, it is magnificent! This slavery is the direct result and manifestation of love. It is co-existent with the noblest freedom. He is free who delights to do what he must do.

The marks of ownership. Paul evidently had in mind his scars as a result of the persecution that he had suffered. He realized that these were the result of faithfulness. Every Christian ought to bear in his own body the marks of ownership. We are not speaking of physical scars, but certainly we are not to consider ourselves completely immune to such! How do we know what might befall us in following Christ? For the present, we are thinking of principles such as:

- Marks of self-denial (Gal. 5:24; 1 Cor. 9:27; Mark 9:43-47).

- Marks of Christ living in us (Gal. 2:20; 5:22; Acts 4:23).

"Bear" is a remarkable word. It suggests more than a sense of toleration and patient endurance. It implies bearing with a sense of triumph as a victorious warrior would show scars as signs of his courage and bravery. With a legitimate triumph, the apostle joyfully bears before men the marks of the Lord Jesus. Let us be happy to bear in our lives the marks of the Lord Jesus.

Whose marks do you bear? There are only two masters—the Christ or the world. The world involves serving the flesh and Satan. Whose initials are in your face? Obey the gospel of Christ and be purchased by Christ (Mark 16:16; Acts 2:38). Yield yourselves to the true Lord so that you might bear the beginnings of the likeness that stamps you as his. May all of us, who profess to be in Christ, leave no doubt about our relationship to Christ. May we in word and deed show that we bear the marks of the Lord Jesus.

The Only Question That Really Matters

In Matthew 21:28-32, we read of the parable of the two sons. This parable is one of the simplest that Jesus ever uttered. It is also one of the most urgent. It is the story of the father who gave to his sons the common command to go work in his vineyard. One son flatly refuses, but later repented and went. The other, while giving a promise of obedience, failed to make his promise good. Jesus boldly applies his story to his audience. "Verily I say unto you, That the publicans and the harlots go into the kingdom of God before you" (v. 31).

The story was timely. It is also timeless. It was needed by the generation then and it is needed by every generation since then. It is perfectly at home among ourselves. It is also a message for us that is just as vital, pertinent, and piercing as it was for those outraged and indignant ears to whom it was first spoken. The truth of this parable has lost none of its compelling urgency. It continues to glow with a red hot earnestness that nineteen centuries have not been able to chill. The question is before us today and it will continue to be before us. "Whether of them twain did the will of his father?"

Why Is the Questioned Asked? Because it happens to be the only question that really matters. This father represents God and to the mind of Jesus the one thing needful is the doing of the will of God. This alone is of supreme importance. The entire Bible is saturated with this conviction. The writer of the books of Kings was not concerned about outward successes or failures of the rulers, but how they stood with reference to the will of God. The first question was always: Did he do the will of God? Did he do what was right in the sight of God? All else is brushed aside in a manner bordering upon contempt. In the New Testament, we find, if possible, an even greater insistence upon the supreme importance of doing the will of God. To yield whole-heartedly to him is Christianity, the heart of it, the whole of it. "Not every one that saith unto me, Lord, Lord, shall enter into the kingdom of heaven; but he that doeth the will of my Father which is in heaven" (Matt. 7:21). Doing the will of the Father is Christianity in its beginning, and in its consummation. It is the highest achievement for time and for eternity. To have an easy time, to avoid opposition, or even to live is not necessary, but it is necessary to be loyal to the will of God. This passionate devotion of Jesus to the will of God accounts for the amazing beauty of his life. Thus, Jesus asked the only question that really matters.

The Command. "Go work today in my vineyard" (v. 28). This command is that given by a father and not by a slave driver. God is not a tyrant. The command that he lays upon every individual is to work in his vineyard, his church (1 Cor. 3:9). He has designated the place and it should be a privilege to work therein. The time is today. We are needed today. It is the only time that we have. Today is the time that we are to make our contribution to life. "But the eyes of a fool are in the ends of the earth" (Prov. 17:24). The fool is so busy seeing the distant, he forgets the here and now. The command recognizes our personal freedom. While God commands, he does not compel us. He will never do violence to the sacred precincts of personality. The door of obedience to his will opens from within. Man must do the opening! (Rev. 3:20).

The Responses. The second son appears to be quite courteous. He gives a ready and seemingly eager reply: "I go, sir." To all appearances, he is respectful, but how disappointing he is! What is fundamentally wrong? Not his courteous manner; not his ready assent to his father's command, but his failure to obey what he said he would do. All else is secondary and actually incidental. He did not do the will of the father. The other son shocks us. He answers with a brazen and brutal reply: "I will not." His reply is one of no respect or courtesy and no hint of obedience. By and by, however, he changes his mind. Maybe the look of the father or perhaps remembrance of his father's sacrifices prompted the change. "But afterward he repented, and went." Now everybody appreciates the beauty of the conduct of this son, but just what is beautiful about it? Not the answer he first gave to his father. Open sin is no compensation for holy living. Not the delay of his obedience. Delay is dangerous. Why do we admire this son? For only one reason: he repented of his ugly and shameful conduct. He said "yes" to his father instead of "no."

God, the Father, commands us to go work in his vineyard. What is your answer? No? Yes, but no action? Yes and righteous action? Let us say "yes" and act today while we have time and opportunity. Tomorrow's sun may never rise! What will it be if we have not done the will of the Father who is in heaven?

The Power of Love

"Jesus answered and said unto him, If a man love me, he will keep my words: and my Father will love him, and we will come unto him, and make our abode with him. He that loveth me not keepeth not my sayings: and the word which ye hear is not mine, but the Father's which sent me" (John 14:23-24). Of all the forces in God's great and wonderful universe, love is the most powerful. Where physical force, the brutal sword, and the biting tongue have miserably failed, love steps in and works wonders. We observe love's power from three viewpoints.

The Power of Love on Ourselves

Every motion, good or bad, reacts upon us. The man we hate suffers as a result of our hatred, but not to the degree that we suffer. The spirit of hatred and revenge hurts the one possessing such a spirit more than those who are the targets of such a spirit.

Bitterness is but a cancer to a man's soul! On the other hand, the man we love is blessed as a result of our devotion, but not to the degree that we are blessed. We are forever reaping what we sow. "It is more blessed to give than to receive" (Acts 20:35). Though our love may not touch and tender the hearts of our enemies, it is never in vain. It helps us! It makes us more Christ-like and fits us for a higher state of existence—it makes us sons of God. "But I say unto you, Love your enemies, bless them that curse you, do good to them that hate you, and pray for them which despitefully use you, and persecute you; that ye may be the children of your Father which is in heaven: for he maketh his sun to rise on the evil and on the good, and sendeth rain on the just and on the unjust" (Matt. 5:44-45).

The Power of Love on Our Fellows

Love's conquering power. "Therefore if thine enemy hunger, feed him; if he thirst, give him drink: for in so doing thou shalt heap coals of fire on his head. Be not overcome of evil, but overcome evil with good" (Rom. 12:20-21). Where drastic, sarcastic methods fail—as they always fail—love wins. Solomon wrote, "A soft answer turneth away wrath: but grievous words stir up anger" (Prov. 15:1). Love disarms the enemy, hushes the cynic, and puts to shame the enemy.

Love's drawing power. Jesus stated, "And I, if I be lifted up from the earth, will draw all men unto me. This he said, signifying what death he should die" (John 12:32-33). In the gospel of Christ we see the great drawing power of love. While hatred repels, love draws people to ourselves, making them our friends, as nothing else will.

Love's binding power. It not only draws men unto us, but also binds them to us. Love is the cement which holds the members of Christ's body together. ". . . that their hearts might be comforted, being knit together in love" (Col. 2:2). The church is united only so long as the members love one another (Heb. 13:1).

The Power of Love on God

Love causes the great spiritual force in the universe to operate in our favor. Love reaches the very throne of the Almighty and moves it, bringing down blessings. The Father comes down and makes his abode with the man who loves him. "If a man love me, he will keep my words: and my Father will love him, and we will come unto him, and make our abode with him" (John 14:23). This is love from man that exhibits itself in obeying or keeping the words of Christ. Love is also the element that refreshes the Divine memory. "For God is not unrighteous to forget your work and labor of love, which ye have ministered to the saints, and do minister" (Heb. 6:10). Finally, God makes all things work together for good to those who love him (Rom. 8:28). The promise is certainly to those who love the Lord.

May we never tire of loving and may we never question the power that love has. "For this is the love of God, that we keep his commandments; and his commandments are not grievous" (1 John 5:3).

The Royal Family of God

Behold, what manner of love the Father hath bestowed upon us, that we should be called the sons of God: therefore the world knoweth us not, because it knew him not. Beloved, now are we the sons of God, and it doth not yet appear what we shall be, but we know that, when he shall appear, we shall be like him; for we shall see him as he is (1 John 3:1-2).

This passage directs our minds to the stately recognition of the love of God that makes us sons. "What manner of love" is a phrase descriptive of the quality of the love—glorious, sublime, immeasurable. Included in the manner of it are the freeness, the greatness, the preciousness, the scope, and the duration. This passage lifts the great future for the sons of God. The world knoweth us not, but God recognizes us and we shall be like Christ when he shall appear.

Let Us Observe . . .
The Great Fact—God has a spiritual family. Though all may be heirs, millions have refused and are refusing their heirship and

have rejected their spiritual birthright. The history of earthly lineage is attested by unquestionable means. The spiritual birthright is attested by a more unquestionable source—the word of God by the Holy Spirit. "For as many as are led by the Spirit of God, they are the sons of God" (Rom. 8:14). And again, "The Spirit itself beareth witness with our spirit, that we are the children of God: And if children, then heirs; heirs of God and joint-heirs with Christ; if so be that we suffer with him, that we may be also glorified together" (Rom. 8:16-17).

The Great Family. If we are children of God, we have entered the family by a spiritual birth. Jesus calls this being born again (John 3:3, 5, 7). Paul states that we are baptized into one body (1 Cor. 12:13). The family of God is the church (1 Tim. 3:15). Hence, when one believes in Christ, repents of sins, and upon a confession that Jesus is the Christ the Son of God is baptized, that one is born again into the family of God. Sonship brings wonderful results. All spiritual blessings are to be found in Christ Jesus (Eph. 1:3). Forgiveness of sins is one of the spiritual blessings: "In whom we have redemption through his blood, the forgiveness of sins, according to the riches of his grace" (Eph. 1:7). Heirship is another! "And if children, then heirs; heirs of God, and joint-heirs with Christ" (Rom. 8:17). Think of the wonderful privilege of prayer! One must be a member of the family to call God Father. The heavenly Father will hear the prayers of his faithful children (1 Pet. 3:12).

Characteristics of the Family

Family Resemblances. In physical families there is a family resemblance manifested in each member. The same is true in the family of God. Godliness is the trait or mark that his spiritual children bear. ". . .denying ungodliness and worldly lusts, we should live soberly, righteously, and godly in this present world" (Tit. 2:12). The rulers "took knowledge of them (Peter and John) that they had been with Jesus" (Acts 4:13). Was it the resemblance that they observed?

Love for the Family. It is natural for one member of the family to love other members. Even greater love should prevail among members of the spiritual family. There should be no place for hatred, jealousy, and ill will in the hearts of members one toward another. The same law that makes one a child of God makes him a brother or sister to every child of God on this earth. "Seeing ye have purified your souls in obeying the truth through the Spirit unto unfeigned love of the brethren, see that ye love one another with a pure heart fervently" (1 Pet. 1:22). Love for the family of God should prompt us to bear one another's burdens (Gal. 6:2), to prefer one another (Rom. 12:10), to do all we scripturally can to keep the family faithful (Gal. 6:1; Jas. 5:19-20), and to rejoice in the family gatherings (Acts 2:42; Heb. 10:25).

Interests of the Family. Physical families have interests in which all the members are to engage. In like manner, members of God's family are to be gravely concerned about royal interest. God's family is to be interested in the spreading of the gospel—the power of God unto salvation. If we are truly interested in the royal realm, we will be spending time, talent, and money on it. Many lost frontiers and provinces would be won for Christ if all who bear his name were concerned about his kingdom. How much interest do you have in spiritual affairs? Aren't you a member of the family?

The Great Future. "But we know that when he shall appear, we shall be like Him." As faithful children of God, we shall one day be gathered with other members of God's family where circles will never be broken . . . blessed thought! "For we know that if our earthly house of this tabernacle were dissolved, we have a building of God, an house not made with hands, eternal in the heavens" (2 Cor. 5:1). Peter spoke of that precious inheritance saying, "to an inheritance incorruptible, and undefiled, and that fadeth not away, reserved in heaven for you, who are kept by the power of God through faith unto salvation ready to be revealed in the last time" (1 Pet. 1:4-5).

We can say with the apostle Paul, "I have fought a good fight, I have finished my course, I have kept the faith: Henceforth there is laid up for me a crown of righteousness which the Lord, the righteous judge, shall give me at that day: and not to me only, but unto all them also that love his appearing" (2 Tim. 4:7-8).

The Saga of Three Beer Cans

This article is about a very unusual subject and perhaps one that does not merit much interest; nevertheless, here is the story. I was mowing the lawn and trimming around the hibiscus in the front of the building. Something caught my eye and, on closer observance, it proved to be a plastic shopping bag with a beer carton with three unused cans. How it got there I do not know! Why it was left there—your guess is as good as mine. The question arose as to what to do with them. For the sake of producing a lesson of some profit to all of us, I was confronted with the following alternatives.

Leave Them Be. Perhaps whoever left them there will return for them. This would suggest that the church lawn serves as a haven and hiding place for something contrary to spirituality as three cans of beer would be. If nothing more, to ignore them would be to leave something undesirable around the building for others to have to confront and deal with. Leaving them for others to reclaim would be bidding God speed to their use of the product.

Use Them Myself. Mind you, we are mentioning possible alternatives and this is one of them. Finders keepers and losers weepers! Take the three cans of beer, cool and drink them. This some individuals would do and have no problem with it. My conscience would be defiled in doing this! The Scriptures teach that Christians are to "abstain from all appearance of evil" (1 Thess. 5:21). "And be not conformed to this world: but be ye transformed by the renewing of your mind, that ye may prove what is that good, and acceptable, and perfect, will of God (Rom. 12:2). How could I respect these Scriptures and countless others in drinking that which can produce drunkenness and ungodliness in my life? Think of a person preaching to others and telling others how they should live and then participating in such practices! How could they expect people to place confidence in their preaching while doing such? "Let your light so shine before men, that they may see your good works, and glorify your Father which is in heaven"

(Matt. 5:16). There are no good works in drinking intoxicating beverages. Beer's alcohol content may be only four to six percent, but beer has something else—Lupulin. This is an active, hypnotic type narcotic. The hop from which it comes is in the same plant family (Moracaea) as the hemp, the source of marijuana. Though drinking the beer was a possible answer to the problem of dispensing with the three cans, that was no answer for me. I abhor such for we are taught to "abhor that which is evil; cleave to that which is good" (Rom. 12:9). So I quickly rule out this alternative and confront another . . .

Give Them To Someone Else. Keep in mind that here were three unopened beer cans that were as usable as the day they were purchased. People drink beer and I know individuals who would probably appreciate the gift of such. I do not condone their practices; nevertheless, they drink beer. Now, this suggests the question—could I give something to someone that I do not believe they should use and understand it is wrong for them to use without partaking of their evil deed? In other words, how could I be free of guilt when I provide for others what I believe is wrong? We need to think seriously about this principle. There have been those who contend they do not drink beer or alcoholic beverages, yet they keep it available for their "friends." If it is something that is wrong, how can I keep myself pure while providing such for others? It is a poor example for one to say, "I don't believe it is right, but I provide it for others." Yes, I could have found those who would have gladly received the three cans, but don't you think they would have laughed at my inconsistency when I tried to tell them I thought it wrong to drink them myself, but gave such to them? Inconsistency causes many lights to go out! "Thou therefore which teachest another, teachest thou not thyself?" (Rom. 2:21).

We are all subject to being careless and overlook practicing what we preach or profess. Such surely impairs our influence for good. Further development of such can produce what Paul condemned in the Cretians: "They profess that they know God; but in works they deny him, being abominable, and disobedient and unto every good work reprobate" (Tit. 1:16). Well, there was at least another possible alternative in dealing with the three cans of beer.

Get Rid of Them. Since they were left on the property without any permission and were violating the rights of others, this was a legitimate alternative. Invariably when such a procedure is suggested, someone cries, "Why destroy something that others desire to use?" In keeping with the law of the land, we should always be ready to destroy what is sinful. No one is advocating a march on the beer parlors or liquor stories to destroy them. To do so would not be in keeping with civil laws that we are to regard. The dispensing of these cans did not fall into such a category. Therefore, I did what I believe most Christians would have done. I placed the carton with the cans in the deepest part of the garbage can and let them go to the trash fill with all other garbage. Actually, this was the only alternative that entered my mind, but as I have tried to point out, there were some other ways of dealing with the solution. You might think this is nonsense and not worthy of taking up space in this book. Perhaps you have a point, but believe me this touches on some things that some people do not want to face. If you don't like what I have said, then I suggest you mow next time and maybe you can confront a similar matter and handle it in the way that is worthy of your better taste! Okay?

The Spiritual Boomerang or God's Law of Retribution

Be not deceived; God is not mocked; for whatsoever a man soweth, that shall he also reap. For he that soweth to his flesh shall of the flesh reap corruption; but he that soweth to the Spirit shall of the Spirit reap life everlasting (Gal. 6:7-8).

A boomerang returns to the one who throws it. It is a curved or angular club used as a missile weapon by the Aborigines of Australia. The boomerang can be thrown so that its flight will bring it back near the place from whence it was thrown—hence, something that reacts on the user. In somewhat similar fashion, our actions act as boomerangs. They return to us. We sow and we reap what we sow. In more refined terminology this is known as the law of retribution. Paul speaks of such in Galatians 6:7-9 under the phraseology of sowing and reaping.

Men appear slow to realize that God's retributive justice is very exacting. It was needful for the apostle to warn the Galatians against self-deception by admonishing them to "be not deceived." Today it is common for some to shake their heads with doubt when confronting this principle of the spiritual boomerang. This is partially due to the fact that they feel that the ungodly prosper as much or more in temporal affairs than the righteous do. They fail to comprehend that the absence of temporal prosperity may be a direct blessing from God which he has arranged for our ultimate spiritual welfare. The real answer is that the culmination of our sowing and evidence of reaping is not here but in eternity. We are living in the seedtime. The fullness of the harvest or reaping is yet to come. Be assured, my friend, that there is a payday coming. The boomerang will return to us.

To the believers of God's word, this law is just as fixed and immutable as God's physical laws. There is a definite analogy between things natural and things spiritual. They both bear the impression of the same divine hand. Numbers who would never think of defying the law of gravitation go heedlessly on with no regard for this fixed law of retribution—a law established by God with the same immutableness as his law of gravitation.

One purpose of the Old Testament Scriptures might be said to be as an example to us that retribution will come (1 Cor. 10:6, 12). King Ahab experienced God's retributive justice. Where dogs licked the blood of faithful Naboth, they also licked Ahab's blood "according unto the word of the Lord which he spake" (1 Kings 21:19; 22:38). Haman built his gallows upon which to hang Mordecai, but the scheme turned upon his own head. Haman and his sons were hanged upon the gallows that Haman had built for Mordecai (Esth. 9:25).

From Galatians 6:7-8, there are certain apparent facts to be gleaned . . .

We Are All Sowing!

This is true of all men. We are sowing at every step and leaving footprints on the sand of time. Thoughts, words, and deeds are the seed. There are two fields in which to sow: (1) unto the flesh, which involves spending our lives in doing the works of the flesh (Gal. 5:19-21); (2) unto the Spirit, which involves a life of well doing wherein the fruit of the Spirit is produced (Gal. 5:22-23).

Sowing, We Shall Reap!

A seed is a prophecy of a harvest and a sower a prophecy of a reaper. Life is action and reaction. The boomerang returns to the thrower and the deed to the doer. Our works, like our shadows, are determined to follow us. A man and his deeds are identical (2 Cor. 5:10; Rev. 14:13). Harvest may be delayed, but the delay does not make it any less certain. Men misinterpret the longsuffering of God. "Because sentence against an evil work is not executed speedily, therefore the heart of the sons of men is fully set in them to do evil" (Eccl. 8:11).

Sowing, We Shall Reap What We Sow!

It is part of a general law that, other things being equal, the same cause always creates the same effect. The offspring resembles the parents whether it is of men, animals, plants, or deeds. Sowing to the flesh yields a harvest of corruption, moral decay, and dissolution of man's being. He who pampers his flesh brings decay to his soul. As one has said, "Hell is sin rotten ripe." Sowing to the spirit yields a harvest of "eternal life." Man is blessed by his good deeds. The life of the apostle Paul represented one sowing to the Spirit (2 Tim. 4:7-8). He lived for Christ in keeping with the truth (Gal. 2:20).

Sowing, We Shall Reap More Than We Sow!

We reap what we sow in kind, but not in quantity. Men reap "thirty, sixty, or a hundredfold" (Matt. 13:23). An evil deed has power to multiply sorrow and shame in our lives and in the lives of others. A righteous deed has the power to multiply love and joy in our lives and in the lives of others. A great educator once said, "We sow a thought and reap a deed; we sow a deed and reap a habit; we sow a habit and reap a character; we sow a character and reap a destiny." We need to constantly be on guard regarding the power of the boomerang!

The Study of God's Word May Be Abused

One of the great privileges afforded man is that of studying the word of God. Earnest study of his word should be a definite feature in the life of everyone professing to follow Christ. There should never develop a time when we feel that we are above studying or learning more of truth. When attitudes of such nature develop, it is evident that the one professing them is heading for a rapid spiritual decline. The Psalmist described the blessed or happy man in Psalm 1, "But his delight is in the law of the Lord; and in his law doth he meditate day and night" (v. 2). The study of God's word is a precious thing, but like other things, we need to be cognizant of the fact that it can be abused. We need to keep the proper perspective and not be guilty of abusing the principle. Bear with me, while a few ways are suggested in which the study of the word of God may be abused.

Studying Only Fragments. It is the failure of some to pick out certain passages from the Scriptures and diligently study such without concern for all the truth. We need to know what the Bible says in completeness about every subject. Jesus said to those Jews which believed on him, "If ye continue in my word, then are ye my disciples indeed; and ye shall know the truth and the truth shall make you free" (John 8:31-32). Continuing in the word involves more than just a fragmental study of it! Paul directed Timothy, "Study to show thyself approved unto God, a workman that needeth not to be ashamed, rightly dividing the word of truth" (2 Tim. 2:15). Even the study of the Old Testament Scriptures helps one to appreciate the New Testament Scriptures that we are to follow in this age (Rom. 15:4; 1 Cor. 10:6, 11).

Studying For Notoriety's Sake. The Pharisees were great lovers of notoriety! They practiced a form of religion to be seen and known of men (Matt. 6:1-5). It is possible for men today to study the word of God that they might be recognized as "profound students." They desire the acclaim of men! Such becomes their purpose in studying the word. Invariably men are suggesting some new concept concerning a principle in the word of God. It would appear that they have a "new revelation" from God! As one has said, "If it's new, it isn't true and if it is true, it isn't new." We can all know more of truth, but there are no "new revelations." We are not professing to judge the intents of a man's heart, but it is highly possible for these "new thoughts" to be with the desire of receiving attention and notoriety more than a search for truth.

By Not Retaining Knowledge. What good is it to study the word and not retain the knowledge? Paul wrote of the Gentiles, "Because that, when they knew God, they glorified him not as God, neither were thankful; but became vain in their imaginations, and their foolish heart was darkened" (Rom. 1:21). Their knowledge of God was of no value when they refused to retain or keep the knowledge in their lives. We need to study to know and to know to do. This suggests the next possible abuse.

By Believing Studying is an End. Study is simply a means to an end. It is not an end within itself. What good is study or knowledge if one refuses to practice the truth? We need to note the words of James, "But be ye doers of the word, and not hearers only deceiving your own selves. For if any be a hearer of the word, and not a doer, he is like unto a man beholding his natural face in a glass: for he beholdeth himself, and goeth his way, and straightway forgetteth what manner of man he was. But whoso looketh into the perfect law of liberty, and continueth therein, he being not a forgetful hearer, but a doer of the work, this man shall be blessed in his deed" (Jas. 1:22-25). One may study the Bible and be able to quote it from Genesis to Revelation, but what good is it to him if he fails to obey it and live by the truth therein? A hearer who does not do is like one building his house on the sand (Matt. 7:24-27).

Using Studying as a Cloak. When any thought or view is advocated in religion, the true disciple of the Lord should be ready to study such in the light of God's word. He should investigate in the light of God's truth. Then, he is to accept or reject what is taught on the basis of what the truth is. I firmly believe that the word of God is plain enough that we can make this discernment with proper study. But there are some who seem to use study as a cloak. Over a period of time, when asked where they stand, their comment is that they are still studying the matter. They haven't come to a conclusion. They are neither for nor against! Brethren, I believe that in many cases such individuals are using study as a cloak for accepting in their heart some false theory. They are hiding behind the statement that we are still studying as a dodge of convictions. Take heed to study for the right reason.

The Untrodden Path

"For ye have not passed this way heretofore" (Josh. 3:4). These were the words of Joshua to the children of Israel. The Israelites were about to cross the Jordan River and enter into the promised land. It was a new experience for them! They had not passed this way before. Having wandered in the wilderness for forty years, they were now on the threshold of realizing the reception of God's promise.

There is a parallel between the position of the ancient Israelites and ourselves in the present time. Whenever we face a new year, we face untrodden paths. "We have not passed this way heretofore." The new year may be compared to an unknown country where none of us has ever been. At times it is good to undertake things that are new to us. The challenge is invigorating to our lives. One of the great concerns of the Lord's people is that of staying alert and watchful. "Watch ye, stand fast in the faith, quit you like men, be strong" (1 Cor. 16:13). The new passage for the Israelites was ordained and directed by God. We must accept the challenge of each new year and walk in its ways as God directs us in his word.

What will we encounter along the untrodden paths? We do not know what the future holds. Modern soothsayers and sorcerers abound who contend that they know. They are false and full of deceptions. In God's arrangement for us, perhaps it is best that we do not know what lies ahead, best that we are not able to look into the future. We are to live each day in the light and strength that the God of heaven gives us. Jesus said, "Take therefore no thought for the morrow: for the morrow shall take thought for the things of itself. Sufficient unto the day is the evil thereof" (Matt. 6:34). I suppose it would be quite frightening for the most of us to contemplate the untrodden paths of each new year if it were not for the elements which God has provided to conquer these untrodden paths. What are some elements to conquer untrodden paths?

A Guide. A good guide brings assurance and confidence. The Israelites were told to follow the ark of the covenant. Who is our guide? The answer is Jesus Christ (John 14:6). He has the qualities that are so necessary in a proper guide: experience or knowledge, loyalty or faithfulness. Jesus fits these perfectly. He is able to guide us through temptations (Heb. 4:14-16), out of sorrows (Matt. 26:36; Heb. 5:7), and through all problems (Col. 2:10). If we are to be benefited, we must follow the guide wherever he leads us!

Certain Provisions. Ample provisions are a necessary concern for a proper journey. We need a chart for the course. The word of God is the true chart that cannot be improved upon! The Psalmist wrote, "Thy word is a lamp unto my feet, and a light unto my path" (Ps. 119:105). Concerning the Scriptures, we read, "All Scripture is given by inspiration of God, and is profitable for doctrine, for reproof, for correction, for instruction in righteousness: that the man of God may be perfect, thoroughly furnished unto all good works" (2 Tim. 3:16-17). The word of God is sufficient to bring us along the untrodden path. We need to stay with the chart and ever be familiar with it.

There is need for proper clothing. The apostle speaks of spiritual clothing in Colossians 3:12-14: "Put on therefore, as the elect of God, holy and beloved, bowels of mercies, kindness, humbleness of mind, meekness, long-suffering; forbearing one another, and forgiving one another, if any man have a quarrel against any; even as Christ forgave you, so also do ye. And above all these things put on charity, which is the bond of perfectness." We are to put on these things. Can you improve upon such a wardrobe?

There is need for food. "As newborn babes, desire the sincere milk of the word, that ye may grow thereby" (1 Pet. 2:2). "And Jesus said unto them, I am the bread of life: he that cometh to me shall never hunger; and he that believeth on me shall never thirst" (John 6:35). Not only is the word of God the chart for the course, it is food for the soul. We need to feed our souls with God's word as we walk the untrodden path of a new year.

Daily Bible Reading. Efforts to teach others and 100% attendance at all services constitute untrodden paths for some who profess to be Christians. Why not start walking in these untrodden paths as far as your life in concerned? Obedience to the gospel of Christ is the untrodden path for the alien. Why not obey the gospel of Christ and walk with Christ in the new year? We may not know what will occur in each new year. But we can certainly know him who does. We need to always stay close to God!

The Valleys of Life

As we think of the Israelites dwelling in a land of hills and valleys, we are made to think of life itself. Life may be said to be a land of hills and valleys. A valley as we all know is a land that lies between mountains, hills, or highlands. There are times when we are walking through the valleys—times when we are on the summit of hills. All of this is contemplated in the word of God. When we speak of the valleys of life, we speak of those places or situations into which all of us sooner or later go and out of which we must come in order to find life to be as bountiful as God has promised that it can be. There is no exception to the rule that men must walk through the valleys of life. We shall endeavor to present some thoughts that are significant and true concerning the valleys of life through which we must pass.

The Valley of Decision (Joel 3:14)

When one becomes accountable to God, he enters the valley of decision (Eccl. 12:1). Every day in our lives some decisions involving right or wrong must be met. All of us are walking in the valley of decision—deciding whether we shall take our stand for Christ or the god of the world, Satan. One cannot evade the responsibility to decide. Jesus said, "He that is not with me is against me; and he that gathereth not with me scattereth abroad" (Matt. 12:30). Great men of God have spoken of the valley of decision (Josh. 24:15; 1 Kings 18:21). Not all Bible characters have made proper and honorable decisions. Rehoboam, the son of Solomon, made a reckless decision (1 Kings 12:4-5, 13-16) A very tragic decision was made by the rich young ruler who loved his earthly possessions more than being a disciple of Christ (Matt.19:16-22). Dear reader, what decision have you made? Whom are you serving?

The Valley of Depression

We mean by the use of this term, the valley into which many of us go on different occasions when our spirits are at a low ebb. "The spirit of a man will sustain his infirmity; but a wounded spirit who can bear?" (Prov. 18:14). This valley is invariably reached in moments of sickness and pain. Strong men have been known to weep in moments of sickness when they had never wept before. There is consolation for the Christian—he has made the right decision in the valley of decision and now has Christ to help him in such times. Faithful men of God have on occasions known this valley. Elijah found a juniper tree in it (1 Kings 19:4-14). John the Baptist found its existence while a prisoner for righteousness' sake (Matt. 11:3-5). Out of this valley has come lives possessing amazing strength. On the other hand, there is another side to this valley of depression—moral weakness. Judas didn't make it out of the valley. These who walk through the valley of moral weakness often experience a lagging of spirit and a troubled mind or heart. How many have said, "I would to God that I had the moral strength to be something beside what I am"?

The Valley of Persecution

If you are a Christian, you are going to be persecuted (2 Tim. 3:12). The valley of persecution awaits those who would follow Christ. There will be those who will revile, speak evil of you, and mock and ridicule your righteousness. In fact, the lack of persecution may be an indication of weakness as a Christian. Stephen walked through this valley. He came out on the sunlit hill of God over yonder (Acts 7:56). We had best prepare to spend some time in this valley if we intend to be the faithful children of God that God would have us be. "Beloved, think it not strange concerning the fiery trial which is to try you, as though some strange thing happened unto you" (1 Pet. 4:12). Don't let persecution defeat you!

The Valley of Death (Ps. 23:4)

One thing can be said of all—they will go through the valley of death (Heb. 9:27). The only thing that will exempt some from going through this valley is that they will be living when the Lord comes (1 Thess. 4:16-17). David spoke of "the valley of the shadow of death" (Ps. 23:4). David had often been in the face of death with Goliath and with Saul. The time is coming and it may be sooner than we think when you and I must walk through this valley. The lyrics of the hymn say, "We are going down the valley one by one, we are going toward the setting of the sun." The victory is in Christ. "O death, where is thy sting? O grave, where is thy victory? The sting of death is sin; and the strength of the sin is the law. But thanks be to God, which giveth us the victory through our Lord Jesus Christ" (1 Cor. 15:55-57).

God permits us to see a faithful life, one which in essence went through these valleys victorious. The Apostle Paul encountered and viewed every valley mentioned (2 Tim. 4:6-8). May each of us faithfully obey his word that we might be victorious in the end. How faithful are you?

The Value of Positive Living

There are factors in life that are opposed one to another, yet the one is dependent upon the other for completeness. Consider that sun and rain are needed for vegetation. Sleep and activity are necessary for a healthy, vigorous life. Negative and positive principles are essential in electricity. Jesus stated a short parable which teaches this truth in a very vivid way. "When the unclean spirit is gone out of a man, he walketh through dry places, seeking rest, and findeth none. Then he saith, I will return into my house from whence I came out; and when he is come, he findeth it empty, swept, and garnished. Then goeth he, and taketh with himself seven other spirits more wicked than himself, and they enter in and dwell there: and the last state of that man is worse than the first. Even so shall it be also unto this wicked generation" (Matt. 12:43-45). The house was cleaned. It remained empty. The unclean spirit returned with seven other spirits more wicked than himself. The last state was worse than the first.

The direct application was to the Jewish nation. "Even so shall it be also unto this wicked generation." They were professing to be righteous in their traditional view, but they were not actively accepting the teaching of Christ that was necessary in their lives to be acceptable with God. They were destined to have their house filled with greater evil than in the beginning by their negative approach to the teaching of Jesus. The truth in this parable is quite applicable to the Lord's people today. The body of a Christian "is the temple of the Holy Ghost which is in you, which ye have of God" (1 Cor. 6:19-20). The temple must be a suitable place for the Lord to dwell. The negative must be applied in eliminating the trash from the temple. The negative precedes the need of the positive. The temple must not be left empty. If left empty, evil will return to it. The positive must be followed in order to see that the house is properly furnished.

Christianity is a complete religion and answers to man's need.

Hence, it is both negative and positive. Jesus Christ, the founder, taught and practiced the negative and also the positive. The church needs to appreciate these two principles. As the gospel is obeyed, one is cleansed from evil, but the house must not remain empty. We seem to have the idea that abstinence from evil is all that is expected of members of the church. The evil spirit found the clean house an attractive place in which to dwell. Satan does not leave us alone just because we are in the Lord's church. Actually, it may be concluded that his attack upon one becomes even more intense. When we were in the world, we were of the "god of this world" which is Satan. Having obeyed the gospel, we broke with Satan and were added to the Lord's church. Satan wants to reclaim his former subjects and does all within his power to cause us to be unfaithful. (1 Pet. 5:8). That is why the house or life of the Christian must be filled with positive deeds. It is not enough simply to emphasize the negative. We must also place concerted emphasis upon the positive. This is where so many of God's children are failing. They have the mistaken idea that, as long as they are not grossly active in committing evil, this alone grants them acceptability before God. The clean house is not enough! We need to have it furnished with positive living.

In the parable, the evil spirit would not have found a dwelling place when he returned if the house had been filled with good things. An empty, swept, and garnished house is very inviting! The Lord has stressed faithfulness to the assembly in order to keep the house filled (Heb. 10:23-25). Christians are to be active in adding the graces that are found in 2 Peter 1:5-8. "And besides this giving all diligence, add to your faith virtue; and to virtue, knowledge; and to knowledge, temperance; and to temperance, patience; and to patience, godliness; and to godliness, brotherly kindness; and to brotherly kindness, charity. For if these things be in you, and abound, they make you that ye shall neither be barren nor unfruitful in the knowledge of our Lord Jesus Christ." These principles constitute some mighty good furniture for the house. Good works are also a part of keeping the house filled. Paul spoke of being "ready to every good work" and "maintaining good works" in Titus

3. By practicing such, we evidence to the world that the house is not vacant (Matt. 5:16).

The evil spirit brought seven other spirits worse than himself when he found the house was empty. We can become unfaithful by not emphasizing positive living to such an extent that the last state of man can become worst than the first. Peter wrote, "the latter end is worse with them than the beginning" (2 Pet. 2:20). If one does not go forward and continue to develop spiritually, he is inevitably destined to become worse (2 Tim. 3:13). We need continually to emphasize the value of positive living in Christ.

The Verb "Continue"

The verb "continue" is a word often used in the New Testament Scriptures. It is associated with admonitions and exhortations directed to Christians. Webster defines "continue" as "1. to last; endure. 2. to go on in a specified condition or course of action. 3. to stay. 4. to keep on; persist." All of these definitions are quite important to the Christian in the hope of heaven. In regard to the Greek word translated continue in Colossians 1:23, *Vincent's Word Studies in the New Testament* says, "The verb means to stay at or with." The New Testament Scriptures are very relevant for people of our generation. By this, we mean that the problems the church and Christians in the New Testament days experienced are in essence the problems that are to be confronted today. People then needed exhortation to continue following the Christ. There were those then who made the start by becoming Christians but showed evidence of falling by the wayside. There were those who even abandoned Christ. We are confronted with the same problems today. So many make the start but fail to continue. I don't know of any congregation but what the principle of continuing is a constant problem. Some congregations may be inclined to ignore that such is a problem, but such an attitude suggests that they really have a problem. Just think what it would be if all who have been baptized into Christ had remained faithful. Buildings would not be large enough to seat those who attend!

The situation may not have been so pronounced at times in some congregations in the days of the apostles, but be assured of this—the problem existed and much is said in the Scriptures about the need for continuing. This would not have been needed if one can't fall from grace or depart from the faith. To the open minded individual, the evidence of the admonition to continue in the Scriptures is sufficient proof that one can cease to be faithful in the Lord after having made the start.

Each January we begin a New Year. What will the new year bring? Fallible man with his finite mind is not capable to give the answer. The one thing that all of us need to be gravely concerned about is that of continuing faithful in the Lord. This is something that we can have control over and should be foremost in our minds. Whatever comes in the days ahead can be properly dealt with as we continue faithful in Christ. The answer is in Christ and we must never forget it. Paul expressed it this way: "I can do all things through Christ which strengtheneth me" (Phil. 4:13). There are empty seats now because some have failed to continue faithful through the year. Perhaps at the beginning of a new year some of these would have been horrified and even offended if one had suggested that they might not continue faithful through the year. But observe what has happened! There is little satisfaction and consolation is saying, "I told you so." This involves souls who are perishing before the Lord in their failure to continue. Notice a few of the principles mentioned in the Scriptures that are associated with the admonition to continue.

The Scriptures Point Christians to the Value of Continuing

In the Faith. After planting the truth in Lystra, Iconium, and Antioch, we read of Paul and Barnabas returning to these cities, "confirming the souls of the disciples, and exhorting them to continue in the faith, and that we must through much tribulation enter into the kingdom of God" (Acts 14:22). Paul and Barnabas were aware of the possibility of these converts not continuing in the faith, hence the value to this exhortation. What good is it to begin something worthwhile and not continue! Continuing in the faith involves following those things which Christ and his apostles have revealed for man to practice. We are not granted the right to do that which is easy and disregard those commands that might be distasteful. The faith has been delivered (Jude 3) and in the teaching of Christ we are to abide (2 John 9-11; Col. 1:23).

In the Word. Jesus said to those Jews who believed on him, "If ye continue in my word, then are ye my disciples indeed; and ye shall know the truth, and the truth shall make you free" (John 8:31-32). Their being disciples indeed, knowing the truth and being made free, depended upon continuing in the word. Paul directed Timothy, "But continue thou in the things which thou hast learned and hast been assured of" (2 Tim. 3:14). This involved the holy Scriptures! The Jerusalem church "continued stedfastly in the apostles' doctrine" (Acts 2:42). Any church or Christian that is to be faithful in Christ must continue in the same (1 Tim. 4:16). Furthermore, the Scriptures point Christians to continuing in brotherly love (Heb. 13:2) and prayer (Col. 4:2). May we continue in the things pleasing to God and never be quitters in what is right!

They Have Already Been Removed

Some years ago, there was a great deal said by the news media concerning a controversy over removing a monument of the Ten Commandments in Montgomery, Alabama. The monument was placed in the rotunda of the Alabama Judicial Building by Chief Justice Roy Moore. The federal courts held that the monument violated the Constitutional ban on government promotion of a religious doctrine. Those who are in favor of the monument not being removed contend that a forced removal would violate the constitutional guarantee of freedom of religion in America. The legal war continued for some time, but the monument was removed.

All of this produces a delicate subject for Christians who truly respect God's word. No one who respects God's word desires to side with the American Civil Liberties Union and atheist groups who are so opposed to religion. It touches one's heart when matters involving the use of God's name, prayer, and evidence of belief in God are being abolished by courts in the country that we love. But think about the dilemma that those who have a zeal for God without knowledge are placing upon those who are truly endeavoring to follow the truth. We are not under the law involving the Ten Commandments. The law with these commandments was given to the children of Israel and bound upon them. The restating of these commandments is found in Deuteronomy 5: "And Moses called all Israel, and said unto them, Hear, O Israel, the statutes and judgments which I speak in your ears this day, that ye may learn them, and keep, and do them. The Lord our God made a covenant with us in Horeb. The Lord made not this covenant with our fathers, but with us, even us, who are all of us here alive this day" (vv. 1-3). The verses that follow make known these Ten Commandments that were part of the covenant that Moses said was made with the children of Israel, "with us, even us, who are all of us here alive this day." When this law was existing, there were prophecies stating that God would give a new covenant.

Jeremiah spoke of this in 31:31-34. "Behold, the days come, saith the Lord, that I will make a new covenant with the house of Israel and with the house of Judah: Not according to the covenant that I made with their fathers in the day that I took them by the hand to bring them out of the land of Egypt." The old covenant with the Ten Commandments was given to the Jews. The new covenant with the teaching of Christ was made available to both Jews and Gentiles as it exists today. Jesus came and fulfilled the old law (Matt. 5:17-18). The Hebrew writer stated, "Then said he, Lo, I come to do thy will, O God. He taketh away the first, that he may establish the second. By the which will we are sanctified through the offering of the body of Jesus Christ once for all" (Heb. 10:9-10). The law with the Ten Commandments has been removed. Paul speaks of this in Colossians 2:14: "Blotting out the handwriting of ordinances that was against us, which was contrary to us, and took it out of the way, nailing it to his cross."

Judge Moore and those who hold his view fail to rightly divide the word of God. They make no distinction between the old and new covenants! They even argue that, if the Ten Commandments are not binding, then we can rightfully engage in all things that they prohibit. The teaching of Christ in the new covenant provides the answer to such argumentation. With the exception of the fourth commandment to remember the Sabbath and keep it holy, Jesus incorporated these principles in the new covenant and even goes further by saying that these may be violated by sins in our hearts. "Ye have heard that it was said by them of old time, Thou shalt not commit adultery: But I say unto you, That whosoever looketh on a woman to lust after her hath committed adultery with her already in his heart" (Matt. 5:27-28). The American colonies were first ruled by England. When the revolution came and gave freedom to the colonies, did this grant them the privilege of doing all things that English law declared immoral? No, because they were now governed by the laws of the new nation that determined moral or immoral matters. In like matter, the new covenant determines how we are to live and not a covenant that was given to the Jews and later removed that the new covenant might exist.

Some years ago, the question was asked in a Bible class regarding what a Christian was called upon to do in being faithful to Christ. A lady who had been a member of the church for a number of years replied by saying that the Christian was to keep the Ten Commandments. Like Judge Moore and others, she evidently was not aware of the fact that the Ten Commandments have been removed. She had no doubt given a deaf ear to the teaching of truth! The monument men erected was removed from Montgomery, Alabama, but God had already, in his word, removed the old law with the Ten Commandments.

There Were Three Crosses

One of the most familiar terms used to designate the place of our Lord's crucifixion is Calvary. Many sermons and songs owe their inspiration to Calvary. The word is found one time in the New Testament, in Luke 23:33. The original word is Golgotha which means "a skull." There were three crosses on Golgotha or Calvary, but we usually refer to the cross of Calvary as one. Two others were crucified with Jesus—Jesus being in the midst (Matt. 27:22-24). The scene on Golgotha represents three death scenes with each scene representing its own peculiar lesson. Let us look at the crosses one by one and the lesson each represents.

The Cross of Impenitence—one dying *in* sin. Over this cross could be written three words:

Lawlessness. This man had been a robber. Disrespect for the law had put him there. He lived in rebellion against the laws of both God and man. He appears to have remained bitter and impenitent to the end.

Hardness. He defied all sacred surroundings. In the presence of incarnate love, the believing centurion, pain wrecking his body and eternity staring him in the face, was yet impenitent. His only appeal was one of contempt! Viewing the Christ, he "railed on him, saying, if thou be Christ, save thyself and us." His dying comrade appealed to him, "Dost not thou fear God, seeing thou art in the same condemnation?" (Luke 23:40).

Carnality. He was not thinking of the salvation of his soul, but of his body (Luke 23:39). He was not thinking of eternal salvation, but temporal salvation. Evidently to him the body was everything. He wanted salvation from the cross, but he wanted it in his own terms. Jesus has not promised to save from the cross, but through the cross (Eph. 2:16). All of us have crosses to bear (Matt. 16:24).

The Penitent Soul—one dying *to* sin. He too had been a lawbreaker. It appears that at the beginning of the execution, he also had reviled the Savior (Matt. 27:43-44). But he had evidently turned and in him we see:

Righteous Indignation (Luke 23:40-41). He rebuked the robber who continued to rail. He vindicated the Lord and this he did in the presence of the Lord's enemies. He was one of the first to vindicate the Christ.

A Sense of Guilt. "We indeed justly, for we received the due reward of our deeds." He bore no hatred toward authorities. He admitted the justice of his own suffering and death in the face of execution.

A Desire For a Place in the Memory of Christ. "Remember me when thou comest in thy kingdom." He called on Jesus for mercy, but made no demands. He expressed no doubt regarding Jesus. In response to his humble cry of faith, he received an infinitely precious promise: "Today shalt thou be with me in paradise."

The Most Popular Thief in the World

Why? Due to the fact that so many religionists look to this thief as their example of salvation. He asked and received! They argue, "Why can't men do the same today?" The answer is in the situation. The thief died while Jesus was living. Jesus had power on earth to forgive sins (Luke 5:24). The Old Covenant was in existence that Jesus nailed to the cross (Col. 2:14-17). The thief was never a subject of the last will and testament of Jesus Christ that is now bound upon men in this age (Heb. 9:15-17). Some would use this thief to destroy the essentiality of baptism. They argue that he wasn't baptized and yet received the Lord's blessing. Why should they be baptized? No one can prove that this man was not baptized under John's baptism and had become a backsliding disciple (Matt. 3:5). But the answer lies in what has already been stated. He died before baptism in the name of Christ for the remission of sins was bound upon sinful men (Acts 2:38). The blessings of salvation through Jesus Christ are obtained today as we obey his will (Mark 16:16). But when obedience unto the Lord is refused, then the multitudes turn their shoes to the thief on the cross.

The Cross of Incarnate Goodness—one dying *for* sin.

Sinlessness. It is almost enough to make us ashamed that we are a part of the human race. Jesus died for our sins, and in a very true sense, mankind spat upon him, pressed the crown of thorns on his head, and nailed him to the cross. He took our place and died for sinful man!

Forgiveness. He prayed for the pardon of his executioners. "Then said Jesus, Father forgive them; for they know not what they do" (Luke 23:34). He gave hope to the requesting penitent.

The crosses of the robbers are typical of two attitudes. They are the impenitent who is untouched and the penitent who breaks down in the presence of Christ. But when we look at the central cross, we see that "in none other is there salvation." Jesus "humbled himself, and became obedient unto death, even the death on the cross" (Phil. 2:8). He died for us!

Therefore

This may appear to be a very unusual title for an article. In fact it is quite unusual. The word "therefore" is a very simple word that we commonly use in our conversation. It is used quite often in the Scriptures and I do not even intend to relate how many times it would be found in the Scriptures. Though it may be a common word to us, it still has a great significance if we will only recognize it. What does the word mean or how do we define it? The *World Book Dictionary* states that the word is an "adv. for that reason; as a result of that; consequently." It further states: "Therefore, consequently, when used to connect two grammatically independent but logically related clauses, indicates that the second follows as a conclusion to the first." From this definition we note that the word brings to our minds conclusions that are to be fathomed and understood.

Notice a few passages that use the word in a very definite manner: "*Therefore* let all the house of Israel know assuredly, that God hath made that same Jesus, whom you have crucified, both Lord and Christ" (Acts 2:36). These are the words of the apostle Peter when he was preaching to those Jews who had a part in crucifying Christ. In verses before this, he had shown by the Scriptures of Psalms 16 and 110 that Jesus was the Christ. David was not speaking of himself, but of Jesus Christ. Having stated these things in logical arguments, he called upon them *therefore* to recognize and accept the conclusion "that God hath made that same Jesus, whom ye have crucified, both Lord and Christ." Notice again where the word plays an important part in grasping the truth that God wants us to recognize: "*Therefore* we ought to give the more earnest heed to the things which we have heard, lest at any time we should let them slip" (Heb. 2:1). In the chapter before, the Hebrew writer speaks of the greatness of Christ and even of his superiority over angels. All of it was stated to help his readers appreciate obedience and submission to the Christ. This being true, we *therefore* are called upon to heed these things lest we at any time should let them slip. This is the conclusion that should be reached. But we submit another passage to help appreciate the significance of this word: "Having *therefore* these promises, dearly beloved, let us cleanse ourselves from all filthiness of the flesh and spirit, perfecting holiness in the fear of God" (2 Cor. 7:1). These promises that are mentioned conclude 2 Corinthians 6. The *therefore* relates to these promises that are for the faithful in Christ who keep themselves cleansed "from all filthiness of the flesh and spirit, perfecting holiness in the fear of God."

Usage of "Therefore" in These Scriptures Conveys Certain Truth

There Are Scriptural Conclusions. The passages to which we referred stated truth to be appreciated and the *therefore* conveyed the conclusions from them. Some people today seem to want the Scriptures in a general way without any conclusions being reached. They, at times, classify such as judging or being dogmatic. They have a horror of such and hence they rule out all conclusions that the word *therefore* would have us to respect. The inspired writers wanted their readers to see the proper conclusions and they did not hesitate to use the word *therefore*. If there are no conclusions to be reached, what value are the Scriptures? They have been given for such. "All scripture is given by inspiration of God, and is profitable for doctrine, for reproof, for correction, for instruction in righteousness: That the man of God may be perfect, thoroughly furnished unto all good works" (2 Tim. 3:16-17).

Man Is Obligated to Accept the Conclusion. *Therefore* reveals our obligation to that which follows the truth that has been stated. Once again, we find people who do not want to view the truth of the Scriptures with a spirit of obligation in their lives. They want to be free of obligations and rule out the significance of *therefore* when some truth is stated. Looking back to 2 Corinthians 7:1, many would no doubt like to inherit the promises, but not with the obligation to cleanse themselves from the filthiness of the flesh and spirit. They do not want the *therefore* that necessitates obligation to the Lord's will.

Therefore Is To Be a Part of True Preaching. Men of God have always dared to present the *therefore* of proper conclusions before their hearers. Generalization may soothe some consciences, but it takes specific preaching to convict the sinner and bring him to obedience to Christ. Paul told Timothy, "Preach the word; be instant in season, out of season; reprove, rebuke, exhort with all longsuffering and doctrine" (2 Tim. 4:2). I can still remember faithful gospel preachers of years gone by and their use of the word *therefore*. I am thinking of faithful men like C.M. Pullias who preached near where I was born. After stating a particular truth from the word of God, his deep voice would vibrate with the word *therefore* in giving the conclusion and obligation that men needed to hear. We should always labor to preach the truth and help people to make the proper conclusion of what God expects of them. This must characterize the spirit of a true servant of God. There are definite consequences that follow the rejection of God and his word. These things must be kept before hearers and this is one of the definitions of the word *therefore*.

I fear for brethren and churches who will not tolerate the *therefore* that is to be an integral part of gospel preaching.

Things That Accompany Salvation

(Hebrews 6:9)

In preparing commodities for the market, producers conserve the off-falls and make of them by-products. A by-product is defined as "something produced in addition to the main product in manufacture." There are by-products in many fields other than manufacturing. It is said that meat packers utilize everything from a pig but the squeal. Think of the many by-products of coal: sulphur, ammonia, light oils and solvents, and coal tar derivatives. Of coal tar derivatives there are many products: intermediates, dyes, medicinals, flavors and perfumes, plastic materials, synthetic rubber. In some commodities, it appears that the by-products of the commodity are as valuable as the product. Coal as a fuel is not as common now as it once was. Are not the medicinal by-products almost (if not) equal to the fuel value of coal? Perhaps so, but we must keep in mind the definite conclusion that there can be no by-products with the product.

The great objective of Christianity is the salvation of the individual's soul. Nothing is secondary to this! To this end, Jesus came into the world (Matt. 1:21; Luke 19:10). Social gospel advocates are all wrong. They fail to see the forest for the trees! One must obey the gospel of Christ to save his soul (Mark 16:15-16; 2 Thess. 1:7-9; 1 Pet. 4:16-17). If you please, this is the real product and we must never lose sight of this great truth. If one fails to save his soul by obeying the gospel, he is a failure and very little else matters. On the other hand, as one obeys the gospel to the saving of his soul, other things develop in his life that we might calmly refer to as the by-products of salvation. These are factors that come about as the results of receiving the product of salvation or things that accompany salvation.

What Are Some of These?

Peace of mind. There are few things in life as dear as peace of mind. As one does the will of God and has the promise of God that his sins are forgiven, that one can experience peace of mind. Consciousness of sins is disturbing to the person with knowledge. Such is the very antithesis of peace of mind. Many a suicide has occurred due to the lack of peace of mind. Men seek it in wealth, pleasures, and worldly fame, but it comes as the result of faithfully trusting in God and his word. Paul wrote, "And the peace of God, which passeth all understanding, shall keep your hearts and minds through Christ Jesus" (Phil. 4:6-7).

Transformation of character and personality. When one obeys the gospel of Christ, he becomes a new creature in Christ. "Therefore if any man be in Christ, he is a new creature: old things are passed away; behold, all things are become new" (2 Cor. 5:17). Being in Christ transforms a man's existence into a life—his house into a home. This principle seems to be apparent in the life of Saul of Tarsus. Before his conversion, he was busily engaged in persecution of the Lord's church. "I verily thought with myself, that I ought to do many things contrary to the name of Jesus of Nazareth. Which things I also did in Jerusalem: and many of the saints did I shut up in prison, having received authority from the chief priests; and when they were put to death, I gave my voice against them. And I punished them oft in every synagogue, and compelled them to blaspheme; and being exceedingly mad against them, I persecuted them even unto strange cities" (Acts 26:9-11). After being saved in Christ, he could write of being "gentle among you, even as a nurse cherisheth her children" (2 Thess. 1:7). In Acts 4:13 we read of the rulers taking "knowledge of them (Apostles) that they had been with Jesus." Among other things, couldn't it have been this transformation quality that they beheld? Yes, salvation is the product, but there are things that accompany salvation and our being in Christ and with Christ.

Joy in living. After obeying Christ, the Eunuch went on his way rejoicing (Acts 8:39). This rejoicing was due to the promise of God that his sins were forgiven. On the same basis, the Philippian jailor who shortly before was on the verge of taking his life, rejoiced after he was baptized (Acts 16:34). Rejoicing in itself is not salvation, but truly it is the result or a by-product of salvation.

Interest in the soul welfare of others. When one's heart has been melted in obedience to the truth, he has a warm heart to the needs of others. Andrew brought Peter to Jesus (John 1:40-42). The Samaritan woman went into the city and told the inhabitants about Jesus (John 4:28-29). When one loves Jesus and his truth, it will express itself in an effort to save others that they might receive the joy that salvation brings. Paul wrote, "Work out your own salvation with fear and trembling" (Phil. 2:12). As we work out our own salvation, the things accompanying salvation will be a part of our lives!

Things That Are To Follow
Teaching

Teaching is the very heart of the religion of Jesus Christ. No one can be saved without being taught the truth. Being saved involves something more than chance or accident! It involves the principle of instruction that every individual must accept. In giving the commission to his apostles, Christ said, "Go ye therefore, and teach all nations, baptizing them in the name of the Father, and of the Son, and of the Holy Ghost: teaching them to observe all things whatsoever I have commanded you: and, lo, I am with you always, even unto the end of the world. Amen" (Matt. 28:19-20). It is evident from this passage that individuals are to be taught. They are then commanded to be baptized and further taught "to observe all things whatsoever I have commanded you." It is impossible for one to come to Jesus except through the medium of teaching. Hear the Christ in John 6:44-45, "No man can come to me, except the Father which hath sent me draw him: and I will raise him up at the last day. It is written in the prophets, And they shall be all taught of God. Every man therefore that hath heard, and hath learned of the Father, cometh unto me." Thus, it is through the hearing and learning process of teaching that one is drawn by the Father to the Christ. There is no other way—man must be taught!

We have said these things to establish in the reader's mind the importance of teaching and to prepare him for what is to follow. We do not by any means intend to minimize the importance of teaching, but at times people use it as a crutch for their weaknesses. We have reference to those who have been taught and have reason to know what is the Lord's will, yet they fail to do it with the excuse that they need more teaching. Perhaps, in one sense, we all need more teaching and never outgrow our need for it; however, many of us have been taught sufficiently regarding particular subjects and our failure to do the will of the Lord in a particular matter cannot be accredited to the lack of teaching. There are things that must follow teaching! Our failure on occasions is due to the lack of these things rather than the lack of enlightenment. What do we have in mind?

Application to the Circumstance

One reads in the Scriptures of certain practices being forbidden by the Lord. The statements are very clear and definite! Some members of the Lord's church can even quote the very passages and then occasions arise that "pass almost under their very noses" without them making the application to themselves. Why didn't the preacher tell me or why didn't someone alert me to the circumstance? Such is often heard! It appears that some who have been taught over and over again must have a picture drawn before them before they make an application of the circumstance to their life. They have just as much an obligation to realize the situation as anyone else does. Do you say that they need teaching? Well, perhaps teaching on not being gullible, but really it is a matter of discernment in such cases that seems to be lacking. The Hebrew writer spoke of those "who by reason of use have their senses exercised to discern both good and evil" (Heb. 5:14). Paul prayed for the Philippians "that your love may abound yet more and more in knowledge and in all judgment (discernment); that ye may approve things that are excellent; that ye may be sincere and without offence till the day of Christ" (Phil. 1:9-10). We need wisdom in applying what we have been taught to the circumstances that arise (Jas. 1:5).

Have Some Conviction

All the teaching in the world is not going to keep a person right with the Lord if he doesn't have conviction enough to live by the Lord's will. Webster defines conviction as "a convincing or being convinced; a strong belief." We hear people express amazement at the failure of some members. They have referred to them as "having been raised in the church" and yet recognize that they really aren't worth "a dime to the church." The problem oftentimes is due to a lack of conviction. The teaching has been adequate but conviction was not developed. Having exerted himself in teaching the Corinthians, Paul admonished them, "Watch ye, stand fast in the faith, quit you like men, be strong" (1 Cor. 16:13). To the Ephesians, he wrote, "Wherefore take unto you the whole armor of God, that ye may be able to withstand in the evil day, and having done all, to stand" (Eph. 6:13). One may teach another until he is blue in the face, but for that teaching to be of value an individual must have some conviction. Deliver me from a man who has the knowledge but lacks conviction. That man will eventually fail the Lord and do harm to the kingdom of God. So many people talk a good religion, but when it comes to standing for the truth and defending what is right, they find it needful to be somewhere else. Paul said in Philippians 1:17 that he was set for a defense of the gospel. This is a statement filled with conviction! With some "taught" individuals, they are set on a *fence* rather than set for a *defense*!

Thinking Too Highly of Ourselves

> For I say, through the grace given unto me, to every man that is among you, not to think of himself more highly than he ought to think; but to think soberly, according as God hath dealt to every man the measure of faith (Rom. 12:3).

There is probably no principle that hinders a man's spiritual life more than thinking "of himself more highly than he ought to think." Humility and lowliness are continually emphasized throughout the entire Bible. In the same respect, pride and haughtiness are strongly condemned in the word of God. This is with the basic objective of encouraging mankind to think of self, as they should, and not to exalt self.

When one thinks of himself more highly than he ought to think, he is placing his soul in great jeopardy. This is true on account of a number of things that one will be inclined to do who would exalt himself. We note a couple of these things:

Belittle the Value of God's Word

To truly appreciate the stream of truth in the Bible, one is to recognize that God's word is higher than man's ways "as the heavens are higher than the earth." Isaiah wrote of God: "For my thoughts are not your thoughts, neither are your ways my ways, saith the Lord. For as the heavens are higher than the earth, so are my ways higher than your ways, and my thoughts than your thoughts" (Isa. 55:8-9). When we think of ourselves more highly than we ought to think, we can place ourselves in the precarious situation of thinking we know as much as God and become a critic of his word rather than a follower of it.

In their worldly wisdom, this was the situation of the Greeks of whom Paul spoke as they viewed the cross of Christ. "For the preaching of the cross is to them that perish foolishness; but unto us which are saved it is the power of God. For it is written, I will destroy the wisdom of the wise, and will bring to nothing the understanding of the prudent. Where is the wise? Where is the scribe? Where is the disputer of this world? Hath not God made foolish the wisdom of this world? For after that in the wisdom of God the world by wisdom knew not God, it pleased God by the foolishness of preaching to save them that believe. For the Jews require a sign, and the Greeks seek after wisdom: But we preach Christ crucified, unto the Jews a stumblingblock, and unto the Greeks foolishness; But unto them which are called, both Jews and Greeks, Christ the power of God, and the wisdom of God" (1 Cor. 1:18-24). We must never forget our position before God. True wisdom is from God's word. We must never forget that God is the Creator and we are but the creatures! "O Lord, I know that the way of man is not in himself: it is not in man that walketh to direct his steps" (Jer. 10:23).

Become Easily Offended

When is it that most people have their feelings hurt and proceed to say and do things that are sinful in God's sight? In most cases, it is when they feel that they have been overlooked or neglected in something that they feel is so great. Who is it who at sometime or another has not been overlooked or neglected? But is this any reason to make a big to do over a little matter and say hateful things about others that will damn our souls unless we truly repent of them? I firmly believe that much of this hurt feeling business would never materialize if individuals stopped thinking of themselves more highly than they should. God's children who are possessed with humility and lowliness are not exalting their feelings, but endeavoring to consider others. They are not wondering why others haven't done such and such for them, but they are seeking ways to help and benefit others. Those who think more highly of themselves than they should never seem to fully grasp this meaning of life. To them, it is like so much water on a duck's back. They still want to know why so and so wasn't done for them and become quite bitter!

More beautiful words and thoughts cannot be found in the Scriptures than that which was written by the apostle Paul in Philippians 2:3-5: "Let nothing be done through strife or vainglory; but in lowliness of mind let each esteem other better than themselves. Look not every man on his own things, but every man also on the things of others. Let this mind be in you, which was also in Christ Jesus."

When we have the mind of Christ, we do not think of ourselves more highly than we ought to think. Individuals can make themselves miserable by thinking more highly of themselves than they ought to. The unhappiness that some have is due to their falling in love with themselves at a very early age of life. When we think like we ought to, we will never find ourselves belittling the word of God or letting ourselves become easily offended. We need to think on these matters and personally apply the lesson!

This World of Superlatives

In this world in which we live, we receive a full course of the superlatives. On every hand, we hear such things as this: the finest of goods, the largest congregations, the highest salaried officials, the most eloquent preachers, the greatest circulation, the best of this and that. On and on it goes! We deal in superlatives with pride and exaltation. As one might suppose by now, the word superlative is defined as "1. superior to all others; of the highest sort; supreme." The emphasis is predominantly upon being number one whether it is *numero uno* in the athletic world or any other endeavor.

Have you run into a fellow lately who told a story in which he was not the hero? When you meet such a man, a man who will admit that he was the defeated party, that he was the one who took a "licking," put his name down in your admiration. This man is not a very common individual. We need to admit that all have come to the point that a little more modesty and little more humility could be used to great advantage in these modern times. Some business firms are realizing this! They are teaching their salesmen that understatement is stronger sales psychology than in overstatement. Jesus taught that humility paid tremendous dividends. He warned, "For whosoever exalteth himself shall be abased; and he that humbleth himself shall be exalted" (Luke 14:11).

Just think of the humble people whom Jesus blessed. The Roman centurion, whose servant was at the point of death, was genuinely humble. Evaluating his humble faith, Jesus said, "I have not found so great faith, no, not in Israel" (Luke 7:9). This humble man viewed himself as not being worthy. "I am not worthy that thou shouldest enter under my roof . . . neither thought I myself worthy to come unto thee" (Luke 7:6-7). Jesus spoke the word and this humble man's request was granted. "And they that were sent, returning to the house, found the servant whole that had been sick" (Luke 7:10). Though this centurion might have had reason to emphasize the superlative since he was a man of authority (v. 8), yet he recognized and displayed unworthiness which made him a great deal different than so many other individuals.

The praying publican, despised by men, went down to his house justified before God in contrast to the proud Pharisee who informed God of his righteousness. "And the publican, standing afar off, would not lift up so much as his eyes unto heaven, but smote upon his breast, saying, God be merciful to me a sinner" (Luke 18:13). No pedestal of pride, no high-mindedness or arrogant indifference was demonstrated by this publican. He was humble at the feet of God, knowing that he needed the mercy of God. And as one might expect, he was justified rather than the proud, arrogant Pharisee who evidenced the craving of the superlative.

Men may deny it, but humility still pays. Humility is a great instructor within itself. It teaches us that the way up is down. No man can ever expect to reach the highest of glory unless he passes through the valley of humility. John Wesley spoke the thought in one of his hymns: "Sink me to perfection's heights."

Humility is a dominant characteristic of most every great soul in human history. The superlative seeker in his craving has lost sight of the standard given by Jesus: "And whosoever will be chief among you, let him be your servant" (Matt. 20:27). Paul reminded the Ephesian elders of his manner of service. "Serving the Lord with all humility of mind" (Acts 20:19).

A soul full of humility will not sit in the scorner's seat. The humble soul does not know its virtues, but is ever mindful of its imperfections. The humble soul recognizes the law of God and gladly submits to it. The humblest and greatest soul that ever lived prayed to his Father, "Nevertheless, not as I will, but as thou wilt" (Matt. 26:39). Humility does not question God, but gladly obeys his every word. A man truly humble in his heart never questions the essentiality of any thing that the Bible teaches is right. Whether baptism is essential is beside the point to a person wanting to do all the will of God. Whether or not one can go to heaven outside of the church does not concern the person who learns that Christ built his church of which one is to be a member. It is enough for the humble heart to know that God approves or desires a thing for him to believe and obey. He obeys from the heart the form of doctrine delivered unto him without hunting a substitute or trying to avoid his responsibility in obeying.

God hates a proud look (Prov. 6:17). "Pride goeth before destruction, and a haughty spirit before a fall" (Prov. 16:18). Without humility, we are bound to underestimate our brother and overestimate ourselves. If we would go to heaven, we need to guard against the emphasis on the superlatives and to humbly do the will of God.

Thou Hypocrite

There is nothing complimentary about these words. They do not convey joy or righteous designation. A person who is a hypocrite has little to offer to anyone in respect of wholesome living. A hypocrite is one who professes something that he does not practice. There are a considerable number of statements in the New Testament regarding the hypocrite. Who do you suppose said more about the subject than any others did? If Jesus was your answer, you were correct. Our Savior recognized hypocrisy in the lives of many with whom he came in contact. Observe a few incidents: "Do not sound a trumpet before thee, as the hypocrites do" (Matt. 6:2). "And when thou prayest, thou shalt not be as the hypocrites are" (Matt. 6:5). "Thou hypocrite, first cast out the beam out of thine own eye" (Matt. 7:5). "O ye hypocrites, ye can discern the face of the sky: but can ye not discern the signs of the times?" (Matt. 16:3). In Matthew 23, Jesus uses the phrase, "Woe unto you, scribes and Pharisees, hypocrites!" at least seven times in exposing their sins. The words of Jesus being relevant, we should not be astonished when hypocrisy is encountered in our dealings with individuals who profess to be righteous.

There May Be Hypocrites in Faith

Some professing to be righteous outwardly are far from such in their hearts. They talk a good faith and in their hearts deny what they are saying. "They profess that they know God; but in works they deny him, being abominable, and disobedient, and unto every good work reprobate" (Tit. 1:15). We need to respect the value of sincerity: "That ye may approve things that are excellent; that ye may be sincere and without offence till the day of Christ" (Phil. 1:10). We may deceive men by our words, but the Lord knows our hearts and he knows when hypocrisy exists.

There May Be Hypocrites Regarding Morals

This may exist when a person speaks out against immoral practices while craving to participate in the sinful practices that are denounced. When given an opportunity, they engage in practicing what they condemn. One may condemn alcoholic consumption, gambling, adultery, fornication, and other immoral practices while secretly engaging in these practices. I have known of gospel preachers strongly preaching against the sin of adultery while in the same period committing adultery with one of the women in the congregation. Thou hypocrite! In one case, when this was discovered, the preacher was asked how he could preach against such while practicing such. His reply was, "I needed the lessons!" He truly needed the lessons with conviction for living a pure life. "Thou that sayest a man should not commit adultery, dost thou commit adultery?" (Rom. 2:22). Temptations abound, but we need to learn to say "No" for yielding is sin.

There May Be Hypocrites in Worship

Jesus had this to say regarding the subject, "Ye hypocrites, well did Esaias prophesy of you, saying, This people draweth nigh unto me with their mouth, and honoureth me with their lips; but their heart is far from me. But in vain they do worship me, teaching for doctrines the commandments of men" (Matt. 15:7-9). By their mouth and lips, they appeared sincere, but their heart was to the contrary. It is possible for individuals to attend service and go through acts of worship without their hearts being in tune with what they are doing. Their heart is far from being sincere in what they are doing. True worship must involve spirit and the truth (John 4:23-24). It is a personal thing to know our own hearts. "For what man knoweth the things of man, save the spirit of man which is in him?" (1 Cor. 2:11). Hypocrisy in any field of endeavor cannot be hid from the individual himself.

When one thinks of hypocrisy, he confronts the abuses and misunderstandings that some have of it. We have confronted those who seem to think that as long as they are not hypocrites, sin is not really sin. Their line of thought seems to be that, if we sin openly and do not try to cover our transgressions with hypocrisy, then we are justified in our deeds. They even boast by saying at least we are not hypocrites. Such may be so, but there is no way that such reasoning can make their sinful deeds justified. We must answer for our sins whether committed openly or in hypocrisy. So many talk about hypocrites in the church. It may be that they do not know what a hypocrite is or even have the ability to spell the word, but they talk of hypocrites in the church. What is their purpose in doing so? Largely, as a "cop out" to keep them from doing what God has for them to do. They do not want to do God's will and try to excuse their responsibility to do so by condemning others as being hypocrites. If hypocrites exist in the church, they will answer to God. But remember, the one who tries to hide behind the hypocrite must be smaller than him!

Thoughts Concerning the Greek Word *Psallo*

Sometime ago, we made mention of having a discussion with an elder of the Christian church concerning the use of mechanical instruments of music in worship to God. Since then, another discussion has taken place in which he invited the preacher of the congregation that he attends to have a part. It was a very lively discussion in which it appeared that they forsook their more time-worn "arguments" and appealed to the Greek word *psallo* to rescue their dying arguments and prove that instrumental music is authorized in the New Testament.

According to them, we were reminded that the New Testament was written in the Greek and there is a Greek word in the New Testament that will give the authority for the use of the mechanical music in worship. We replied that the New Testament has been translated into English and no translation of that word includes mechanical music. *Psallo* in various forms occurs five times in the New Testament. Ephesians 5:19: "Singing and making melody (*psallontes*) with your heart." Romans 15:9: "Sing (*psallo*) unto thy name." 1 Corinthians 14:15: "Sing (*psallo*) with the spirit and sing (*psallo*) with the understanding." James 5:13: "sing praises" (*psallein*).

The study of the Greek language is not to be ignored or denied. But always remember, the ripest scholars have studied and reviewed the Greek. These are the very ones who have translated the Greek into the English language. One hundred one of America's ripest scholars gave to us our American Standard Version of the Greek text, translating the Greek into the English. Forty-seven of the most brilliant scholars in King James' day presented the English world with the Authorized or King James Version. A faithful and accurate translation of the Greek into the English was wanted and ordered. These one hundred and forty eight translators of distinguished abilities, with one accord, rendered *psallo* in the New Testament to mean "sing." "Sing," "sing," "sing," "make melody," and "sing praises" in the five times it is used in the New Testament. But the advocates of mechanical music in worship are not satisfied. They still crave their idol and insist that the word *psallo* includes a mechanical instrument of music. In essence, they conclude that the most renowned scholars of the Greek language were actually in error as to the real meaning of their translation of *psallo*.

The lexicons give the root meaning of *psallo* to be "to pull, rub, strike, or vibrate." The carpenter *psallos* the carpenter's line when he lets it go to make the chalk line. The archer *psallo's* the string of the bow when he pulls the bow string and lets the arrow fly. *Psalloing* of the hair and the beard involves the practice of pulling the hair and stroking the beard. In like manner, a musician takes an instrument and strikes its strings or chords. This is *psalloing*, but it occurs on the instrument named. It is not the instrument that makes the *psalloing*, but rather the act performed on it. It is the height of absurdity and an extreme abuse of grammar to make the object of a verb a part of its definition. Since Paul said *"psallo* the heart" (Eph. 5:19), the heart is that which is *psalloed* in worship and not a mechanical instrument.

When Paul said *psallo*, one might as well say that he meant to pull the hair as to contend that he meant to play on a harp, organ, or any other mechanical instrument. When Paul said in Ephesians 5:19 *"psalloing* with the heart unto the Lord," the worshiper's heart is the object of the *psalloing*. The verb *psallo* does not include the object of the verb. The object must be named! In the New Testament, the human heart, rather than some mechanical instrument is connected with singing and Paul named it. He specified the instrument in addition to the verb *psallo*. As an example of this, it is profitable to think of the word "baptize." It means to dip or immerse, but it requires an object or element. The particular element must be named in addition to the word. We possibly could dip a man in grease, oil, or even sand, but the New Testament reveals that we are to baptize with water. In so doing the element of water is named with the verb and that eliminates grease, oil, or any other substance.

When a Christian sings, according to Ephesians 5:19, his heart responds to the melody of the song and he has *psalloed* with the heart. God placed the instrument on the inside of man and every worshiper can and must *psallo*." However, if *psallo* means to play a mechanical instrument, then every worshiper must get one, bring it to service and play it. Otherwise, the organist will be the only one who is *psalloing*. Such a perversion of the word is just another futile effort to justify worship that has not been ordained of God. God would have us to sing and make melody in our hearts. What one worshiper is to do, all others are to do. Be content with the will of God and never endeavor to pervert it!

Three Valuable Words

As one comes to the end of one year and the beginning of another, it is appropriate to consider taking an inventory. Business firms will be doing this in view of the coming new year. Christians should give consideration to taking a spiritual inventory. Three words are very helpful in one conducting a proper spiritual inventory. We are thinking of retrospection, introspection, and prospection. Let us consider these words in view of our lives.

Retrospection: "to look backward; contemplation of the past." There are some things that we ought to forget as we look back on a year.

- Our injuries (Matt. 18:21-22). Perhaps we have had some.
- The past that hinders (Phil. 3:12-14). "Forgetting those things which are behind."
- The lower for the higher (Col. 3:1-3). "Seek those things which are above."

There are some things we should never forget.

- Our debts (Rom. 12:8).
- Our debts of gratitude. The butler forgot about Joseph after an obligation to remember him (Gen. 40). Christians are debtors to preach the gospel (Rom. 1:14-16). Children should show gratitude toward their parents (Eph. 6:1-3). Parents have a debt of gratitude toward children (Eph. 6:4).
- What we owe God. For our lives and the blessings that we receive (Acts 17:27-28; Ps. 103:1-2). Men are prone to be ungrateful toward God. "Where are the nine?" (Luke 17:11-17).
- The good we hear (Heb. 2:1-3; Jas. 1:23-25).
- The cleansing from old sins (2 Pet. 1:9).

Introspection: "To look within; self-examination; appraising ourselves; taking stock." We should estimate our strength and weakness, our mental abilities and mental weakness, our good habits and bad habits. The gospel requires a looking within (1 John 2:8; 1 Cor. 11:28; 2 Cor. 13:5). With many professed Christians, introspection is too rare a process. How would our souls look if we had a photograph? Would we be ashamed? Would it make us blush for our friends to see it? We look into a mirror to see our face. We need to carefully and prayerfully look into the word of God to see our hearts (Jas. 1:23-25). It is quite possible that we may find that our hearts are not right in the sight of God (Acts 8:21). We may need to repent and confess sins (1 John 1:9).

Prospection: "Looking ahead; looking forward." We must not linger too long on the past. We may find ourselves desiring to return. Israel is an example of this. Stephen spoke of Israel and their regard for Moses, "To whom our fathers would not obey, but thrust him from them, and in their hearts turned back again into Egypt" (Acts 7:39). They evidently dwelt too long upon the past. We need to move forward. Jesus said, "No man, having put his hand to the plow, and looking back, is fit for the kingdom of God" (Luke 9:62). We have already dealt with retrospection with its merits and faults. The emphasis now is upon prospection. The words of the apostle Paul are quite appropriate regarding this theme: "Brethren, I count not myself to have apprehended: but this one thing I do, forgetting those things which are behind, and reaching forth unto those things which are before, I press toward the mark for the prize of the high calling of God in Christ Jesus" (Phil. 3:13-14). Paul was "forgetting those things which are behind" and was "reaching forth unto those things which are before."

Prospection carries the idea of purpose and planning. Purpose and planning should be a definite part of the life of a Christian. All of it, of course, is to be done with a deep reverence for the Lord's will. "For that ye ought to say, If the Lord will, we shall live, and do this, or that" (Jas. 4:15). Planning is an element of success in any field of activity. We shouldn't attempt to ignore it as regarding our spiritual lives. Christians should have plans for the future with scriptural goals and objectives. The wise man wrote, "Where there is no vision, the people perish" (Prov. 29:18). By vision, was he referring to revelation or foresight for the future?

Football announcers speak a great deal about momentum. The Lord's people need spiritual momentum and they need to retain it. The proper objectives help us to possess this spiritual momentum. In the coming year we need to look away from the world and see more of Jesus Christ. We need to look less at the things which are seen, and more at the things which are not seen. "While we look not at the things which are seen, but at the things which are not seen: for the things which are seen are temporal; but the things which are not seen are eternal" (2 Cor. 4:18). How is your spiritual inventory? Does it come up to the standard that the Lord requires?

Touching Jesus

In Mark 5:25-34, we find the account of a woman who had an issue of blood for twelve years. She had spent all that she had and, instead of getting better, she grew worse. She had been to many physicians and all of them had failed to affect a cure. It is not the physical side that we want to concern ourselves with altogether just here. Jesus was her only hope! He had been performing many wonderful cures. She heard about him and she said in verse 28, "If I may touch but his clothes, I shall be whole." The same is true with us regarding sin. Jesus is our only hope! If we fail to touch Jesus, the Savior, we will be eternally lost. She literally touched him. Our touch is figurative, but it definitely involves scriptural concepts. We notice four important things:

The Touch of Need. This woman realized her need of the Master. So many people do not realize that they need a Savior. Many, no doubt, would come to the Lord if they only realized their need and saw their lost condition. I heard of a Bible teacher who was teaching a class of children and some of them came to the class with dirty hands. He wanted to let them know their condition. The next day, he came to the classroom early and placed a vase of snow white lilies on the table. When the children came in, they saw them at once. They went up to smell them and in so doing they placed their hands beside the white blossoms. They at once saw the condition of their hands. The next day they came to the class with clean hands. Members of the church must live such clean upright lives that the world can see the difference between their sordid, sin-stained lives and the lives of those that are walking with Jesus. We can never expect to lead people to a knowledge of their need unless we live on a higher plane than those in the world. Luke wrote, "The former treatise have I made, O Theophilus, of all that Jesus began both to do and teach" (Acts 1:1). Jesus not only taught people how to live, but showed them as well. We must teach, but teaching without practice does not carry much weight.

The Touch of Purpose. In the multitude, many people had no doubt touched Jesus that day but they received no recorded benefit. Why? They had no definite purpose in their touch. This woman came for the one purpose—to touch Jesus. Things that we do that are pleasing in the sight of God must be done with a definite purpose in mind. In Acts 19:1-5, Paul found a group of disciples who had been baptized, but they had been baptized for the wrong purpose. "And he said unto them, Unto what then were ye baptized? And they said, Unto John's baptism" (Acts 19:3). They had obeyed John's baptism that was no longer valid. John taught Jews to look forward to the Christ that should come. Inasmuch as Christ had at this time already come, been crucified, buried, and arisen from the dead, they were no longer to look forward to these events being fulfilled. They had already been fulfilled! They needed the right purpose in their baptism. They needed to be baptized into Christ (Gal. 3:26-27). "When they heard this, they were baptized in the name of the Lord Jesus" (Acts 19:5). We need to touch Christ with the right purpose. What purpose did you have when you were baptized? Was it in keeping with Mark 16:16 and Acts 2:38 or with a purpose that is not in keeping with the truth?

The Touch of Faith. This woman did not have a doubt in her mind. She said, "If I may touch but his clothes, I shall be whole" (v. 28). She had an unwavering faith, a faith that did not question and did not hesitate in accepting the truth. We, too, must have that kind of faith in the power of Jesus. He was then, and is now, all powerful. He acknowledged, "All power is given unto me in heaven and in earth" (Matt. 28:18). Since all power is in the hands of our Lord, why should we have a doubt about being accepted if we come according to his will? Read the account of the conversion of the Eunuch in Acts 8. He manifested no doubt in doing what he was told to do. The same may be said of Saul in Acts 9 as he followed the directions of the Lord. The faith of this woman led her to come to Jesus and touch him. Her faith was active which brings us to the next thought . . .

The Touch of Obedience. An active faith leads us to obedience. This conclusion cannot be escaped. Needing Jesus is not enough. Every soul needs the Lord Jesus, whether he knows it or not. He might even realize his need. I have heard men say, "I know I ought to be a Christian" but that is not enough. They might even believe that Jesus is the Son of God, but that is not enough to save them. Peter stated, "Neither is there salvation in any other: for there is none other name under heaven given among men, whereby we must be saved" (Acts 4:12). Jesus saves those who obey his gospel (Mark 16:16; Gal. 3:26-27). When we do this, we touch Jesus that our sins might be forgiven. Have you touched Jesus?

Translations or Interpretations?

In the last decade or so, the public has been exposed to a number of translations of the Bible in modern language or as some refer to it, in the language of our day. I suppose such terminology is directed in contrast with the King James Version which is not considered in the language of our day or modern language with its "thy, thou, thine, wit, etc." I am no worshiper of the King James Version which was produced in 1611 by the order of King James of England. I also do possess a little more knowledge of the origin of versions than to say that it was the version that Paul "carried around in his hip pocket." On the other hand, I use this version and consider it to be a good translation of the Bible. Now don't get me wrong! There are other good translations of the Scriptures in perhaps more readable style than the King James Version. Scholars of repute contend that the American Standard Version which was translated in 1901 is perhaps the most accurate translation available along with the New American Standard Version which has in more recent years been made available.

One of the better approaches to studying the word of God is to compare the different translations. In comparing them, one is able to have a very good insight into the meaning of a particular verse or passage. I have found *The New Testament in Twenty-Six Versions* to be a profitable help in the study of the N.T. and through the years, I have ordered such for individuals who have come to appreciate the work in their study of the Scriptures. Perhaps by now, readers of this article are able to conclude that I am not opposed to other translations of the Scriptures. However, I am opposed to some that do not represent legitimate translations and are in themselves more interpretations than translations.

The Jehovah's Witnesses have produced the *New World Translation* which is far more of an interpretation than a translation of the New Testament Scriptures. They have evidently produced such "to prove" their doctrine and though they contend that it was translated by legitimate scholars of the Hebrew and Greek languages, you will surpass what I have been able to do if you get them to tell you who these so-called scholars are. In 2 Peter 3:10, rather than the earth and the works that are therein being burned up at the coming of Christ, this translation (?) renders that they will be discovered. Makes a lot of sense, doesn't it? They can't stand the truth of the earth being destroyed at the day of the Lord or coming of Christ. According to their false doctrine, the earth will be renovated to be the home of the righteous. Hence, they represent an interpretation rather than a translation.

The American Bible Society has produced *Good News for Modern Man*. It is a production in modern English that "reads well," but among other errors it is filled with an effort to justify the doctrine of salvation by faith alone. As an example, in the rendering of Romans 1:17, the word "alone" is injected into the text making it appear to the reader that faith alone or faith without obedience to the gospel commandments is sufficient for salvation.

I have come in contact with a translation from the Tyndale House Publishers known as *The Living New Testament Illustrated*. In fact, the same publishers also make available the entire Bible as *The Living Bible Illustrated* and entitle the volume *The Way*. In examining this work, I noticed 1 Peter 3:21. In the KJV, the first of the verse reads: "The like figure whereunto baptism doth also now save us." Other reliable versions concur in the fact that baptism does also now save us. But in this version, we read the following: "That, by the way, is what baptism pictures for us: in baptism we show that we have been saved from death and doom by the resurrection of Christ." There is a world of difference in saying that something saves than saying that something pictures that we have been saved. Here again, in my estimation, is an example of interpretation rather than a legitimate translation. In an effort to disallow that baptism is necessary for one to be saved or that baptism does also now save us, the producers of this volume have baptism picturing that one has already been saved from death and doom. To render 1 Peter 3:21 in such a manner is to deny the very best work of Greek scholars and the finest of translations available to man. Furthermore, it is to place this verse concerning baptism in conflict with all other passages that reveal baptism as being essential to salvation (Mark 16:16; Acts 2:38; 22:16; Gal. 3:26-27; Rom. 6:3-5). Yes, some translations read easy and smooth, but we need to use care less they read us into hell in leading us to reject the simple plan of salvation that God has for us to obey. Take care—don't be taken in or deceived!

Troubled Hearts

> Let not your heart be troubled: ye believe in God, believe also in me. In my Father's house are many mansions: if it were not so, I would have told you. I go to prepare a place for you, And if I go to prepare a place for you, I will come again, and receive you unto myself; that where I am, there ye may be also (John 14:1-3).

Much is being spent today in research concerning heart disease. Heart operations and transplants have become accepted realities with a number of people. We find ourselves marveling at the progress that has been made in treating heart disease. This form of heart disease and its ailments need rightful attention. But not all heart trouble is physical. There is also the spiritual heart, yea the heart that the gospel message pricked in Acts 2:37.

Jesus was referring to the spiritual heart when he told his apostles, "Let not your heart be troubled" (John 14:1). He repeated the phrase in verse 27 and added the words "neither let it be afraid." We speak of heart specialists in reference to the diseases of the physical heart. Jesus is the greatest of all heart specialists for he deals with the greater of hearts—the spiritual heart. It is a common occurrence to witness those whose hearts are troubled. Their words and their actions are indicative of their troubled hearts. Jesus came into the world to relieve, not to burden. He wants our hearts to be calm. He wants our souls to be serene, not troubled. When Christ disturbed individuals, it was for their good. He who stilled the water came to calm troubled hearts.

Troubled Hearts Are A Result Of . . .

Sorrow—severance of tender ties. The disciples felt that they were loosing a friend. Christ knew their thoughts and realized how heavy their hearts were. The application of this text has been the source of great comfort to myriads as they have bid farewell to loved ones taken in death.

Despair—disappointment. Being slow to comprehend the true mission of the Lord, they could see only the view of Christ leaving them. They felt that their plans and aspirations for the future had gone astray. Disappointment today is the cause of many troubled hearts. We fail to see the unseen as we should (2 Cor. 4:18).

Sin and shame. Perhaps there is nothing that has caused more troubled hearts than sin and the shame that follows. The pathetic note is that so many fail to recognize that they might do something about it (Rom. 6:23).

What Is Christ's Remedy For A Troubled Heart?

At a time when Christ was burdened, he offered consolation to others instead of seeking it. Jesus takes delight in comforting his disciples and desires to lighten the burden of a heart that is heavy and troubled. The remedy is faith—"ye believe in God, believe also in me." There must be faith in God who has promised a home for his children on high. "Without faith it is impossible to please Him" (Heb. 11:6). There must be faith in the Christ, who as the mediator, stands between us and God. There is no approach to God except through the Son of God. "I said therefore unto you, that ye shall die in your sins: for if ye believe not that I am he, ye shall die in your sins" (John 8:24). "Jesus saith unto him, I am the way, the truth, and the life: no man cometh unto the Father, but by me" (John 14:6).

The belief that brings comfort to disciples is not a mere assent to propositions, but trust in a person, distinguished by love and obedience. Faith apart from obedience can be everything else but comforting. In many respects, such troubles the heart more than if a person were completely void of faith. Do you question this? The chief rulers believed on Christ but they would not confess him. "Nevertheless among the chief rulers also many believed on him; but because of the Pharisees they did not confess him, lest they should be put out of the synagogue: For they loved the praise of men more than the praise of God" (John 12:42-43). Loving the praise of men more than the praise of God was their hindrance. Would you conclude that such hearts were filled with serenity as a result of faith? Quite to the contrary! Saul of Tarsus believed before Ananias came to him and directed him to be baptized that his sins might be washed away. But it was not until his faith obeyed in being baptized into Christ that his troubled heart was comforted (Acts 22:16; Rom. 5:1; Gal. 3:26-27).

Faith as a remedy for the troubled heart is entirely too simple for many people. One can point another to the remedy but no one can make the other accept it. Nevertheless, it is still available! "And the peace of God, which passeth all understanding, shall keep your hearts and minds through Christ Jesus" (Phil. 4:7). This comes through continued obedient faith and we must never forget it.

Truth and Consequences

Truth has its consequence. There is a definite price to pay when one follows truth. Truth in religion is God's word. Jesus prayed to the Father, "Sanctify them through thy truth: thy word is truth" (John 17:17). The principle of cause and effect is very prevalent regarding the truth. When one follows the truth, he is to be prepared to accept possible consequences that develop from following the word of God. Jesus referred to such in Matthew 10:34-36, "Think not that I am come to send peace on earth: I came not to send peace, but a sword. For I am come to set a man at variance against his father, and the daughter against her mother, and the daughter-in-law against her mother-in-law. And a man's foes shall be they of his own household." Again, from Luke 14:26, "If any man come to me, and hate not his father, and mother, and wife, and children, and brethren, and sisters, yea, and his own life also, he cannot be my disciple." These and numerous other passages in the Scriptures reveal that truth has its consequences! But what possible course can men take when they are confronted with the consequences?

The individual may refuse to obey the truth due to fear of the consequences. The chief rulers mentioned by Jesus are examples of this. "Nevertheless among the chief rulers also many believed on him; but because of the Pharisees they did not confess him, lest they should be put out of the synagogue: For they loved the praise of men more than the praise of God" (John 12:42-43). For fear of the Pharisees and losing their seat in the synagogue, they would not confess their faith in Christ. They loved men's praise more than the praise of God. Such a course was tragic! The only hope man has for eternal life with God is to obey the truth. Nevertheless, we are persuaded that many people refuse the truth for fear of the consequences. We should have faith enough to obey God and let him help us with the consequences or let the consequences take care of themselves!

Men may endeavor to change the truth to modify the consequences. God's truth can never be changed! We are not the designers of truth. Paul wrote of the Galatians: "I marvel that ye are so soon removed from him that called you into the grace of Christ unto another gospel: Which is not another; but there be some that trouble you, and would pervert the gospel of Christ. But though we, or an angel from heaven, preach any other gospel unto you than that which we have preached unto you let him be accursed. As we said before, so say I now again, if any man preach any other gospel unto you than that ye have received, let him be accursed" (1:6-9). Men may pervert the gospel of Christ and preach another gospel, but the truth of God's word remains the same. "For ever, O Lord, thy word is settled in heaven" (Ps. 119:89). The power of sentiment induces some to feel that family and fleshly ties are the greatest in the world. Jesus taught to the contrary, "He that loveth father or mother more than me is not worthy of me: and he that loveth son or daughter more than me is not worthy of me" (Matt. 10:36). Let some one say that to follow the truth would make their home unhappy or even destroy the peace of family ties, and invariably he finds sympathy among some brethren to the extent that they would justify him in not obeying the truth to lessen the consequence. We all have our crosses to bear! "Then said Jesus unto his disciples, If any man will come after me, let him deny himself, and take up his cross, and follow me" (Matt. 16:24). Regardless of how sentimental we might be, the truth is the truth and no one can faithfully alter the truth to lessen the consequences.

Men may obey the truth regardless of the consequences. This is the honorable thing to do. This is the real meaning of faith! When we obey the truth, we should prepare our hearts for the acceptance of the consequences. Our choice before God is that of accepting or rejecting his truth. In all things, we must possess the Spirit of Christ. "Now if any man have not the Spirit of Christ, he is none of his" (Rom. 8:9). Paul wrote, "Let this mind be in you, which was also in Christ Jesus" (Phil. 2:5). Christ followed the truth of his Father and suffered the consequence of the agony of the cross (Heb. 5:8-9; 12:1-2). The writer of Proverbs admonishes his readers, "Buy the truth, and sell it not" (Prov. 23:23). So many people still think that they can float to heaven on a bed of ease. In sentiment, they want the truth, but the consequences they would deny. They want the crown but not the cross. Beloved, when we are prone to be weary of the price of truth, stop and think of what the consequences will be for those who do not obey the gospel (2 Thess. 1:6-9). Let us resolve always to obey the truth and trust in God to help us endure the consequences (1 Cor. 10:13).

Twisting the Picture Won't Help the Scene

We once read of a New York enthusiast who had an outstanding collection of etchings, one of them being the Leaning Tower of Pisa, which hung over his writing desk. For a long time he noticed that it persisted in hanging crooked despite the fact that he straightened it every morning. At last he spoke to the maid, asking her if she were responsible for its lopsided position each morning. "Why, yes," she said, "I have to hang it crooked to make the tower hang straight."

Perhaps you wonder why reference is made to such an account as this. Simply this: That is exactly how a lot of people, not recognizing the real position and beauty of the Scriptures, deal with the Bible. They twist the word of God in order to justify their own actions and doctrines hoping to make them all appear right. Peter stated that Paul wrote some things hard to be understood, "which they that are unlearned and unstable wrest (twist, NKJV), as they do also the other scriptures, unto their own destruction" (2 Pet. 3:16).

The denominational doctrine of salvation prior to and without baptism is such a twisting of the Scriptures. Its position is that "he that believeth and is saved may be baptized." But such is plainly the wrong view of the thing, because Jesus said that instead of salvation being before baptism, it was exactly the other way around: "He that believeth and is baptized shall be saved" (Mark 16:16). Whoever has the impression that salvation is before or without baptism has a perverted view of it. The Galatians were reminded: "For ye are all the children of God by faith in Christ Jesus. For as many of you as have been baptized into Christ have put on Christ" (Gal. 3:26-27). Salvation is only to be found in Christ and only those baptized into Christ are in Christ where this salvation is to be obtained. It takes a great deal of twisting to keep from seeing that baptism is essential to salvation!

Prayer is one of the most glorious privileges God ever granted to mankind. But here again a beautiful privilege is twisted to justify the actions and doctrines of men. The Scriptures teach that prayer is granted to those who obeyed the Lord. Contrary to this, alien sinners are told repeatedly to "pray for the Lord to save you, pray for the Holy Spirit, pray for remissions of sins." All this, an alien sinner is advised to do by people who possess more zeal than knowledge. To instruct a sinner to pray is to lead him into a thing the God of heaven has not even suggested that anyone but a child of his do. We note what Peter said about prayer, "For the eyes of the Lord are over the righteous, and his ears are open unto their prayers: but the face of the Lord is against them that do evil" (1 Pet. 3:12). The wise man wrote, "He that turneth away his ear from hearing the law, even his prayer shall be abomination" (Prov. 28:9). The individual who instructs an alien sinner to pray for remission of sins is twisting the word of God. The Scripture says with reference to the sinner's obtaining the remission of his sins, "Repent, and be baptized every one of you in the name of Jesus Christ for the remission of sins and ye shall receive the gift of the Holy Ghost" (Acts 2:38).

It is a serious thing to tamper with the word of God (Gal.1:6-9). But that is just what so many people continue to do. They twist the truth in order to justify their own actions and doctrines. Jesus stated, "He that rejecteth me, and receiveth not my words, hath one that judgeth him: the word that I have spoken, the same shall judge him in the last day" (John 12:48). One of the impossible things is trying to deceive God. "Be not deceived; God is not mocked: for whatsoever a man soweth, that shall he also reap" (Gal. 6:7). It is a foolish thing to twist any portion of the Scripture to fit our deeds, for in the judgment we will surely meet the word of God in all of its purity. And friend, twisting the picture won't help the scene. "For we must all appear before the judgment seat of Christ; that every one may receive the things done in his body, according to that he hath done, whether it be good or bad" (2 Cor. 5:10).

"Unto the Jews I Became As a Jew"

(1 Corinthians 9:20-21)

If there is any passage in the Bible that gives support to the common phrase, and an even more common practice, "in Rome do as Rome does," I suppose it would have to be this passage. If there is a passage which strengthens the concept that teaching, preaching, and practice are to be suited to the people, again, I suppose this passage would be the one most likely used by those of such a persuasion. As one might conclude, there is probably no passage in the Bible that is mo re abused and misrepresented than this from 1 Corinthians 9:20-21. Every passage has its truthful meaning and this one falls short of proving what some individuals contend it proves.

The apostle's action in other places proves that he did not intend to convey in these verses that teaching and practice should be suited to the people. His action in Galatians 2:1-5 toward those who would command Titus to be circumcised is in conflict with such a view. "To whom we gave place by subjection, no, not for an hour; that the truth of the gospel might continue with you" is not language of truth compromising or designing teaching to please the people. Think of the occasion when Paul rebuked Peter for not eating with the Gentiles when the Jews came (Gal. 2:11-14). Had Paul forgotten the teaching of 1 Corinthians 9:20-22? By no means! However, if the passage teaches what some believe it does, he must have forgotten it or brazenly acted contrary to it to do what he did in withstanding Peter to the face "because he was to be blamed." Some people need to be reminded of the word of Paul to Elymas in Acts 13:10 when he referred to this sorcerer as "thou child of the devil, thou enemy of all righteousness."

The entire tenor of the teaching of Christ is opposed to this passage teaching that preaching and practice should be flexible to suit the likes and dislikes of hearers. In our Lord's prayer in John 17, he relates that his disciples "are not of the world, even as I am not of the world. I pray not that thou shouldest take them out of the world, but that thou shouldest keep them from the evil. They are not of the world, even as I am not of the world" (John 17:14-16). In these words, there is not any solace for the view that the disciples can have their actions so flexible as to "in Rome do as the Romans do." Furthermore, the admonitions of the Spirit through the inspired writers of the New Testament Epistles, are in definite conflict with such a flexible view. Paul wrote, "be not conformed to this world" (Rom. 12:2), and that Christians are "a peculiar people" (Tit. 2:14). Jude felt it needful to exhort Christians to "earnestly contend for the faith" (Jude 3).

What did Paul have in mind by writing these words in 1 Corinthians 9:20-21? We have talked about what he did not mean, but what did he mean or have in mind? In this chapter, Paul is defending his right to be supported in his preaching. He proves this principle by three illustrations and an example from the Old Testament (1 Cor. 9:7-9). Though he had this power or right, he chose not to use it. His reward or happiness was to preach without charge. In order that the Corinthians might realize and believe his words, he further added that this was in keeping with his life as stated in verses 19-22. Paul said that he had, on occasions, assumed four different relations: as a Jew, under the law, without law, as the weak. The end or purpose was "that I might gain the more."

In matters of indifference and custom, the apostle carried no prejudices. He observed circumcision where it did not interfere with the liberty of the Gentiles (Acts 16:3). To those without law (the Gentiles), he respected their opinions and made innocent concessions when it did not conflict with faith. Paul referred to "the weak" in Romans 14 as pertaining to the eating of meat and esteeming one day above another.

To appreciate what the apostle had in mind, we need to understand that there are matters of faith and matters of indifference. Matters of faith are regulated by the word of God and one cannot be flexible in such matters in being true to God. Indifference is regulated by opinion and in such an area, one can unto the Jews be as a Jew. In matters of indifference, many concessions can be granted that others might be gained to the faith. This principle is not without danger at times. From what is stated in 2 Corinthians 12:13, it would appear that it had not resulted in the desired end that Paul had intended for the Corinthians. His comment was, "forgive me this wrong."

It should be the Christian's desire to gain all to Christ. Concessions in matters of indifferences may open their hearts to receive the matters of faith. People are gained to Christ when they are converted to Christ. This is only done when individuals obey the gospel of Christ (Mark 16:16; Acts 2:38). There can be no concessions in matters involving obeying the will of God. To do so is to deny loyalty to God!

Victory Over Circumstances

Many are pessimistic and discouraged over their circumstances which they feel limit their abilities. An observation of the latter years of the apostle Paul's life would be an encouragement for us to find victory over circumstances. Paul, along with many of the early Christians, was frequently bound in prison "for the word of God and the testimony of Jesus." This was his lot when he wrote a number of epistles. He referred to these bonds: "For which I am an ambassador in bonds" (Eph. 6:20). "So that my bonds in Christ are manifest in all of the palace" (Phil. 1:12-13). "Remember my bonds" (Col. 4:18). It was natural for his bonds to hinder him in some way, even in his writings; but, as his friends remembered that he was in bonds, they would understand and could pray for him.

We all have bonds in some fashion and quite often need encouragement. Sometimes we say we could have done better, had it not been for some unavoidable and disturbing influence that hindered us. Have you ever contemplated victory over circumstances? In a sense, the businessman has a bond of work, the professional man his appointments, the invalid his illness, the mother her home duties, and the poor man his poverty. Many things they would like to do if it were not for their bonds or obligations. We need to take lessons from Paul's bonds and not let these "bonds" in our lives defeat us. Observe these lessons that are suggested by Paul's bonds:

His bonds were not disgraceful to him. He was not in prison because he had done wrong, but because he would not do that which he knew to be wrong. His chain was a symbol of principle! Our bonds, unless brought on by wrongdoing, are not disgraceful and we should patiently accept them. Rather than to view the bonds as being disgraceful, we need to look up and realize that in all legitimate circumstances, we can be beneficial to the truth and the Lord's cause. Now hear this: "wherein I suffer trouble, as a evildoer, even unto bonds; but the word of God is not bound" (2 Tim. 2:9).

His bonds didn't prevent him from being useful. Paul may have been saddened by the fact that he was kept from his travels, yet he was made to see that his imprisonment had been an advantage to him. He evidenced this fact in writing to the Philippians: "But I would ye should understand, brethren, that the things which happened unto me have fallen out rather unto the furtherance of the gospel; so that my bonds in Christ are manifest in all the palace, and in all other places; and many of the brethren in the Lord, waxing confident by my bonds, are much more bold to speak the word without fear" (Phil. 1:12-14). Some of Paul's rarest opportunities came to him during the time that he was in bonds. As he wrote, "but the word of God is not bound" (2 Tim. 2:9). It was during such times that he was privileged to preach to the jailer, Felix, Agrippa, Onesimus, and Caesar's household.

Every child of God should remember that the Lord can make all things work together for good, if he will only do his best whatever his circumstances might be. Bitterness and a sour disposition should never be allowed to dominate us when bonds come. Furthermore, we are extremely poor judges of ultimate results. In the day of final reckoning, those who felt that they were doing very little because of their circumstance may find that they have done a great deal.

His bonds did not mar his happiness. Having been beaten and in prison; yet we read, "at midnight Paul and Silas prayed, and sang praises unto God" (Acts 16:25). If we will allow him to, Christ can bring happiness to us. It matters not in what kind of a situation we may be placed. An individual who understands this principle will say, "If I must live in this place, I will develop it." "If this is my lot, then I will make the best of it." Any average person can master any set of circumstances, if he will allow the Lord to lead him. "Not that I speak in respect of want: for I have learned, in whatsoever state I am, therewith to be content. I know both how to be abased, and I know how to abound: every where and in all things I am instructed both to be full and to be hungry, both to abound and to suffer need. I can do all things through Christ which strengtheneth me" (Phil. 4:11-13).

His bonds did not lessen his reward. Anyone's responsibility is measured by his abilities plus his opportunity. We often connect reward with activity, but Christ connects it with faithfulness and character. If we have done our best within our limitations, that is what the Lord requires of us and our reward will be far beyond our ability to ask or think. "I have fought a good fight, I have finished my course, I have kept the faith: Henceforth there is laid up for me a crown of righteousness which the Lord, the righteous judge, shall give me at that day: and not to me only, but unto all them also that love his appearing" (2 Tim. 4:7-8). What a beautiful reward!

Victory Over the World

For whatsoever is born of God overcometh the world: and this is the victory that overcometh the world, even our faith. Who is he that overcometh the world, but he that believeth that Jesus is the Son of God ?(1 John 5:4-5).

These words were addressed to Christians living within the

borders of the great Roman Empire. When we consider their circumstances, these words were nothing short of amazing. They occupied humble positions. They were surrounded by a society which tolerated evils and vices that beggar description. I personally do not believe the corruptness of our society equals that which was characteristic of the Roman Empire. The power of Rome was irresistible, yet John said that these Christians were overcoming the world. They were saints in Caesar's household (Phil. 4:22).

John, more than any other of the New Testament writers, dwells on the concept of overcoming—of gaining victory. The word "overcometh" is used five times in the epistle of 1 John. Each of the letters to the seven churches of Asia, as found in the first of Revelation, is concluded with the thought of overcoming. As an example, the epistle to the church at Ephesus is concluded with the admonition: ". . . To him that overcometh will I give to eat of the tree of life, which is in the midst of the paradise of God" (Rev. 2:7).

What Is the Foe That Challenges the Believer?

Though there are many instruments that oppose Christians and the Lord's church, yet opposition may be described in the word "world." The word is used in various senses in the Scriptures and it is important to note these various senses so that this foe may be properly recognized. "World" is used in the sense of:

1. Creation of the universe (John 17:5).

2. To denote the earth as a single planet of the universe, as the home of humans (Mark 16:15).

3. To designate the inhabitants of the earth (John 3:16).

4. To denote affairs, endowments, advantages, pleasures which stir desires, seduce from God and are obstacles to the cause of Christ (Matt. 16:26; Jas. 4:4; 1 John 2:15-17).

John was referring to definition #4—to all the forces which are antagonistic to the spiritual life (Gal. 1:4; 2 Tim. 4:10). This was the world that these Christians were overcoming and the one which we must overcome. Society may not appear the same, but the principle of opposition is always the same.

The Conflict—Not Any Easy One!

The world is a gigantic power. It is not easily resisted. The world does not always attack in the same manner. With the early Christians, the assault was more of a direct nature (John 16:1-3; Matt. 5:10-11; 2 Tim. 3:12; 1 Pet. 4:14). We may expect the assault to come upon us by offers of compromise, appeals to interests, or appeals to our desires and passions. Whatever its methods, the attack comes when we are worn out by cares, duties, and troubles—when we are "cumbered about much serving" (Luke 10:40). There is one thing for sure, if we are not overcoming the world, then the world is overcoming us. We are either fighting the current or flowing with the stream. When we are induced to accept the views and maxims of the world instead of God's word, we are being overcome rather than overcoming. Paul admonished the Colossians: "Beware lest any man spoil you through philosophy and vain deceit, after the tradition of men, after the rudiments of the world, and not after Christ" (2:8).

The Conqueror—"Even Our Faith"

Our wisdom and strength can never conquer the world. The faith is the conquering principle. Faith comes "by hearing, and hearing by the word of God" (Rom. 10:17). Faith is that force within the soul, which leads one to deny the world and cling to God. The eleventh chapter of Hebrews begins with a definition of this wonderful principle called "faith" and proceeds in abounding with illustrations of how faith can lead men to deny the world and follow God. The virtue of the Christian's faith lies in the object. It is our Christ-centered faith that gives the victory. With our faith in the Lord, the world loses its power over us. "But thanks be to God, which giveth us the victory through our Lord Jesus Christ" (1 Cor. 15:57). To overcome the world, one must have faith to obey the gospel, to be born again, and continue in faithful obedience as a Christian (1 John 5:4; John 3:3-5; Mark 16:16; 1 Cor. 15:58). Victory is a wonderful thing and victory over the world is a wonderful achievement. We can all have that victory in faithfully following Jesus. As one has said, winning is not everything, but losing is nothing. Let's labor to defeat the world and not be classed with those who are losers!

Waiting For the Rapture?

The subject of the rapture has become a rather popular one with many in the denominational world. Tim LaHaye's apocalyptic novel, *Left Behind,* and his other writings have intensified belief in what is designated "the rapture." This is the belief that believers in Jesus are plucked from the earth while the others suffer through a cataclysmic, seven-year battle between the Christ and the antichrist. It is quite common to read bumper stickers that convey that the drivers are waiting for the rapture or their vehicles will be destroyed in the rapture. There are also bus benches in the Bradenton area advertising that the rapture will occur in 2007. Under the title, "Are You Rapture Ready," Shelby Corbitt of Oneco, writes on the Internet: "The rapture of the church (God's children) will happen during the SUMMER OF 2007 and could be anytime from June 21-September 21. This means Jesus Christ is coming in the eastern sky and call all His children up to Heaven, leaving all the sinners and unbelievers behind—this is not the end of the world—but it will be the beginning of terrible tribulation for those left behind" (www.2007rapture.com).

To my knowledge, the word "rapture" is not found in any versions of the Scriptures. The word "rapture" is from the Latin word *vapare* which means to "take away" or "snatch out." Webster defines the word as "a state or experience of being carried away with overwhelming emotion." With such a definition in mind, we find the word and its different forms innocently used in the lyrics of many spiritual songs that we sing. The use of the word in this respect does not endorse the period or doctrine of the rapture that is embedded in premillennial teaching.

The doctrine or rapture theory is unscriptural and false to the core. Consider how it is contrary to the Scriptures:

It teaches too many comings of Christ. The theory has two comings of the Lord within a seven year span. The rapture has Jesus coming *for* the saints, and then coming *with* the saints. The Hebrew writer speaks of his coming a second time, but never twice within a seven year period. "And as it is appointed unto men once to die, but after this the judgment: So Christ was once offered to bear the sins of many; and unto them that look for him shall he appear the *second time* without sin unto salvation" (Heb. 9:27-28). His first appearing was when the Word was made flesh and dwelt among men (John 1:14). His second appearing will be for the universal judgment (Acts 17:31; 2 Tim. 4:1).

It denies Christ's universal coming. The rapture depicts only a portion of humanity seeing Jesus when he comes. The Scriptures speak to the contrary. "When the Son of man shall come in his glory, and all the holy angels with him, then shall he sit upon the throne of his glory: And before him shall be gathered all nations" (Matt. 25:31-32). "All nations" very definitely means more than just a portion of humanity. "Behold, he cometh with clouds; and every eye shall see him, and they also which pierced him: and all kindreds of the earth shall wail because of him. Even so, Amen" (Rev. 1:7).

It contradicts plain passages such as John 5:28-29. "Marvel not at this: for the hour is coming, in the which all that are in the graves shall hear his voice, and shall come forth; they that have done good, unto the resurrection of life; and they that have done evil, unto the resurrection of damnation." This passage teaches that the righteous dead and wicked will come forth at the same hour. Those who hold the rapture theory have the righteous dead raised to meet the Lord in the air and there remain for seven years. The wicked dead are not raised, but are left in the tomb. The rapture theory has a seven-year interval. Premillennialism has a thousand-year interval between the resurrection of the two classes. If my arithmetic is correct, that means 1,007 years between the resurredtion of these two classes. The Lord said the hour is coming when both classes, the righteous and the wicked dead, would be resurrected. Who will we believe—Jesus Christ, the Son of God, or those advocating the rapture theory?

It is contrary to its "proof" text. 1 Thessalonians 4:16-18 is quoted by those believing in the rapture as scriptural proof for its coming. "For the Lord himself shall descend from heaven with a shout, with the voice of the archangel, and with the trump of God: and the dead in Christ shall rise first: Then we which are alive and remain shall be caught up together with them in the clouds to meet the Lord in the air: and so shall we ever be with the Lord. Wherefore comfort one another with these words." In all fairness, the Greek word rendered "caught up" conveys the thought of rapture. But this lacks much in being proof of the rapture theory. It seems the Thessalonians were anxious in regard to those who had died in Christ. At the coming of the Lord, what would be their condition? Through the Spirit, Paul assures them that "we which are alive and remain unto the coming of the Lord shall not prevent (go before) them which are asleep" (v. 15). But they will be raised first and then with the righteous living will be caught up in the clouds to meet the Lord in the air and then they would ever be with the Lord. This would not involve some seven years while a tribulation, that is unknown in the Scriptures, exists on the earth. When Paul says "the dead in Christ shall rise first," he is not distinguishing this event from a second premillennial coming after a tribulation, which the rapture advocates teach. He is simply saying the dead will rise first before the living in Christ ascend to meet the Lord. Both of these will occur at the one resurrection of the dead. If you are waiting for the rapture, you will be waiting in vain. Such is not taught in the Scriptures! We need to be preparing and waiting for the second coming of Christ and the judgment to come.

Was Apollos A False Teacher?

And a certain Jew named Apollos, born at Alexandria, an eloquent man, and mighty in the scriptures, came to Ephesus. This man was instructed in the way of the Lord; and being fervent in the spirit, he spake and taught diligently the things of the Lord, knowing only the baptism of John. And he began to speak boldly in the synagogue: whom when Aquila and Priscilla had heard, they took him unto them, and expounded unto him the way of God more perfectly (Acts 18:24-26).

These verses constitute our introduction to Apollos. Everything that is stated regarding him is quite commendable with the exception of the participle phrase, "knowing only the baptism of John." How he came to know the baptism of John, I do not know. How he did not know that it had served its scriptural purpose and was no longer present truth, I do not know. However, from this account regarding him, I do conclude that he was still preaching the baptism of John and calling upon individuals to conform to it. John the Baptist preached to Jews and "baptized with the baptism of repentance, saying unto the people, that they should believe on him which should come after him, that is, on Christ Jesus" (Acts 19:4). The baptism of John was unique! It was a forerunner of Jesus in preparing people for his mission and the advent of his kingdom. It looked forward to the cross and the death of Christ for the sins of the world. After the death of Christ and the coming of the kingdom, all people have the privilege of looking back to the cross and having their sins forgiven in obeying the gospel of Christ. But Apollos knew only the baptism of John, years after the death of Christ. He was teaching something that was once truth, but had ceased to be due to its fulfillment.

More could be said about the character of Apollos and the baptism of John. However, our question is: "Was Apollos a false teacher?" On more than one occasion, I have preached that he was and later learned that some members of the church disagreed.

Having tried to discuss it with them, it never seemed definite why they defended him as not being a false teacher. It could have been on the basis of his outstanding qualities. In consideration of such qualities, they felt his preaching the baptism of John should be overlooked as being error. It would appear that somewhere along the line, brethren have gotten the idea that a false teacher is one who is teaching error on many things and just one thing, like knowing only the baptism of John, should not cause him to classified as a false teacher. How much error can one teach and still be teaching the truth? How much poison can one receive without his body being effected? We are called upon to "buy the truth, and sell it not" (Prov. 23:23). This involves all the truth and not just a portion that might appeal to us.

It might be that some refuse to view him as a false teacher because there is no evidence of his insincerity. All preachers and teachers of God's word are to be sincere in what they teach. However, a person can be sincerely wrong! Think of Saul of Tarsus! He persecuted the church and caused people who followed Jesus to be put to death. He did such, thinking that he should do many things contrary to the name of Jesus Christ (Acts 26:9). Many of us have at times given directions to individuals. Though sincere in our actions, we pointed them on the wrong road. Did our sincerity assure them of reaching their destination? Certainly not!

Apollos was teaching something that was no longer truth. Some excuse him from the classification of a false teacher due to the fact the Scriptures do not say that he was. Aquila and Priscilla having heard him, "they took him unto them, and expounded unto him the way of God more perfectly." This godly couple recognized truth from error and knew that Apollos needed correction. Why would there be need to teach one the way of God more perfectly unless they were wrong? There are cases in the Scriptures where it is quite evident that false teaching has been done, but those doing so are not called false teachers. In 2 Timothy 2:17-18, one reads of Hymenaeus and Philetus teaching that the resurrection is past already; and overthrew the faith of some. It is obvious that what they taught was false, but we do not read of them being labeled false teachers. Their false teaching identified them as false teachers! They were teaching something that was false and overthrew the faith of some.

If one today began to teach the baptism of John, would this be recognized as truth that will save an individual's soul? If Apollos was not false in what he preached, then a preacher today should not be identified as a false teacher in preaching the same. When Paul came to Ephesus, he found those who had received the baptism of John. When they heard the truth concerning the baptism of John, they were baptized in the name of the Lord Jesus (Acts 19:1-5). They had been falsely taught and they needed to know the truth and obey it. This they did in being right with God. Verses 27-28 imply that Apollos received the truth and went to Achaia preaching it!

We Have An Enemy

We may not be aware of this enemy, but it certainly exists. We are thinking of self. We may have enemies who are more easily recognized than self. This is one of the factors that contributes to the danger that self can do to us. Many people are prone to blame everyone and everything for their failures when the real failure is self. They have not conquered self and in turn it is doing all it can to conquer them. This enemy penetrates further than any other foe and can bring destruction when others might fail. All other foes who confront the Christian must have assistance from self before an individual is conquered. Satan cannot defeat one until he has the cooperation of self. When the child of God handles self in the proper manner, there is nothing that Satan can do to cause him to deny the faith. Self is far more successful than any other enemy. This enemy can keep one from obeying the gospel, from worshiping acceptably, and from living the life that the Lord expects of a faithful child of God.

We have thus far said a great deal about how potent this enemy is and what it can do. The question is, "How may this enemy be handled or defeated?" The Scriptures give us the answer and there are a number of directions as to what one is to do with self. We notice a few of these . . .

Deny Self. "Then said Jesus unto his disciples, If any man will come after me, let him deny himself, and take up his cross, and follow me" (Matt. 16:24). One of the requirements of following Christ is that an individual will deny himself. This is required as one becomes a Christian and the denial must continue if one is to live a faithful life in Christ. Ordinarily, we use the word "self-denial" in a restricted sense. We use it to mean doing without something or giving up something. For instance, a week of self-denial is a week when we usually do without certain pleasures or luxuries in order to contribute to some good cause. However, that is only a very small part of what Jesus meant by self-denial. To deny self means in every moment of life we are to say "no" to self and to say "yes" to God. To deny oneself means once, finally, and forever to dethrone self and to enthrone God. To deny oneself means to obliterate self as the dominant principle of life and to make God the ruling principle of one's life. The life of constant self-denial is the life of constant assent to God.

Never Exalt Self. "For I say, through the grace given unto me, to every man that is among you, not to think of himself more highly than he ought to think; but to think soberly, accordingly as God hath dealt to every man the measure of faith" (Rom. 12:3). Problems of vanity and pride arise due to the fact that so many of us think more highly of ourselves than we ought to think. Think of the many church problems and ill feelings among brethren that possibly could have been eliminated if lowliness and humility had prevailed in the place of those thinking of themselves more highly than they should! One of the more beautiful passages in the epistles of Paul is found in Philippians 2:3-5—a passage that many of us have never known in practice! "Let nothing be done through strife or vainglory; but in lowliness of mind let each esteem other better than themselves. Look not every man on his own things, but every man also on the things of others. Let this mind be in you, which was also in Christ Jesus." When these admonitions are followed, an individual will not be exalting self. He will be handling self in a way that will not permit self to defeat him. "Humble yourselves in the sight of the Lord, and he shall lift you up" (Jas. 4:10).

Keep Self. John wrote, "We know that whosoever is born of God sinneth not; but he that is begotten of God keepeth himself, and that wicked one toucheth him not" (1 John 5:19). John speaks of a Christian keeping himself and in so doing Satan "toucheth him not." This is what we have mentioned previously in this study. Satan cannot touch one if that person keeps himself. To overthrow one, Satan must have the help of self that he does not receive when one keeps himself. Paul spoke of keeping self in these words, "but I keep under my body, and bring it into subjection: lest that by any means, when I have preached to others, I myself should be a castaway" (1 Cor. 9:27). Peter spoke of Christians being "kept by the power of God" (1 Pet. 1:5). Man is to keep the faith and as he does so, he is kept by the power of God. We are to resist temptations, but when we yield to them and sin, we are to confess our sins with the confidence that the Lord "is faithful and just to forgive us our sins, and to cleanse us from all unrighteousness" (1 John 1:9). This is part of keeping ourselves and defeating self. We may deny that this enemy exists and when we do so, we are playing into the hands of Satan. God would have us to properly evaluate self and keep it in subjection that we might continue to be pleasing to him.

What About Doubt?

Webster defines doubt as "to be unsettled in opinion or belief; be uncertain or undecided." Doubt might be said to be opposed to assurance and peace of mind. With caution and in a limited sense, it might be said that it is good at times for an individual to experience doubt. We are told to "prove all things; hold fast that which is good" (1 Thess. 5:21). Doubt has sometimes caused individuals to examine their religious positions and find them not in keeping with the word of God. The sincere ones, having come to the knowledge of truth, were obedient to truth and have the peace of mind that God intends for them to have. Perhaps all of us, at one time or another, have experienced doubt which was good for us. It motivated or encouraged us to correct that which was robbing us of peace of mind that God desires for his people to enjoy.

Though doubt sometimes brings good results, it is not to be denied that doubt in itself is misery. Who can say that they were happy while doubt engulfed their heart? Regardless of the situation or endeavor of life, doubt represents misery. Think of a husband or wife who doubts the fidelity of his/her mate! Is this man or woman happy as he/she should be in his/her married life? It is quite to the contrary! Use whatever example or illustration that you might desire. The result pictures doubt and misery to be hand in hand.

We come now to the heart of what we have in mind regarding the subject of doubt. On occasions, we have known people who have professed to obey the will of God while experiencing doubt about what they have done and continually being governed by doubt. We have reference to some who have professed to be Christians for years and yet on some of the most fundamental subjects, they say "we still don't know what the truth is." They even profess to study and be searchers, but they are still in doubt. Novices are not the ones we have in mind. The firmness of some true novices would even put these people to open shame! We are talking about some who might well fit the description of those Paul spoke of as "ever learning, and never able to come to the knowledge of the truth" (2 Tim. 3:7). Be it understood that, for a limited time, doubt can serve an admirable function in one's life, but we fail to accept the thought that doubt can prevail in one's life and be an asset.

The truth is available to all men and we are confident that it is not hidden to anyone who desires it and is ready to pay the price for it. Paul wrote, "But if our gospel be hid, it is hid to them that are lost: In whom the god of this world hath blinded the minds of them which believe not, lest the light of the glorious gospel of Christ, who is the image of God, should shine unto them" (2 Cor.

4:3-4). Jesus stated in the Sermon on the Mount, "Ask, and it shall be given you; seek, and ye shall find; knock, and it shall be opened unto you: For every one that asketh receiveth; and he that seeketh findeth; and to him that knocketh it shall be opened" (Matt. 7:7-8). Does this mean that one must seek throughout his entire life in order to find what constitutes the truth he is to obey in order to be saved? Must one remain in doubt the greater part of his life while seeking to find? Such reasoning would defeat the concept of assurance, confidence, and peace of mind that the Scriptures vividly portray. Those who were the converts in the book of Acts were people who appear to have obeyed the gospel the first time it was preached to them. It was not so complicated that they had to spend a lifetime studying to find the truth before they could remove the doubt in their lives. Some one is ready to say, "Oh, but they didn't have to confront the various doctrines that we do today." Error has always existed. They had to confront Judaism that seemed to have an influence on people in a sense as great as anything we might picture in prevailing error today. Perhaps, we have hit upon one of the grounds of doubt! It appears that some feel that they have to know all the error in the world to know what is truth. Be it understood that it is good to know something about false teaching, but one can read the Bible and know the truth regardless of what one knows of false doctrine.

I firmly believe that anyone who continues in doubt about the fundamental principles of God's will toward man is affected by something other than lack of plainness of the Scriptures. There were Jews who came to Jesus and said unto him, "How long dost thou make us to doubt? If thou be the Christ tell us plainly. Jesus answered them, I told you and ye believed not: the works that I do in my Father's name, they bear witness of me. But ye believe not, because ye are not of my sheep, as I said unto you" (John 10:24-26). These accused Jesus of causing them to doubt by not being a plain teacher. The Lord told them the reason for their lack of faith: "Ye are not of my sheep." They were not humble enough to condescend to the obedience required in accepting the truth in God's word. When we doubt, we need to examine ourselves in the light of the word of God. We need to look inward where the problem usually lies! God wants all of us to have peace and not doubt!

What About the Heathen?

What will become of the heathen who never heard the gospel? Of all questions that are asked concerning Bible themes, this is one of the most frequent. We would like to think that most people ask this question with a sincere desire to settle their minds on the subject and be able to teach others the truth on the matter. However, we are prone to believe at times that it has arisen in Bible discussions in an effort to cast reflections upon the teaching of truth and God, endeavoring to prejudice people against the gospel. They wish to use the question to make it appear that God is unfair if he doesn't save an individual who doesn't know the will of the Lord. Brother R.L. Whiteside has some good comments on this question and we quote the following from his commentary on Romans (23):

> If a person understood the real purpose and philosophy of the gospel, he would never ask that question. To set such questioners to thinking, we ask: What would have become of the same heathen, if there had never been any gospel? The gospel was designed to save a world already condemned. It is only in a relative sense that people are lost because they do not obey the gospel. Primarily people are lost because they are sinners. To illustrate: a boat is rushed out to rescue a drowning man. He refuses to be rescued, and is drowned. Now, why did he drown? "O", some one replies, "he drowned because he would not get in the boat." Wrong. The boat had nothing to do with his drowning; he drowned because he was in the water, and he would have drowned just the same had there never been a boat. Of course, his refusing to be rescued made his drowning a case of suicide. Just so with the sinner. The gospel is sent out to rescue the perishing. When the sinner refuses to be rescued, it intensifies his guilt and shows it to be a case of spiritual suicide. But the gospel had nothing to do with his perishing; he would have perished had there never been a gospel. The boat was a means of rescue, and so is the gospel.

A few Scriptures come to my mind in regard to this question: "But the scripture hath concluded all under sin, that the promise by faith of Jesus Christ might be given to them that believe" (Gal. 3:22). "And the times of this ignorance God winked at; but now commandeth all men every where to repent" (Acts 17:30). "Seeing it is a righteous thing with God to recompense tribulation to them that trouble you; And to you who are troubled rest with us, when the Lord Jesus shall be revealed from heaven with his mighty angels, In flaming fire taking vengeance on them that know not God, and that obey not the gospel of our Lord Jesus Christ: Who shall be punished with everlasting destruction from the presence of the Lord and from the glory of his power" (2 Thess. 1:6-9). These Scriptures reveal that all are concluded under sin and all are called upon to repent. Furthermore, vengeance from the Lord will be rendered upon those who do not know him and refuse to obey the gospel of Christ. It would appear that these Scriptures should be plain enough in supplying the answer to the question for one who is ready to accept the word of God as authority. But I fear the trouble with many is that they are not ready to let the word of God settle the matter for them. They think God should think as they think and do not realize the truth of Isaiah's statement: "Let the wicked forsake his way, and the unrighteous man his thoughts: and let him return unto the Lord, and he will have mercy upon him; and to our God, for he will abundantly pardon. For my thoughts are not your thoughts, neither are your ways my ways, saith the Lord. For as the heavens are higher than the earth so are my ways higher then your ways, and my thoughts than your thoughts" (Isa. 55:7-9).

Another thought: If one is exempted because he does not know the will of God, why bother in trying to teach "the heathen"? The teacher would be doing them more damage than good! When the truth is presented to them, they might not obey and thus be lost wherein (according to some) their ignorance and lack of knowledge would excuse them. Certainly, one can see the fallacy of contending that ignorance is excusable. It is not so with the laws of the land. When one violates a law, ignorance of that law does not exempt that individual from its penalty. If ignorance and lack of knowledge will exempt "the heathen," then let's all be of that category and have our salvation assured. God will do right and he is a righteous judge! Whatever may be said of "the heathen," we need to consider our lives and those of us who know the will of God. So many who talk about "the heathen" have not obeyed the gospel and are not living in keeping with God's will. They express concern for those who have not known the will of God, but what about concern for themselves and for others who know it and have not obeyed it? We suggest again that some are possibly more concerned in offsetting the power of the gospel than they are about truly being concerned about what will happen to "the heathen."

What Baptism Does Not Do

This is a scriptural approach to the subject. In 1 Peter 3:21, Peter mentioned to his readers what baptism did and also what it did not do. "The like figure whereunto even baptism doth also now save us, (not the putting away of the filth of the flesh, but the answer of a good conscience toward God,) by the resurrection of Jesus Christ." Much is said in the word of God and by gospel preachers concerning the importance of water baptism, yet there are some definite things which baptism does not do.

It is well to study this lesson for more than one reason. One reason is that denominationalists claim that members of the church of Christ are fanatics on the subject of water baptism. To hear them, one would think that the members of the Lord's church consider baptism to do it all and be everything. A lesson of this nature might help to silence such unwarranted statements. Why do they think that members of the church of Christ say so much about baptism? It could well be due to the fact that they say so little about the matter, that by comparison, it seems like so much. It is also good to study this lesson due to the fact that some members could possibly be found placing entirely too much importance on baptism to the disregard of other things! By the action of some members, one might be led to think that baptism does it all. That appears to be about all some have done as far as the kingdom of God and service to Christ is involved. Yes, there are those who abuse baptism by over emphasizing what it does, but we must always remember that the abuse of a thing does not destroy the proper use of it.

What Baptism Does Not Do

It does not put off the filth of the flesh. This is evident from Peter's words in 1 Peter 3:21. "Filth" refers to that which is dirty, physically defiled. Baptism does not "wash sin from the skin" and is not to be confused with a bath for the body or a ceremonial cleansing of the flesh as ordinances practiced under the Old Covenant.

It does not change a man's heart. A change of heart is essential to man's salvation. His intellect, emotions, and will are to be changed. Such a change is brought about by faith in Jesus Christ, not in baptism. ". . . purifying their hearts by faith" (Acts 15:9).

It does not destroy a man's inclination to sin. If one's love for sin is to be destroyed, it will be in "godly sorrow working repentance unto salvation" (2 Cor. 7:10). If a man doesn't have godly sorrow toward sins before baptism, he is not going to acquire such in being baptized. Some have questioned their conversion when, after baptism, they were again tempted to do wrong. Baptism does not exclude an individual from being tempted. Christ's greatest temptation came after he was baptized (Matt. 4).

Baptism does not suffice for obedience to other commands, either before or after. Every command which God has given has its own definite purpose in those who are obedient. Denominational people are inclined to make prayer suffice for other commands that they fail to obey. We might find ourselves doing the same with the command of baptism. Baptism is not repentance and it will not suffice for repentance. Some people seem to be of the persuasion that they can be obedient to baptism and that takes care of every sinful relationship. What of the meaning of repentance? Baptism doesn't wash away a sinful relationship. It is in repentance that we forsake such and in life bring forth the fruits of repentance. To be right before God, we must learn to keep every commandment of God in its proper perspective.

It does not assure salvation for the future. ". . . baptism doth now save us" (1 Pet. 3:21). The Bible speaks of salvation past, present, and future (Mark 16:16; Phil. 2:12; 1 Pet. 1:4-5). Baptism is the line of demarcation giving one remission of past sins (Mark 16:16). Our "observing all things" (Matt. 28:19) assures present and future salvation. We must add to our faith (2 Pet. 1:5-11).

It does not grant a deliverance from persecution, affliction, sickness, or death! Those who were obediently baptized suffered as much or even more than others did (2 Tim. 3:12). Think of faithful Stephen (Acts 7:54-60). Baptism as it is accompanied by faith, repentance, and confession of Christ affords one deliverance from past sins—not from persecution.

Let's never be guilty of abusing any of the commandments of God. Let's leave them where God placed them. Baptism is a condition of salvation (Acts 2:38; 1 Pet. 3:21). We have no promise of heaven without it—*but it doesn't do it all!*

What Can The Righteous Do?

"If the foundations be destroyed, what can the righteous do" (Ps. 11:3). The setting of this Psalm seems to be when David was confronting some very trying times. It could have been when Saul was pursuing him or later when his son, Absalom, was endeavoring to take the kingdom from his father. It would also appear that David's counselors or advisers looked upon his situation as being desperate and advised him to "flee as a bird to your mountain" (v. 1). They considered the foundations were being destroyed and the cause of the righteous being hopeless.

We live in a time when many foundations have been destroyed and many others are being severely shaken. These foundations involve matters of morality and decency. Many people do not view fornication, adultery, abortion, and homosexuality as sinful. They ignore the foundation of truth concerning morality and decency that is prevalent in the word of God. The church of Christ is not exempt from foundations being destroyed. Congregations are practicing things that are not taught in the word of God and feel no constraint to follow the pattern of truth that constitutes our acceptability with God. In years gone by, we heard men of God stand in the pulpits and preach forceful lessons on the establishment of the church, authority in Christ, the necessity of baptism, the horror of sins, and many other subjects that are foundations of truth. Are they being preached today as they once were? In many pulpits, they are being ignored and replaced with what the membership desires to hear rather than the truth.

If the foundations be destroyed, what can the righteous do? Rather than wring our hands in despair and actually do nothing, there are things that the righteous can do. We think of a few of them:

The righteous can remain righteous. The righteous are those who have obeyed the gospel of Christ and been added to the Lord's church (Rom. 1:16-17; Acts 2:47). The Psalmist relates that "all commandments are righteousness" (Ps. 119:172). When one follows the commandments of the Lord, he is righteous before the Lord. Whatever may happen, we must keep on being righteous and respecting the foundations that the unrighteous ridicule. There is no time or place to give up in contending for the faith.

The righteous can be vexed. Peter speaks of Lot, "And delivered just Lot, vexed with the filthy conversation of the wicked: for that righteous man dwelling among them, in seeing and hearing, vexed his righteous soul from day to day with their unlawful deeds" (2 Pet. 2:7-8). To be vexed conveys the thought of being troubled, distressed, or even tormented. The sins of Sodom caused Lot's righteous soul to be vexed. The righteous today should view the sins that cause foundations to be destroyed in such a manner. Sin is no light matter and we must never sanction anything that is a transgression of God's law.

The righteous can be separate. We do not have to partake with those who are destroying foundations. "Wherefore come out from among them, and be ye separate, saith the Lord and touch not the unclean thing; and I will receive you" (2 Cor. 6:17). "And be not conformed to this world: but be ye transformed by the renewing of your mind" (Rom. 12:2). The righteous can remain separate! These verses would have no real significance if this were not so.

The righteous can keep their light shining. Darkness needs the light. "Let your light so shine before men, that they may see your good works, and glorify your Father which is in heaven" (Matt. 5:16). We can keep appreciating the foundations that others destroy and rejoicing when these things are preached. There is need for boldness in helping others see that there are still those who are righteous in living right.

The righteous can keep teaching the truth. Paul gave the beautiful charge to Timothy: "I charge thee. . .Preach the word; be instant in season, out season; reprove, rebuke, exhort with all longsuffering and doctrine" (2 Tim. 4:1-2). Others may destroy foundations, but we can keep on preaching the truth that upholds the foundations. Preaching the word is that which can stem the tide of digression and keep the church true to the Lord.

The righteous can keep trusting in the Lord. That seems to be David's reply to those who suggested that he flee as a bird to his mountain. "The Lord is in his holy temple, the Lord's throne is in heaven: his eyes behold, his eyelids try, the children of men" (v. 4). The Lord is on his throne in heaven. Some have asked, where was God on September 11, 2001? He was and is on his throne in heaven. We may wonder why he permits certain things, but God rules and we need to always keep trusting him. He knows what he is doing!

What Does It Mean To Become a Christian?

This is a very important question, one that all individuals would do well to consider. Consideration of the question might help some sinful soul become a Christian and help the indifferent Christian become more faithful. There is a tendency for all of us to take the privileges and blessings of the Lord too lightly. It is good often to prayerfully consider fundamental questions of this nature.

It must mean much for one to become a Christian for that is what God wants all men to be (Acts 11:26; 26:28; 1 Pet. 4:16). Certainly God does not desire for us to become something that is not characterized with great meaning! As one follows the teaching of the Scriptures, he will become a Christian. A Christian is the only thing that the Scriptures obeyed will constitute one. When one follows the word of God without subtraction and addition, he will become a Christian. When one takes a little of the word, combined with the doctrines of men, he will become something other than a Christian. This is what has happened to so many today and they have only been deceived rather than obedient to God. It must mean much to be a Christian for it costs much to become one. "Then said Jesus unto his disciples, If any man will come after me, let him deny himself, and take up his cross, and follow me" (Matt. 16:24). Denial, cross bearing, and courage to follow Christ are not without cost! There is the cost of being a Christian—but friend, have you ever stopped to consider the cost of not being one? I know it must mean much to be a Christian because it cost the Lord his life that men might become Christians. To say that it doesn't mean much to be a Christian is tantamount to saying that the death of the Lord was insignificant.

What Does It Mean For An Individual To Become a Christian?

It means making the only sensible plan of preparation for the future. The Christian is the only one truly preparing to meet the future and cope with death (Mark 8:36-37; Heb. 9:27).

It means making your time and talents count for the glory of God and the good of man. The land of indecision and doubt has been abandoned when one obeys the Christ and becomes a Christian. No more aimless drifting, no more idleness, and no more wasted days. Life is now filled with usefulness and meaning. "Whether therefore ye eat or drink, or whatsoever ye do, do all to the glory of God" (1 Cor. 10:31). Only a Christian can do this (John 15:5; Matt. 12:30).

It means that you are crossing a line into the service of God and out of the service of Satan. ". . . who hath delivered us from the power of darkness, and hath translated us into the kingdom of his dear Son" (Col. 1:13). One takes upon himself the name of Christ to represent the gospel to the world. He must always be concerned with "walking worthy of the vocation" (Eph. 4:1).

It means that you are surrendering an old allegiance never to resume it. ". . . let us lay aside every weight, and the sin which doth so easily beset us, and let us run with patience the race that is set before us" (Heb. 12:1). The weight may be previous religious affiliations, friends who are evil, or business that is dishonest (Matt. 5:16).

You are admitting that you have been lost, a sinner, and needed Christ to save you. Realization of the words of Paul in Romans 3:23, "for all have sinned and come short of the glory of God." You know that you are unable to save yourself and are humble enough and sincere enough to obey Christ. It means that you know you are not perfect and are trying to overcome your faults.

It means one is pledging himself to live like Christ. The very meaning of the word "Christian" is to partake with Christ (1 Pet. 2:21). One is to strive to be like Christ, to do as the Christ did, to act like Christ did, and to think as Christ thought. "Look not every man on his own things, but every man also on the things of others. Let this mind be in you, which was also in Christ Jesus" (Phil. 2:4-5).

It means blessed assurance. Having become a Christian, one is now a child of God with all the family blessings (Rom. 8:16-17; 1 John 3:2). He now has the confidence that God will hear his prayer (1 John 5:14), he is assured that God will be with him (Rom. 8:31-32), he has the hope of heaven (1 John 2:25; 2 Tim. 4:7-8).

Yes, it means much to be a Christian! Have you become one (Mark 16:16; Acts 2:38)? Are you living faithfully (1 Cor. 15:58)?

What Doth The Lord Require Of Thee?

(Micah 6:8)

This is one of the great questions in the Scriptures. The prophet, Micah, represents the people as asking him to tell them how to appease the offended Lord, and to obtain his favor. He represents the people as asking, "Shall I come before him with burnt offering with calves of a year old? Will the Lord be pleased with thousands of rams? With ten thousands of rivers of oil? Shall I give my firstborn for my transgression? The fruit of my body for the sin of my soul?" (vv. 6-7). Then, in verse 8, the prophet answers in his own person the questions in verses 6 and 7 under the heading, "What doth the Lord require of thee?"

I Observe Some General Facts In This Question

The Lord will forgive those who have offended him. The prophet depicts Israel as asking, "What does the Lord require?" These were God's children who had proven unfaithful.

The Lord has requirements for his people. These requirements are established by the Lord. He is the one who has been sinned against and he has the right to determine what man must do to be forgiven. The Lord's requirements are never impossible for man to comply with. John states that his commandments are not grievous (1 John 5:3).

The Lord's requirements are precise and exacting. Man is never to be left in doubt as to what the Lord requires. This principle is quite evident throughout the Scriptures. The prophet stated what the Lord required with exactness: "to do justly, and to love mercy, and to walk humbly with thy God."

There is a personal obligation to these requirements. ". . . and what doth the Lord require of thee?" The emphasis is upon "thee." Requirements must be met by the individual. They are without respect of persons. The king and queen, the rich and the poor have the same requirements (Acts 10:34-35).

The requirements are the same in principle in all the ages, but the commandments that must be followed to produce these principles have varied in God's dealings with man. What constituted doing justly for the Israelites is not the same in every respect for the Christian. The Israelites were to follow the law of Moses with its ceremonies while the Christian is under the law of Christ (Jas. 1:25).

The requirements are of the external and internal nature. Though they be basically internal, the external must not be denied. The Israelite was to bring his sacrifice to God; however, it was to be something more than a formal service. Formal obedience or sacrifice is no good without the heart. In this age we are to worship God in spirit and in truth (John 4:23-24). There are always two sides of every act of obedience. We must do what God has required, and we must do it from the proper spirit or heart. Obedience without love is nothing. "And though I bestow all my goods to feed the poor, and though I give my body to be burned, and have not charity (or love), it profiteth me nothing" (1 Cor. 13:3). Again, "For in Jesus Christ neither circumcision availeth any thing, nor uncircumcision; but faith which worketh by love" (Gal. 5:6).

What Doth The Lord Require Of Thee?

Do Justly. This involves the fairly demanded duties both toward God and toward men. Doing justly requires that rectitude and uprightness should characterize us in all our relationships. We are not to seek to damage the reputation of another. The "Golden Rule" is to be acted upon (Matt. 7:12). We are unjust in dealings with God when we withhold time, wealth, and influence which we are able to devote to him. Think about this brethren!

Love Mercy. This involves not only showing mercy, but also loving it. Mercy is more than justice, just as a "good man" is more than a righteous man. The parable of the good Samaritan demonstrates one who shows mercy (Luke 10:30-37). Here was one who became involved in the need of another. He didn't put the man in the ditch and leave him half dead, but he certainly did what he could to get him out and relieve his pain. So many of our deeds seem to lack the element of mercy. We need to be willing to go beyond the strict rights which others may claim of us. Sweet mercy is nobility's true badge.

To walk humbly with thy God. To do such requires humble obedience to the will of God in all that he has for us to do. This truly involves faith in God (Heb. 11:6; Gal. 2:20; 2 Cor. 5:7). It is faith that motivates one to do what God has for him to do (Mark 16:16; Acts 2:38; Rev. 2:10). It signifies agreement. "How can two walk together except they agree?" (Amos 3:3). It means beautiful fellowship (1 John 1:6-7). Are you doing what the Lord requires of thee? Think! Doing what the Lord requires of thee is that which determines who will be in heaven. Heaven will be the home of those who have responded to God's requirements. It is so easy for us to manufacture what God requires rather than to listen to what is stated by God in the Scriptures. We should never lose sight of the fact that it is the Lord who does the requiring. We may wonder sometimes why he requires what he does. Even then, we must leave the "why" with the Lord and be content with doing what he says!

What Is Jesus To You?

There is nothing selfish in the principles of Christianity. One Christian cannot rejoice over blessings conferred upon him that were not granted to others as Christians. Yet one's relation to Christ is individual and personal. I must concern myself with what he is to me. Everyone who has heard of Jesus can give an answer to this question. The answers may vary, but no one is exempted from the question. Even for him to mean nothing is something and this is the ungrateful answer some might give.

The subject is: What is Jesus to you or what does he mean to you? "Mean" is defined as "degree of importance in influence or effect." The effect Christ has on us may be contrary to what he would desire. What ought to make him dear to us often makes him mean less. He should mean happiness, peace, and hope to those who profess to follow him, but at times such is not the case. Be it understood that the failure is not with the Lord. The failure is in the hearts of men. Their halfhearted, conditional surrender to Christ is not sufficient to make him mean happiness, peace, and hope. Hence, to some Christ means:

Sorrow and Misery. The Rich Young Ruler is an example of this. "He went away sorrowful" (Matt. 19:22). Why did Jesus mean sorrow to him? He loved his possessions more than following Christ. There are two types of sorrow—godly and worldly (2 Cor. 7:10). It is good to have godly sorrow for such motivates repentance, but the sorrow of the world "worketh death." It has been said that a person is never the same after having knowledge of Christ. Obedience to him brings ultimate peace and hope, while rejection fosters sorrow and misery.

A Disappointment. To the majority, Christ meant a disappointment to his own people. "He came unto his own, and his own received him not" (John 1:11). By many he was labeled a deceiver, fraud, and blasphemer. This was largely due to a misunderstanding of his mission. In John 6:66, we read, "From that time many of his disciples went back, and walked no more with him." It is quite obvious that Christ didn't mean much to these who turned from him. Having heard him speak of their obligation to eat of his body and drink of his blood, they doubtlessly experienced disappointment in his teaching and his mission—"they walked no more with him." Some now in coming to Christ are disappointed. The disappointment is no fault of the Christ. Through faulty teaching, some have been led to expect things that Christ has never promised. Their disappointment stems from lack of teaching or incorrect instruction that has created a misunderstanding of his mission.

A Burden. How can Christ become a burden to one? When one knows enough about Christ and his word to realize that it is true and the love of the world keeps enticing him, it is possible to have just enough religion for it to be burdensome. One may know what Christ expects and what is right, but yield to the pull of the undercurrent of a sinful world to follow its lustful pleasures. Be it understood that Christ brings happiness and peace; however, these come with wholehearted acceptance, not half-hearted obedience. In his beautiful invitation, Christ said, "Come unto me, all ye that labour and are heavy laden, and I will give you rest. Take my yoke upon you, and learn of me: for I am meek and lowly in heart: and ye shall find rest unto your souls. For my yoke is easy, and my burden is light" (Matt. 11:28-30). We need to have the attitude and disposition of Paul, "I am crucified with Christ: nevertheless I live; yet not I, but Christ liveth in me: and the life which I now live in the flesh I live by the faith of the Son of God, who loved me, and gave himself for me" (Gal. 2:20).

For Emergency Only. In sorrow, sickness, or bereavement, Jesus is turned to, but not before such things occur. Christ means to some people what a spare tire or life preserver means to them—something that is not turned to or called upon until in time of need or distress. Perhaps this thought is characterized by the account of the drowning man who is reputed to have prayed: "Lord, I have never called upon You for help before and if you save me this time, I'll never bother You anymore." Certainly, Christians are to look to the Lord in times of distress, but this is not the only time. He is to mean something more to us than "For Emergency Only."

Friend, what does Jesus really mean to you? Why don't you pause long enough now to truly answer the question? What does the inventory of your heart reveal? Remember, he desires to mean happiness, peace, and hope. The failure is not with Jesus if these things are not found in our lives. We need to examine our faith in the word of God!

What Motivates You?

Cause and effect are very prevalent in our course of life. There are definite principles that prompt or cause us to act. Such involves the subject of motivation. Webster defines "motivation" as "a motivating; a providing of a motive; inducement." Our thoughts, words, and deeds are to an extent governed and controlled by motivation. Motive is extremely important in being pleasing unto God. In many respects this is one of the unique features of the kingdom of God and of our being acceptable in his sight. The world lays emphasis upon "getting the job done." In many cases, an employee might please his employer by adequately completing the assigned task regardless of the motive that was in his heart. We are aware of the fact that exceptions to this statement might be found in the business world, but there are absolutely no exceptions to the principle in the kingdom of God. One must be guided by the proper spirit or motive to be pleasing in the sight of God. It is not enough just to act! What is in your heart? What motivated you to act?

Jesus said: "Take heed that ye do not your alms before men, to be seen of them: otherwise ye have no reward of your Father which is in heaven" (Matt. 6:1). Again, "And when thou prayest, thou shalt not be as the hypocrites are: for they love to pray standing in the synagogues and in the corners of the streets, that they may be seen of men" (Matt. 6:5). Was it right and proper to pray and give alms? Certainly so! The act was not condemned. Jesus was condemning their motive. They were doing what they did "to be seen of men." They were not motivated by the proper spirit. If we ever hope to be pleasing in the sight of God, we must give great heed to the motive in our hearts. Paul wrote, "Some indeed preach Christ even of envy and strife; and some also of good will: the one preach of contention, not sincerely, supposing to add affliction to my bonds: but the other of love, knowing that I am set for the defence of the gospel" (Phil. 1:15-17). Two classes of preachers are mentioned. Both classes preached Christ!

The difference was in the motivation! Envy, strife, contention, and insincerity characterized the one class. On the other hand, good will and love were the noble motivations of the other. What a difference motivation can make!

There are false and unholy motivations that can control us. It is quite possible to act through a motive of:

Spite. This is a rather small word that is very potent. It is defined as "dislike or hatred for another person, with a wish to annoy, anger, or defeat; petty malice." When some people are told something is wrong, it is possible that some go ahead to perform the act in spiteful rebellion to those who pointed it out to them. How many times this has been practiced by young people who were rebelling at parental authority! Congregations have been known to have had their beginning out of the motivation of spite. These are composed of individuals who opposed the truth and were determined to have their way in spiteful rejection of the truth. I once knew a brother who gave heavily when a preacher of his liking preached and refused to contribute when it was not to his liking. It is certainly a shameful motivation to do something simply to show your brethren that it can be done. Some years ago, I read a letter in which a brother was lamenting the action of brethren in dividing a congregation. He commented that it was done through "spit." Like mine, his proof reading left much to be desired. He doubtlessly meant "spite," but it is possible that he wasn't too far off target.

Convenience. With some folks, it is simply the more convenient thing for them to do or teach what they do. They sometimes inherit a situation and for convenience, they do what they do. Some preachers in particular congregations are doing and saying certain things because they can't stay there and do and say otherwise. They are motivated by convenience rather than an open minded spirit of love for the truth. Such people are to be pitied! Whoever it might be, God knows their hearts and is always aware of their motive (Gal. 6:7-9).

Novelty. The spirit of novelty has its effect upon prompting people to act. As some come into the kingdom of God, it is a new thing to them that thrills them as a new toy might do to a child. They appear zealous and eager! For a while, there isn't enough that they can do or find to do. But later, they are about as cold as they were hot some time before. Perhaps they are like the frozen cat that the veterinarian revived by giving it gasoline. The cat jumped up and ran brilliantly around and over the room. Then it fell over. You are to ask, "Was it dead?" No, it simply ran out of gas! Novelty is a poor motivation and substitution for conversion. We soon run out of gas. Paul wrote of the proper motivation, "For in Jesus Christ neither circumcision availeth any thing, nor uncircumcision; but faith which worketh by love" (Gal. 5:6). ". . . and though I give my body to be burned, and have not charity, it profiteth me nothing" (1 Cor. 13:3).

What Offends You?

There are various definitions of the word "offend." We are thinking of Webster's definition: "3: to cause to feel vexation or resentment usu. by violation of what is proper or fitting." It may be said that what offends an individual largely denotes the character of that person. The immoral filth that is so prevalent in the world does not offend or disturb numbers of people. They can even laugh and revel in pornography, nudity, and acts of sexual immorality. They accept profanity and lewd recitations without any feeling of resentment or vexation. Perhaps Jeremiah confronted this attitude when he wrote, "Were they ashamed when they had committed abomination? Nay, they were not ashamed, neither could they blush: therefore they shall fall among them that fall: at the time that I visit them they shall be cast down, saith the Lord" (Jer. 6:15; 8:12). Though the word "offended" is not mentioned, doesn't the phrase, "they were not ashamed, neither could they blush" convey the same thought?

John the Baptist sent messengers to Jesus asking, "Art thou he that should come, or do we look for another?" Jesus concluded his reply by saying, "And blessed is he, whosoever shall not be offended in me" (Matt. 11:6). From this statement, it is apparent that Jesus knew that there would be those who would be offended in him. He promises a blessing to those who would not let this happen to them. In the night in which he was betrayed, Jesus said to his disciples, "All ye shall be offended because of me this night: for it is written, I will smite the shepherd, and the sheep of the flock shall be scattered abroad. But after I am risen again, I will go before you into Galilee. Peter answered and said unto him, Though all men shall be offended because of thee, yet will I never be offended" (Matt. 26:31-33). That which followed was the threefold denial that Peter made of Jesus which suggested that he was offended above others in Christ. The scribes and Pharisees were offended in Christ when he refused to follow their traditions of washing hands, etc. "Then came his disciples, and said unto him, Knowest thou that the Pharisees were offended, after they heard this saying?" He had spoken the truth and offered no apology for it. "But he answered and said, Every plant, which my heavenly Father hath not planted, shall be rooted up" (Matt. 15:11-15).

It is quite evident that when Jesus lived on earth many people were offended in him. We should never be surprised to find people today who are offended in Christ. There are those who are offended in what he taught. He taught that only few would be saved (Matt. 7:13-14). The few are those who believe in him and are baptized for the remission of their sins (Mark 16:16; Acts 2:38). He only built one church (Matt. 16:18), and the saved are added to it in obedience to his gospel (Acts 2:47). Jesus never taught that one has the right to his own belief and the church of his choice. All of this is offensive to the broadminded of our day. They want a Christ that doesn't offend them and have set about to manufacture such in refusing the Christ revealed in the Scriptures.

We should never be ashamed of the gospel of Christ. We should defend it and not be offended at the truth regardless of the circumstances. When faithful brethren endure offences for the cause of Christ, those who are faithful in Christ should also be offended by the ungodly actions. I believe Paul had such in mind when he wrote, "Who is weak, and I am not weak? Who is offended, and I burn not?" (2 Cor. 11:29). Evidently, he burned with indignation when the faithful were mistreated and his heart went out to them.

When Christ and the truth are abused, God's people should be offended at such action. However, such is not always the case. In fact, there are occasions when some who profess to be Christians become offended when the false teachers and perverters of the truth are opposed. They are more concerned with feelings and sentiments than they are for truth being upheld. Also, there are projects and human institutions that Christians endorse. We are not saying that they are wrong or that they have no right to exist. However, we must realize that they are not the church and they must never have priority over the church that Jesus built and for which he died. But here is the thing that is disturbing—let someone offer some criticism over how these projects or institutions are conducted and observe how brethren become offended by their remarks. These same people have been known to calmly accept criticism of the Lord and his church, but such is not the case when fault is found with their school or some other human institution. A faithful gospel preacher recently mentioned to me that he had offered some words of disfavor regarding some practices of a college that brethren support. The elder, to whom he mentioned such, according to his words, went into orbit. He was gravely offended that anyone would question practices of this college. Would he have been so affected if this were spoken to him about the church? He has never been known to be! What offends you, my brother?

What Was I, That I Could Withstand God?

"What was I, That I could withstand God?" (Acts 11:17). These words were asked of the apostle Peter to the Jews, "they of the circumcision" who contended with him regarding his preaching to the Gentile household of Cornelius. In Acts 10, we read of the household of Cornelius receiving the word of God. An angel of the Lord appeared unto Cornelius and directed him to send for Peter for "he shall tell thee what thou oughtest to do." When Peter came to Caesarea and the house of Cornelius he "wentest in to men uncircumcised (Gentiles), and didst eat with them" (Acts 11:3). The gospel was preached to the Gentiles for the first time (Acts 15:7-9). On Peter's visit to Jerusalem, the Jews contended with him concerning his work with the Gentiles. He rehearsed the matter from the beginning, relating how God had given them the like gift as he did unto the apostles, and then spoke these words, "What was I, that I could withstand God?"

In speaking these words, Peter was using them to justify his actions. God had given Peter and the six Jewish brethren, whom he had brought with him from Joppa, evidences that the Gentiles had a right to receive the gospel as well as the Jews. Hence, Peter was saying, "What could I do other than assist the Gentiles in obeying, since it was God's will that they be permitted to do so?" "Withstand" is defined as "to stand against; to oppose or resist, with either physical or moral force." It is a grave and tragic undertaking for men to withstand God.

The Phrase Might Be Uttered To Signify . . .

Man's weakness and God's strength. What was Peter's view as compared to God's design? What is man compared to God? The prophet wrote, "For my thoughts are not your thoughts, neither are your ways my ways, saith the Lord. For as the heavens are higher than the earth, so are my ways higher than your ways and my thoughts than your thoughts" (Isa. 55:8-9). But man has ever been slow in recognizing his position before God.

Man's submission and God's authority. Peter did not desire to oppose God's will. One should never attempt to withstand God. His will is for our own good! "Not my will but thine be done" should characterize our existence. We must reverence the thought that God is withstood when his word, as preached by his servants is refused (1 Sam. 8:7; Luke 10:16).

An explanation for one's religious activities. Why did you obey the gospel? One very pertinent and scriptural reason was that one did not desire to withstand God. To refuse to obey is to withstand or fight against God (Mark 16:16). Why are you a Christian? The answer again might well involve the fact that man did not desire to oppose God and his will. God would have all men to be Christians. Becoming a Christian involves obeying the will of God (Acts 11:26; 26:28). Why are you faithful in worship and striving to live like Christ? This again, involves withstanding or refusing to withstand God! Those who refuse to forsake the assembling of themselves together show respect to the will of God (Heb. 10:25) and do not wish to withstand God. We would that all members of the church of Christ could appreciate this principle as they should. Some evidently feel that they are only withstanding the elders, preachers, or some other human being by refusing to assemble and live godly lives. When we refuse the will of God in any respect, we are withstanding God.

What Was I To Withstand God? I Was:

Ungrateful. Considering all the blessings of God, the least we could do is to submit to his will. Jesus asked, "Where are the nine?" Only one leper possessed enough gratitude for his cleansing to come back and thank Christ. When men continually withstand God, they are in the same ungrateful attitude as the nine. God would have us give thanks for all things (1 Thess. 5:18). We should always be thankful for the privilege of doing his will and never be so ungrateful as to attempt to withstand God.

Foolish. The rich farmer omitted God from his plans. There was no recognition of God in his prosperity. God addressed him as "thou fool" (Luke 12:20). Two builders are mentioned in Matthew 7:24-27. One was wise and the other foolish. The wise builder obeyed the will of God and did not withstand God's will. The foolish was quite to the contrary. He failed to obey after having heard the will of God. He was the foolish builder. It is foolish to deny the will of God or refuse to obey such. The will of God has always been for man's happiness. Look at the gross unhappiness in the world! How many are truly obeying God's word? Foolish people!

Let's never attempt to withstand God, but always endeavor to do his will in all things and in all times.

Where Is It Condemned?

We were told by "an elder" of the Christian church that he was still looking for the Scripture that condemned the use of mechanical music in worship. By Scripture, he had in mind a particular passage that used the words, "thou shalt not" or a thought kindred to such. In the course of the conversation, he was told that the passage that condemns it in the New Testament is the passage that also condemns infant baptism, the burning of incense, the practice of polygamy, and many other items that he probably views as being unscriptural. The passage is, "Whosoever transgresseth, and abideth not in the doctrine of Christ, hath not God. He that abideth in the doctrine of Christ, he hath both the Father and the Son" (2 John 9). The doctrine or teaching of Christ is expressed in the New Testament. By commandment, apostolic example, or necessary inference, the authority of Christ is established. Anything that is not in the doctrine of Christ is condemned by the principle that we abide in the doctrine of Christ. The doctrine of Christ authorizes singing (Eph. 5:19; Col. 3:16). There is no authorization in the doctrine of Christ for the use of mechanical music in acceptable worship to God.

Though doubtlessly inconsistent at times, this gentleman operated on the basis that the Scriptures only condemned by expressly stating that a practice was wrong. He has never truly realized the power of the silence of the Scriptures. We are called upon to respect what God has said and also respect what he has not said! The word of God reveals the mind of God toward man (1 Cor. 2:10-13). What God wants or desires of man is stated in the Scriptures. The things written aforetime for our learning in the Old Testament emphasize the value of respecting the silence of God's word. Cain did not respect it and his unlawful offering was rejected of God (Gen. 4:5; Heb. 11:4). Nadab and Abihu did that which God "commanded them not" and were punished of God. They offered "strange fire" that was an infringement upon the silence of the Scriptures (Lev. 10:1-2). Had this gentleman been present, his approach to how the Scriptures condemn wouldn't have saved Nadab and Abihu. He would have said go ahead without respect for the silence of the Scriptures that gave no authorization for the "strange fire."

I firmly believe that the most singular difference and exacting distinction between faithful churches of Christ today and other religious groups concerns respecting the silence of the Scriptures. This principle constituted the difference between Martin Luther and Ulrich Zwingli. Both reformers contended that the Scriptures were the authority in religious matters. However, Luther contended that they were permitted to do anything other than that which the Scriptures expressly condemned. On the other hand, Zwingli advocated that they were only permitted to do those things which the Scriptures authorized. One might see that Zwingli advocated a respect for the silence of the Scriptures which Luther failed to do. This principle of respecting the silence of the Scriptures and only doing that which is authorized accounts for much of the distinction between what we recognize as "liberals" and "conservatives" in the church today. The liberals contend that "such and such" is not expressly condemned by the Scriptures; hence, it is all right to practice such. The faithful reason in respect to 2 John 9 and many other passages that "such and such" is condemned by the fact it is not authorized by the Scriptures by commandment, apostolic example, or necessary inference. This is the plea of truth manifested in the potent phrase, "Speak where the Bible speaks and be silent where the Bible is silent."

A Failure to Respect the Silence of the Scriptures Is A Rejection Of...

Authority (Matt. 28:18). Authority is the right to command. If men are permitted to do other than that which is authorized, how can there be submission to true authority? We have authority for singing (Eph. 5:19). The expression of one thing is the exclusion of all others. Hence, Ephesians 5:19 authorizes singing and excludes the use of mechanical music.

The Existence of a Pattern (Heb. 8:5). If one contends that an act can be performed that is not condemned, then the value of a pattern is denied. A pattern is what one desires. It is not what else will be all right. The sum total of what God says about any subject constitutes the pattern that we are to follow to be acceptable with him. When we respect the existence of a pattern, we respect the silence of the Scriptures.

Walking By Faith. "So then faith cometh by hearing, and hearing by the word of God" (Rom. 10:17). It is impossible to walk by faith and do something God has not authorized. To deny and fail to respect the silence of the Scriptures is to ignore the value of walking by faith. Let us do what God says and not what he hasn't said (Heb. 12:25).

When Is One Guilty of Being Factious?

People are very good at giving their own definition to words and contending that the Scriptures support their definitions. We have said many times that so much depends upon the definition that we give to words. Many times there would be less tension, enmity, and heartaches among brethren if they would come to a scriptural definition of the terms they use and be consistent in the use of the terms before proceeding with any discussion. Where is the individual that has not at one time or another condemned someone for using a definition for a word that he would approve in himself on other occasions?

These thoughts are important in determining just who is or when a man is factious. Now, are we talking about factious in God's sight or some definition that we might attach to the word or even a definition from *Webster's Dictionary*? According to one conception of the word, a factious man is one who causes a disturbance by vehemently objecting to certain matters or procedures that others might tolerate or condone. Those who tolerate such procedures might view the objector as being one who is factious! And well might he be in the light of that definition! But would such a person be wrong in the sight of God or be a factious man before God? Not necessarily! Suppose he sees where the word of God is being perverted or neglected and conscientiously cries out for his brethren to return to the Old Paths and speak where the Bible speaks and be silent where it is silent. On the basis that he is right in his contention, he would be considered faithful rather than factious in the sight of God. But many people find it convenient to ignore this principle with their judgment of others and yet contend for the same on other occasions when their actions are questioned. Is a man factious today when he speaks out against unscriptural practices which are being disguised under the heading of unity in diversity? Certainly not in the sight of God! However, in the sight of brethren who endorse such, he might well be branded as factious on the basis that he objects to and opposes what they believe to be all right.

W.E. Vine writes in his *Expository Dictionary of New Testament Words* concerning *erithia* which is translated faction that factious "denotes ambition, self-seeking, rivalry, self-will being an underlying idea in the word; hence it denotes party making. It is derived, not for *eris*, strife, but from *erithos*, a hireling; hence the meaning of seeking to win followers, 'factions,' so rendered in the R.V. of 2 Corinthians 12:20, A.V., 'strifes'; not improbably the meaning here is rivalries, or base ambitions." From these statements it would appear that the factious man is one who through self-will, etc. seeks to win followers in a manner of party making. The underlying conception is that he does such by "speaking perverse things" (Acts 20:30) or things contrary to the will of God. So it is reduced down like everything else is in the sight of God as to who is preaching the truth and who is not! When a man is contending for the truth of God's word and has the truth, that man is not a factious man in the sight of God. We need to be alert to one who is factual in the Scriptures and not deem him factious when he desires that the truth be followed.

Some time ago I read the charges that two elders in a congregation brought against the third elder. They contended that he was factious and never related any falsehood or perversion of the word of God that he was guilty of teaching. Actually he was endeavoring to encourage the other elders along with himself to do their duty as shepherds of the flock in the light of the word of God. He may have been factious in their eyes but where is such a one condemned in the word of God? Mind you, here was a case where the two elders would endorse a brother in a liberal congregation for objecting to the procedures when most of the congregation might deem him factious. They would refer to such a brother as being faithful for standing up for "a thus saith the Lord" and then turn around and condemn a fellow elder in the congregation wherein they served as being factious or a heretic (Tit. 3:10) who simply pleads for them to follow a principle of truth that they were failing to do in the word of God.

It seems with some of us, the difference in our eyes of being factious or faithful is based upon "who is wearing the shoes." If our sins are pointed out, that man is factious in so doing, but when we do it and have to stand up for the truth then we are faithful. Selah! We could easily say more if space permitted, but we conclude with this observation: If contending for the faith makes one factious, we ought to endeavor to be so more and more. "Beloved, when I gave all diligence to write unto you of the common salvation, it was needful for me to write unto and exhort you that ye should earnestly contend for the faith which was once delivered unto the saints" (Jude 3). May we keep on doing it!

When It Comes To Push and Shove

This is a phrase that is often spoken and it conveys some thoughtful considerations. These words suggest action and determination in the lives of individuals. We have encountered members of the church who leave the impression that they are strong in the Lord. However, when they are called upon to stand for their convictions, they display an entirely different attitude that is void of conviction. In other words, so many of us are strong in the Lord until it comes to the time for pushing and shoving. It is so much easier to talk a good faith than it is to practice one. As one endeavors to follow Christ, there will be trying times and times when we will be called upon to declare upon whose side we are. "Then said Jesus unto his disciples, if any man will come after me, let him deny himself, and take up his cross, and follow me. For whosoever will save his life shall lose it: and whosoever will lose his life for my sake shall find it" (Matt. 16:24). Again, "No man can serve two masters: for either he will hate the one, and love the other; or else he will hold to the one, and despise the other. Ye cannot serve God and mammon" (Matt. 6:24). Jesus said that there was a cross for men to bear as they followed him. He never promised to remove the cross. He makes us aware of it and calls upon us to bear it.

The Scriptures speak of those who professed to follow Christ, but when they were called upon to push and shove, they chose not to do so. The disciples mentioned in John 6 were of this classification. Having heard Jesus speak of their responsibility to eat of his flesh and drink of his blood, there were those who considered such to be a hard saying. "From that time many of his disciples went back, and walked no more with him" (John 6:66). They didn't have the spirit that would prompt them to be a part of pushing and shoving. They wanted no part of such. These may have been following Jesus for the loaves and fishes. Jesus said of some: "Verily, verily, I say unto you, Ye seek me, not because ye saw the miracles, but because ye did eat of the loaves, and were filled" (John 6:26). Evidently, they wanted what would come with little or no effort on their part. They wanted no part of pushing and shoving as a philosophy of life.

Well, how about Demas? "For Demas hath forsaken me, having loved this present world, and is departed unto Thessalonica" (2 Tim. 4:10). This is the same Demas of whom Paul had spoken with admiration on previous occasions (Col. 4:14; Phile. 24). As Paul wrote the book of 2 Timothy, he did so as a prisoner in Rome. No doubt, if he ever needed true companionship, it was such a time as this. Was he able to count on Demas? No! "For Demas hath forsaken me, having loved this present world." Some commentators would have us believe that Demas didn't depart from the faith. He was only guilty of forsaking Paul. I believe he also departed from Jesus on the basis that he loved this present world. I don't read in the Scriptures of individuals being true to Jesus and at the same time loving this present world. John tells us to love neither the world nor the things that are in the world and, if we do, they have not the love of God in them (1 John 2:15-17). Whether you accept this thought or not, it is quite definite that he had forsaken a brother who had need for him. When the time of pushing and shoving arose, he chose to forsake Paul. That was his answer to what he would do when it comes to push and shove.

I recall occasions when, as a young preacher, I was told of things that needed to be corrected and people who needed to be rebuked. Without thinking thoroughly upon the matter, I have permitted myself to be engaged in doing so. When there were brethren upset by the rebukes, those who had encouraged it to be done washed their hands with Pilate saying they had no part of it. There was the proverbial limb that was cut off behind me. When faced with unfavorable results, they wanted no part when it came to push and shove. Through the years, I have tried to use the wisdom of telling others when they suggest it needs to be done, let's do it together and not evade the responsibility of pushing and shoving when the need arises. Some years ago, we knew a brother in Miami whose favorite expression was, "I'm set for a defense." When things arose that required the push and shove, it was obvious that he was "set on a fence" rather than for the defense of truth.

Let's not be pessimistic! The Scriptures reveal those who knew the meaning of when it comes to push and shove. Read with me from Romans 16: "Greet Priscilla and Aquila my helpers in Christ Jesus: Who have for my life laid down their own necks, unto whom not only I give thanks, but also all the churches of the Gentiles" (Rom. 16:3-4). What had they done? "Who have for my life laid down their own necks." When it came to push and shove, Priscilla and Aquila stood firm for the truth and for Paul, a servant of truth. Whenever and whatever the occasion, we need always to be ready to push and shove for the progress of truth and never cowardly oppose it. How about it? Are we doing it?

When Right Becomes Wrong

Few words are more often used than the words right and wrong. The words, or their equivalents, are used by all persons and nations. There is a great difference when deciding what is right and what is wrong. Ancient Sparta encouraged theft. Plato recommended the murder of weak and sickly children. He spoke of drunkenness at the feast of Bacchus as proper and even praiseworthy. Stoics commended suicide as a cardinal virtue. The obligation of marriage was generally disregarded by the ancient philosophers.

Man has definitely needed a standard to determine what is right and wrong. "O Lord, I know that the way of man is not in himself: it is not in man that walketh to direct his steps" (Jer. 10:23). God has given man the standard in the Scriptures inspired of God. "All Scripture is given by inspiration of God, and is profitable for doctrine, for reproof, for correction, for instruction in righteousness: that the man of God may be perfect, thoroughly furnished unto all good works" (2 Tim. 3:16-17). Right is that which is approved of God and regulated by the Scriptures. Wrong is anything contrary to the word of God. But what do we mean by the phrase, "when right becomes wrong"? The phrase seems to be definitely contradictory! Often individuals emphatically state that "right can't be wrong." Yet, there are some practices right in themselves but practiced under certain conditions and circumstances, they become wrong in the sight of God.

Right becomes wrong when liberty is used as a stumblingblock to others and offends the conscience of a weak brother. Paul stated this truth in discussing the eating of meat offered to idols (1 Cor. 8:7-13). The meat, which the apostle referred to, was that which had previously been offered in worship to idols. Such sacrificial meat was so plentiful that a Christian could hardly avoid using it unless he refrained from meat altogether. The strong brethren were made bold to eat such meat, contending that the idol could in no way contaminate it. Others, having less knowledge and not being able to shake off the power of old practices, could not free themselves from their former reverence for the idol. To such, the sacrificial meat was part of a real sacrifice and was contaminating. The truth was that the idol did not contaminate the meat, as those with knowledge contended, yet they were to respect the conscience of the brother whose conscience would be violated if he ate of meats sacrificed to idols. Thus, right became wrong if it wounded the weak conscience of the brother for whom Christ died (v.13). It would appear the principle may be applied to many modern amusements and indulgences which the strong regard as harmless today but which they refrain from practicing less they endanger the weaker lives (Rom. 14:21).

Right may be wrong when something morally right is assumed and practiced as a religious practice. Some things such as stealing, lying, and adultery are immoral. Anything immoral is both morally and religiously wrong. There are some things right morally but religiously wrong. It is morally right to eat fruit; however, Adam and Eve sinned by so doing. Why? Because that which was morally right was in that incident a transgression of God's law. It is morally right to wash hands before eating; however, in so doing the Pharisees and Scribes rejected the commandments of God. They added to the word of God and bound something religiously that God had never authorized (Mark 7:6-9). Many people have the idea that an act morally right is equally religiously right, but such is not so! Sprinkling water does not violate any moral law; however, when sprinkling is substituted for baptism, it is wrong. Within itself, instrumental music does not violate any moral law. On this basis, many say that they see no harm in using instrumental music in the worship. Looking at it from a moral viewpoint, it is not wrong, but religiously it is. Why? Because we are taught in the Bible to sing and there is no authority in the New Testament for the use of mechanical music in worship unto God (Eph. 5:19; Col. 3:16; 2 John 9-11). Titles for honor and exaltation are not morally wrong, but they are wrong when used in a religious sense (Matt. 23:9; Ps. 111:9).

Right becomes wrong when civil and divine laws conflict. The word of God teaches God's children to "be subject unto the higher powers" (Rom. 13:1-7). We are to be obedient to the laws of the land (1 Pet. 2:13-17). This is right in the sight of God. But what if the law of the land would have Christians to violate the law of God? "Then Peter and the other apostles answered and said, We ought to obey God rather than men" (Acts 5:29). This was the reply given to those authorities who were telling them to no longer preach in the name of Jesus Christ. In such a case, the right of obeying civil authority had become wrong. We must always remember that we are only right as we have the approval of God and that approval comes from the authority of the Scriptures.

Wherefore Rebuke Them Sharply

"Wherefore rebuke them sharply, that they be sound in the faith" (Tit.1:13). These words were from the apostle Paul and directed to Titus concerning his work among the Cretians. Let us observe a few of the words in this admonition that we might appreciate it more.

Rebuke. This was the action that Titus was to take. Webster defines the word as "to address in sharp disapproval; reprimand." There is a definite place for rebuking in the pattern for gospel preaching. Paul charged Timothy, "Preach the word; be instant in season and out of season; reprove, rebuke, exhort with all longsuffering and doctrine" (2 Tim. 4:2). Preaching to rebuke is as needful as preaching to reprove and exhort. Again, Paul admonished Timothy in regard to elders that sin, "Them that sin rebuke before all, that others also may fear" (1 Tim. 5:20). A gospel preacher that shuns to rebuke, when rebuking is needed, does not properly comprehend the work of an evangelist.

Them. Naturally "them" refers to those who were to be the objects of the rebuke. Beginning with verse 10, we note to whom the "them" refers. "For there are many unruly and vain talkers and deceivers, specially they of the circumcision: whose mouths must be stopped, who subvert whole houses, teaching things which they ought not, for filthy lucre's sake. One of themselves, even a prophet of their own, said, The Cretians are always liars, evil beasts, slowbellies." Paul agrees with the Cretian prophet by saying, "The witness is true." Here were individuals evidently in fellowship with the Lord's church that certainly were a long way from being righteous. To stop these was a part of the things that were "wanting" in Crete, as well as ordaining elders in every city who would be able to "convince the gainsayers" and be a part of rebuking such false teachers as occasions arose. The rebuke is the offensive weapon against those who are teaching things which they ought not. If their mouths are to be stopped, rebuking is the means that God has ordained to bring about such an end.

Sharply. This adverb refers to the intensity of the rebuke. It wasn't to be administered mildly. "Rebuke them sharply" was the admonition given Titus. The souls of these who needed rebuking were truly at stake. What they were doing was affecting others. The souls of others could be led astray by their false teaching. It was a severe matter that needed sharp rebuking. The false teacher cannot save himself or anyone else that heeds the false doctrine that he propagates. No sin is more condemned in the word of God than the sin of false teaching.

That They May Be Sound in the Faith. These words constitute the purpose of the rebuking. "That they may be sound in the faith" was the desired end of the rebuking. The "they" must refer to those who were teaching things which they ought not to have been teaching. When one considers the individuals mentioned in verses 10-12, he might be prone to say nothing could help them. Such was not the view of the Holy Spirit. The Spirit directed Paul to tell Titus to rebuke them that they may be sound in the faith, that they might cease their erroneous practices and follow the truth. The means to the end was rebuking.

So many in the Lord's church have never realized the value of the proper rebuke. They are prone to view it as lack of love for the one rebuked and to contend that the one rebuking does not have the spirit of Christ. They fail to appreciate the rebuke as a God-given instrumentality to bring soundness in an individual's spiritual life. These people needed to be sound in the faith. I definitely believe that they professed to be a part of the faith, but were unsound in the faith. Perhaps some would not heed the rebuke and continue on in their unsoundness. The responsibility that Titus had was to rebuke them sharply. We are responsible before God in doing what God has for us to do and not that of determining the results. Of those who would not heed the rebuke, doubtlessly Paul wrote, "A man that is a heretic, after the first and second admonition, reject; knowing that he that is such is subverted, and sinneth, being condemned of himself" (Tit. 3:10-11). A person in error deserves the respect of receiving a good rebuke. He has the right to expect it from those who are faithful to God.

We should not weary of rebuking when it is needed, and the Lord's people should be optimistic toward the desired end—that the rebuke will bring about repentance that produces soundness in the faith. All of us need to adhere more closely to the word of God and trust less in the wisdom of men. Rather than thinking it will drive men away to rebuke them sharply, we should trust that it will make them sound in the faith. "Reprove not a scorner, lest he hate thee: rebuke a wise man, and he will love thee" (Prov. 9:8).

Who Wears the Shoes?

This may appear to be a rather strange title for a subject dealing with spiritual matters. One may even look upon the subject with amazement. What does such have to do with those things that would affect my soul? On the other hand, if we stop and think for a moment we find ourselves familiar with this phrase and the usage of it. People are inclined to play favorites and what they approve and condemn depends upon who the individuals are, or as our subject indicates, "Who wears the shoes?" Are you with me now? This deals with the subject of respect of persons or partiality that is condemned in the Scriptures. "But if ye have respect to persons, ye commit sin, and are convinced of the law as transgressors" (Jas. 2:9), and again, "I charge thee before God, and the Lord Jesus Christ, and the elect angels, that thou observe these things without preferring one before another, doing nothing by partiality" (1 Tim. 5:21). These and numerous other passages in God's word point us to the fact that we should not be governed by "who wears the shoes" in what we endorse or condemn.

The Shoes Should Not Make A Difference
When I Am Wearing Them. How often we see failures in others that we never recognize in ourselves We are given to approving

things in ourselves that we condemn in others. In our own eyes, we are guiltless while doing the same things which we abhor in others. "Therefore thou art inexcusable, O man, whosoever thou art that judgest: for wherein thou judgest another, thou condemnest thyself; for thou that judgest doest the same things" (Rom. 2:1). We should never be so naïve as to think that the shoes we wear grant us priorities to do things that are not permissible in God's word. By doing so we can find ourselves being hypocritical and portraying a poor example to those with whom we have contact. "For if a man think himself to be something, when he is nothing, he deceiveth himself. But let every man prove his own work, and then shall he have rejoicing in himself alone, and not in another" (Gal. 6:3-4). "But be ye doers of the word, and not hearers only, deceiving your own selves" (Jas. 2:21). We need to examine our lives and avoid being deceived into thinking that our lives or the shoes we wear grant us immunity from what we criticize in others.

When Those of My Family Wear Them. There have been occasions when individuals have condemned others and strongly denounced their behavior. They defended their actions by showing from the Scriptures that these people had sinned and violated the word of God. Amen. But wait a minute When some of their family practice the same sins, then things are different. With the same fervor with which they condemned others, they now attempt to justify those of their immediate family who are doing the same things. The difference is in who wears the shoes This scenario has been known regarding divorces and remarriage. Others were condemned until it came home to one's own family and then it's entirely different. This has been known in rearing children. Condemn others for their failure in rearing their children to behave, but you had better not say anything to them about their children or children in their family. There are many other categories or subject matters which would illustrate what we have in mind, but it still comes down to "Who wears the shoes?" "For I am come to set a man at variance against his father, and the daughter against her mother, and the daughter in law against her mother in law. And a man's foes shall be they of his own household. He that loveth father or mother more than me is not worthy of me: and he that loveth son or daughter more than me is not worthy of me" (Matt. 10:35-37).

When My Friends Wear Them. With few possible exceptions, all of us have friends. There are those in the church who we feel closer to and relate to more than to some others. We have been known to be irritated by some while others doing and saying the same things do not bother us. When our friends get out of step with the Lord, if we aren't exceedingly careful we are prone to justify them while we might condemn others who are practicing the same. We are faced again with the adage, "Who wears the shoes?" No one is denying having friends and feeling a fondness for them, but we should be cognizant of their failures and mistakes just as surely as we would be of others with whom we are not so friendly. Actually, a true friend is one who helps his friend overcome his mistakes and be penitent of them (when such is needful), rather than helping one to justify or deny them. There have been occasions when some individuals have spent considerable time in rebuking others for their conduct and then turn right around and give the silent treatment or even justification to their friends who engage in sins that are even more prevalent. Don't you feel that Paul was a friend of Peter, yet look at how Paul confronted Peter regarding his dissimulation: "But when Peter was come to Antioch, I withstood him to the face, because he was to be blamed. For before that certain came from James, he did eat with the Gentiles: but when they were come, he withdrew and separated himself, fearing them which were of the circumcision" (Gal. 2:11-12). Who wore the shoes did not deter Paul from doing what was needed in pointing out Peter's error. When such is needed whether it be friend or foe, "Wherefore rebuke them sharply, that they may be sound in the faith" (Tit. 1:13).

We need to be fair and honest with all men. Partiality and favoritism can cause us to lose our influence among others and even bring about the losing of our souls. Help us Lord!

Whom Shall We Please?

This constitutes a very great question. Everyone is constantly trying to please someone. Our very lives are fashioned around the one or ones whom we are endeavoring to please. Are we striving to please the right person or persons? This is a question that all of us should gravely consider The salvation of our souls is involved in the answer to this question. Whom should we strive to please?

Not Ourselves. Self is the person most individuals are striving most to please, and ordinarily, the last person whom they should strive to please. Writing to the saints at Rome, Paul admonished them, "We then that are strong ought to bear the infirmities of the weak, and not to please ourselves. Let every one of us please his neighbor for his good to edification. For even Christ pleased not himself; but, as it is written, The reproaches of them that reproached thee fell on me" (Rom. 15:1-3). There is a definite reason why Christians should not endeavor to please themselves. Self-pleasers have been the tragedy makers and the heart breakers of the ages. From the beginning of man's existence, the blackest of sins have been committed through man's effort to please himself. Furthermore, Christ pleased not himself: "even as the Son of man came not to be ministered unto, but to minister, and to give his life a ransom for many" (Matt. 20:28). Christ left us an example "that we should follow in his steps" (1 Pet. 1:21). Just think, if Christ had pleased himself, we would have no Savior. One is to deny self in following Christ (Matt. 16:24), and this attitude is to continue with him throughout his life as a follower of Christ.

Our Neighbor. "Let every one of us please his neighbor for his good to edification" (Rom. 15:2). The design or arrangement of Christ is to get us away from ourselves. To create in our hearts an interest in others is the surest way to get us away from ourselves. The statement is qualified. One should be alert to please his neighbor for his good to edification. There are folks who are pleased when others pamper them, but pleasing that pampers is not for one's ultimate good. It simply spoils them and will eventually present much heartache. Let us please our neighbor by loving him as ourself (Mark 12:29-31). Jesus taught the parable of the good Samaritan to teach just who is our neighbor and that he is to be ministered to when in need (Luke 10:30-37). We also please our neighbor in God's appointed way by building him up in character—"for his good to edification."

Our God. To please God and win his approval should be the paramount goal of our life. Regardless of what we might accomplish in this life, if we fail to please God, then our life here has been a failure. There are many people who are concerned about pleasing men and so unconcerned in reference to pleasing God. It appears that their first thought is in regard to pleasing self and men. This they readily do at the expense of disfavor with God. They evidently think that they can treat God in whatever way they might choose and at the same time stifle their consciences into believing that God will accept them.

Foremost in the hearts of the true servants of God has been their desire to please God and not man. Paul wrote, "But as we were allowed of God to be put in trust with the gospel, even so we speak; not as pleasing men, but God, which trieth our hearts" (1 Thess. 2:4). Again, "For do I now persuade men, or God? Or do I seek to please men? For if I yet pleased men, I should not be the servant of Christ" (Gal. 1:10). A preacher of the gospel who is more concerned about pleasing men than God is not fit to preach the gospel. No one should desire the displeasure of anyone, but when it comes to a matter of truth and error, the true servant of God has no alternative but to preach the truth regardless of the consequences. Many of the ills that are in the church of the Lord today have come about due to the fact that some have never really stopped to consider that they are to please God in preaching his truth rather than to court the approval of man and his desires.

Before Christ we must give an account. "For we must all appear before the judgment seat of Christ; that every one may receive the things done in his body, according to that he hath done, whether it be good or bad" (2 Cor. 5:10). To please God requires considerable effort in trust and obedience, but it will all be more than worthwhile in that day when we are called to give an account. How thankful will the righteous be that they pleased God in their life, that in that day they can stand approved of God. Have you stopped to consider just whom you are pleasing? The salvation of your soul might well depend upon your consideration of the question.

There are occasions when we decline to do what God desires for us to do. We offer explanations for our refusal, but what is the real explanation? Doesn't it evolve around the thought that we are more determined to please ourselves than God? God doesn't ask or expect impossible things of any of us. What he expects of us, we can perform. It is a lack of faith when we cry that he expects too much of us. Satan wants us to view God's commands in that manner. The real answer lies in our own selfishness in determination to please ourselves rather than wholeheartedly submitting to God. The next time you find yourself not doing what God wants you to do or not being where God wants you to be, ask yourself, "Who are you pleasing?"

Why Are Not All Prayers Answered?

This is a question that occupies the minds of many sincere praying people. A misunderstanding of this question has caused doubt in the faith of some. It has even caused some to cease praying due to the fact that they thought, "What's the use?" Others have been known to give up entirely because they felt their prayers were not answered. A misunderstanding of this question has also given oil for the fires of infidelity. We need a thorough understanding of the scriptural teaching concerning prayer. Like all biblical subjects, it has been abused and none of us is overburdened with faith in prayer. But let us consider:

Do we have the right to expect God to answer our prayers? In a definite statement, Peter wrote, "For the eyes of the Lord are over the righteous, and his ears are open unto their prayers: but the face of the Lord is against them that do evil" (1 Pet. 3:12). A lesson from creation emphasizes that God will answer prayers. If God took interest enough to create us, shouldn't the same interest be manifested in our cries of need now? There is also the lesson from redemption! Granted that God took interest enough in the race to redeem it, he must, in the very nature of things, love us enough to heed our cries. The father and son (child) relationship requires that God answer his children's prayers. Jesus stated in these words, "Or what man is there of you, whom if his son ask bread, will he give him a stone? Or if he ask a fish, will be give him a serpent? If ye then, being evil, know how to give good gifts unto your children, how much more shall your Father which is in heaven give good things to them that ask him?" (Matt. 7:9-11). Examples abound in the Scriptures of those whose prayers were answered by God. James refers to the prayers of Elijah saying, ". . . The effectual fervent prayer of a righteous man availeth much. Elijah was a man subject to like passions as we are, and he prayed earnestly that it might not rain: and it rained not on the earth by the space of three years and six months. And he prayed again, and the heaven gave rain, and the earth brought forth her fruit" (Jas. 5:16-18). Elijah was subject to like passions as we are! He was not above our condition of life. God heard and answered his prayer. God hears and answers the prayers of obedient children today. That's the lesson that God would have us learn from his reference to Elijah.

Why are some prayers not answered? Why aren't some of our requests granted?

The petitioner may not be a righteous person. The Scriptures teach that "the effectual fervent prayer of a righteous man availeth much" (Jas. 5:16). The righteous are those who keep the commandments of God (1 Pet. 3:12; Ps. 119:172). The righteous are those who are in the right spiritual condition. They have obeyed the gospel of Christ (Mark 16:16) and are living faithfully as children of God. We should stop to consider whether or not the prayer has come from a righteous heart. Under the Old Testament, there were occasions when the children of God were unrighteous and upon such occasions, God would not hear them (Isa. 1:15; 59:1-2).

The prayer is not effectual fervent, or one prayed in earnest. Remember that James said, "The effectual fervent prayer of a righteous man availeth much" (Jas. 5:16). A fervent prayer is one that is warm, earnest, and that comes from the heart. Elijah's prayer was one that was "prayed earnestly." For our prayer to be effectual and fervent, it must be prayed in faith (Jas. 1:6-7). We must believe that God is and that he hears and answers his children's prayers.

We might expect God to do it all, or expect prayer to do it all. Jesus taught his disciples to pray for daily bread, but he also taught in the words of the Spirit, "if any would not work, neither should he eat" (2 Thess. 3:10). God feeds the robins, but he doesn't put the worm in their mouths. If we depend upon our prayers alone to suffice and make no effort ourselves, our life will be a delusion. Prayer "availeth much" but doesn't suffice for the whole of our existence before God. God's people must prayerfully work at being faithful in the service of God. Have we expected our prayers to avail too much?

To grant the request might not be best for us. Some times, God answers by not answering. He answers by saying "No"! I have many things in this life for which to be thankful. One of these is that God has not responded in granting some of my foolish requests. At the time, they did not appear foolish, but later, it was obvious that they were. God knows what is best, far more than we do! Paul asked the Lord three times to remove his thorn in the flesh. Rather than it being removed, he was told, "My grace is sufficient for thee" (2 Cor. 12:7-9). We need to believe that God will answer our prayers. We need to pray often and we need to check the circumstances before we contend that God has failed us!

Why Didn't Paul Heal Epaphroditus?

A few evenings ago the phone rang and a brother was calling with a Bible question. It seems he was teaching the book of Philippians in a neighboring city and desired some help regarding Epaphroditus who is introduced to Bible readers in the second chapter of Philippians. It appears that Epaphroditus had become seriously ill after coming to Rome to be with Paul. "For indeed he was sick nigh unto death: but God had mercy on him; and not on him only, but on me also, lest I should have sorrow upon sorrow" (Phil. 2:27). "Because for the work of Christ he was nigh unto death, not regarding his life, to supply your lack of service toward me" (Phil. 2:30). The teacher was anticipating being asked in his class, "Why didn't Paul heal Epaphroditus as he had done for others in the New Testament?" Think of the case of the father of Publius that had occurred some time before on the island called Melita: "And it came to pass, that the father of Publius lay sick of a fever and of a bloody flux: to whom Paul entered in, and prayed, and laid his hands on him, and healed him. So when this was done, others also, which had diseases in the island, came, and were healed" (Acts 28:8-9). From this account and others, it is quite evident that Paul had received of God power to heal. Back to the question, "Why didn't Paul heal Epaphroditus? Why was it that God was called upon to show mercy upon him?"

Some one might suggest that Epaphroditus didn't possess faith enough for Paul to heal him. What is said of this man points to his being strong in the faith. Paul speaks of him as "my brother, and companion in labour, and fellowsoldier, but your messenger, and he that ministered to my wants." Again, "Because for the work of Christ he was nigh unto death not regarding his life" (Phil. 2:26, 30). If these statements do not convey evidence of true faith on his part, what words would? Furthermore, healing was done at times when there was no real evidence on the part of the one being healed that the one had faith. Back to the case of the father of Publius and those healed on the island of Melita that has previously been mentioned. It would be presumptuous to argue that they had faith. Yet, Paul healed them. The matter of faith does not seem to be a part of answering the question.

Not only the case of Epaphroditus, but others in the life of Paul were not healed that might cause some to have problems in dealing with the "Why?" What about Trophimus? ". . . but Trophimus have I left at Miletum sick" (2 Tim. 4:20). From what is said regarding this man, we conclude that he was a faithful servant of God. If faith was required to be healed, he evidently was not lacking. The statement implies that Paul could have used him in helping with his labors, but he had to leave him at Miletum sick. The question is before us, "Why didn't he heal Epaphroditus and Trophimus?"

From what we read in 1 Timothy 5:23, it would appear that Timothy had some problems that could have needed healing. Rather than heal Timothy, Paul wrote unto him, "Drink no longer water, but use a little wine for thy stomach's sake and thine often infirmities" (1 Tim. 5:23). We might not be able to pinpoint his problems, but it does appear that he needed help "for thy stomach's sake and thine often infirmities." Paul did not miraculously heal him, but gave him a remedy for his problem. It might be termed as a prescription: "Drink no longer water, but use a little wine." It would appear to be an elliptical statement: Drink no longer water only, but also use a little wine. Why didn't Paul heal him and not bother with a possible slow remedy for his ailments?

We focus now upon Paul's famous thorn in the flesh. Though no one is certain, it would appear that this involved some infirmity of the flesh. He had besought the Lord three times to remove whatever it was from him. "And he said unto me, My grace is sufficient for thee: for my strength is made perfect in weakness. Most gladly therefore will I rather glory in my infirmities" (2 Cor. 12:9). Why didn't Paul heal himself or have one of his fellow laborers who had the gift of healing to relieve him of this infirmity?

The answer that I gave the teacher was that, in the case of Epaphroditus and these other cases, to heal them did not come under the purpose of divine healing. Miraculous divine healing as portrayed in the New Testament was for the purpose of confirming the word. The word then was in the man and not available as it is now recorded in the New Testament Scriptures (Heb. 2:3-4). Though the healed person was benefited, the primary benefit was pointing viewers to the spoken word. This evidently would not have occurred in the case of Epaphroditus or these others!

Why Gaddest Thou About So Much?

(Jeremiah 2:36)

These words constitute a portion of the rebuke from God directed to backsliding Israel. Gad was the seventh son of Jacob and head of one of the tribes of Israel. The tribe was rather nomadic, restless, and lacking in stability. The phrase, "gadding about" evidently originated from the transient habits of the tribe of Gad.

To be a "gad about" is to be something that is not commendable. We should never desire such a reputation. We should strive to be dependable, trustworthy, and stable in all of our endeavors. "Gadabouts" did not become limited to Israel. We are aware of the fact that modern "gadabouts" exist. Observe a few of these:

Domestic Gadabouts. Many, dissatisfied with home life, go far and wide in search of pleasure. Some people never seem to settle down. I remember talking to an elderly man about obeying the gospel of Christ. His reply was, "I am not ready to settle down yet!" At a time when one foot was in the grave and another on a banana peeling, he still felt that he wasn't ready to live a sober and righteous life in Christ Jesus. Many broken homes are the definite results of domestic gadabouts. The husband or the wife, and in some cases, both of them aren't content to be faithful to their obligations. The restraints are too much. The bright lights beckon! The word of God commands "young women to be sober, to love their husbands, to love their children, to be discreet, chaste (not chased, bkt), keepers at home, good, obedient to their own husbands, that the word of God be not blasphemed. Young men likewise exhort to be sober minded" (Tit. 2:4-6). Great damage is done by domestic gadabouts! Many children suffer because of gadabout parents.

Gadabouts In Employment. Some do not stick to one job for any length of time. They are always looking for "greener pastures" or "the pot of gold at the end of the rainbow." I personally know of an individual who had at least ten different jobs in the span of ten or fifteen years. In the beginning of each employment, he stated that he had found what he was looking for in life, but after a few months, he felt the company had failed him and he found himself seeking other employment. It was always the failure of others in their mistreatment of him. He never seemed to look in the mirror and see his lack of stability. Professing to be a Christian, his lack of stability has hurt the church rather than his life being an asset to the Lord's work.

As one has said, "Looking for a soft job is a job for a soft man." Be it understood that readjustments are necessary at times, but with many they are just a habit or the consequence of natural discontent. "Not that I speak in respect of want: for I have learned, in whatsoever state I am, therewith to be content. I know both how to be abased, and I know how to abound: everywhere and in all things I am instructed both to be full and to be hungry, both to abound and to suffer need. I can do all things through Christ which strengtheneth me" (Phil. 4:11-13). Evidently, some professed Christians do not know that these words are in the word of God. *Do you?*

Religious Gadabouts. To visit about at times is good and fairness cannot condemn such in moderation, but at times it can get to be ridiculous! For members to be true to the word of God, they need to be true and faithful in a local church. The Bible knows nothing about "members-at-large." Such are members who visit about all the time and are not members of a local congregation or at least have practically forgotten they were recognized as members. People of this nature say, "Well, we worship where we go!" So much for that, but if you are gone practically every Lord's day or at practically all of the services, what good are you to the local church? Why some members deny the scripturalness of being "members at large" and advocate being identified with a local church, yet by visiting about so much, they can virtually be what they deny is right. We need to realize what it means to be on the team and bear our part of the responsibilities. What if every member were like you, what type of a local church would exist with so many who are religious gadabouts?

And then there are those who are constantly changing membership from one congregation to another, not because of a matter of faith or conviction, but more to some discontentment caused by a trivial incident which they magnify. Rather than following the teaching of Matthew 18:15-17, they "pack their bags" to another congregation. Where will they go next? Actually, with the attitude they possess, they mean very little wherever they go. Let's have conviction and stability! Readjustments are sometimes necessary, but beware of your gadabouts!

Wisdom To Know The Difference

A prayer appeared in a religious periodical which caught my eye. It was worded something like this: "Help me Lord to follow what is right and to abstain from what is wrong and grant me the wisdom to know the difference." There is much involved in the last phrase, "grant me wisdom to know the difference." At times the conscientious individual finds it somewhat difficult to find the difference. Making a difference requires wisdom in many other principles other than right and wrong. These principles are related to the life of a Christian and have a bearing on proper devotion to God. It is tragic at times not to know the difference! There is a great need for wisdom in our lives. It is defined as "ability to judge soundly." Wisdom has been said to be the proper application of knowledge. Solomon requested wisdom and in so doing he pleased God by his request (1 Kings 3:9-10). James points us to asking God for wisdom and we sorely need to make this a practice in our prayers (Jas. 1:5). The writer of Proverbs relates that it is better to get wisdom than gold (Prov. 16:16).

We need wisdom to know the difference regarding principles of which we are familiar and at times have encountered difficulty in determining when we are following the proper one. These are principles that at times we are inclined to discern most easily and oftentimes unjustly in others, but not so easily with ourselves (2 Cor. 13:5). Notice a few of these principles that we have in mind.

Worry and Concern. We are definitely taught in the Scriptures against the sin of worry (Matt. 6:25, 28, 34; Phil. 4:6; Luke 10:41). On the other hand, children of God are fervently exhorted to be concerned over our deeds and the deeds of others (Matt. 6:33). In our determination not to worry, we must also guard against not becoming slothful and unconcerned. "Worry" is defined as "to feel or express great care and anxiety . . . to fret." "Concern" is "interest in or care for any person or thing." The Christian is not to fret or be despondent in his concern or interest less he be found practicing worry rather than concern. Is that perfectly clear? I seriously doubt it and that is the point; we need wisdom to know the difference concerning the principles involved. It is so convenient to tell someone not to worry and then do the same thing yourself. We are prone to define our worry as concern and strongly condemn someone else for the practice we condone in ourselves. Give us wisdom to know the difference.

Conservative and Lacking Faith. There is virtue in conservation but not at the expense of God. Jesus stressed great sacrificial belief. God was to be placed first above all. Our faith in God is "to launch out into the deep" (Luke 5:4). As we read of the life of Christ, we recognize that in some respects he was conservative. He asked his disciples to pick up the fragments after feeding the four and five thousand (John 6:12; Matt. 15:37). In teaching discipleship, Jesus taught the value of counting the cost (Luke 14:28-33). May we be conservative in those things that are approved by the Lord and may we never be lacking in the faith that pleases God. May we never desire a faith that will "involve little risk" and attempt to hide our cowardliness under the guise of conservatism. Lord, give us the wisdom to know the difference! I firmly believe that conscientious individuals recognize the problem at times and need to seek God's help in knowing the difference.

Fanaticism or Faithfulness. A fanatic is generally defined as one governed or produced by too much zeal. One must be careful in using the word. God's people are to be zealously faithful (Tit. 2:14). It is always easy to brand someone a fanatic just because he stresses some work and differs with another. Would not many people refer to Paul and the early Christians as being fanatics? Yet God called them faithful! There are those in our time who brand members of the Lord's church as being fanatic in teaching baptism or being fanatic in stressing attendance and giving. In comparison to the lives of those crying fanatic, I suppose these would be so classified, but by God's standard they are doing his will and being faithful in his sight. So many are so indifferent and lazy that, in their eyes when anyone evidences zeal at all, then they have become fanatics. Paul prayed for his countrymen who had zeal without knowledge (Rom. 10:1-3). The zeal that they displayed was not pleasing in the sight of God. They were establishing their own righteousness and were not submitting to God's righteousness. They were not faithful and in a degree of fairness would it not be proper to refer to such zeal as fanatical? The false prophets of Baal who cut themselves and cried out to Baal from morning to evening might be classified as fanatics (1 Kings 18:28-29).

We can't say more than was stated in the beginning. God help us to know what is right. Help us to abstain from wrong—give us the wisdom to know the difference. We sorely need wisdom!

Is This Like You?

My idea of visitation? Everyone comes to see me.
My idea of sympathy? Everybody suffers with me.
My idea of a sinner? The man I don't like very much.
My idea of a meek man? The man who yields to me.
My idea of a contentious man? The man who disagrees with me.

My idea of a wise man? The man who agrees with me.
My idea of unity? Everybody doing what I say.
My idea of cooperation? Everybody working with me.
My idea of a good sermon? One that fits and hits everyone else but me.

Abundant Life

Why The Bible? (1)

The Bible is here and is the most remarkable book in the world—the book of the ages. It has been the most bitterly fought of all the books published. The Bible has been proven to be "an indestructible book." There are more copies of it today than ever before. It is almost an exception to find a home that does not possess a Bible. To understand "Why the Bible" we need to know "from whence" came the Bible. It is here—it just didn't happen! An axiomatic truth is that every effect must have its own adequate and sufficient cause. Evil men would not have written it. The Bible condemns them! Good men could not have written it. No dramatist can draw taller men than himself! A stream does not rise higher than its source! If man wrote it, he manufactured a God and a Christ higher than himself. The only plain explanation is that the Bible was produced, as it claims, by the inspiration of God. "All Scripture is given by inspiration of God" (2 Tim. 3:16). Peter gives us a definition of inspiration in 2 Peter 1:20-21: "Knowing this first, that no prophecy of the Scripture is of any private interpretation. For the prophecy came not in old time by the will of man: but holy men of God spake as they were moved by the Holy Ghost." The Holy Ghost moved men of God to speak and write the Scriptures (Eph. 3:3-5; 2 Thess. 2:15). The Bible is here! There is a purpose behind all of God's ways—nothing walks with aimless feet, hence, why did God give the Bible? First, from negative viewpoints...

Not As An Instrument For Worldly Wisdom. Some appear to read the book with the desire to be known as persons of leading thought. To them it is a novelty and source of a conversation piece.

Rather than its precious precepts being read to serve as a guide of one's life, they are read and used in thirst for distinction—a source of cultural jest and amusement. "Let no man deceive himself. If any man among you seemeth to be wise in this world, let him become a fool, that he may be wise. For the wisdom of this world is foolishness with God: for it is written, He taketh the wise in their own craftiness. And again, The Lord knoweth the thoughts of the wise, that they are vain" (1 Cor. 3:18-20).

Not As A Proving Ground For Doctrine. There are individuals who assume certain theories and then read the Bible to force it into some recognition of their theories. Men seem to find it difficult to realize that the Bible is the doctrine. It reveals what we are to believe and follow—the doctrine that we are to accept. "All Scripture is given by inspiration of God, and is profitable for doctrine, for reproof, for correction, for instruction in righteousness; that the man of God may be perfect, thoroughly furnished unto all good works" (2 Tim. 3:16-17). The Scriptures are for *doctrine*. They provide the doctrine rather than provide a proving ground for the theories and doctrines of men. Almost anything can be "proved" by the man who wants to find the proof. There are those who believe in salvation by faith only. They turn to the Bible and "prove" their doctrine by John 3:16. In so doing they must completely ignore the many passages that speak of obedience (Heb. 5:8-9; Matt. 7:21-23; Rom. 6:17-18; Jas. 2:24). The Bible reveals truth to those who read it honestly and with an open mind. When a person's mind is already fixed, his reading of the Bible is usually to substantiate what he already believes rather than to know the doctrine of Christ. Paul speaks of God sending strong delusion to those who receive not the love of the truth that they might be saved. "And with all deceivableness of unrighteousness in them that perish; because they received not the love of the truth, that they might be saved. And for this cause God shall send them strong delusion, that they should believe a lie: That they all might be damned who believed not the truth, but had pleasure in unrighteousness" (2 Thess. 2:10-12). We must read and study the Bible to know what God wants us to do and not for what we want to do!

Not As A Subject Of Our Criticisms. The Bible has been criticized more than any other book available to man. It has stood the criticisms and will continue to stand them. However, we need to appreciate the thought that the Bible is to be our critic rather than the target of man's criticisms. Remember that Paul said the Scriptures are "for doctrine, for reproof, for correction, for instruction in righteousness" (2 Tim. 3:16). Reproof, correction, and instruction suggest that their value involves being a critic of our lives, as we need to let them be. The Hebrew writer said, "For the word of God is quick, and powerful, and sharper than any two-edged sword, piercing even to the dividing asunder of soul and spirit, and of the joints and marrow, and is a discerner of the thoughts and intents of the heart" (Heb. 4:12). We need to read it and let it be our critic. We need to heed its commands, warnings, and admonitions rather than to set ourselves up as critics of the word of God. Our view of "Why the Bible?" will largely determine the manner of lives that we live. When we consider the Bible as God speaking to us, we will be more inclined to do what the Bible teaches us to do. On the other hand, when we look upon it as just a good book produced by man's design, our regard for its importance will most likely not be shown in our lives. Many people in the religious world really do not understand the purpose of the Bible. This is one of the explanations for their being something religiously that is not authorized by God. Also, after all the teaching and preaching that some members of the Lord's church have heard, there are still those who do not properly understand "Why the Bible?"

Why The Bible? (2)

In the last article we began to consider the answer to this very important question, "Why the Bible?" For an individual to gain the most from the Bible, he needs to properly understand God's purpose in giving us the Bible. I doubt seriously if any man can be benefited by the Bible in the way that God intends for him to be benefited if that man fails to understand the true purpose of the

Bible. Unfortunately, there are many who do not realize the proper purpose of the Bible. Like most everything else, the Bible has been the subject of abuse rather than the proper use. There are those who abuse the Bible rather than use it for the purpose that God intended. The abuse of a thing does not destroy its proper use and we should be aware of this regarding any principle.

We pointed out in the previous article that the Bible is not to be used as an instrument for worldly wisdom, not as a proving area for doctrines; or as a subject for our criticisms. The Bible presents the doctrine that we are to follow (2 Tim. 3:16-17). It determines the doctrine that man is to accept rather than man designing some theory and turning to the Bible in some perverted way for justification of the theory. The Bible has been criticized more than any other book available to man. I suppose that this will continue as long as man exists. It has stood the criticisms and you can be assured that it will continue to stand them. However, we need to understand that the Bible has been given to be our critic rather than the subject of our criticisms (Heb. 4:12). The person who persists on being the critic of God's word will doubtlessly never be benefited from the word in God's intended purpose for man. Don't you agree?

While we are viewing "Why the Bible?" negatively or from the viewpoint of why it was not given, it might be profitable to mention a couple of more factors along this line. The Bible has not been given . . .

To Create Unhappiness, Misery, Or Sorrow. Why mention this factor? Because there are those who seem to think that their unhappy state is due to the Bible. As a whole, unhappiness, misery, and sorrow are the products of sin. Though the Bible reveals sin and man's condition before God, yet the Bible does not make man a sinner. The Bible reveals the remedy for sin and admonishes man to accept such in the gospel of Christ. If the Bible does bring unhappiness at any time, it is in the like manner of a patient confronting an operation. The individual is sick already. The operation is for the purpose of relieving the ailment. There are those in the sickness of sin who read the Bible. They realize their condition and are confronted with what has to be done to relieve it. This naturally causes a certain amount of anxiety and unhappiness, but as one conforms to the direction of truth, then he can be benefited. The operation is for the good of the individual that the ailment might be corrected. David wrote, "The statutes of the Lord are right, rejoicing the heart" (Ps. 18:8). The Bible has been given to bring happiness, not to create unhappiness. Men are guilty of falsely accusing the Bible when they allege that it creates unhappiness, misery, and sorrow. The weakness is prevalent with so many in blaming other things for the actual condition rather than to truthfully recognize where the fault lies.

For the Property of a Favored Few. The Bible is to be read by all men. All men have the God-given right to read it and follow the teaching therein. No man has any right to tell an individual that he is not to read the word of God. Yet, there are those who advocate that the Bible and the reading of it is for a favored few. 2 Peter 1:20-21 has been used to substantiate such a false theory. "Knowing this first, that no prophecy of the scripture is of any private interpretation. For the prophecy came not in old time by the will of man: but holy men of God spake as they were moved by the Holy Ghost." The private interpretation mentioned in verse 20 refers not to the reception of the word but rather to how the prophecy of the Scripture originated. Read the next verse! "For the prophecy came not in old time by the will of man: but holy men of God spake as they were moved by the Holy Ghost." The emphasis is upon how the word came or how it was produced rather than man's reception of it! Notice the absurdity of using this passage to teach that man is not to personally study the word of God. By so doing, one is taking a passage from the Bible that only the favored few can understand to teach persons that they are not to read the Bible with the hope of understanding what they read. In other words I read this passage to teach me that I can't understand what I read. How could I ever conclude this if I couldn't understand what I read? Catholic hierarchy has been known to use this passage to teach people that the Scriptures are not to be understood by the "laity" but only by the favored few.

Luke speaks of God's nobility in Acts 17:11. "These were more noble than those in Thessalonica, in that they received the word with all readiness of mind, and searched the scriptures daily, whether those things were so." The Scriptures were searched and this pleased God. These Scriptures were not and still are not the property of a favored few. The Bible is to be followed. To do this men must read it and know of God's will. "Study to shew thyself approved of God, a workman that needeth not to be ashamed rightly dividing the word of truth" (2 Tim. 2:15). "And beside this, giving all diligence, add to your faith virtue; and to virtue knowledge" (2 Pet. 1:5). "But grow in the grace and in the knowledge of our Lord and Saviour Jesus Christ" (2 Pet. 3:18). How can one grow in knowledge if one cannot read the Bible for himself and understand what he is reading? If you don't read and think for yourself, someone will do it for you and that is what many religious teachers desire to do. Don't let it happen!

Why The Bible? (3)

In two previous articles, we have considered some observations pertaining to why the Bible has been given from a negative viewpoint or from the view of why it hasn't been given. Many people have a perverted view of the purpose of the Bible. We are to use the Bible and refrain from misusing it. There is such an abuse of the Bible in our times that we are prone to feel that lessons of this nature are quite valuable. From the negative consideration, we have pointed out that the Bible has not been given for the purpose of serving as an instrument for worldly wisdom, not as a proving ground for doctrines, not as a subject of our criticisms, not to create unhappiness or misery, and not as the property of a few favored people. It would not be difficult to find individuals who so use the Bible in these perverted purposes. To have such a misconception of the word of God is a tragic thing. A person who handles the Scriptures for a wrong purpose is destined to forfeit his right to the blessings of God.

Why Has the Bible Been Given or Made Available To Man?

God and man's condition before God. For knowledge concerning God, one is dependent upon the Bible. Other books may speak of God but what true knowledge that is presented therein has come from the Bible. "The heavens declare the glory of God; and the firmament showeth his handiwork," but the Bible reveals God and his attributes. All men have manifested some recognition of a Supreme Being. Without the Bible man gropes in darkness for the revelation of whom this Supreme Being is and how he is to be served. The Bible reveals that man has sinned and come short of the glory of God (Isa. 59:1-2; Rom. 3:23). This is revealed in simple, easy to understand language. There is no incentive to obey God until one fully realizes his lost condition. The world desperately needs to be told what it means to be lost for time and eternity (2 Thess. 1:7-8). The Bible contains this information in language that accountable beings can comprehend and obey.

That God desires our salvation. The Bible makes it abundantly clear that God desires to save all men (1 Tim. 2:4). God desires for all men to come to repentance (2 Pet. 3:9; Acts 17:30). His love for the world is universal. His invitation is to all (John 3:16; Matt. 11:28-30; Rev. 22:17). Man needs to know these facts. The Bible reveals them. Where would we be concerning such needed information if it weren't for the Bible?

What God has done for our salvation? Step by step the plan of God is revealed to show what God has done to make salvation available for man in this age. The call of Abraham, the giving of the Law, the message of the prophets, the ministry of John, the labors of the Lord, his death, burial, and resurrection, and the establishment of the church (Acts 2), all these things are revealed in the Bible to lead us back to God and help us appreciate what God has done to make our salvation available. Where would we be without the Bible?

What God would have us to do. God has the right to prescribe the conditions wherein man might be saved by him. There is no promise of salvation apart from what God has said in his word.

The only true basis of anyone knowing of sins being forgiven is that which is derived by knowledge from the word of God. Where the Bible has not gone, then there has not gone the directions from God as to what an individual is to do that he might be saved. Many religionists today speak of believing the Bible, but they view it as being "a dead letter." They feel that God's Spirit is operating separate and apart from the word. Here again are people who do not properly understand the purpose of the Bible. If men can be saved by some direct operation of the Spirit upon their lives, then why give the Bible in the first place? If it is "a dead letter," as they claim, what real good is there for the Bible to exist at all?

I recall some years ago hearing a college professor affirm that the Spirit brings salvation apart from God's word. During his comments, he referred to the missionaries that his particular denomination had in foreign countries laboring to preach the word to the populace in these countries. The question was placed before him as to the purpose of these missionaries. If men are saved apart from the word, why did men need the word and why have men to preach it? In somewhat of a feeble effort to be consistent with his theory that the Spirit saves without the word, he contended that these missionaries taught the people a better way of life or standard of life. He appeared to have uttered something about giving them bathtubs, etc.

It takes the word for people to be saved. The Bible reveals the conditions (Mark 16:16; Acts 2:38; 22:16; Gal. 3:26-27). We are certainly converted by the Holy Spirit. This is brought about by the word of the Spirit, which directs us in what to do and is revealed in the Bible. An angel appeared to Cornelius and told him to send for Peter who would tell him what he ought to do (Acts 10:1-6). Why was Peter sent for if the Spirit saves people without people knowing the word of God? Peter's mission to Cornelius was to tell him words whereby he and his house might be saved (Acts 11:14). God has chosen the foolishness of preaching to save them that believe (1 Cor. 1:21-24). The word of God is quick and powerful (Heb. 4:12), and it is all we need to know in order to obey God, be pleasing in his sight, and live in such a way as to be faithful unto death. We need to be steadfast in thanking God for his word and using the Bible in the proper manner. We must be users of the word and not abusers of it. How thankful are you that God has given us the Bible? Thankful enough to obey?

Why the Early Church Gave Liberally

As one reads the New Testament, there are many characteristics about the early church which will impress him. One of these characteristics is the great liberality of its members. The historian Luke gave a glowing tribute to the Jerusalem church in these words, "Neither was there any among them that lacked: for as many as were possessors of lands or houses sold them and brought the prices of the things that were sold, and laid them down at the apostle's feet: and distribution was made unto every man according as he had need" (Acts 4:34-35). Paul spoke highly of the generosity of the Macedonians, "Moreover, brethren, we do you to wit of the grace of God bestowed on the churches of Macedonia; how that in a great trial of affliction, the abundance of their joy and their deep poverty abounded unto the riches of their liberality. For to their power, I bear record, yea, and beyond their power they were willing of themselves" (2 Cor. 8:1-3).

What accounted for their liberality? As we notice the things for which they were responsible, perhaps we can be prompted to possess more liberality in our lives.

How Do We Account For Their Liberality?

They gave themselves. After speaking highly of the generosity of the Macedonians, Paul added these words, "And this they did, not as we hoped, but first gave their own selves to the Lord, and unto us by the will of God" (2 Cor. 8:5). They first gave themselves to the Lord. They were genuinely converted. It might be figuratively said that their pocketbook was baptized with them. When one is converted, the matter of giving material goods will be easy. One reason why so many are stingy and covetous is that they have not been converted to the Lord. They have not first given themselves. When we are converted, liberality becomes a part of our life.

They had a background conducive to liberality. The Jerusalem church was composed mainly of Jews. The tithes, offerings, gifts, and sacrifices of the Jews under Judaism are all well known facts. The Old Testament abounds with such teaching. Having this background, it was an easy matter for them to be liberal with their giving under the New Testament. With many today, the background has not been so conducive. We need teaching and liberality needs to be impressed upon us.

They recognized the principle of stewardship. They realized that theirs was not theirs, but that they were taking care of God's possessions and would some day have to account for the way they handled them. Our stewardship of God's possessions is affirmed often. "As every man hath received the gift, even so minister the same one to another, as good stewards of the manifold grace of God" (1 Pet. 4:10). "Let a man so account of us, as of the ministers of Christ, and stewards of the mysteries of God. Moreover it is required in stewards, that a man be found faithful" (1 Cor. 4:1-2). "What? Know ye not that your body is the temple of the Holy Ghost which is in you, which ye have of God, and ye are not your own? For ye are bought with a price: therefore glorify God in your body, and in your spirit, which are God's" (1 Cor. 6:19). "But godliness with contentment is great gain. For we brought nothing into this world, and it is certain we can carry nothing out" (1 Tim. 6:6-7). Knowing that what we are using is the property of another causes us to exercise extreme caution. Have you considered your stewardship? Perhaps the failure to do so accounts for your lack of liberality!

They lived in the shadow of the cross. Some of them had been eyewitnesses of the death of Christ, the proof of God's love. This was liberality at its greatest—this made them want to give. We are centuries removed from Calvary, but those events should be real to us. One of the greatest hindrances of liberality today is a failure to truly appreciate the death of Christ on the cross. We need to realize that God so loved that he gave and that Christ loved the church and gave himself for it. When "we love Him because He first loved us," we can joyfully consecrate what we have to his cause.

No Stingy, Covetous Person Will Enter Heaven

We need to learn the lesson of being liberal in our giving. "But this I say, He which soweth sparingly shall reap also sparingly; and he which soweth bountifully shall reap also bountifully. Every man according as he purposeth in his heart, so let him give; not grudgingly, or of necessity: for God loveth a cheerful giver" (2 Cor. 9:6-7). Have we learned it?

Wind Conscious More Than Christ Conscious

"But when he saw the wind boisterous, he was afraid; and beginning to sink, he cried, saying, Lord, save me" (Matt. 14:30). "Beginning to sink" is an arresting and tragic phrase. A few moments before, Peter was daring that which, to our minds, seemed impossible. With the light of faith in his eyes, Peter planted his feet on the word "come" and began to walk on the water to go to Jesus. His success proved to be short lived. His faith changed to fear and his victory changed to defeat. It is a pitiful sight to see anyone drowning. It is even more sorrowful to see a person sinking spiritually.

This sinking man is a picture of much that we see in the church today. It represents those who have not given over the fight, yet they do not seem to be getting anywhere. They are simply counting time and idling along. It represents those who are not living as victoriously as they once did. Their religion is more a thing of weight than joy. They have no real desire to work in the vineyard. The worship services are more a source of criticism than joy and edification. It might even represent those who have quit trying altogether. According to their own lives, they are not simply sinking, but the waters of utter defeat are rolling over them.

What was the explanation for Peter's "beginning to sink"? How did he come to be sinking? It does not appear from his lack of interest or effort. This is the case of many today. They have simply lost interest. They often bewail the fact that they are getting very little out of their religion. How can they expect to get a great deal out of it when they are putting so little into it? We generally receive in proportion to what we put into a thing. Nor was Peter's failure born of the difficulty of the task. The task was difficult to the point of impossibility. Peter said, "Lord, if it be thou, bid me come unto thee on the water. And he said, Come. And when Peter was come down out of the ship, he walked on the water, to go to Jesus" (Matt. 14:28-29). Jesus invited Peter to come. He supplied what was needed for Peter to walk on the water and he would have continued to supply what was needed.

Peter's failure was due to his becoming wind conscious rather than Christ conscious. Peter "saw the wind boisterous." The hindrances so completely filled his horizon that he saw nothing of what was helpful. This is largely our trouble. We become wind conscious rather than Christ conscious. Problems make us depressed and bewildered. The need of the hour is not blindness. We need to face the facts, but not to the point of over emphasizing our difficulties. On occasions, Christians behold the winds of unpopularity, old habits, doubt, fear, and worry over temporal affairs and offences that are hurled upon them. In taking their eyes off the Christ, they see these winds and find themselves "beginning to sink."

Peter took his eyes off the right object. We are ever to look to Christ, "looking unto Jesus the author and finisher of our faith; who for the joy that was set before him endured the cross, despising the shame, and is set down at the right hand of the throne of God" (Heb. 12:2). "But we see Jesus, who was made a little lower than the angels for the suffering of death, crowned with glory and honour; that he by the grace of God should taste death for every man" (Heb. 2:9). Others have begun to sink when they beheld other things and looked the wrong way. There was Eve in the garden of Eden who was tempted by the serpent. "And when the woman saw that the tree was good for food, and that it was pleasant to the eyes, and a tree to be desired to make one wise, she took of the fruit thereof, and did eat, and gave also unto her husband with her; and he did eat" (Gen. 3:6). And let us not forget Lot's wife. She disobeyed God by looking back on the city of Sodom and suffered the consequence of being turned into a pillar of salt. Jesus did not ignore this history, but exhorted his followers to "Remember Lot's wife" (Luke 17:32).

The beauty of this narrative is that Peter turned defeat into victory. How was this accomplished? Not by denying or ignoring the difficulties. He frankly faced the fact that he was "beginning to sink." He realized his true situation and made no effort to ignore it. Some people seem to never realize their true situation and are not aware that they are sinking. One of the definite prerequisites of being saved is that one becomes aware of his need to be saved. So many are satisfied to such an extent that they do not realize their sinking position to do anything about it. Peter turned his eyes from the wind to fix them on Christ. He recognized Christ's power to save. He asked the Lord to save him. Jesus today stretches forth his hand to sinking men through the gospel of Christ; it is the power of God to save. We must be obedient to Christ and continue to be more Christ conscious and less wind conscious.

With Regard To Bitterness, Don't Confuse It!

We have been told on occasions to take heed and not let ourselves become bitter. We have also found ourselves exhorting others to follow the same advice or admonition. Such is a very healthy and profitable admonition for it is founded on the word of God. "Let all bitterness, and wrath, and anger, and clamor, and evil speaking be put away from you, with all malice" (Eph. 4:31). In the heat of conflict, it is quite easy for the individual to lose sight of the objective and permit himself to become bitter. There is need for constant vigilance and self-examination in order that we keep ourselves free of bitterness. We should never be offended when some brother exhorts us to be careful to abstain from the sin of bitterness. Spiritual battles may be fought and the conflict may rage without bitterness! It may be difficult in some instances, but when is the life of a Christian really easy?

With regard to bitterness, let's be careful to abstain from it and let's also be careful not to confuse it! What do we mean by "confuse it"? Simply this . . . it appears that some have the idea to do some things that God ordains is actually to manifest bitterness. They are prone to neglect such practices under the "justification" that they do not want to give anyone the idea that they are bitter. Though absurd, it can happen!

It Is Possible To Confuse Bitterness With . . .

A Firm Unmovable Spirit. One may have such a spirit and never be bitter. The Christian is called upon to "be ye stedfast, unmovable, always abounding in the work of the Lord" (1 Cor. 15:58). Some wishy-washy characters want to brand firmness in the truth with bitterness. Perhaps, it's like the subject of gossiping. We never gossip—it's always the other fellow. In like manner, we are always firm with the proper spirit, but the other fellow has let himself become bitter. Who wears the shoes makes a great deal of difference! Don't you agree? Or perhaps, I have become bitter by making such a remark. And have you ever noticed, it is not the character who agrees with us that we consider bitter, but the one with whom we disagree. Wonder why?

Sincerity and Frankness. Again, we emphasize that one may be sincere and frank in word and deed without succumbing to the spirit of bitterness. The deeds of the Christian should be free of hypocrisy. We don't have to be a "sneak" to do the work of the Lord. The apostle wrote of sincerity: "that ye approve things that are excellent; that ye may be sincere and without offense till the day of Christ" (Phil. 1:10). Again, he spoke of boldness and frankness:

"We were bold in our God to speak unto you the gospel of God with much contention" (1 Thess. 2:2). At the same time, he could write: "But we were gentle among you, even as a nurse cherisheth her children" (1 Thess. 2:7). Certainly this excluded bitterness! We do not have to be a hypocrite to abstain from bitterness. There is no premium on being "sneaking sweet"!

A Determination to Apply the Truth. Truth is to be applied to individuals and situations that arise! The Scriptures will not jump up and apply themselves. Someone has to love the Scriptures enough to make proper application of them. In fact, to refuse to apply the truth is actually to deny the value of truth. What value is it to preach that baptism is for the remission of sins and then refuse to admit that the unbaptized are lost? In like manner, many people say they believe the truth and then when the application time comes, they are not "set for a defence of the gospel." They profess to be sound in the faith without making application of truth. It would appear that they are set on the fence rather than being prepared to defend the gospel or being "set for a defence of the gospel" as God expects of his people.

Paul wrote, "And have no fellowship with the unfruitful works of darkness, but rather reprove them. For it is a shame even to speak of those things which are done of them in secret" (Eph. 5:11-12). If application is not involved, yea if application is not necessary, then what meaning is there to these words? There are the unfruitful works of darkness in which individuals engage. No fellowship is to be granted to those who are involved in such, "but rather reprove them." However, when application is made, there are those who view those doing so as being motivated by bitterness. Though professing to be sound in the faith, their "soundness" lies in words rather than truly applying the truth to situations that arise. Time corrects some things, but time does not make one sin right of which an individual has not repented. We need continually to apply the truth. Such is to be done and certainly can be done without bitterness of heart. In putting away bitterness, let's be careful not to put away some precious principles from God's word under the guise of doing away with bitterness. While washing the baby, take heed that the baby is not thrown out with the bath water.

Work Out Your Own Salvation

After referring to the obedience and exaltation of Jesus Christ, Paul, in Philippians 2:12, exhorts the Philippians to obey that in time they too may be exalted. The saints at Philippi had been obedient. Paul had beheld their obedience when he was in their company. He was admonishing them to continue "not as in my presence only, but now much more in my absence." He was urging them to go ahead in obeying while he was absent from them. Their necessary obedience was described in the phrase, "work out your own salvation with fear and trembling."

As one might expect, this passage is often misapplied and falsely used to mean something contrary to what Paul meant. We recall a young man who quoted this phrase to justify his being left alone. At the time, he wasn't interested in the truth or anyone helping him know the truth. He felt it was something he had to work out for himself without any direction or assistance. Actually, it was a screen for him to be left alone. The Philippians had already obeyed the gospel of Christ. They knew that they weren't going to heaven of their own devising. "O Lord, I know that the way of man is not in himself: it is not in man that walketh to direct his steps" (Jer. 10:23). It is impossible for one to know of salvation without the help of others. Whether man is taught orally or by reading the word, it is still the word of God that must be brought to his mind that he might know the will of the Lord in order to be obedient. "For whosoever shall call upon the name of the Lord shall be saved. How then shall they call on him in whom they have not believed? And how shall they believe in him of whom they have not heard? And how shall they hear without a preacher?" (Rom. 10:13-14).

Denominationalists use the phrase in an effort to show that there is not one law of obedience which God expects all men to obey.

They contend that no one has the right to say that anyone hasn't obeyed the will of God. It is something that man has to work out or design for himself. He may do it one way while someone else does it another, but regardless, both get the job done. These people are assuming something that the verse does not say. We are to work at what God has told us to do in obedience and not something apart from his direction (Gal. 1:6-9; 2 John 9). Truth is truth in the will of God and this truth is available for all to obey. Williams' translation renders this phrase: "Working clear down to the finishing point of your salvation." Paul had seen them obey the gospel and become Christians, now he wanted them to finish what they had started.

Some have been known to affirm from this passage that, by grace one becomes a child of God, then he no longer needs grace but is saved by "working out his salvation." By the grace of God, we are saved from our past sins (Eph. 2:8-9) and by grace, we continue to stand acceptable before God (Tit. 2:11-12; 2 Pet. 3:18). This "working out" does not annul the need for grace. It involves man's part in continually receiving the grace of God as we follow the will of God.

This Passage Does Teach . . .

Salvation is essentially an individual matter between each man and God. "Your *own* salvation." The burden of obedience cannot be accepted by another (Acts 2:40; Gal. 6:5). Man has sinned and he is the one who must obey to be saved (Isa. 59:1-2; 2 Cor. 5:10).

Salvation has its divine and human side. Verses 12-13 of this chapter refer to man working and God working. Many religionists condemn men working in salvation. They term is "salvation by works." Such people have a hard time dealing with Acts 10:35; 2:40; Philippians 2:12; Hebrews 5:8-9; James 2:26 to just mention a few verses. Man is encouraged in his work by God's cooperation. "God worketh in you to will and do of his pleasure." We must not ignore our part in accepting God's grace.

Salvation has its different tenses. Salvation is stated in the New Testament as a thing already accomplished, in the state of accomplishment, and that yet is to be accomplished. Hence, we note the three tenses—past, present, and future. Observe in Paul's writings: past (Eph. 2:11-12), present (Phil. 2:12), and future (Rom. 13:11). Many church members talk about and rejoice in forgiveness (Mark 16:16) and look forward no doubt to future salvation (1 Pet. 1:4-5). However, they fail to think of the present. How are we now? Are there things lacking in our spiritual health? "Work out your own salvation with fear and trembling" refers to the present. We need to work out our salvation now to keep alive and take care of the future.

This salvation comes by conscious activity and struggle. This is suggested by the words "with fear and trembling." The life of a Christian is not a mystic and indolent quietism, which moves neither hand nor foot. This life is represented as a life of watching, of struggle or combat. "But I keep under my body, and bring it into subjection: lest that by any means, when I have preached to others, I myself should be a castaway" (1 Cor. 9:27). "Fight the good fight of faith, lay hold on eternal life, whereunto thou art also called, and hast professed a good profession before many witnesses" (1 Tim. 6:12). Salvation is man's supreme end and goal. Think on these things, brethren!

Ye Shall Be Free Indeed (1)
John 8:36

All creatures are lovers of freedom. It is a cherished possession that should be greatly appreciated, but many times it is simply taken for granted until one is deprived of it. Men have fought and died to obtain freedom. This country was founded upon the principle of freedom. The four freedoms have long been a revered thing in past generations—freedom from want, fear, freedom of speech, and religion. These principles should be honored and men should be exceedingly grateful to live where they are available to the citizens; however, Jesus spoke of freedom that was far more important than these. Jesus brought to the world the meaning of true religious freedom. This is freedom that so few in this country have actually realized! Jesus spoke of freedom that comes through truth saying, "and ye shall know the truth and the truth shall make you free" (John 8:32). Though men often boast of the religious freedom that this country affords its citizens, yet myriads are still in bondage. They have not obeyed Christ to obtain the freedom that he bestows upon his true followers. We should be grateful for the freedom to worship God that this country grants its citizens, but never guilty of thinking such is the extent of the freedom that Christ offers men. The true meaning of religious freedom is available to men regardless of what freedom a particular country may or may not extend to its citizens.

What Freedom Does Christ Offer?

Freedom From Sin. After stating that the truth shall make you free, the Jews answered, "We be Abraham's seed, and were never in bondage to any man: how sayest thou, Ye shall be made free? Jesus answered them, Verily, verily, I say unto you, Whosoever committeth sin is the servant of sin" (John 8:33-34). Jesus was speaking of freedom from sin. In later years, as the gospel was preached in fact, Paul reminded the Roman saints, "But God be thanked, that ye were the servants of sin, but ye have obeyed from the heart that form of doctrine which was delivered you. Being then made free from sin, ye became the servants of righteousness" (Rom. 6:17-18). Their being free from sins was based upon their obedience to the gospel. As penitent believers on a confession of faith in Christ, they were baptized into Christ that they might be freed from their sins (Rom. 6:3-5; Gal. 3:26-27; Acts 2:38; 22:16). In verse 22 of Romans 6, Paul stated, "But now being made free from sin . . ." Have you experienced this freedom?

Freedom From Condemnation. Sin brings or produces condemnation. When one is freed from sin, he can rejoice in freedom from the condemnation that sin produces. "There is therefore now no condemnation to them which are in Christ Jesus, who walk not after the flesh, but after the Spirit. For the law of the Spirit of life in Christ Jesus hath made me free from the law of sin and death" (Rom. 8:1-2). The law of sin and death brings condemnation. In obedience to the gospel, the law of the Spirit of life in Christ made these saints free from condemnation. They were in Christ Jesus, but needed to take heed continually to walk in the Spirit and not after the flesh. To walk after the flesh was to sin and place themselves again in condemnation. "For God sent not his Son into the world to condemn the world; but that the world through him might be saved. He that believeth on him is not condemned; but he that believeth not is condemned already, because he hath not believed in the name of the only begotten Son of God" (John 3:17-18). How many are truly free from condemnation?

Freedom From the Law of Moses. The Jewish Christians were in a position truly to appreciate such freedom. To the Galatians, Paul wrote, "Christ hath redeemed us from the curse of the law, being made a curse for us: for it is written, Cursed is every one that hangeth on a tree" (Gal. 3:13). Again, "Stand fast therefore in the liberty wherewith Christ hath made us free, and be not entangled again with the yoke of bondage" (Gal. 5:1). The yoke of bondage was in reference to the law of Moses that some at that time were inclined to submit to again. Peter referred to the law in this degree when the discussion arose concerning the circumcision of the Gentiles, "Now therefore why tempt ye God, to put a yoke upon the neck of the disciples, which neither our fathers nor we were able to bear?" (Acts 15:10). Christ nailed this law of bondage to the cross. "Blotting out the handwriting of ordinances that was against us, which was contrary to us, and took it out of the way, nailing it to his cross" (Col. 2:14). He has made it available for man to exchange the yoke of bondage for his rest giving yoke (Matt. 11:28-30). There are religionists today who desire to follow portions of the law of Moses. Actually they are in essence desiring bondage rather than the freedom that is in Christ. "Christ is become of no effect unto you, whosoever of you are justified by the law; ye are fallen from grace" (Gal. 5:4).

Ye Shall Be Free Indeed (2)
John 8:36

In last article, we mentioned that all creatures are lovers of freedom and that freedom is one of man's dearest possessions. Men have made the supreme sacrifice for freedom and we should continually treasure the freedom that is prevalent in this country. However, there are many people who boast of being free who have never experienced the freedom that Christ offers to mankind. There are multitudes who are still in slavery. They have never obeyed the Christ, and regardless of what their citizenship affords them, they are still in bondage to sin and condemnation. In the last article we referred to the fact that Christ and obedience to him affords an individual freedom from sin and the condemnation that sin brings. No one is "free indeed" until he has obeyed the gospel of Christ. Paul wrote, "But God be thanked, that ye were the servants of sin, but ye have obeyed from the heart that form of doctrine which was delivered you. Being then made free from sin, ye became the servants of righteousness" (Rom. 6:17-18). These saints at Rome had become free from sin by obeying the gospel of Christ. As baptized penitent believers, they had put on Christ and were blessed with the liberty or freedom that is in him (Gal. 3:26-29).

What Freedom Does Christ Offer?

Christ grants men freedom from other principles as well as from sin, condemnation, and the Law of Moses which were mentioned in the last article. We desire to emphasize in this article that Christ extends to his followers freedom from . . .

The Rudiments of the World. The expression "rudiments of the world" is found at least twice in the book of Colossians. "Wherefore if ye be dead with Christ from the rudiments of the world, why, as though living in the world, are ye subject to ordinances, (touch not; taste not; handle not; which all are to perish with the using;) after the commandments and doctrines of men?" (Col. 2:20-22).

Paul was reminding these brethren that they were dead from the rudiments of the world and hence freed from them. Now why were they still being in subjection to such and placing themselves in bondage? Again, in Colossians 2:8, Paul calls upon them to "beware lest any man spoil you through philosophy and vain deceit after the tradition of men, after the rudiments of the world, and not after Christ." These passages bring to mind that Christians can be freed from bondage at one time and then permit themselves to be enslaved again as the conduct of many proves. The "rudiments of the world" doubtlessly refer to fleshly ordinances. The ordinances approved by Christ are the only ones to which the Christian is to be subject. These ordinances an individual can conscientiously obey while having the freedom that is his in Christ Jesus.

Freedom From Sectarianism. The religious activities of multitudes are controlled by the teaching of various sects of which they are the members. Most people in the religious world view religion through sectarian or denominational approaches. Any thing resembling a sect is condemned in the word of God! In fact, the original word that is translated "sect" is in other places translated "heresy" or "factions." Paul refers to the word "factions" in the works of the flesh mentioned in Galatians 5:19-21 and says those who do such things shall not inherit the kingdom of God. So many poor souls today have been deceived in sectarianism and have never found the freedom that is in Christ Jesus. They are bound to what their church or sect teaches rather than following the simple truth in Christ. When their Bible is read, it is read with the interpretation that their church or sect places upon any particular subject. Is such freedom? It is bondage rather than freedom in Christ.

Freedom From Human Creeds. Closely related to freedom from sectarianism is freedom from human creeds. The various sects have their human creeds, prayer books, confessions of faith, or catechisms. Members of these particular churches or sects are made members of the various denominations by following their human creed. The Bible is interpreted in the light of their creed. The Bible and the Bible alone is the only "creed" that anyone needs in religion. The followers of any given human creed are obligated to preach in accord with it. They have not the freedom to fully preach God's word. They are in bondage to the dictates of the creed and their preaching and teaching must concur with it. Paul told Timothy to "preach the word" (2 Tim. 4:2). He had the Christ given freedom to preach completely the truth as in God's word. "All Scripture is given by inspiration of God, and is profitable for doctrine, for reproof, for correction, for instruction in righteousness: that the man of God may be perfect, thoroughly furnished unto all good works" (2 Tim. 3:16-17). Christians have the freedom to use God's word as such. As God's children, we should always be aware of the freedom that we have in Christ and teach others that they might also have it.

Ye Shall Be Free Indeed (3)

John 8:36

For the last two articles we have been discussing the freedom that is to be found in Christ Jesus. Christ does not grant an individual freedom *to* sin, but he affords one freedom *from* sin. So many folks have the wrong concept concerning the subject of freedom. To them any restraint upon their activities is a violation of freedom. They crave a life of licentiousness without any restraint as their definition of freedom. This was the prevalent view of the "hippie" generation. Paul cautioned the Galatians regarding the abuse of liberty that they had in Christ. "For, brethren, ye have been called unto liberty; only use not liberty for an occasion to the flesh, but by love serve one another" (Gal. 5:13). Sin committed by one professing to be in Christ is just as much sin as sin committed by one who is an alien sinner. In his invitation to man, Jesus offered freedom from a galling yoke of bondage, but he still had a yoke for man to bear in the freedom that Christ makes possible. Hear him, "Come unto me, all ye that labor and are heavy laden, and I will give you rest. Take my *yoke* upon you, and learn of me; for I am meek and lowly in heart: and ye shall find rest unto your souls" (Matt. 11:28-30).

People confuse rebellion with freedom. Restraint is vital to man's well being and where no restraint exists there is virtually anarchy. One that has such a spirit does not know Christ. A follower of Christ takes the yoke of Christ and wears it joyfully. This yoke is for our own good and to rebel against it constitutes tragedy. When some professed followers of Christ state that they are tired of people telling them what they should do, in most cases they are including Christ and what his yoke stands for, as well as the brethren who are only trying to steer them right. They are symbolizing a freedom that is not to be found in the Lord.

In the last article, we mentioned that Christ offers freedom from the rudiments of the world, sectarianism, and human creeds. It is our purpose in the space that remains to suggest a freedom that often we fail to realize. We are speaking of freedom from fear. Yes, in Christ there is freedom from fear. It requires faith in our hearts to appropriate this freedom, and our constant fears could be due to lack of genuine faith. Notice the passages which speak of freedom from fear:

Of Enemies. "Let your conversation be without covetousness; and be content with such things as ye have: for he hath said, I will never leave thee, nor forsake thee. So that we may boldly say, The Lord is my helper, and I will not fear what man shall do unto me" (Heb. 13:5-6). Again, "And fear not them which kill the body, but are not able to kill the soul, but rather fear him who is able to destroy both soul and body in hell" (Matt.10:28).

Of Failure. "Draw nigh unto God, and he will draw nigh to you. Cleanse your hands, ye sinners; and purify your hearts, ye double-minded" (Jas. 4:8). As we draw near to God, failure can be turned to success. If God is for us, who can be against us? Certainly God will be for those who draw nigh unto him! "A man that hath friends must show himself friendly: and there is a friend that sticketh closer than a brother" (Prov. 18:24). That friend is Jesus Christ!

Of Starvation. "Therefore I say unto you, Take no thought for your life, what ye shall eat or what ye shall drink; nor yet for your body, what ye shall put on. Is not the life more than meat, and the body than raiment? Behold the fowls of the air: for they sow not, neither do they reap, nor gather into barns; yet your heavenly Father feedeth them. Are ye not much better than they?" (Matt. 6:25-26). The Christian is to be active in laboring for his daily food, but his mind is not to be burdened with worry. He has the promise of his heavenly Father's providential care. "But seek ye first the kingdom of God, and his righteousness; and all these things shall be added unto you" (Matt. 6:33). Do you realize this freedom that is available in Christ Jesus? Remember—it requires faith!

Of Burdens. Jesus said that under his yoke, the burden is light (Matt. 11:30). Peter wrote, "Humble yourselves therefore under the mighty hand of God, that he may exalt you in due time: casting all your care upon him; for he careth for you" (1 Pet. 5:6-7). God wants our cares! He urges us to cast them upon him. With the abilities that God has given us, we are to do what we can. What we cannot do in confronting our burdens, we are to have the faith to cast them upon the Lord. We have a Savior who truly cares for us!

Of Death. Perhaps this is the greatest fear that human beings confront! Referring to the value of Christ's death, the Hebrew writer said, "He might destroy him that had the power of death, that is, the devil: and deliver them, who through fear of death were all their lifetime subject to bondage" (Heb. 2:14-15). Paul said of Christ: ". . . who hath abolished death, and hath brought life and immortality to light through the gospel" (2 Tim. 1:10). Christ offers his people victory over death (1 Cor. 15:57). Yes, it requires faith to appreciate the freedom that Christ offers!

Yes, It Certainly Does!

Before me is a clipping taken "From the Teacher's Notebook" by Paul R. Van Gorder, Associate Teacher. Evidently this was clipped from some religious magazine in which Mr. Van Gorder edits a question and answer column designated "From the Teacher's

Notebook." He is asked, "Does Mark 16:16 teach that one must be baptized in order to receive salvation?" His answer was, "No, it does not! The second clause of the verse makes this quite clear, for it declares, '. . . he that believeth not shall be damned.' If baptism were essential to salvation, it would be included in such passages as John 3:16, Acts 16:31, Ephesians 2:8-9, and Romans 10:9-10. We must be careful never to form a doctrine on one isolated phrase of one verse when many other Scripture references state the doctrine clearly." So there you have this gentleman's answer to the question which is a very common denominational answer to such a query. Let us examine his conclusions.

The Second Clause. In the first clause, Jesus was speaking of salvation. "He that believeth and is baptized shall be saved." The conditions being that one is to believe the gospel and be baptized so that he might be saved. Belief plus baptism equals salvation! In the second clause, Jesus is speaking of damnation. "But he that believeth not shall be damned." If one does not believe, there is nothing that he can do to be pleasing to the Lord (Heb. 11:6). The clause does not say he that believeth not and is not baptized shall be damned! No need for that—for if one doesn't believe he could never be scripturally baptized in keeping with the command of Christ to be saved. If an individual will not take the first step (beliefh), then there is no need of talking to him about the second (baptism). Hence, to be saved one must believe and be baptized, but to be damned he only has to disbelieve. The door is closed on everyone who fails to believe. Friends, the second clause does not say or imply that baptism is not necessary in order to be saved. It appears that this man should have seen that! Was he mean or green, dishonest or actually ignorant?

Van Gorder said that, if baptism was essential for salvation, it would be included in such passages as John 3:16, Acts 16:31, Ephesians 2:8-9, and Romans 10:9-10. I never cease to be amazed at some of the arguments (?) that people make to try to avoid the simple truth that Christ taught. This man must follow the view that baptism must be in every passage of Scripture mentioned in order for it to be essential to salvation. The Scriptures reveal God's truth, but no one passage contains all truth. All passages are true, but not all the truth is in any one passage to the disregard of others. Surely this man would not deny that an individual must repent in order to be saved. All right, where does John 3:16 say anything about repentance? The verse does not mention repentance and thus according to his reasoning on baptism, then repentance is not necessary to salvation because John 3:16 doesn't mention it. See how people condemn themselves in refusing to accept the truth of Christ! As others would say, doubtlessly he would argue that believing in John 3:16 includes repentance and to that we would add that is also includes baptism. In Acts 16, after telling the jailor to "believe on the Lord Jesus Christ, and thou shalt be saved, and thy house," Paul and Silas spoke the word to him and his house and the jailor took them the same hour of the night and washed their stripes and was baptized, "he and all his straightway." This showed what was included in believing on the Lord Jesus Christ to be saved. Repentance was evidenced in washing stripes, and baptism was performed in the same hour of the night. Mr. Van Gorder concluded that baptism was not included before hearing the sermon to the jailor and seeing what faith prompted them to do to be saved.

He also refers to Ephesians 2:8-9 as saying if baptism were essential it would be included therein. When one reads Acts 19, he reads of the account of these Ephesians being saved "by grace through faith" and what was included. Not only did it include baptism, but it involved some being baptized again who had not been baptized scripturally or for the right purpose (Acts 19:1-5). Acts 19 is the finest commentary that one can obtain on what Ephesians 2:8-9 included. All of this was preaching and action in keeping with the terms of the Great Commission stated in Mark 16:15-16.

Our friend writes, "We must be careful never to form a doctrine on one isolated phrase of one verse when many other Scripture references state the doctrine clearly." Wonder why he doesn't practice this principle? He writes as though Mark 16:16 is the only passage or clause that mentions baptism. Has he not read 1 Peter 3:21, Galatians 3:26-27, 1 Corinthians 12:13, Acts 2:38, Romans 6:3-4 as well as others? We are to take all the Scriptures and when we do we will see that one is to believe, repent, and, upon a confession of faith, be baptized to be saved.

The Scriptures can be understood and there is no need for an average intelligent person being deceived by false teaching. "Wherefore be ye not unwise, but understanding what the will of the Lord is" (Eph. 5:17). We recognize that some Scriptures are more difficult to understand than others. Peter wrote concerning some of the things that Paul wrote, ". . . in which are some things hard to be understood, which they that are unlearned and unstable wrest, as they do also the other scriptures, unto their own destruction" (2 Pet. 3:16). The plan of salvation, or what one must do to be saved, is not one of the things hard to be understood. If one doesn't want the truth, he can listen to false teachers confuse God's simple truth and be led to destruction. Salvation depends upon people being honest enough to see the truth and obey it.

You Never Mentioned Him To Me

The songbook that we use, *Sacred Selections for the Church,* has a number of old songs that might be rather new to many of us. One of these rather beautiful old hymns has the following lyrics:

> When in the better land
> Before the bar we stand,
> How deeply grieved our souls will be
> If any lost one there
> Should cry in deep despair:
> You never mentioned Him to me.
> You helped me not the light to see,
> You met me day by day,
> You knew I was astray;
> Yet, you never mentioned Him to me.

Yes, this is a beautiful hymn, but at the same time it is something more! The truth it conveys is terrifying! There are so many of us who have acquaintances that we meet day by day, yet how often we neglect mentioning Christ and the truth to them in a manner befitting the gospel of Christ that we are supposed to love so dearly. I firmly believe that this is the failure of so many of us in the Lord's church today. Every time the song is sung, it strikes at the responsibilities that are ours in endeavoring to teach the gospel to the lost. The truth that these lyrics convey is before us! Doesn't it disturb your conscience? Can you truly say that you have made an honest effort to teach the truth to all with whom you have had daily contact?

Why Is It That We Do Not Mention Him More Than We Do?

I'm just too busy. Too busy at what? Making money? Having a good time? Too busy taking care of a home? It is easy to make ourselves believe that we are too busy when we do not really want to do the work of the Lord. Whom do we think we are fooling? Suppose God has said that he was too busy to send Christ to this world that we might be saved. God was not too busy to exhibit his love and make salvation available for us. Surely, we should never get too busy to pass on the story of his love to others. Yet, you never mentioned him to me! We won't be too busy to die and stand in the judgment of God!

It won't do any good. This is defeatism at its best. This is a triumph for Satan! As long as Christ and his church have friends with such an attitude as this, they'll have no need for enemies. With some, it possibly will not do a great deal of good, but what about others? If we fail to try, how do we know it wouldn't do any good? Furthermore, as Christians we have the obligation to warn whether the warning is accepted or not. The words of the prophet Ezekiel are applicable, "When I say unto the wicked, Thou shalt surely die; and thou givest him not warning, nor speakest to warn the wicked from his wicked way, to save his life; the same wicked man shall die in his iniquity; but his blood will I require at thine hand. Yet if thou warn the wicked and he turn not from his wickedness, nor from his wicked way, he shall die in his iniquity; but thou hast delivered thy soul" (Ezek. 3:18-19). Every time I read this passage I find myself thinking of the lyrics of this song that has suggested this article.

I'm doing my part. Just what are you doing? "I go to services, pray often, give of my money, and even help about caring for the building. I think this is just about all God expects of me." When can an individual truthfully and conscientiously say that he is doing his part? So many times the part that we are doing is composed of those things that come the easiest. If we aren't careful, we can build our own criteria of righteousness and ignore what the Lord tells us to do. The philosophy of how little we can do and still please God has become far more popular than the spirit of doing more and seeing our joy ever increase in God's sight. "You never mentioned Him to me" is the cry of the lost. Are we going to make an effort to justify ourselves by saying, "I was doing my part and it didn't include trying to teach you"? Think!

I've tried and I failed. No doubt this is so and as you try again, you may fail again. Are you going to admit that you are a failure? Think of salesmen and what they have to encounter. A fisherman is not going to have fish for dinner with his bait on the dock. He must keep the bait before the fish. The illustration may be crude, but the lesson is sound. Try again and again! Instead of quitting in the work of the Lord just because you have failed a few times, why not analyze the cause of failure? At the least, may it be said, you mentioned him to me. This is something all of us can do and the work is very important!